Resurrection and Spirit

Resurrection and Spirit

From the Pentateuch to Luke-Acts

Brian W. Lidbeck

WIPF & STOCK · Eugene, Oregon

RESURRECTION AND SPIRIT
From the Pentateuch to Luke-Acts

Copyright © 2020 Brian W. Lidbeck. All rights reserved. Except for brief quotations in critical publications or reviews, no part of this book may be reproduced in any manner without prior written permission from the publisher. Write: Permissions, Wipf and Stock Publishers, 199 W. 8th Ave., Suite 3, Eugene, OR 97401.

Wipf & Stock
An Imprint of Wipf and Stock Publishers
199 W. 8th Ave., Suite 3
Eugene, OR 97401

www.wipfandstock.com

PAPERBACK ISBN: 978-1-7252-6701-5
HARDCOVER ISBN: 978-1-7252-6702-2
EBOOK ISBN: 978-1-7252-6703-9

Manufactured in the U.S.A. 10/29/20

All translations are the author's, unless otherwise stated.

Scripture quotations marked (ESV) are from the The Holy Bible, English Standard Version®, copyright © 2001 by Crossway, a publishing ministry of Good News Publishers. Used by permission. All rights reserved.

Scripture quotations marked (NIV) are taken from the Holy Bible, New International Version®, copyright © 1973, 1978, 1984, 2011 by Biblica, Inc.™ Used by permission of Zondervan. All rights reserved worldwide. www.zondervan.com.

Scripture quotations marked (NRSV) are from the New Revised Standard Version Bible, copyright © 1989 by the Division of Christian Education of the National Council of the Churches of Christ in the U.S.A. Used by permission. All rights reserved.

To Diane
With gratitude, love, and affection

Contents

Preface | ix
Acknowledgments | xi

1. Introduction | 1
2. The Spirit, Creation, and Luke-Acts | 9
3. The Spirit, Prophecy, and Luke-Acts | 31
4. From Death and Barrenness to the Resurrected King | 53
5. Beyond Grave Expectations: Moses, the Prophets, and Luke | 86
6. The Center of Luke-Acts: Lord and Christ | 118
7. The Resurrection and the Spirit as Identifiers of the Lord Jesus Christ | 143
8. Resurrection and Spirit: The Risen Lord Bestows the Spirit | 166
9. Conclusion | 203

Bibliography | 209
Author Index | 221
Index of Ancient Documents | 225

Preface

STUDENTS OF LUKE'S TWO volumes have benefited from the publication of a plethora of monographs on the Holy Spirit and related Lukan emphases in recent decades. For many years now, scholars have debated the nature of Luke's doctrine of the Spirit (pneumatology). Is his pneumatology focused on conversion and initiation into Christ, charismatic empowerment, or a combination of the two? Attempts to answer this question have certainly shed light on Luke's two volumes. At the same time, some other important themes in Luke's volumes have not received adequate attention. Only in recent years was the first significant monograph on Luke's doctrine of the resurrection released. In addition, Luke's pneumatology has often been studied somewhat independently of his other important themes. This work attempts to examine two of Luke's most important emphases, resurrection and Spirit, in tandem and in relation to his Christology. The biblical-theological approach employed here also recognizes Luke's emphasis on eschatological fulfillment and works to avoid isolating these Lukan themes from the Hebrew Scriptures. Consequently, this study traces the development of the two themes from the Pentateuch, through other key Old Testament passages, and to Luke-Acts. The discussion ultimately focuses on the Pentecostal narrative and examines how resurrection and Spirit converge there in identifying Jesus as Lord and Christ.

Acknowledgments

THIS PROJECT BEGAN AS a doctoral dissertation at the Assemblies of God Theological Seminary in Springfield, Missouri. I would like to express my gratitude to the faculty and staff of the Seminary for their instruction, guidance, and encouragement. Special thanks go to Dr. James Railey and Dr. James Hernando, who served on my dissertation committee and provided valuable commentary on the dissertation. I must also thank my esteemed project supervisor, Dr. Douglas Oss, for opening up for me a whole new world of understanding in biblical theology and for providing direction and oversight throughout the writing process.

Those who engage in a project of this magnitude realize how crucial it is to have a team of supporters. I have benefited from the enthusiastic support of many friends at Fountain of Grace Church and Grand Rapids First Church. The staff and students at Northpoint Bible College in Grand Rapids, Michigan, have continually expressed love and support for me and enthusiasm for this project. They are an inspiration!

The author's name appears on this book, but the intangible contributions of others are everywhere contained within it. My wife, Diane, in particular, has provided incalculable amounts of prayer, sacrifice, grace, and encouragement. Christ accompanies me through her love.

1

Introduction

THE PURPOSE OF THIS study is to explore the relationship between two of Luke's most prominent themes in his gospel and Acts: the resurrection and the Spirit. By studying the two themes together and drawing heavily from the Hebrew Scriptures that Luke uses as his foundational source, one sees Luke's theology more holistically, gains fresh insights into his pneumatological interests, and better understands his perspective on the resurrection of Christ. This approach can then serve as a basis for additional study and comparison with Paul's complementary teaching on these subjects.

The thesis of the following study is that (1) Luke frames his two volumes in an eschatological context in keeping with the perspective of the Hebrew Scriptures, and this context provides a point of intersection for resurrection and Spirit; (2) he views the Spirit as the divine agent who advances God's plan through creative and charismatic acts, but especially by anointing a Messiah in fulfillment of an Old Testament leadership and Davidic pattern; (3) the concept of resurrection has roots in the Pentateuch, and the resurrection of the anointed one is a fulfillment of Scripture, a reversal, and a royal exaltation; (4) the Spirit anoints Messiah's followers to proclaim the message of his resurrection and reign to all nations; (5) the themes of resurrection and Spirit intersect in identifying Jesus in accordance with Luke's central point that Jesus is Lord and Christ (Acts 2:36); and (6) the themes of resurrection and Spirit converge in the Pentecostal narrative, for it is through the resurrection as part of the complex of exaltation events that Christ's divine status becomes evident and that he exercises the divine prerogative of pouring out the Spirit.

The primary notion that Christ's resurrection and the Spirit both serve Luke's purpose in glorifying Jesus as Lord and Christ relativizes other significant themes. Thus, important emphases such as prophetic inspiration receive attention as the means by which the Spirit advances God's plan, but prophetic inspiration and charismatic events are viewed as means to an end and not as ends in themselves. Likewise, this study acknowledges Luke's use of cultic images in relation to Pentecost but emphasizes how Luke uses such images to focus on Christ. Luke employs temple and priestly images in order to point to the exalted status of Christ and does not necessarily use them in the same way that Paul does.

The Reason for Resurrection and Spirit

Even the mention of the Holy Spirit in a study on Luke-Acts could immediately call into question the need for yet another journey on this well-trodden path. The Spirit in Luke-Acts has received an outpouring of scholarly attention for several decades and is recognized by all as a major theme in Acts. The abundance of references to the Spirit (there are about seventeen direct references to the "Spirit" [πνεῦμα] in Luke's gospel and fifty-seven in Acts) demonstrates Luke's obvious interest in the topic.[1] Martin Mittelstadt has chronicled much of the history of the debate over Lukan pneumatology in his work *Reading Luke-Acts in the Pentecostal Tradition*. He notes the surprise of François Bovon that not only have Lukan studies not ceased, but that Lukan theology has advanced, in part due to the arrival of Pentecostal theologians.[2] Yet, while the breadth of Lukan studies has expanded tremendously, the debate over a proper Lukan pneumatology still rages, and the existence of that continued debate is evidence that there is still room for greater clarity and more work.[3]

---

1. By comparison Matthew mentions the Spirit twelve times, Mark six times, and John seventeen times. Luke also refers to the Spirit in other ways, especially as a promise (Luke 2:49; Acts 1:4; 2:33, 39), as a gift (Acts 1:4; 2:38; 10:45; 11:17; cf. 15:8), and in close association with power (Luke 1:49; Acts 1:8). I will also argue that Jesus as the Christ ("anointed one") must be included as a significant element of Luke's pneumatology.

2. Mittelstadt, *Reading Luke-Acts*, 10–11.

3 Although this is an oversimplification, the main positions on Lukan baptism in the Spirit can be summarized by James Dunn's early position on conversion-initiation, Robert Menzies's Pentecostal position on prophetic empowerment, and Max Turner's moderating approach of charismatic conversion. A host of other authors fall somewhere along the conversion/empowerment spectrum, and some Pentecostals of a

Introduction

One might assume that a subject as prominent as the resurrection would have been studied exhaustively in Luke-Acts by now. After all, Luke directly mentions the subject with his typical resurrection terminology sixty-two times.[4] References to resurrection in general include four resuscitations apart from Easter (Luke 7:11–17; 8:49–56; Acts 9:40–41; 20:9–10), discussions with the Sadducees (Luke 20:27–37; Acts 23:8), mention of the final resurrection (Luke 14:14; Acts 24:15), and a figurative resurrection (Luke 15:32). Jesus's resurrection is foreshadowed in the story of the rich man and Lazarus (Luke 16:31) and is reflected via a double entendre in the raising up of a paralyzed man (Acts 3:6–7). Use of "the Name" of Jesus implies his resurrection (e.g., Acts 3:6, 16; 4:7, 10, 12, 30; 5:29, 40), and the title "Lord" implies his resurrection and exaltation (Acts 2:36; 4:33). Also, the "word" of the Lord became closely associated with Christ's resurrection and the complex of saving events early in Acts (2:22, 40, 41; 4:29, 33). Not only the pre-ascension appearances (Luke 24; Acts 1:1–11) but also the post-ascension appearances of Jesus testify to his resurrection (Acts 7:56; 9:3–16; 10:13–15; 18:9–10; 23:11).[5]

Yet Lukan studies have by no means exhausted Luke's teaching on resurrection. The standard Lukan commentaries and theologies address resurrection in Luke-Acts, but "a perusal of the vast array of research on Luke-Acts reveals a startling lacuna: not one monograph has been devoted to the subject of the resurrection in Luke-Acts as a whole, and relatively few essays have been devoted to the subject."[6] Kevin Anderson's *"But God Raised Him from the Dead"* has gone a long way in filling that lacuna, but there is still room for further study.

---

more revisionist persuasion have sought to thoroughly integrate Lukan pneumatology with the rest of the New Testament and have moved more in the direction of Turner. See Dunn, *Baptism in the Holy Spirit*; Menzies, *Empowered for Witness*; Turner, *Power from on High*.

4. The verb ἀνίστημι ("to rise") refers to resurrection nineteen times, thirteen of which refer specifically to Jesus's resurrection. In its seventeen occurrences, the noun ἀνάστασις ("resurrection") always refers to resurrection (if one includes the reference in Luke 2:34, but see the later discussion). It refers directly to Jesus's resurrection four times and implies his resurrection five times. Luke uses the verb ἐγείρω ("to rise up") sixteen times in reference to resurrection, and ten of these refer to Jesus's resurrection. The verb ζάω ("to live") refers to resurrection about nine times and describes Jesus's resurrection on four occasions. The noun ζωή ("life") clearly refers to Jesus's resurrection on one occasion. Thus, Luke uses the above terms in reference to resurrection about sixty-two times and to Jesus's resurrection a total of thirty-seven times.

5. The list offered here is a sampling and is not exhaustive.

6. Anderson, *"But God Raised"*, 1–2.

Even a cursory reading of Luke-Acts reveals the prominence that Luke gives to resurrection (especially the resurrection of Christ) and to the Holy Spirit. Due in part to the influence of the Pentecostal and charismatic movements, a host of books on the Spirit and, particularly, on the Spirit in Luke-Acts have flooded the market. Such specialized studies have their place, but there is a danger in isolating a single Lukan theme from his larger purposes, other emphases, and the broader biblical story. Some authors have noticed this danger and made an attempt to establish their pneumatology on a stronger, broader biblical footing or have expanded the study of pneumatology by examining it in relation to other subjects. Roger Stronstad sought to demonstrate the Old Testament roots of Lukan pneumatology; the subtitle of the second edition of his book emphasizes this: *The Charismatic Theology of St. Luke: Trajectories from the Old Testament to Luke-Acts.*[7] Martin Mittelstadt studied Lukan pneumatology in light of Luke's suffering theme,[8] and Youngmo Cho endeavored to shed light on the uniqueness of Luke's pneumatology by examining the themes of Spirit and kingdom and comparing Luke's handling of these themes to Paul's treatment of them.[9]

Despite the advances, however, a need still exists for a more thoroughly christocentric Lukan pneumatology. Studying the themes of resurrection and Spirit in tandem results in a more christologically oriented pneumatology. Luke helps his audience understand that the Spirit is the divine agent who advances the plan of God by anointing the Messiah to proclaim salvation and by empowering believers to proclaim the resurrection of Christ and his lordship over the nations.

Still, examining these two themes together is not enough. A third theme, which is really a Lukan presupposition and framework for his two volumes, rapidly emerges in this study, and that is his eschatology. Spirit and resurrection are two crucial elements of Lukan eschatology. From the birth narratives forward, the Spirit is a key player in fulfilling Hebrew expectations of a coming Messiah, and resurrection is the definitive, restorative event signaling the fulfillment of Hebrew hopes and the arrival of the eschaton. Therefore this study must place a heavy emphasis on

---

7. Stronstad, *Charismatic Theology of St. Luke*. Stronstad more fully develops some of the seminal ideas of earlier Pentecostal scholars such as Anthony D. Palma, who says, "Glossolalia is a specialized form of the gift of prophecy." Palma, *Spirit*, 76. Note especially Palma's discussion of Num 11, Joel 2, and Pentecost in chapters 2 and 6.

8. Mittelstadt, *Spirit and Suffering in Luke-Acts*.

9. Cho, *Spirit and Kingdom*.

the role of eschatology in the Third Gospel and Acts, and eschatology by its very nature requires a thorough investigation of the Old Testament's progress in revelation. Thus, this study places a premium on developing an Old Testament eschatology in order to shed light on Luke's perspective and to avoid reading his themes in isolation from the worldview that spawned them.

Methodology

Luke wastes no time in striking the eschatological note when he writes of "the things that have been fulfilled among us" (Luke 1:1).[10] Because Luke has set the agenda for us up front, it is necessary to thoroughly exam how the Hebrew Scriptures inform Luke's eschatology and his doctrine of the Spirit and resurrection. Therefore this study employs a biblical-theological approach to trace how the Spirit functions as the divine agent who advances the story toward the resurrection of Christ and, ultimately, the resurrection of his followers. The seeds of these themes are buried in the soil of the Pentateuch; thus the argument traces key developments of the doctrine of the Spirit and of the resurrection from the Pentateuch to Luke-Acts.

The biblical-theological approach employed here implies several presuppositions. It implies the acceptance of the proposition that the Bible has an underlying unity to it and that Christ is at the center of this unity.[11] It implies a supernatural worldview in which God is advancing a redemptive plan in history. There is a metanarrative to history that can be discerned in the Scriptures. Thus, this study does not assume some commonly held views such as a second-century-BC date of Daniel, which is based largely on the modern critical notion that the author uses *vaticinium ex eventu* (prophecy after the fact). The following argument also challenges the assumption that resurrection is an invention of Intertestamental Judaism.[12] Furthermore, the approach to this study contests many

---

10. All translations are the author's unless otherwise noted.

11. For a discussion of biblical theology by authors who hold a high view of the authority of Scripture, see Carson, "Current Issues in Biblical Theology"; Vos, *Biblical Theology*, 11–27.

12. The number of scholars whose sympathies lie along these lines are too numerous to mention, but Geza Vermes could speak for many: "In the Judaism of the Old Testament, resurrection made only a few late and foggy appearances, probably not before the end of the third century BC. It was not asserted definitely before the time of

of the fundamental ideas of the documentary hypothesis, such as the idea that early Israelite religion had no eschatology, that Israel evolved from polytheism to monotheism, that messianism only came later in Israel's history, and that the Pentateuch is merely a piecemeal product of human authors of various times rather than the product of a divine mind.[13]

This study also presupposes that Luke-Acts is a two-volume work written by a single author and most likely identified as Luke the physician (Col 4:14). Luke writes with the intention of continuing the story of redemptive history and therefore narrates the events with a theological purpose.[14] A variety of methods such as grammatical-historical exegesis, literary criticism, and redaction criticism help shed light on Luke's perspective, but Luke-Acts is studied primarily as a whole, finished product that offers unique insights into the progress of God's plan. Comparisons with Paul's complementary instruction reveal the contributions of each author, but one author's work does not hold a superior position in the canon nor serve as the primary interpretive lens of another author's work.

In order to demonstrate Luke's theological continuity with the Pentateuch and the emergence of his emphases from there, this work gives ample attention to the Spirit and resurrection in the Pentateuch. Because there are far more clear references to the Spirit in the Old Testament than there are to resurrection, representative passages on the Spirit are selectively chosen for discussion. Most resurrection passages in the Old Testament receive attention because they are less numerous, highly controversial, and have not been frequently studied from the pneumatological and Lukan perspective of this work. Pentecost receives substantial attention, as the two themes converge there. Because of the biblical-theological orientation of this project, a large portion of the study focuses on the implications of Old Testament antecedents for Luke's pneumatology and doctrine of the resurrection.

---

the Maccabean revolution in the 160s BC, and even from then on its acceptance grew slowly and remained far from universal." Vermes, *Resurrection*, xv–xvi.

13. Vos expounds on the inconsistencies between Old Testament eschatology and Julius Wellhausen's views. See chapter 3 especially in Vos, *Eschatology of the Old Testament*.

14. See the classic study by I. Howard Marshall, *Luke: Historian and Theologian*.

Introduction

Summary

The themes of resurrection and Spirit most clearly converge in and around Luke's Pentecostal narrative, but the Old Testament provides the essential theological ingredients that allow the two themes to merge into a celebration of Christ's lordship in Luke-Acts. Along the way there are glimpses of the convergence of the two themes, but the primary way they intersect is through the eschatological and prophetic perspective of the Old Testament. Consequently, chapters 2–5 begin in the Pentateuch, with chapters 2–3 focused on pneumatology and chapters 4–5 devoted to resurrection. Each chapter explores how the Mosaic worldview serves as a foundation for Luke's pneumatology or for his doctrine of the resurrection. Chapters 6–8 build on this foundation and show specific ways in which the Spirit and resurrection complement one another in Luke-Acts.

More specifically, chapter 2 focuses on the Spirit's role in creation. The Torah's eschatological perspective comes into view immediately, as the Spirit acts to bring emptiness to fullness. Luke sees the significance of this and records the Spirit's role in the conception of Jesus. Moses also depicts the Spirit as a sanctuary builder with the ultimate goal of enabling God and humanity to dwell together. Thus, the Spirit is associated with the divine presence.

Chapter 3 highlights various passages in the Pentateuch that demonstrate the prophetic aspect of the Spirit's work, an element shared with Luke. Numbers 11 receives attention because of this emphasis and because of its eschatological and Lukan implications. The discussion shows that Numbers 11 also incorporates other themes and has christological significance. The prophetic activity of Joseph, Balaam, and Joshua is also examined with an eye on Christology.

Chapter 4 argues that the notion of a resurrection has its roots in the Torah and that this doctrine logically results from the Pentateuch's eschatological moorings associated with God's plan to bring restoration from the fall. The connection between death and barrenness receives attention, and the study traces the theme from Abraham and Sarah to the Lukan birth narratives. The books of 1 and 2 Samuel substantially advance the story through Hannah's answered prayer, her praise, and the story of an anointed king; therefore, the chapter emphasizes these books as a foundation for Lukan Christology and pneumatology.

Chapter 5 continues the discussion on the resurrection and explores the individual eschatology of the Pentateuch as a basis for Luke's view of the resurrection of Jesus and that of his followers. The investigation moves to the prophets Hosea, Isaiah, Ezekiel, and Daniel and demonstrates how they build on the resurrection principles rooted in the Pentateuch. They flesh out the picture by further clarifying the reality of resurrection and developing the centrality of Christ as one who both experiences this great reversal of death and brings reversal for those who live under his rule.

Chapter 6 identifies the center of Lukan theology, further developing the royal and messianic implications of the Old Testament and Judaism and focusing on Jesus as Lord and Christ (Acts 2:36). This chapter demonstrates how the message of the kingdom of God and the expression "word of God" focus largely on Jesus's resurrection.

Chapter 7 highlights how Luke's pneumatology and the preaching of the resurrection converge in identifying Jesus as Lord and Christ. The Spirit identifies Jesus as the expected Messiah through inspired prophets such as Simeon, through prophetic praise, and through the ministry of John the Baptist. This chapter contains an overview of resurrection in Luke's gospel and addresses some significant passages, but the bulk of the discussion on resurrection highlights the resurrection preaching in Acts.

Chapter 8 examines how the Spirit and the resurrection come together in fulfilling Old Testament expectations of an eschatological reversal and the experience of God's presence in Lukan thought. The discussion focuses on Jesus's resurrection and exaltation as the defining reversal in which his royal identity is manifest. His worthiness to exercise the divine prerogative of pouring out the Spirit becomes evident. This chapter also explores how Luke employs cultic imagery in order to describe the Pentecostal outpouring and highlight the christocentric nature of the event.

Chapter 9 concludes the study by highlighting the major areas where the Spirit and resurrection converge in Lukan thought and by offering some reflection on the implications of this for critical scholarship and the Pentecostal debate.

2

The Spirit, Creation, and Luke-Acts

THE PENTATEUCH CONTAINS ABOUT fifteen references to God's Spirit (רוּחַ),[1] although it is sometimes difficult to discern whether the Spirit of God is intended or the human spirit, the wind, or a spiritual being.[2] The Genesis account immediately mentions the Spirit in 1:2, but it is evident from later passages that the activity of the Spirit is assumed by the audience in several passages where he is not mentioned. The following discussion focuses on the Spirit in creation. In connection with this, one observes the eschatological orientation of the Spirit's work as the agent who advances God's agenda as well as the Spirit's role as a sanctuary builder.[3] This view of the Pentateuch has a direct bearing on Luke's eschatological worldview, the prominent place he gives to the Spirit's role in the miraculous conception of Jesus, and some of the language of Pentecost.[4]

---

1. Gen 1:2; 2:7; 41:38; Exod 15:8, 10; 28:3; 31:3; 35:31; Num 11:17, 25–26, 29; 24:2; 27:18; and Deut 34:9. The Hebrew term occurs 38 times in the Pentateuch and 394 times in the Old Testament.

2. Throughoutng I use the uppercase "S" to distinguish between the divine Spirit and other uses of רוּחַ. The common addition of the phrases "of Yahweh" or "of God" to "Spirit" indicate that the Hebrews did make a distinction between the divine Spirit and other spirits, and the commentary of New Testament writers makes the distinction even more obvious. Associations with divinity justify using the capital "Spirit" in some contexts.

3. The following argument directly contradicts the history of religions approach of Charles, who says that "since early Yahwism possessed no eschatology of its own, the Israelite was left to his hereditary heathen beliefs." Charles, *Eschatology*, 52.

4. The argument assumes that the bulk of the Pentateuch was written by Moses and that minor editorial additions do not detract from the essential unity of each book and

The Spirit and Creation

"In the beginning" (Gen 1:1) is more than a fitting phrase at the commencement of a book; it is an eschatological statement that implies both a story in progress and an end.[5] That the final chapter of the Bible obviously alludes to the Genesis creation account (e.g., "the tree of life"; Rev 22:2) verifies that a divine plan was already in motion and that a consummation was in view.[6] Indeed, "the correlate of eschatology is creation,"[7] and "there is an absolute end posited for the universe before and apart from sin."[8] This is fundamental to a doctrine of the Spirit and of resurrection. Genesis 1:2 immediately positions the Spirit in the role of the eschatological agent who turns the wasteland into a place of worship. There has therefore been something inherently prophetic about the operation of the Spirit from the outset, not so much in the formal sense of the word, but in the eschatological sense. That is, the Spirit knows the plan of God and propels it into the future. This prophetic/eschatological aspect of the Spirit's activity has a bearing on Luke's view, for numerous authors have noted the prophetic emphasis in Luke-Acts, and some have emphasized that Judaism primarily understood the Spirit as the prophetic Spirit.[9] But the origin of Luke's emphasis on prophecy is deeper than Judaism and even the commonly recognized prophetic utterance passages in the Hebrew Scriptures (e.g., Num 11:25–26, 29; 1 Sam 10:6, 10; 2 Chr 15:1; 20:14; 24:20; Joel 2:28–29); it is rooted in the identity of the Spirit as the eschatological agent who advances God's plan. Therefore it is no surprise when Luke opens his gospel with an allusion to eschatological fulfillment and numerous references to the Spirit and prophecy (e.g., 1:1, 41–42, 67–79; 2:25–35).[10]

---

the unity of the Pentateuch's story line.

    5. Sailhamer, *Genesis Unbound*, 47.

    6. Sailhamer, *Genesis Unbound*, 48. That this is so also differentiates the hermeneutic employed here from other approaches that do not hold to the unity of the Scriptures or do not allow the New Testament authors to have an authoritative voice in interpreting Old Testament passages.

    7. Vos, *Eschatology of the Old Testament*, 1.

    8. Vos, *Eschatology of the Old Testament*, 73.

    9. See Turner, *Power from on High*, 119–37, for a discussion of the prophetic Spirit in Judaism. Turner argues that the Spirit in Judaism was not strictly prophetic but also associated with ethics.

    10. Vos, *Eschatology of the Old Testament*, 75. Here Vos also points out that the tree of life also contained "a prophetic element" in that it held out the possibility and goal

The Hovering Spirit

Several observations point to the identification of the רוּחַ אֱלֹהִים ("Spirit of God") as the divine Spirit rather than as a wind or breath in Gen 1:2.[11] First, the author identifies him as the "Spirit of God," and every one of the thirty-two occurrences of אֱלֹהִים in Gen 1 refers to God, including the occurrences in verses 1 and 3.[12] Second, the later allusion to Gen 1:2 in the Spirit's power overshadowing Mary (Luke 1:35) assumes that the Holy Spirit is in view. Third, the progress from "formless and empty" (תֹהוּ וָבֹהוּ; Gen 1:2) to order and fullness more naturally lends itself to divine agency than to an impersonal force. Fourth, the dependency of the account of the construction of the tabernacle upon the creation account suggests that the same Spirit at work in Exodus (e.g., 31:5) was at work in Genesis.[13] Fifth, the context of Deut 32:11, the second of only three places in the Old Testament where רחף ("hover") is found (Gen 1:2; cf. Jer 23:9), strongly suggests the activity of God.[14]

In this Song of Moses he refers to God as the Creator of the Israelites (Deut 32:6), the one who found them "in a wilderness land and in an empty [תֹהוּ] and howling waste"—a clear reference to Gen 1:2.[15] In this wilderness the Lord cares for Israel like an eagle hovering over its young (Deut 32:11). The simile likely refers to the pillar of a cloud by day and fire by night.[16] Yet in this prophetic song Israel forsakes its God, participates in idolatry, and faces judgment. But the Lord is sovereign: "'See now

---

of eternal life even before the fall (Gen 3:22). But with the fall, resurrection became the means by which the original goal of God's dwelling with humanity for eternity could ultimately be achieved. Thus, even though resurrection per se does not occur in the creation account, the concept is completely consistent with God's eschatological purpose.

11. E.g., Schmidt is among the many who translate רוּחַ as "wind" in Gen 1:2. Schmidt, *Schöpfungsgeschichte der Priesterschrift*, 73.

12. This view is in contrast to those who posit that אֱלֹהִים has a superlative force here and translate the phrase as "mighty wind." Richard E. Averbeck points out that the רוּחַ אֱלֹהִים never means anything but the Spirit of God in the Old Testament. Averbeck, "Breath, Wind, Spirit," 32.

13. Sailhamer, *Pentateuch as Narrative*, 87.

14. In addition, this verb occurs in the *piel* participle in both Gen 1:2 and Deut 32:11and emphasizes continuous action. This more easily lends itself to the activity of a living being than to a wind. See Hildebrandt, *Old Testament Theology*, 35; Kaiser, "Pentateuch," 4.

15. In the Pentateuch the noun תֹהוּ ("formless") is only found in Gen 1:2 and Deut 32:10.

16. Van Pelt and Kaiser, "רחף," 1098.

that I, I am he, and there is no god besides me; I kill and I make alive; I have wounded and I will heal; and there is none that can deliver out of my hand'" (Deut 32:39). He will restore Israel and ultimately fulfill his purposes despite their failings. The Septuagint translates the four verbs of the two merismic phrases as future verbs (ἐγὼ ἀποκτενῶ καὶ ζῆν ποιήσω πατάξω κἀγὼ ἰάσομαι) so as to render the phrase, "I will kill and I will make alive; I will wound and I will heal." But the third verb is a perfect verb in the Hebrew text (מָחַצְתִּי; "I have wounded"), and the switch from it to the imperfect verb (אֶרְפָּא) highlights the final verb and turns it into a clear promise of restoration: "I have wounded and I will heal."[17]

This is an amazing promise in light of the deplorable state of Israel envisioned here: they are devoid of strength, and there is no one left among them (Deut 32:36).[18] Several elements in the Hebrew text of verse 39 highlight God's absolute and unique authority over life and death, including the attention-grabbing "see now" (רְאוּ עַתָּה), the change in the narrative to the first person, and the repetition of "I" (אֲנִי). While this passage does not directly detail an individual eschatology or a physical resurrection, it certainly builds a theological basis for the concept, particularly when one reads that the certainty of vindication for Israel comes from the declaration "As surely as I live forever" (v. 40). Death is no barrier to the eternal God—a concept basic to Jesus's claim that God remains in fellowship with the patriarchs and raises the dead (Luke 20:37–38).

The linguistic and thematic ties between the Genesis account and the Song of Moses provides somewhat of a frame around the Pentateuch. Genesis narrates the creation, the agency of the hovering Spirit in bringing order from an empty wasteland, the fall of humanity, and the promise of future restoration (3:15). Deuteronomy 32 describes the creation of Israel, the rescue of the nation from the howling wasteland, the hovering presence of God, the rebellion of the nation, and the promise of future restoration.[19]

Some salient points from the above comparison deserve mention. First, the two passages tie together several items of particular interest

---

17. Block also notes how the imperfect makes this a promise. Block, *Deuteronomy*, 766.

18. Kalland sees 32:39 as "a reference to his creative power and his power to rescue from death illustrated by his rescue of the nation of Israel when no one remains (v. 36)." Kalland, "Deuteronomy," 214.

19. John Rea also notices the connection between the hovering Spirit at creation and the creation of a new nation in Deut 32. Rea, *Holy Spirit in the Bible*, 29.

in this study, including an eschatological outlook, creation, the activity of the Spirit, and the need for restoration. In the second passage the restoration amounts to a national resurrection. Second, the intentional recapitulation of Genesis in Deuteronomy suggests a narrative unity to the Pentateuch, which in turn suggests that the Hebrew people had an early foundational knowledge of God's sovereignty over life and death and of his ability to reverse death. Third, in this light, Ezekiel's depiction of Israel's national restoration with vivid resurrection terminology does not seem so original (Ezek 37:1–14). The rabbis sometimes used some questionable hermeneutics in passages such as Deut 32:39 while attempting to demonstrate that resurrection is taught in the Torah, but their instincts were largely correct, for even Ezekiel drew from the implications of such passages.[20]

The Design of the Spirit

The Spirit's agency in transforming the land from "formless and empty" (תֹהוּ וָבֹהוּ; Gen 1:2) to ordered and full associates him with eschatological progression. Lloyd Neve suggests that the conjunction in the phrase "and the Spirit of God" (וְרוּחַ אֱלֹהִים) could be a *waw* adversative, establishing a contrast between the barrenness of the land prior to the Spirit's activity and the fullness afterward.[21] The context confirms this suggestion. Throughout the creation narrative the author highlights the arrival of light, new life, beauty, and symmetry and then reaches a climax in the creation of humans in the image of God. The cadence of the Hebrew text itself and the Hebrew literary devices employed (such as rhyme, repetition, and alliteration) reflect the nature of the subject matter described; a "crown of beauty" replaces ashes (Isa 61:3 NIV). Gordon Wenham notes numerous indicators of this in the text, such as the correspondence between the first three and second three days of creation, the repetition of

---

20. See the rabbi's comments on Deut 32:39 in bSan 91b. The Babylonian Talmud also says that "all Israel have a portion in the world to come," except for certain persons such as those who hold "that resurrection is not a biblical doctrine," which is literally translated as, "that resurrection is not intimated in the Torah." Brauner, *Online Soncino Babylonion Talmud Translation*, bSan 90a and n31. Notice the rather forced interpretation of various passages in bSan90b. Also notice how Rabbi Judah the Patriarch correctly grasped the eschatological significance of the exodus deliverance, but he resorted to eisegesis in his interpretation of Exod 15:1. See Levenson, *Resurrection and the Restoration of Israel*, 27.

21. Neve, *Spirit of God in the Old Testament*, 63.

the number seven and the occurrence of multiples of seven, the formulaic manner in which the creation days are presented, and the chiastic construction of Gen 1:1—2:3.[22]

Later biblical writers confirm the eschatological significance of the creation story when they allude to the "formless and empty" (תֹהוּ וָבֹהוּ) phrase of Gen 1:2 and use the same two nouns in other eschatological contexts. The prophets incorporate the same two nouns to describe the devastation of the approaching international day of vengeance (Isa 34:11) and the ruination of the land of Judah (Jer 4:23). Just as in the Genesis account, the sin of humanity results in a reversal of the order and beauty of creation and the wasting of the land.[23] With this background in mind, the multiple mentions of the Spirit in the Lukan birth narratives should alert the reader that God's agent of creation is advancing his agenda in a fresh, creative act (1:15, 35, 41, 67; 2:25, 26).

Sailhamer argues that the author of Genesis largely emphasizes the inhabitability of the land with the expression "formless and empty" because God is in the process of making the land a fitting place for humanity to dwell and because the broader context of the Pentateuch focuses so much on the covenantal promised land.[24] He finds much support for his thesis in the prophetic books, and the contrast between "empty" (תֹהוּ) and "inhabited" in Isa 45:18 is particularly impressive.[25] Continuity exists between this passage, the themes of Deut 32, and the creation account. In Isa 44–45 God promises to raise up Cyrus to rebuild Jerusalem and the temple (44:28; 45:13), and God will do this because he is the only God (45:6; cf. Deut 32:39).[26] As in Deut 32:39, this passage emphasizes the absolute sovereignty of God over all things, especially creation and the fortunes of humanity: "I form the light and create darkness, I bring prosperity and create disaster; I, the LORD, do all these things" (Isa 45:7 NIV). References to God as Creator, the one who "created the heavens" and who "made the earth" (v. 18), occur throughout this passage. He created the earth to be inhabited; he will perform a re-creation to make Judah an inhabited place again, and he invites "the ends of the earth" to

22. Wenham, *Genesis*, 2:4–7.
23. So also Hildebrandt, *Old Testament Theology*, 31.
24. Sailhamer, *Pentateuch as Narrative*, 84–89.
25. Sailhamer, *Pentateuch as Narrative*, 85n11. Beale seems to agree that inhabitability is a major emphasis in the Genesis account. Beale, *Temple and Mission*, 81–82.
26. Numerous scholars have commented on how the Genesis account contrasts with ancient cosmologies and with the polytheism of Egypt and the oriental nations.

turn to him and be saved (v. 22). Jacob's thirsty land and dry ground will have water: "I will pour out my Spirit on your offspring, and my blessing on your descendants" (44:3 NIV).

At this juncture it is important to note that the Spirit is revealed to be an eschatological agent from the earliest mention of him forward. It is also abundantly clear that sin destroys the good designs of the Spirit, necessitating eschatological visitations of his presence to renew life and, ultimately, to fulfill the original purposes of God in a new creation. Luke's reference to the creative activity of the Spirit in Mary's womb (Luke 1:35; cf. Gen 1:2), his announcements of eschatological reversal for Israel (Luke 1:47–55, 68–79), the prominence he gives to the role of the Spirit in the eschaton (e.g., 3:16; 4:16–21; Acts 2:17–21), and the close association he sees between Christ's return and eschatological refreshing and restoration (3:18–21) indicate that his perspective is steeped in the foundational elements of the Pentateuch's eschatological pneumatology.

The Spirit as Sanctuary Builder

Mention of the "generations" (תוֹלְדוֹת) in Gen 2:4 as well as the shift in the narrative makes it apparent that this verse serves as a division marker, but Wenham correctly asserts that this first unit (1:1—2:3) also functions as an introduction to the entire Pentateuch.[27] The previous argument that Gen 1 connects with Deut 32 supports his assertion. This is a significant observation because the author immediately calls attention to the Spirit by giving him a prominent position at the beginning of an introduction to such an important work. From a literary perspective, this suggests that the Spirit in some way governs the activities in the narrative to follow. While the Pentateuch mentions the Spirit from time to time, it is more important where he is mentioned than how often he is mentioned.[28] Although the repeated references to the Spirit in Luke-Acts make Luke's interests more evident, the same principle applies there. Luke seldom mentions him in the body of the gospel, yet the frontloading of references to him removes all doubt that the Spirit is active throughout the life of Christ. And in Acts, the location of the Spirit's outpouring at Pentecost serves as a narrative lens through which the reader understands the rest of the book.

---

27. Wenham, *Genesis*, 1:5.

28. Frank Macchia makes this same point regarding the occurrences of glossolalia in Acts. Macchia, "Groans Too Deep for Words," 149–73.

Thus, it is incumbent upon the reader to pay careful attention to what follows in the narrative, and Genesis reveals that the author casts the Spirit in the role of a sanctuary builder. He depicts the garden of Eden as a sanctuary where humanity is blessed and God is worshipped, Adam as an archetypal priest-king of the garden commissioned to enlarge its boundaries (Gen 2:15), and sin as the spoiler of the good creation. That the author intended such a picture becomes evident when one views the Pentateuch as a whole and notices the similarities between Eden and the construction of the tabernacle. Numerous scholars have remarked on those parallels, and the following discussion summarizes some of the key points.

Eden as Tabernacle

Michael Fishbane draws attention to the verbal parallels between the creation account and construction of the tabernacle (Gen 1:31; 2:1–3; cf. Exod 39:32, 43; 40:33). "Thus, 'Moses saw all the work' which the people 'did' in constructing the tabernacle; 'and Moses completed the work' and 'blessed' the people for all their labors."[29] Fishbane follows this observation with another noteworthy insight: "There is the arresting fact that the desert tabernacle was erected on the first day of the first month of the year (Exodus 40:2, 17)."[30] Sailhamer notes that both the creation account and the tabernacle construction are marked by seven acts introduced with "And God said" (Gen 1:3, 6, 9, 14, 20, 24, 26) or "And Yahweh said" (Exod 25:1; 30:11, 17, 22, 34; 31:1, 12).[31]

The presence of gold also stands out in both "sanctuaries" (Gen 2:11–12; Exod 25:3, 11), and both feature precious stones as well (Gen 2:12; Exod 25:7). In keeping with Near Eastern tradition, cherubim guard the entrance of the garden of Eden (Gen 3:24); they also appear over the mercy seat (Exod 25:18–22) and in the tabernacle curtains (26:1), and they guard the Most Holy Place in Solomon's temple (1 Kgs 6:23–28).[32] The location of the cherubim suggests that the garden of Eden was entered from the east, as were later temples and Ezekiel's eschatological temple (Ezek 40:6).[33] Likewise, Ezekiel depicts the future temple as the

---

29. Fishbane, *Biblical Text and Texture*, 12.
30. Fishbane, *Biblical Text and Texture*, 12.
31. Sailhamer, *Pentateuch as Narrative*, 299.
32. Wenham, "Sanctuary Symbolism," 21.
33. Beale, *Temple and Mission*, 74.

source of a river of life (47:1–12; cf. Rev 22:1–2) in a manner reminiscent of the river that flowed from Eden (Gen 2:10; cf. Ps 1:3; 46:5).[34]

Exodus 25:31–40 describes in detail the tree-like design of the tabernacle's golden lampstand. The best candidate for an original pattern for this piece of furniture is the tree of life (Gen 2:9; cf. Josephus, *Ant.* 3.145).[35] Between the close of the tabernacle's description in Exod 31 and the second detailed description as each item was built according to the divine plan (Exod 35–40), the idolatrous sin of the Israelites disrupts and temporarily halts progress on the tabernacle. Similarly, the fall in Gen 3 interrupts the harmony in the narrative and the progress toward eternal fellowship with God.[36] Perhaps the most obvious similarity between Eden and later sanctuaries is the fundamental purpose of them, that is, to fellowship with and worship the King, whose glory fills the sanctuaries. The sharing of the *hithpael* form of הלך ("walk back and forth") between Gen 3:8 and Lev 26:12 reinforces this central idea.[37] In Leviticus God promises to reward the obedience of his people with nothing less than his presence. He promises to put his tabernacle (מִשְׁכָּן) among them (26:11) and, in parallel, he promises to walk among them (וְהִתְהַלַּכְתִּי; v. 12; cf. Deut 23:15; 2 Sam 7:6–7).

Adam as Priest-King

Some scholars also hold that the author of the Pentateuch presents Adam as an archetypal priest-king made in God's image and acting as King Yahweh's vice-regent.[38] Evidence for this rests in part on the translation of the two infinitives in Gen 2:15, לְעָבְדָהּ וּלְשָׁמְרָהּ ("to work it and keep it"), but also on verbal echoes in later priestly texts, contextual considerations, and the command given to Adam in the following verse.[39] It is likely that

---

34. Wenham, "Sanctuary Symbolism," 22; Beale, *Temple and Mission*, 72–73. Beale lists several ways in which later writers described Eden as a sanctuary as well as similarities between later biblical temples and Eden (pages 66–69).

35. Beale, *Temple and Mission*, 71.

36. Sailhamer also notes this in *Pentateuch as Narrative*, 299.

37. Wenham, "Sanctuary Symbolism," 20.

38. E.g., Beale, *Temple and Mission*, 82–83.

39. Beale gives substantial attention to this issue and argues that the contextual considerations are determinative in finding priestly overtones in the depiction of Adam. Beale, *Temple and Mission*, 66–70. For a summary of how others have grappled with the significance of the Hebrew infinitives, see Beale, *Temple and Mission*, 67n89.

more than just cultivation and taking care of the Garden is in view. The second verb could anticipate Adam's role in guarding the garden from evil intruders (3:1).[40]

Wenham notes that "the only other passages in the Pentateuch where these verbs are used together are to be found in Num 3:7–8, 8:26, 18:5–6, of the Levites' duties in guarding and ministering in the sanctuary."[41] He rightly makes this connection, and Num 18:7 is an important one to add to the list. However, the two verbs also occur together in Deut 11:16 and 12:30, where the Lord commands the Israelites to watch that they do not serve other gods, and in 13:4 (v. 5 MT): "You shall walk after the LORD your God and fear him and keep [תִּשְׁמֹרוּ] his commandments and obey his voice, and you shall serve [תַעֲבֹדוּ] him and hold fast to him" (ESV).[42] The requirement of obedience in 13:1–5 is squarely based on Gen 2:16–17: "And the LORD God commanded the man, saying, 'You may surely eat of every tree of the garden, but of the tree of the knowledge of good and evil you shall not eat, for in the day that you eat of it you shall surely die'" (ESV).[43] Keeping God's covenant is a basic qualification for the Israelites to be "a kingdom of priests" (Exod 19:5–6). The author of Genesis views God's instructions to Adam in 2:15–17 as a pattern both for the Levitical priesthood and for the general priestly obligations of the nation.

Martin Buber suggests that the final editor of the Pentateuch intentionally drew the parallels between the construction of the tabernacle and creation in order to instruct humanity to continue and expand on the work of creation.[44] Beale picks up this thought and, based on Adam's identity as "a priest-king in God's image" and the commission given to Adam and Eve to "be fruitful and multiply and fill the earth and subdue it, and have dominion . . ." (Gen 1:28 ESV), holds that "it is plausible to suggest that they were to extend the geographical boundaries of the garden

---

Sailhamer translates the phrase as "to worship and obey," emphasizing the relational aspect of Adam's purpose. Sailhamer, *Genesis Unbound*, 82–83.

40. Kline, *Kingdom Prologue*, 54–55, 65–67.

41. Wenham, "Sanctuary Symbolism," 21.

42. Although the latter texts from Deuteronomy do not directly apply to priestly duties, they do not detract from Wenham's primary observation, for each of these passages occur in the same section of Deuteronomy where God urges covenant fidelity and warns against apostasy.

43. Beale also notes the similarity between the instructions given to Adam and those given to Solomon upon the completion of the temple (1 Kgs 9:1, 6–7). Beale, *Temple and Mission*, 68.

44. Buber, *Die Schrift und ihre Verdeutschung*, 39.

The Spirit, Creation, and Luke-Acts

until Eden covered the whole earth."[45] He further lists the numerous repetitions of this commission in Genesis and notes the connection between the commission and the building of what he calls "small sanctuaries."[46]

Thus, Moses presents the Spirit as the agent involved in constructing the first sanctuary and expanding it over all the earth. This function of the Spirit becomes even more evident during the construction of the tabernacle under Moses. Significantly, the sovereign King who dwells in the sanctuaries entrusts a vice-regent with priestly duties and with the expansion of the kingdom beyond the borders of the initial sanctuary. One can observe similar threads intertwining when Christ comes and recapitulates Adam's life yet reverses his failure (Luke 3:38—4:13), acts as a priest bestowing the blessing of the Spirit (24:50–53), and sends out his disciples to expand his kingdom to the nations (Acts 1:8).[47]

The Spirit and the Tabernacle of Rest

The writer of Hebrews speaks of more than the cessation of physical labor when referring to a rest of salvation and a final eschatological goal (Heb 4:1–13). The author quotes Ps 95:11 in verse 3: "As I swore in my wrath, 'They shall not enter my rest'" (ESV), which is a loose quotation of Num 14:30 and Deut 1:35. However, in the latter passages the Lord actually forbids them to enter the land. That the land and rest are used interchangeably shows that the promised land was supposed to have been a place of rest, a sabbatical destination. In Exodus the Sabbath commandment is based squarely on the creation account (Exod 20:8–11; Gen 2:1–3), but the writer supports the same commandment with a reference to the exodus in Deut 5:12–15. The Israelites escaped the clutches of Pharaoh by a fresh, creative act of God to enter into a new rest at a new sanctuary in the promised land. Vos correctly notes that God's rest (from the verb שׁבת; Gen 2:2) involves "fulfillment" and "consummation" and is inherently relational in orientation.[48] Thus, after the fall the Sabbath gains an even more evident eschatological flavor because a salvific work must take place in order to make relationship and Sabbath rest possible.

---

45. Beale, *Temple and Mission*, 81–82.
46. Beale, *Temple and Mission*, 94–96.
47. This thought will receive further discussion in chapter 8.
48. Vos, *Eschatology of the Old Testament*, 105.

The repeated appeals to Pharaoh to let Israel go in order to worship God (e.g., Exod 3:18; 4:23; 8:20; 9:13) were no mere ploy to escape bondage; those statements embody the purpose of the entire redemptive plan of God and the particular goal of Exodus. The book climaxes with God's glory descending on the tabernacle, but along the way idolatry brings progress to a halt and interrupts the plan.[49] Exodus 25–30 records the Lord's instructions for building the tabernacle and its furnishings. Just prior to the golden calf episode, the text devotes attention to Bezalel's filling with the Spirit (31:1–11) and then the admonition to observe the Sabbath (vv. 12–18). When the golden calf debacle is finally in the rearview mirror, tabernacle construction commences, and the renewed narrative begins with a fresh admonition to observe the Sabbath (35:1–3), offerings for the building project (vv. 4–29), and reference to Bezalel's filling with the Spirit (35:30—36:7). William Dumbrell observes that "the Sabbath command . . . is restated at the beginning of chapter 35 to emphasize the continuity of chapters 35–40 with 25–31."[50] In addition to that, the Sabbath as the symbol of divine/human fellowship serves as a frame providing a sharp contrast with the idolatrous acts that rejected Yahweh's royal rule and denied him a dwelling place in Israel's midst (25:8). The writer heightens this contrast further by locating the "Spirit of God" (רוּחַ אֱלֹהִים; 31:3; 35:31) adjacent to the Sabbath passages and forming an inclusio around Israel's sin. The agent of sanctuary building will have no truck with idolatry and rebellion.

The importance of the Spirit's influence in the construction of a sacred place receives added emphasis in Exod 28:3: "You shall speak to all the wise in heart, whom I have filled with the Spirit of wisdom [מִלֵּאתִיו רוּחַ חָכְמָה], that they make garments for Aaron to consecrate him to serve me as priest." The following points suggest that the Spirit of God is in view. First, the terminology is very similar to 31:3 ("and I have filled him with the Spirit of God, with wisdom"; וָאֲמַלֵּא אֹתוֹ רוּחַ אֱלֹהִים בְּחָכְמָה), where the Spirit of God is directly mentioned. Second, although Bezalel is singled out as the leader, the Spirit's enabling of others also seems to be implied in verse 6. Third, the use of the first-person singular with "filled" only occurs in 28:3 and 31:3 in the Pentateuch, and in both cases God is the subject of the *piel* verb מלא ("fill"). Fourth, the sheer uniqueness of God's filling a human being in the Pentateuch suggests that something more than mere talent is intended.

49. Dumbrell, *End of the Beginning*, 43–44.
50. Dumbrell, *End of the Beginning*, 44.

Filled to Build

The verb מלא ("fill") occurs fifty-eight times in the Pentateuch.[51] In contrast to God's blessing on the sea creatures, his command to them to "fill" the waters (Gen 1:22), and the divine charge to man and woman to fill the earth (v. 28), the Hebrew verb refers to the land as filled with wickedness in Lev 19:29 and violence in Gen 6:11, 13. The blessing on Noah and the repetition of 1:28 after the flood (9:1) emphasize all the more the contrast between the blessing of fullness and abundance versus the curse of sin. A similar contrast with death and oppression occurs in the opening chapter of Exodus. Despite the death of Joseph and the entire previous generation (Exod 1:6), the Israelites multiplied and "the land was filled with them" (v. 7). "But a new king arose over Egypt" (v. 8). In Deuteronomy the coming prosperity and fullness in Canaan is contrasted with the slavery in Egypt (Deut 6:11–12).

The initial uses of the verb מלא ("to fill") are determinative for interpreting the significance of the fullness of the Spirit, especially when one considers the strong contrast between the "I have filled him" and "he has filled him" frame (Exod 31:3; 35:31) with the intervening idolatry of Israel. The forces of violence, wickedness, death, evil rulers, enslavement, and idolatry continually assault God's plan of blessing, yet his Spirit actively works to establish a worshiping, Sabbath community.

The two records of Bezalel's filling with the Spirit are practically identical for several verses in the Hebrew text (Exod 31:1–6; 35:30–34), except that the latter text records the filling as an accomplished event. It is also noteworthy that the second record expands on the Spirit's gifting and enablement and adds the inspiration to teach to Bezalel's and Oholiab's

---

51. Thirteen of these have a temporal aspect and record the completion of a span of time: Gen 25:24; 29:21, 27–28; 50:3; Exod 7:25; 23:26; Lev 8:33; 12:3, 6; 25:30; Num 6:5, 13. Van Pelt and Kaiser note that the term sometimes describes the fulfillment of God's promises in the Old Testament (e.g., 1 Kgs 8:15). Van Pelt and Kaiser, "מלא," 940. More often the term has a spatial aspect. A handful of times the verb is used for common purposes such as filling a jar with water: Gen 21:19; 24:16; 26:15; 42:25; 44:1; Exod 2:15. On a couple of occasions the term is associated with judgment, as flies and locusts filled the Egyptians' houses (Exod 8:17; 10:6). Eleven times the term occurs as part of an idiom ("fill the hands") describing the ordination of the priests (28:41; 29:9, 29, 33, 35; 32:29; Lev 8:33; 9:17; 16:32; 21:10; Num 3:3). Hamilton gives a brief but helpful discussion of the idiom. He notes that in Lev 8:22 the noun alone means "ordination." Hamilton, *Exodus*, 493. The priest's breast piece was also to be filled with precious stones (Exod 28:17; cf. 39:10).

repertoire.[52] In general, chapters 35–40 recapitulate chapters 25–31, as Moses and the Israelites build the tabernacle in accordance with the heavenly pattern (25:8–9) and the divine command (39:42–43), but it is striking how the Sabbath guidelines along with the filling of the Spirit bracket the interruption in the narrative.

Bezalel apparently experienced a continual relationship with the Spirit, yet his filling experience did not initiate him into membership in the covenant community but empowered him to build God's sanctuary and thereby advance God's plan.[53] This latter point is the more significant point in the Pentateuchal narrative. God personally fills Bezalel with the Spirit of God (רוּחַ אֱלֹהִים), and this direct agency highlights the importance of the event. The "filled" terminology (Exod 35:31) recalls the abundance associated with creation and God's blessing, and the phrase "Spirit of God" (רוּחַ אֱלֹהִים) and the Spirit's agency in building a new sanctuary ties this project to Gen 1:2. In addition, sin disrupts the progress toward the intended Sabbath rest in both narratives and on numerous other occasions as well.

The primary purpose for which God filled Bezalel with the Spirit comes to fruition at the climax of Exodus. "Then the cloud covered the tent of meeting, and the glory of Yahweh filled the tabernacle [מָלֵא אֶת־הַמִּשְׁכָּן]. And Moses was not able to enter into the tent of meeting because the cloud settled on it [כִּי־שָׁכַן עָלָיו הֶעָנָן; ὅτι ἐπεσκίαζεν ἐπ' αὐτὴν ἡ νεφέλη, LXX], and the glory of Yahweh filled the tabernacle [מָלֵא אֶת־הַמִּשְׁכָּן]" (40:34–35). In the final three verses (36–38) the author emphasizes the presence of the cloud by day and fire by night in the plain view of the Israelites. The repetition of "filled" is especially appropriate with its strong association with the blessing of God's presence in creation as well as associations with the Spirit. The Spirit has overseen the construction of a divine dwelling place and made it possible for the Israelites to worship the God who dwells in their midst.

Some of the emphases discussed above receive more detailed treatment below and in later chapters, but a few preliminary comments on

---

52. Hess finds significance in the names of Bezalel ("in the shadow of God") and Oholiab ("tent," "protection of God"). He also sees connections between their calling to build a tabernacle and the creation sanctuary. Hess, "Bezalel and Oholiab," 165–67.

53. The nature of Bezalel's filling makes for an interesting ontological discussion. One might observe that generalizations regarding the sporadic and temporary endowments of the Spirit do not apply to Bezalel—someone who was filled not only to perform tasks on a continual basis but who was also entrusted with a teaching responsibility.

how these observations inform Lukan thought are in order. First, one expects that the "filled with the Holy Spirit" terminology at Pentecost (Acts 2:4) carries at least some of the theological weight of Bezalel's experience of divine enablement and of the tabernacle's filling with the divine presence. Second, one can better appreciate the magnitude of the Pentecostal event in light of Yahweh's direct impartation of the Spirit on Bezalel, as Jesus himself exercises the divine prerogative and directly bestows the Spirit on his waiting disciples. Third, while Luke does not emphasize sabbatical terminology, his eschatological orientation is entirely consistent with the concept (Acts 3:21). Fourth, Luke insists that repentance must precede the experience of the eschatological blessing of the Spirit (2:38; 3:19, 24–26; 5:31–32). Sin must be dealt with in order for God's ultimate purposes to come to fruition.

Overshadowing, Filling, and Luke-Acts

The prophetic function of the Spirit in Luke's opening chapters has received substantial attention, but the angel's announcement to Mary has never quite seemed to fit with an understanding of the Spirit in Luke-Acts as strictly inspiring prophetic utterance. "And the angel answered and said to her, 'The Holy Spirit will come upon you [ἐπελεύσεται ἐπὶ σὲ], and the power [δύναμις] of the Most High [ὑψίστου] will overshadow [ἐπισκιάσει] you; therefore the holy one to be born will be called the Son of God'" (1:35). The Greek verb ἐπισκιάζω ("overshadow") occurs only nine times in the Scriptures, thus Luke draws attention to Exod 40:35 (LXX) via shared terminology and to Gen 1:2 via shared concept.[54] Luke signals to his readers that the same Spirit who brought form from chaos and tabernacled in Israel's midst has come to bring life to Mary's womb and advance God's eschatological plan.

In Luke 1:35 the Holy Spirit parallels the power of the Most High and the coming upon parallels the overshadowing. This makes for a

---

54. Three of the occurrences are in the parallel accounts of the transfiguration (Matt 17:5; Mark 9:7; Luke 9:34). Luke uses it in reference to Peter's extraordinary healing miracles (Acts 5:15), and the remaining occurrences are found in the Septuagint (Exod 40:35; Ps 90:4; 139:8; Prov 18:11). Nolland also sees Lukan dependency on Exod 40:35. Nolland, *Luke 1—9:20*, 54. Rea connects these texts to new creation in Christ: "By this common figure of the hovering and overshadowing presence of God's Spirit, the original creation, the creation of God's covenant nation and the new creation in Christ are linked together." Rea, *Holy Spirit in the Bible*, 29. For an overview of various understandings of the background of ἐπισκιάζω, see Bock, *Luke*, 1:121–23.

fascinating mixture of Exod 40:35 and Isa 32:15 as well as an anticipation of Acts 1:8. Isaiah describes the radical reversal that fructifies the desolate land when "the Spirit from on high comes upon you" (ἐπέλθῃ ἐφ᾽ ὑμᾶς πνεῦμα ἀφ᾽ ὑψηλοῦ) (32:15 LXX). The extremely rare combination of ἐπέρχομαι ("come upon") and πνεῦμα ("Spirit") occurring in Luke 1:35, Isaiah 32:15, and Acts 1:8 strongly suggests an intentional tie between these passages.[55] The use of the similar adjectives ὑψηλός ("high," (Isa 32:15) and ὕψιστος ("Most High," Luke 1:35) confirm the notion that Luke draws from Isaiah, and Acts 1:8 seems like an obvious reflection of Luke 1:35: "But you will receive power [δύναμιν] when the Holy Spirit comes upon you [ἐπελθόντος]" (Acts 1:8a). Images of new creation, divine presence, reversal, and power all converge in Luke 1:35, and the focal point of all these images is the Davidic Christ.[56] The presence of the Spirit accomplishes in Mary's womb a miraculous generation of the preexistent, royal Son of God (vv. 31, 32, 35) through whom the Old Testament's anticipation of the restoration of God's presence will take place. The shared terminology in Acts 1:8 indicates that the disciples participate in bearing the transformative presence and power of God with the coming of the Spirit at Pentecost. Their testimony is christocentric ("my witnesses") and focuses on the resurrection of Jesus (v. 22). Through their testimony to the risen and exalted Davidic king, the nations are exposed to the glory of God and begin to experience a taste of the final restoration.

The other early references to the Spirit in the Lukan birth narratives have associations with prophecy. Although prophecy is not directly mentioned in conjunction with John the Baptist's filling (1:15), John will function like the prophet Elijah (v. 17). The utterances of Elizabeth (1:41–45), Zechariah (1:67–79), and Simeon (2:25–35) are clearly prophetic. Luke even depicts Mary in the prophetic role when she voices the Magnificat (1:46–55). But Mary's initial encounter with the Spirit in 1:35 is not primarily prophetic; the overshadowing Spirit signals the divine presence and functions in power to bring in the Messiah in an act of new creation. As with Gen 1:2, the Spirit in Luke 1:35 has a literary and theological prominence in the narrative.[57] Although Luke will certainly

---

55. These two Greek words also occur together in Num 5:14, 30; Job 1:19; 4:15 (LXX), but the divine Spirit is not in view in these passages.

56. Green also notices the "christological repercussions" of Luke 1:35. Green, *Gospel of Luke*, 90.

57. Luke 1:35 is Luke's third mention of the Spirit (assuming one considers "the Spirit and power of Elijah" in 1:17 as a reference to the divine Spirit), but the emphasis

emphasize the prophetic role of the Spirit, the more basic operation of the Spirit is to bring about the eschatological plan of God. Therefore the entire narrative of Luke-Acts reflects the theology of the Pentateuch on a fundamental level. The references to prophecy highlight a specific function of the Spirit and the means by which the Spirit carries out his greater role—to move fallen creation toward "the time of the restoration of all things" (Acts 3:21).

Luke's use of "filled" (πίμπλημι) also indicates the broader dimensions of the Spirit's purposes in Luke-Acts. Luke nearly has a monopoly on the use of this verb in the New Testament; he uses it twenty-two times.[58] The compound ἐμπίπλημι ("to fill," "to satisfy") seldom occurs in the New Testament (Luke 1:53; 6:25; John 6:12; Acts 14:17; Rom 15:24), but in each case it distinctly connotes satisfaction, such as in the sense of satisfying hunger. Gerhard Delling remarks on how strange this is, given the absence of this distinction between the verbs in the Old Testament, where both Greek terms translate the Hebrew words מלא ("to fill") and שׂבע ("to satiate").[59] Consequently, it does not matter a great deal that the Septuagint uses the compound ἐμπίπλημι rather than πίμπλημι in the key references to Bezalel's (Exod 28:41; 31:3; 35:31) and Joshua's (Deut 34:9) filling with the Spirit (cf. Mic 3:8; Isa 11:3; Sir 39:6). Luke employs πίμπλημι in the angel's announcement that John the Baptist "will be filled with the Holy Spirit, even from his mother's womb" (Luke 1:15), in reference to Elizabeth's filling with the Holy Spirit (v. 41), and in describing Zechariah's filling with the Spirit and prophesying (v. 67).[60] Roger Stronstad rightly notices the strong ties between the "filled with the Spirit" expression and prophetic utterance in Luke-Acts.[61] For Luke, "filled with the Spirit" does function as a technical phrase for prophetic empowerment. At the same time, several observations regarding the broader

---

on Jesus's miraculous conception gives v. 35 a prominence that rivals even John's filling from birth (1:15).

58. Apart from Luke, only Matthew uses the term and only on two occasions (22:10; 27:48).

59. Delling, "Πίμπλημι, Ἐμπίπλημι, Πλησμονή," 128–29.

60. Other references to πίμπλημι in connection with the Spirit in Acts include 2:4; 4:8, 31; 9:17; 13:9.

61. He concludes that "Luke uses the term, 'filled with the Spirit,' to describe neither moral behavior nor Christian service in general, but rather as a technical term to describe the office of the prophet, on the one hand, or to introduce prophetic speech (a pneuma discourse), on the other hand." Stronstad, *Spirit, Scripture and Theology*, 98.

biblical use of "filled with the Spirit" suggest that prophetic connections alone do not exhaust the meaning of this Lukan expression.

First, none of Luke's most likely septuagintal sources for this phrase focus on prophecy. The Spirit fills Bezalel for tabernacle construction (Exod 28:3; 31:3; 35:31) and the Spirit fills the ruler from the "root of Jesse" (Isa 11:1) with "the fear of God" (v. 3).[62] Second, although the filling with the Spirit in Luke-Acts consistently relates to various forms of prophetic/inspired utterance (Luke 1:17, 41, 67; Acts 2:4; 4:8, 31; 9:17; 13:9, 52),[63] Luke also indicates that the disciples "were filled [ἐπληροῦντο] with joy and the Holy Spirit" (Acts 13:52). The Spirit-empowered preaching is evident both before and after this statement, but the fruit of joy evinces the supernatural, emotional enabling of the Spirit in the face of persecution (13:50). Third, the Septuagint uses πίμπλημι to describe how the tabernacle "was filled with the glory of the Lord" (δόξης κυρίου ἐπλήσθη) when the cloud "overshadowed" (ἐπεσκίαζεν) it (Exod 40:34–35). Seeing as Luke already refers to this passage when he describes the overshadowing of Mary (1:35), this passage probably also influenced his perspective on "filling," in which case eschatological restoration of God's presence is in view.

Fourth, just as מלא ("to fill") has a broader use in describing the completion of time in the Old Testament, so Luke (and Luke alone) uses πίμπλημι to describe the fulfillment of events in the birth narratives.[64] This is quite significant because Luke only uses the term in this manner in the birth narratives, and he has a strong concentration of allusions to eschatological fulfillment in the opening chapters. Luke's use of the cognate verb πληροφορέω ("to fulfill") in the opening verse sets the tone for both volumes. He uses πίμπλημι to indicate the end of Zechariah's temple service (Luke 1:23), the arrival of the time for Elizabeth to give birth (v. 57), the arrival of the time for Mary to give birth (2:6), the time for Jesus's circumcision (v. 21), and the end of the time of Mary's and Joseph's purification (v. 22). In addition, Gabriel says that his words "will be fulfilled [πληρωθήσονται] at their appointed time" (1:20). Luke uses the future

---

62. The Septuagint evinces the Jewish understanding of Isa 11:1 as referring to a specific ruler to come. Instead of the "branch" of the Masoretic text, the Septuagint has the term ῥάβδος ("rod" or "staff").

63. Most of the passages in Acts do not immediately or expressly mention prophecy, but the larger context bears out the prophetic (and often) charismatic aspect of the filling.

64. Delling, "Πίμπλημι, Ἐμπίπλημι, Πλησμονή," 130.

passive of another cognate verb, πληρόω, to prophesy a fulfillment but then uses πίμπλημι to record the actual fulfillment (v. 57). This mixing of cognates gives the impression that more than the mere passage of time is in view; the narrative has an air of divine appointment and redemptive fulfillment. So while Luke knows that πίμπλημι can mean either "filled" or "fulfilled," it is possible that he intends his readers to see shades of "fulfillment" when reading about "filling." In any event, there are enough pointers in the Lukan and septuagintal context to indicate that the phrase "filled with the Spirit" not only signifies prophetic utterance, but also implies a range of associations including eschatological fulfillment.[65]

The goal of the prophetic empowering is of even more interest in this study than the prophetic means, and the inherently eschatological nature of the phrase "filled with the Spirit" grows in significance with the realization that the prophetic utterances of those described in this manner focus on Christ.[66] The Spirit fills John the Baptist to restore backsliders and prepare the way for the Lord (Jesus) (Luke 1:15-17). Elizabeth proclaims the lordship of Mary's baby (v. 43). Zechariah gives praise for salvation through one from the line of David (v. 69). Peter explains the Pentecostal tongues (Acts 2:4) as a prophetic response (v. 17) to the resurrection of the Davidic king (vv. 24-35), whom "God has made . . . both Lord and Christ" (v. 36). The resurrection of "Jesus Christ" features as the central issue in Peter's Spirit-filled response to the Jewish leaders (4:8-13). The aftermath of the prayer meeting earthquake and Spirit's filling of the believers centers on testifying "to the resurrection of the Lord Jesus" (vv. 31-33). Upon Saul's filling, he preached that "Jesus is the Son of God" (9:20). Even Saul's pronunciation of judgment on Elymas resulted from his interfering with the preaching about Jesus and also led to the proconsul's belief in Jesus (13:6-12). Finally, the Lord Jesus bore witness to the message preached by Paul and Barnabas by granting miraculous signs (14:3; cf. 13:52). In short, "filled with the Spirit" becomes a christocentric phrase that, especially in Acts, often accentuates the resurrection message of Christ. This phrase bursts with eschatological, pneumatological,

---

65. Luke actually uses πίμπλημι to speak of the fulfillment of Scripture (21:22), and only a few verses later πληρόω serves a similar purpose (v. 24). This is not to suggest that Luke makes no distinction between an individual's filling with the Spirit and the fulfillment of certain events, but to point out that Luke draws from the Old Testament well in associating eschatological development with the filling of the Spirit.

66. The Old Testament expectation of a last-days outpouring of the Spirit make any mention of the Spirit in the New Testament inherently eschatological.

and christological significance. Luke views all the Spirit's activity as christocentric, for the eschatological blessings only arrive through him.

The various theological associations accompanying the "filled with the Spirit" phrase prompt one to consider the implications of this for the disciples at Pentecost. The phrase carries too much theological weight to limit it only to prophetic utterance, although it surely does signify that. One must consider the christological implications of prophetic tongues as a response to the enthronement of God's vice-regent. Inherent in this is also an eschatological fulfillment in that God has often filled people with his Spirit in order to move his plan a step closer to the final Sabbath rest. In addition, it is very difficult to isolate "filled with the Spirit" from the images of divine presence that accompany it in the Old Testament. The disciples are therefore bearers of the divine presence who prophetically announce the arrival of a new stage in God's plan and salvation through Jesus Christ. Chapters 6–7 discuss this in greater detail.

One additional note on the ultimate filling that the tabernacle filling anticipates deserves mention. "But truly, as I live, and as all the earth shall be filled [וְיִמָּלֵא] with the glory of the LORD, none of the men who have seen my glory and my signs that I did in Egypt . . . shall see the land that I swore to give to their fathers" (Num 14:21–23a ESV). This passage occurs on the heels of Moses's intercession and the twelve spies' report on Canaan. Of course the two notable exceptions to the prohibition were Caleb and Joshua, who "wholly followed after Yahweh" (lit. "filled after"; מִלְאוּ אַחֲרֵי; Num 32:12; cf. Deut 1:36), in contrast to the other spies, who did not "wholly follow after" the Lord (Num 32:11). This is an uncommon use of מלא ("to fill") in the Old Testament, but it is an appropriate way to describe Caleb, who had "another spirit" and "wholly followed after" the Lord (הָיְתָה רוּחַ אַחֶרֶת עִמּוֹ וַיְמַלֵּא אַחֲרָי; Num 14:24), as well as Joshua, who "was filled with the Spirit of wisdom" (מָלֵא רוּחַ חָכְמָה; Deut 34:9; cf. Exod 28:3; 31:3; 35:31). While the developing narrative singles out Joshua as the next pneumatic leader of Israel (Num 27:18), the nexus of filling terminology, the general oversight of the Spirit (Gen 1:2), the concern with God's coming glory (Num 14:21), the word רוּחַ ("spirit") applied to Caleb, and the shared spiritual condition of Caleb and Joshua suggests that more than merely a different disposition motivates Caleb; the divine Spirit enables him to see God's provision of the new "sanctuary." God's glory will fill the land, and he will use Spirit-filled people like Caleb and Joshua to move history in that direction.

Some versions translate the *niphal* imperfect verb וְיִמָּלֵא of Num 14:21 as a present tense, signifying that God's glory already fills the earth (e.g., NIV, HCSB). But the future is the better translation, for the glory that already appears at the tent of meeting (14:10) will one day cover the earth (cf. Isa 11:9; Hab 2:14). The denial of the promised land to the disobedient was also a denial of an anticipatory experience of the final restoration, yet neither the sin of the Israelites nor the judgment upon them will finally derail the plan of God. The very life of God himself assures the certainty of the achievement of the eschatological goal, for the eternally living, omniscient, and omnipotent God has the ability to see the future and guide history toward its goal.[67] It is this eschatological worldview Luke builds on when he grants a prominent position to the overshadowing Spirit in Luke 1:35 and when he fills men and women with the Spirit.

Summary

Genesis 1:2 presents the Spirit as a creative agent who prepares a sanctuary and as an eschatological agent who advances God's plan to bring restoration to fallen humanity. The repetition of themes from Gen 1 in Deut 32 demonstrates that the Spirit plays a role in bringing what amounts to a national resurrection to Israel. This frame around the Pentateuch gives a glimpse of God's resurrection power and points to an eschatological connection between resurrection and Spirit. This eschatological perspective is foundational to Luke's theology (Luke 1:1), and the frontloading of the Spirit in both Gen 1 and Luke 1 further invites the reader to compare how the Spirit exerts influence over each narrative. Moses depicts the Spirit as having a role in building the sanctuary of Eden and Adam as a viceregent with responsibility for expansion of the Edenic sanctuary. This is not unlike Christ's exalted role as Lord in Acts 2 and the missiological emphasis connected with his reign. Additional associations between the Spirit and sanctuaries occur through Bezalel's filling in order to craft the tabernacle and God's filling the tabernacle with his divine presence. Luke adopts the terminology of filling and employs it throughout Luke-Acts, especially at Pentecost. Luke also adopts the overshadowing language of

---

67. Vos argues along similar lines that "a God who cannot create cannot consummate things because he is conditioned by something outside himself that will not lend itself to him for the execution of a set purpose and for the plastic handling of what is antecedently given to him toward that end." Vos, *Eschatology of the Old Testament*, 1.

Exod 40:35 (LXX) in his account of Gabriel's announcement to Mary (Luke 1:35). There is therefore an element of eschatological new creation and divine presence in the birth narrative in addition to the emphasis on the Spirit's role in inspiring prophecy.

The Lukan perspective on pneumatology relies quite heavily on the Pentateuch at a fundamental level. His pneumatology is eschatological in orientation and involves elements of new creation, divine presence, and prophetic inspiration. The christocentric nature of Pentateuchal pneumatology is in the developing stage, but Luke realizes that he stands in the application phase of history, so his employment of "filled with the Spirit" is eminently christocentric. It is precisely around this focal point of Christ that resurrection and Spirit merge at Pentecost (as discussed in chapters 7 and 8 below). The next chapter investigates the nature of Spirit-inspired prophesying in the Pentateuch and the influence of this pneumatology on the Lukan narrative.

3

The Spirit, Prophecy, and Luke-Acts

THIS CHAPTER ANALYZES THE prophetic elements of pneumatology in the Pentateuch and focuses especially on Num 11–12. Prophetic utterance as an immediate response to the coming of the Spirit has received substantial attention from others, but the following discussion investigates the nature of the prophesying and provides comparisons with Luke's account of Pentecost. The discussion elucidates some of the eschatological, ethical, and christological elements in Numbers and the rest of the Pentateuch and describes some of the implications for Luke's Pentecostal pneumatology.

Because eschatology says something about the nature of God, it follows that the Spirit of God will not only have an eschatological orientation but also a fundamentally prophetic role as the agent who carries out the divine plan. That is, the very nature of the Spirit's roles as the divine mover of God's plan and as an eschatological agent involves knowledge of the future and the ability to direct history. In this general sense, every activity of the Spirit is prophetic, yet the Spirit is also closely associated with prophecy in the particular sense of granting supernatural revelation and inspired utterance. The author of the Pentateuch portrays the Spirit as the one who inspires prophetic activity, and the creation account lays the foundation for this role.

Immediately following the record of the Spirit's "hovering" (מְרַחֶפֶת; Gen 1:2) activity, Genesis records, "And Elohim said, 'Let there be light,' and there was light" (v. 3). A series of similar prophetic statements brings creation to completion (vv. 6, 9, 11, 14, 20, 24, 26). Hildebrandt notes the difficulty of translating רוּחַ ("S/spirit") as "breath" in 1:2, because such a rendering does not square well with the movement indicated by the active participle of רחף ("hovering"). He also notes the theological significance of the literary placement of the Spirit adjacent to the divine, creative word: "The passage is emphasizing the actual, powerful presence of God, who brings the spoken word into reality by the Spirit. Thus, the Spirit and the word work together to present how the one God is responsible for all that is seen in the physical universe."[1] The prominent position given to the Spirit, the emphasis on his activity, and his close proximity to the creative word strongly suggests his agency in accomplishing the prophetic word. Although this is not, strictly speaking, the Spirit inspiring prophetic utterance, it is a strong enough association with the prophetic word to temper any surprise when the reader later encounters the Spirit inspiring prophecy.

The early chapters of Genesis contain other prophetic elements. The prophetic warning that Adam "will surely die" if he eats of the tree of the knowledge of good and evil interrupts the pleasant story with death and has a sobering effect on readers who are already experiencing the fulfillment (Gen 2:17). Adam names his wife Eve because he understands the promise of a seed as a certain, future event (3:15, 20), and Vos calls attention to the prophetic element of the tree of life.[2] Those who eat of it will "live forever," and that experience denied to Adam and Eve in the moment will ultimately be realized by many through redemption (v. 22). A prophetic view of things is fundamentally connected to creation and eschatology, and Genesis later connects the Spirit with prophecy in the life of Joseph in order to preserve the fledgling nation of Israel.

Joseph and the Prophetic Spirit

Psalm 105 refers to Abraham, Isaac, and Jacob as "prophets" (v. 15) and specifically reviews how Joseph's predictions were fulfilled (vv. 17–19). This psalm has in mind God's rebuke of Abimelech for taking Abraham's wife and the statement that Abraham is a prophet (Gen 20:6–7). Other items in the Genesis narrative, such as Abraham's visionary experience (15:12–21), also make Abraham's prophetic status evident. Likewise, in the story of Joseph, his dreams, interpretations, and predictions of the

---

1. Hildebrandt, *Old Testament Theology*, 35.
2. Vos, *Eschatology of the Old Testament*, 75.

future identify him as a prophet.³ It is appropriate that the psalmist identifies the patriarchs as "anointed ones" (Ps 105:15) and that the author of Genesis identifies Joseph as a pneumatic. Pharaoh says of him, "Can we find a man such as this, in whom is the Spirit of God [רוּחַ אֱלֹהִים]?" (Gen 41:38). Thus, there is a clear connection between the prophetic/revelatory gifting and the Spirit in the Joseph cycle.

Some translators, doubting that a pagan ruler would recognize the Spirit of God, opt for "the spirit of God" (e.g., NIV; Gen 41:38).⁴ But there are good reasons to believe that Pharaoh credited Joseph's gifting to the Spirit of God and that the author of Genesis intended his readers to also understand the reference as such. The reader has not seen the phrase "Spirit of God" (רוּחַ אֱלֹהִים) since Gen 1:2. This close identification with the Spirit in creation suggests that the same Spirit continues to act on behalf of the chosen seed. And as for Pharaoh, he readily recognizes God's activity: "God has made all this known to you" (41:39). This follows from Joseph's repeatedly crediting God as the source of revelation: "Joseph answered Pharaoh, 'It is not in me; God will give Pharaoh a favorable answer'" (v. 16 ESV; cf. vv. 25, 28, 32). Unless Pharaoh was exceedingly slow, he would have realized the truth of Joseph's claim by the time he comments on the source of Joseph's wisdom.

John Levison also translates the phrase as "spirit of God," but for different reasons than some others do. He calls attention to the association of the רוּחַ ("S/spirit") with wisdom and discernment (v. 39) and rejects the notion that Joseph experiences a charismatic endowment. "There is not the slightest indication in the narrative of Joseph to suggest that Joseph's ability to interpret dreams, his rise to power, or his capacity for plotting and planning is due to moments of inspiration. His is, rather, a life lived well, wisdom articulated well, discernment executed well."⁵ Levison's explanation of Bezalel's filling summarizes his primary concerns: "It may require a measure of historical self-discipline to resist reading the words 'filled with (the) spirit of God' as an endowment aimed at equipping Bezalel to construct the tent of meeting. It requires putting aside the influence of misleading bifurcations that arose through the misapplication of Herman Gunkel's fresh thesis, as well as later Jewish references to

---

3. Evidence of Joseph's prophetic ability begins with his dreams in Gen 37:1–11, and these charismatic elements become a central element in the continuing narrative.

4. Kaiser challenges the note in the *NIV Study Bible*, which says that a pagan ruler would not speak of the spirit in Joseph as the divine Spirit. Kaiser, "Pentateuch," 8.

5. Levison, *Filled with the Spirit*, 51.

filling with the spirit and the language of Pentecost (Acts 2:4)."[6] The "bifurcations" Levison alludes to especially include the distinction between the human spirit and the divine, wonder-working Spirit.[7] He views the breath of life in humans as the same spirit that fills Bezalel and Joseph. Thus, Joseph's "ability to interpret dreams is practiced" and he "has experience in the art of dream interpretation."[8]

Levison's challenge to Hermann Gunkel and those influenced by him has some merit.[9] There has been a tendency to view the Spirit in the Old Testament largely in terms of his "coming upon" in a momentary empowering experience to the exclusion of those passages pointing to a continual indwelling experience (e.g., Joseph, Bezalel, and David). Levison also takes seriously the life-giving and sustaining aspects of the Spirit's work, and he does attempt to look afresh at the evidence through Hebrew eyes.

But there are also some substantial problems with his approach. First, while Gunkel runs the risk of too severely dividing Pauline and Lukan pneumatology into two pneumatologies, Levison faces the same problem in dividing the Old Testament Spirit from the New Testament Spirit. In his view, the New Testament does indeed have a charismatic pneumatology, but this pneumatology is a new development arising from the influence of Greek culture.[10] Thus, the continuity between the testaments is lost. Second, when Levison fails to note the broad semantic range of רוּחַ ("S/spirit") and identifies the human spirit with the divine Spirit, it creates more problems and questions than it solves. For example, it seems difficult to reconcile Paul's ontological discussion of the presence of the Spirit as the defining mark of the believer as opposed to the absence of the Spirit in the unbeliever (Rom 8:9). Problems also arise when one tries to explain how the Spirit can leave Saul and an evil spirit from the Lord can come upon him (1 Sam 16:14). Third, Levison apparently does not view the רוּחַ of Gen 1:2 as the Spirit of God, for he ignores this passage throughout his book and completely omits it from his discussion of Joseph, citing Gen 6:3 as "the only other reference to the spirit of God in Genesis."[11]

---

6. Levison, *Filled with the Spirit*, 66–67.
7. Levison, *Filled with the Spirit*, 8–9.
8. Levison, *Filled with the Spirit*, 50.
9. See Gunkel, *Influence of the Holy Spirit*.
10. Levison, *Filled with the Spirit*, 326–28.
11. Levison, *Filled with the Spirit*, 48.

Omission of this passage handicaps his entire pneumatology and hampers his understanding of Joseph's prophetic gifts. Fourth, Levison's emphasis on Joseph's "practice" of interpreting dreams is inadequate for explaining Joseph's knowledge of the future. His approach tends to underemphasize the supernatural manifestation and overemphasize human ability.

Admittedly, it is difficult to define the precise relationship between the divine Spirit and the human spirit, as the latter is certainly a product of the former in some sense.[12] But to completely remove the identity markers between the divine Spirit and the human spirit and to also ignore the unusual charismatic influence of the divine Spirit disregards the full biblical testimony and results in confusion.

Levison rightly points out that Joseph experiences an abiding presence of the Spirit.[13] The recurrence of charismatic manifestations and the phrase "Yahweh was with him" (Gen 39:2–3, 21, 23; cf. 1 Sam 10:6, 7, 13–14, 18; 18:12, 14) point in this direction. As Num 11 suggests, the author of the Pentateuch apparently had no scruples about affirming both the reality of an ongoing experience of the Spirit's presence and times of charismatic and prophetic empowerment. He also assumed that his audience had no difficulty embracing this perspective.

Joseph's experience exemplifies the coexistence of several themes associated with the Spirit's enablement, such as wisdom, leadership, and prophetic revelation, but one must keep in view the larger purpose of the Spirit's activity. In the Genesis narrative God sovereignly raises up Joseph to preserve the seed of the chosen people in order to fulfill his promise. For the fledgling nation it is a matter of life and death; Jacob sends his sons to Egypt in search of food so they "may live and not die" (42:2). It is somewhat ironic that in the middle of the Joseph story the author rehearses the sordid details of the sins of Judah's family (ch. 38). Judah himself does not show proper regard for the chosen seed when he marries a Canaanite and later seeks out a prostitute.[14] No thanks to Judah himself, the seed continues through his family line (49:10). Joseph clearly demonstrates superior character through most of the story, and through him the nation survives (42:2, 20). The author rehearses this history so

---

12. Averbeck also argues for a distinction between the human spirit and divine Spirit while noting their conceptual similarities. Averbeck, "Breath, Wind, Spirit," 29–31.

13. Levison would not capitalize the term, viewing such a translation as anachronistic.

14. Sailhamer, *Pentateuch as Narrative*, 209–10.

that the Israelites entering Canaan would see how God has sovereignly worked through the power of his Spirit to protect their national identity and birth a nation for his glory. Once again it is in the midst of human sinfulness and even the deaths of those in the chosen line (Er, 38:7; Onan, v. 10; Judah's wife, v. 12) that the Spirit propels his plan into the future. This mixture of the Spirit's eschatological orientation and charismatic enablement is consistent with the prophetic experience of the seventy elders (Num 11) and with Luke's emphasis on fulfillment and prophetic inspiration (Acts 2:16–18).

The Seventy Elders and the Prophetic Spirit

The Divine Presence

God's presence among his people remains a central issue in Numbers. This is evident in the organization of the Israelite's encampment (Num 1:53), the prominent position given to the ark along with the corresponding association with God's presence (10:33–36), the charge to maintain purity in the camp followed by Yahweh's statement "I dwell among them" (5:3), and the emphasis on God's visible manifestation of his presence in the cloud (9:15–23). This reality provides the backdrop for the numerous complaints of the people in Numbers, so that Num 11 begins with the attention-arresting comment that "the people complained about their hardships [רַע] in the hearing of the LORD" (v. 1 NIV).[15] The fire from Yahweh at Taberah presumably comes directly from the fiery cloud; the fiery cloud of God's divine presence becomes the fire of divine judgment (vv. 1–3).

The Israelites themselves further impede the progress of God's plan when they complain about the food supply. Again, the whining was "in the ears of Yahweh" (בְּאָזְנֵי יְהוָה; Num 11:18; cf. v. 1) and God decrees to Israel, "You shall not eat just one day, . . . but a whole month, until it comes out at your nostrils and becomes loathsome to you, because you have rejected the LORD who is among you [בְּקִרְבְּכֶם] and have wept before him, saying, 'Why did we come out of Egypt?'" (vv. 19–20 ESV). Ronald Allen appropriately comments and translates, "The language is

---

15. The Hebrew root רַע occurs as an adjective in verses 1 and 10, as a verb in verse 11, and as a noun in verse 15. Roger Cotton suggests that the repeated use of the root indicates that Moses was guilty of the same kind of complaining the Israelites were practicing. Cotton, "Pentecostal Significance of Numbers 11," 4.

emphatic and gripping: 'Surely you have rejected Yahweh who is among you!'"[16] Timothy Ashley also captures the seriousness of Israel's grumbling when he notes that "the wish to go back to Egypt was a wish to go back to a time before Yahweh was in their midst, and thus was rebellion against him."[17] The centrality of the issue of God's presence is further reflected in Moses's reply to God's promise of meat: "There are 600,000 people on foot, of whom I am in the midst [בְּקִרְבּוֹ]" (v. 21). This reply purposely and sarcastically mirrors God's claim to be present and makes all the more poignant Moses's doubts about God's ability to provide.[18] It is important to note that even in a passage so well known for its emphasis on the prophetic aspect of the Spirit,[19] the broader picture of God's intention to dwell with his people is still in view.

Some scholars have noticed that when God "takes" (אצל; "lay aside," "reserve," "withdraw," "withhold"; Num 11:17, 25)[20] from the Spirit on Moses and puts the Spirit on the seventy elders, the text assumes that Moses has been functioning under the power of the Spirit all along.[21] In addition, Isaiah appears to allude to the activity of the Spirit in this passage as well as to the general superintendence of the Spirit throughout the Mosaic period. "He lifted them up and carried [וַיְנַשְּׂאֵם] them all the days of old . . . But they rebelled and grieved his Holy Spirit" (Isa 63:9b, 10a ESV). The word נשא ("carry") occurs five times (Num 11:12 [2x], 14, 17 [2x]) when Moses complains about having to carry the people, but Isaiah suggests that God and his Spirit were involved in the carrying. Isaiah 63:11 probably refers to Num 11:17; in both passages God "set" (שׂים) his Spirit on them or among them. Finally, "The Spirit of Yahweh gave them rest" (Isa 63:14); thus the Spirit's continued activity is evident.[22]

16. Allen, "Numbers," 793.
17. Ashley, *Book of Numbers*, 212.
18. Milgrom, *Numbers*, 88.
19. E.g., see the discussion in Levine, *Numbers 1–20*, 324, 328–43.
20. Brown, et al., "אצל," 69.

21. Hildebrandt points out that a variety of activities have been accomplished by the Spirit, including the miraculous events. If this is so, and if Num 11 is paradigmatic for Luke, then one should also expect the Spirit's involvement in the performance of miracles in Luke-Acts. Hildebrandt, *Old Testament Theology*, 108; Cotton, "Pentecostal Significance of Numbers 11," 6.

22. One might also see the general assistance of the Spirit in Neh 9:20, where the text says, "You gave [נָתַתָּ] your good Spirit to instruct them and did not withhold your manna from their mouth and gave them water for their thirst." However, Num 11:25 uses the same Hebrew term and is probably the referent.

The Spirit Rests on the Elders

Numbers 11:25 records that Yahweh descended in a cloud, the Spirit "rested" (בְּנוֹחַ; ἐπανεπαύσατο, LXX) on the seventy elders, and the elders subsequently "prophesied" (וַיִּתְנַבְּאוּ) for a limited period of time. The use of the Hebrew verb נוח ("rest") is of particular interest because, not only does the Spirit also rest on Eldad and Medad (v. 26), but the prophets observe that the רוּחַ ("S/spirit") of Elijah rests (נָחָה; ἐπαναπέπαυται, LXX) on Elisha (2 Kgs 2:15), and the Spirit of Yahweh rests (וְנָחָה; ἀναπαύσεται, LXX) on the branch of Jesse (Isa 11:2).[23] This resting of the Spirit has clear associations with the prophetic activity of the seventy elders in Numbers and with the miraculous works of Elijah and Elisha, but the resting of the Spirit associated with the branch surpasses charismatic activity and encompasses the kind of leadership qualities required of Moses and transferred to the seventy elders: "And the Spirit of the LORD shall rest upon him, the Spirit of wisdom and understanding, the Spirit of counsel and might, the Spirit of knowledge and the fear of the LORD" (Isa 11:2 ESV). Isaiah anticipates a Messiah who functions as a prophetic figure in the tradition of Moses and Elijah and who embodies the wisdom of Joseph.

The shared terminology between Num 11:25 and 2 Kgs 2:15 is significant because Luke depicts Jesus as the fulfillment of the ministries of both Moses and Elijah.[24] The shared language of the Spirit between Num 11 and Isaiah is quite impressive, so that Luke's pneumatology follows lines of continuity drawn from Num 11 to the prophets Elijah and Elisha to Christ and also from Num 11 via Isaiah to Christ.

The latter claim regarding Isaiah finds support in the shared terminology of "setting" (Num 11:17; Isa 63:11) and "resting" (Num 11:25; Isa 11:2), as described above. Another of Isaiah's most important messianic passages employs a term (נתן; "give," "place") from Num 11: "I will place [נָתַתִּי] my Spirit on him" (Isa 42:1b). Moses wishes "that Yahweh would place [כִּי־יִתֵּן] his Spirit on them" (Num 11:29b). This endowment

---

23. Notice that these passages are tied together by similar terminology in both the Hebrew text and the LXX. The LXX uses ἐπαναπαύομαι (Num 11:25–26; 2 Kgs 2:15) and its cognate ἀναπαύω (Isa 11:2).

24. E.g., see Luke 4:24–27; 9:30; Acts 1:9; 3:22.

of the Spirit on Isaiah's "servant" (42:1) is highly significant for Luke, as he refers to Jesus as the "servant" (Acts 3:13, 26; 4:30) and "your holy servant Jesus, whom you anointed [ἔχρισας]" (4:27); he refers to Isa 42:1 at Jesus's baptism (Luke 3:22); and he combines Isa 42:7 with 61:1 to form the programmatic text of Luke 4:18–19: "The Spirit of the Lord is upon me, because he has anointed [ἔχρισέν] me . . ." It is this Davidic (Isa 11:1), anointed (61:1) servant (42:1) who passes through death (53:8–9) yet experiences prolonged days (53:10) and exaltation (52:13; 53:10–12). Not only does Luke draw directly from Num 11 for some of his pneumatic themes, but he also relies heavily on Isaiah, who builds on the language of Num 11.

Prophecy, Ecstasy, and Numbers 11

Opinions vary as to the nature of the prophesying in Num 11:25–26. Walter Kaiser and Leon Wood suggest that singing was included.[25] Wenham goes so far as to hypothesize that the men were engaging in something like the tongues of Acts 2.[26] Some employ the term "ecstatic" as the word of choice[27] while others insist that ecstasy was not involved.[28] Ashley simply refuses to speculate at all.[29]

Some of the discussion revolves around the Hebrew verb נבא ("prophesy"), occurring three times in the *hithpael* (often used to indicate intensive action) in Num 11:25–27. Some scholars see the use of the *hithpael* form of the verb as signifying some kind of charismatic or visible manifestation.[30] Ashley sees a varied use of the *hithpael* form of the verb; sometimes it describes ecstatic activity (1 Sam 10:5–6, 10, 13; 19:20–21,

---

25. Kaiser, "Pentateuch," 9; Wood, *Holy Spirit*, 111.

26. Wenham, *Numbers*, 109.

27. E.g., Budd, *Numbers*, 128; Milgrom, *Numbers*, 89; Montague, *Holy Spirit*, 15; Robert Koch holds that the account has its origin among ecstatic prophets who sought to legitimize their ecstasy by deriving it from Moses. Koch, *Geist Gottes*, 43.

28. Harrison, *Numbers*, 188–89; Cole, *Numbers*, 193.

29. Ashley, *Book of Numbers*, 214.

30. Cotton holds that this is not the common form of the verb, that "this form of the verb was used of visible physical demonstrations of some kind," and that the use of this verb "strongly suggests that God used a visible, Spirit-empowering, prophetic event to publicly confirm his authorization of, power upon, and intimate involvement in these leaders' ministries." Cotton, "Pentecostal Significance of Numbers 11," 7.

23–24), and other times there is "no hint of such behavior (Ezek. 37:9; Jer. 26:20)."[31]

The verb נבא ("prophesy") occurs 115 times in the Old Testament and only occurs in the *hithpael* (28 times) and *niphal* (87 times). (The *niphal* stem of the verb express simple action.) It is challenging to discern any well-defined, distinctive use of the *hithpael* because the picture is not uniform. In general, Numbers, 1 Samuel, 1 Kings, and 2 Chronicles employ the *hithpael* form, while the *niphal* predominates in 1 Chronicles, Jeremiah, Ezekiel, Joel, Amos, and Zechariah.[32] It is difficult to generalize about the use of נבא in the Pentateuch because it is only found in Num 11:25–27. One may claim the use of the *hithpael* at Saul's filling in the presence of the musical prophets in 1 Sam 10:5–6, 10, and 13 as a good example of ecstasy, yet the author employs the *niphal* in verse 11 and disrupts the continuity. Saul's prophesying under the influence of an "evil spirit" (18:10), the prophesying of his soldiers (19:20, 21 [2x]), and his prophesying when he was stripped of his robes (vv. 23–24) holds more promise for an ecstatic theme. However, if Saul's stripping of his royal robes symbolizes a posture of humility before God and Samuel and accentuates the role of Yahweh as the true King of Israel and David as his new choice, then the event has an internal logic to it and is not just a misfit story of a naked, raving maniac.

The frenzied prophesying of the prophets of Baal certainly deserves the word "ecstatic" as an appropriate descriptor (1 Kgs 18:29), but a few chapters later the *hithpael* is used of both Micaiah and the false prophets to describe intelligible, verbal prophecy (22:8, 10, 18), and the verb form switches to the *niphal* at one point when summarizing the message of the false prophets (v. 11).[33] So also in Jer 2:8 and 23:13 the prophets prophesy by Baal, yet the former passage uses the *niphal* and the latter the *hithpael*. Likewise, Jeremiah 14:14 and 26:20 both use the two forms interchangeably in a single verse. It is, however, noteworthy that in a book that more commonly employs the *niphal* verb form, Shemaiah employs the *hithpael* when he attempts to cast aspersions on Jeremiah by labeling

---

31. Ashley, *Book of Numbers*, 214.

32. The former group accounts for twenty-one of twenty-eight occurrences of the *hithpael* and the latter group accounts for eighty-three of eighty-seven occurrences of the *niphal*.

33. The same pattern occurs in the parallel passage of 2 Chr 18:7, 9, 17, where verse 11 is in the *niphal*. Note also that the *hithpael* is used to describe an intelligible prophecy in 2 Chr 20:37.

him a "madman" and an imposter prophet. This may suggest that this form was thought to more suitably apply to bizarre behavior.

Ezekiel uses the *niphal* form of נבא ("prophesy") thirty-five times and the *hithpael* only twice (13:7; 37:10). This is not too surprising when one observes that Ezekiel uses the verb as an imperative twenty-seven times, and the *hithpael* form of נבא is never used in the imperative in the Old Testament. Nonetheless, it is interesting to note that Ezekiel dials up the *hithpael* to describe those who prophesy out of their own imaginations (13:7) and when he prophesies the coming of breath to the army of dry bones (37:10). Given Joel's apparent dependence on Num 11:25–27, one would expect to see the *hithpael* form of the verb in Joel 3:1 (MT), but once again the *niphal* form appears. Thus, the biblical picture is complex.[34]

The preceding overview lends itself to the following conclusions. First, the Old Testament does not unilaterally equate the *hithpael* form of נבא ("prophesy") with ecstasy. Second, "ecstasy" needs more precise defining because scholars apply the term so broadly in the Old Testament and often assume the biblical picture is monolithic and consistent with extrabiblical pagan practices.[35] But for the biblical prophets, ecstasy appears to be a state of heightened awareness of God's presence and sensitivity to God that enables them to receive and dispense divine communications. This state may or may not be accompanied by music, an extreme level of enthusiasm, or physical manifestations in the prophet. In short, ecstasy among the biblical prophets is not lunacy, and the fanatical activities of some pagan prophets (1 Kgs 18:29) is not characteristic of those functioning under the influence of the Spirit.[36] Third, the *hithpael* in Num 11 is an appropriate form of the verb to use but does not, by itself, necessarily indicate ecstasy. The *hithpael* plus the contextual remarks of the observers suggests ecstasy according to the definition offered above, but it does not suggest a wild, pagan form of ecstatic activity.

---

34. Wilson, "Prophecy and Ecstasy," 321–37. Wilson's entire argument is based on the diversity of the biblical picture on this matter.

35. Wilson, "Prophecy and Ecstasy," 324. Wilson also notes the need for a definition as well as the problem of failing to distinguish ecstasy as "the *means* by which divine-human communication takes place" and the "*observable behavioral characteristics*" (italics original) of the inspired person.

36. Hildebrandt suggests that Old Testament prophets who "experience ecstasy do so as a by-product of the conscious reality of God's presence and Spirit. The OT focus is on the verbal utterances of the prophets." Hildebrandt, *Old Testament Theology*, 162.

Perhaps Yahweh's description of typical prophecy in Num 12:6 indicates the nature of what transpired among the seventy elders: "If there is a prophet among you, I the LORD make myself known to him in a vision; I speak with him in a dream" (ESV). Given Joel's later association of this type of revelation with prophecy (3:1–2 MT), the Israelite audience's understanding of Moses as a prophet who receives revelation and communicates it, and the commentary in 12:6–8, it is reasonable to think that the seventy had some kind of revelatory experience and verbally expressed those revelations in the hearing of the bystanders. The similarity in prophetic experience to that of Moses caused consternation in Joshua (11:28); thus the seventy elders and the disciples of Pentecost were ecstatic prophets in the tradition of Moses but not in the tradition of pagan lunatics. The nature and content of prophecy in the Pentateuch serves as a general guide for what one might expect in Num 11. Joseph prophesied particular events for the larger purpose of preserving the fledgling nation of Israel (Gen 37:5–11; 50:19–21). Jacob prophesied about the future of Israel and a coming ruler (49:10). Balaam likewise prophesied of a coming ruler (Num 24:17) as well as the blessing on Israel and the continuation of the Abrahamic promise (v. 9). Moses and Miriam prophesied in songs of praise to God for his saving acts in the exodus (Exod 15:1–21). Given this larger context and the specific calling of the seventy to assist Moses in leading Israel on their journey to Canaan, one can surmise that the prophesying likely involved praise for God's saving acts and sovereign care of Israel, glimpses of future blessing in Canaan, or perhaps even some foretelling of a coming Messiah. However, the specific manifestation of other tongues in the Mosaic era is extremely unlikely when one considers the missiological symbolism of speaking in tongues. Prophetic activity prior to Christ only anticipates the global ramifications of the promise to Abraham (Gen 12:1–3), but the actual launching of the international mission at Pentecost in consequence of the Messiah's enthronement calls for an appropriate missiological symbol—glossolalia.[37]

Nevertheless, the nature of the prophecy outlined above is consistent with Peter's explanation of the tongues of Pentecost.[38] The speaking in tongues does not result from an excessive imbibing of wine but results

---

37. Keener also supports a missiological understanding of the symbolism of tongues. See his list of others who make this missiological connection. Keener, *Acts*, 1:823n385.

38. Marshall is among those who observe that "the descent of the Spirit on the people and their consequent speech has a model in Num. 11:25." Marshall, "Acts," 531.

from the inspiration of the Spirit (Acts 2:13). The utterance is prophetic in nature, associated with revelations such as visions and dreams (vv. 17–18), an expression of praise directed toward God (v. 11) in response to Christ's resurrection and enthronement (v. 36), and symbolic of the nations the disciples are empowered to reach (1:8). Thus, Num 11 provides an excellent backdrop to Pentecost because in both cases the ecstasy is supernatural in nature but not lacking an internal logic and clear redemptive purpose. This sort of ecstasy is neither lunacy nor the result of intoxication.

Prophesying "in the Camp"

Many scholars rightly concur with Cotton that the Spirit's resting upon the elders in conjunction with the prophetic response indicates divine authorization of them as God's chosen leaders.[39] The prophetic response has a certain sign value to it. But more controverted is the question of the significance of Eldad and Medad continuing to prophesy "in the camp"—a phrase emphasized by its three occurrences. Not only do the two "remain in the camp," but they "prophesy in the camp" (Num 11:26), and Joshua echoes the narrator's voice when he tells Moses they are "prophesying in the camp" (v. 27). Wenham focuses on the results of the event, that "the phenomenon became more widely known and allowed Moses to give it his public approval."[40] Cole also emphasizes the publicity aspect of the event but adds that "the inclusion of this account evidences the power of God in accomplishing his purposes among his people."[41] Montague opines that "the anecdote about Eldad and Medad seems aimed against attempts to restrict the working of the Spirit to official channels."[42] Montague moves in the right direction.

Cotton includes several of the ideas intimated above in his analysis of the episode with Eldad and Medad: "This strongly suggests that God wanted to show the sovereignty of the Spirit and he wanted this empowering experience to move beyond any leadership establishment to the general population. Thus, Numbers 11 provided for the leaders of Israel what

---

39. Cotton, "Pentecostal Significance of Numbers 11," 6–7; Allen, "Numbers," 794; Stronstad, *Charismatic Theology of St. Luke*, 23; Wilson, "Prophecy and Ecstasy," 331. Milgrom calls it "divine validation." Milgrom, *Numbers*, 89.

40. Wenham, *Numbers*, 109.

41. Cole, *Numbers*, 194.

42. Montague, *Holy Spirit*, 15.

God wants for all his people, all who will receive him."[43] The concept of a universal empowering and prophetic experience is woven into the fabric of this passage by (1) the repetition of "in the camp"; (2) the shocking contrast (apparently noticed by Joshua) between the restriction of revelatory, pneumatic experiences to the tent (and in association with the cloud) and the prophetic overflow in the camp; (3) Moses's question "Are you jealous for my sake?," which exposes Joshua's mentality of limitation; and (4) Moses's wish for a universal, prophetic, pneumatic experience among God's people: "Would that all the LORD's people were prophets, that the LORD would put his Spirit on them!" (11:29 ESV). Joshua's eagerness to protect Moses's unique position may also hint that Joshua views Moses's endowment with the Spirit as a mark of exalted status reserved for royal type personages. Moses's response is shocking because it promotes the notion that God will one day exalt all his people to ruler status.

Thus, the democratization of the Spirit in Joel 3:1–2 (MT) is fundamentally connected with Num 11 and is a continuation of an ancient theme. Once again, the eschatological theme (never far removed from the narrative) surfaces and gives the reader a glimpse of the bigger plan. Luke not only adopts the specific fulfillment of this passage in the Pentecostal outpouring of Acts 2, but he also embraces the eschatological perspective and theological patterns inherent in the Pentateuchal narrative (more on this below).

The Spirit and Morality

Generally speaking, Gunkel is correct when he observes that in Luke-Acts and in the Old Testament character is a "prerequisite" for the prophetic Spirit but not induced by the Spirit.[44] The same applies to faith.[45] This is certainly true in Num 11, for the elders do not become members of the covenant community based on reception of the Spirit, and their empowering experience is definitely charismatic in nature. But perhaps Gunkel has overstated the case a bit. He observes exceptions in the Old Testament where morality is attributed to the Spirit (Isa 11:1, 2; 28:6; 32:15–20; Ezek 36:27; Ps 51:13; 143:10),[46] and the force of his claim that the summary

---

43. Cotton, "Pentecostal Significance of Numbers 11," 9.
44. Gunkel, *Influence of the Holy Spirit*, 20.
45. Gunkel, *Influence of the Holy Spirit*, 17.
46. Gunkel, *Influence of the Holy Spirit*, 19.

statement in Acts 2:42–47 does not contain "one syllable to indicate that the ideal state of the community described derives from the Spirit"[47] is mitigated by the implications of a narrative reading of the text.[48]

In Num 11, one must ask how the context of grumbling and discontent relates to Moses's wish that every member of the community might be a prophet. Presumably, Moses believes that people who are endowed with the prophetic Spirit and who are functioning in that capacity will not only relieve him of leadership responsibilities but will replace grumbling with theocentric and edifying speech.[49] While the prophetic and functional elements of the narrative remain central, Moses's wish also suggests that the moral implications should not be entirely divorced from the charismatic elements. Thus, Miriam's and Aaron's moral failure in opposing Moses (Num 12) is all the more shocking, as neither lived up to her or his prophetic calling (Exod 4:16; 15:20) and both failed to realize the eschatological significance of the Spirit's anointing on themselves and on Moses.[50] The expectation of an association between morality and the Spirit creates tension in the reader of the stories of Balaam, Samson, and Saul, for even if Yahweh unexpectedly gives his Spirit to an unworthy person, the encounter with the Spirit should be personally transforming. So although Gunkel and those who have followed him are correct that faith precedes the coming of the Spirit in Luke-Acts, it is not necessary to completely divorce the ethical implications of the Spirit's work from charismatic events. Surely Luke did not intend to isolate the Pentecostal outpouring from the character of the Christian community (Acts 2:42–47).

Moses, Christ, and Lukan Dependence on Numbers 11–12

Stronstad has summarized some of the programmatic elements of Num 11 in relation to Pentecost, including the transfer of the Spirit, the functional

47. Gunkel, *Influence of the Holy Spirit*, 16.

48. In other words, the prominent location of Pentecost in Acts suggests that the character of the early church has been influenced by this event. See Tannehill, *Narrative Unity*, 2:44.

49. Cotton also sees this kind of moral connection with the Spirit here. He also points out Caleb's "different Spirit" (Num 14:24) as an example of this connection. Cotton, "Pentecostal Significance of Numbers 11," 9.

50. Milgrom gives evidence, such as the listing of Miriam's name first, that she was the "principal instigator of the gossip." Milgrom, *Numbers*, 93.

role of leadership, and the prophetic response to the Spirit's arrival.[51] But beyond Moses's prophetic wish, the episode also shows its eschatological mooring by emphasizing the uniqueness of Moses as a prophet. Yahweh descends to the entrance of the tent in a cloud and directly chastises Aaron and Miriam, referring to Moses as "my servant," calling him "faithful," and affirming a unique "face to face" relationship with him (Num 12:5–8; cf. 1 Cor 13:12). Milgrom observes that Num 12:6–8 forms a chiasm with the middle section focusing on Moses's uniqueness.[52] The editorial note on Moses's extreme humility (v. 3) anticipates that of David (1 Sam 18:18, 23) and of Christ (Matt 21:5), as the mention of Moses as "servant" (Num 12:7, 8) also anticipates David (2 Sam 7:5, 8; Luke 1:69; 4:25) and Christ (Isa 52:13; Acts 3:13, 26).[53] That Yahweh transfers the Spirit from Moses to the seventy also highlights Moses's uniqueness and anticipates Christ's exaltation and outpouring of the Spirit. The eschatological implications of Moses as a unique prophet are made more explicit in Deut 18:15: "Yahweh your God will raise up for you a prophet like me from among you, from your brothers—you will listen to him." Peter quotes this passage in Acts 3:22, connects it with the eschatological renewal, employs a double entendre with the words "raise up" in order to highlight Christ's resurrection, and so identifies Christ as the "prophet like Moses."[54]

Luke draws substantially from the Pentateuch's eschatology, and his dependence on Num 11–12 may extend beyond the Pentecostal items previously mentioned. For example, Luke constructs his narrative in Acts in such a manner as to alternate between attacks on the church from without and compromise and problems within. This sounds very much like Numbers. Luke emphasizes unity in the body, but also records the struggle to maintain it and the threats to it. Numbers does the same. In particular, Acts 6 contains several similarities to Num 11–12. In both passages there is complaining and quarrelling over food (manna/daily food distribution to widows), and in both passages Spirit-filled men help with troubleshooting. Additionally, in both passages women are involved in the conflict (Miriam/Grecian and Hebraic Jews), and in both passages there is a racial element in the tension (Moses's Cushite wife/Grecian and

51. Stronstad, *Charismatic Theology of St. Luke*, 66.

52. Milgrom, *Numbers*, 95.

53. Clowney, *Unfolding Mystery*, 98. Clowney makes the connection between Moses, David, and Christ as servants. The Hebrew term for "servant" in the passages cited is עֶבֶד, but three different Greek terms translate it in the examples cited.

54. This use of a double entendre receives further discussion later.

Hebraic Jews). Luke seems to view the early days of the church as somewhat analogous to those of the Israelites.

It appears that Luke is thoroughly invested in the Pentateuch's narrative theology, pneumatology, and eschatology. Numbers 11–12 has a significant christological element that Luke employs. Though Luke heavily emphasizes the prophetic and charismatic elements of Num 11, he is not unaware of the ethical implications of the Spirit's activity (Acts 2:44–45) and the strong association of divine presence inherent in an outpouring of the Spirit (2:3).[55] Such themes find further expression in the experience of Joshua and, to some extent, even in the pagan prophet Balaam.

The Spirit in Joshua

One cannot say for certain when Joshua first received his anointing with the Spirit. In Num 27:18 Yahweh instructs Moses: "Take Joshua the son of Nun, a man in whom is the Spirit [אִישׁ אֲשֶׁר־רוּחַ בּוֹ], and lay your hand on him" (ESV). The laying of Moses's hand on Joshua signifies recognition of anointing for leadership but not causation of such. Neither does the group of seventy elders empowered with the Spirit (Num 11:25) appear to include Joshua. However, the Hebrew text indicates that the Spirit was "in him" and that he was "filled with the Spirit of wisdom" (מָלֵא רוּחַ חָכְמָה; Deut 34:9).[56]

Several items are worth noting regarding Joshua's equipping with the Spirit. First, both the language and the ongoing activities suggest that, like Moses, Joshua experienced a continual indwelling with the Spirit. Second, Moses's request for a replacement leader and his shepherding terminology ("so Yahweh's people will not be like sheep without a shepherd"; Num 27:17b) reinforces and continues the leadership theme

---

55. Menzies argues that the textual problem in Luke 10:1 is best resolved by translating "seventy" rather than "seventy-two." Although this is the minority reading, he believes that the text alludes to Num 11:24–30 rather than to the nations of Gen 10. He makes several noteworthy points, although Luke 10:1–17 never directly mentions the Spirit. Menzies sees a Num 11 allusion as significant so that Luke anticipates the Pentecostal outpouring and the universal mission of the church. Menzies, *Language of the Spirit*, 73–82.

56. The second reference in Deut 34:9 ("for Moses had laid his hands on him") could be understood as causation, but it does not easily square with Num 27:18. It is likely that the Deuteronomy passage refers to the Numbers passage but does not intend to indicate that Num 27 identifies Joshua's initial filling.

highlighted in Num 11.⁵⁷ Third, the language of Deut 34:9 (מְלֵא רוּחַ חָכְמָה; "filled with the Spirit of wisdom") is very similar to that referring to the artisans in Exod 28:3 (מִלֵּאתִיו רוּחַ חָכְמָה; "I have filled with the Spirit of wisdom"). The terminology not only describes divine enablement but also carries associations with the filling of the tabernacle (Exod 40:35), the filling of tabernacle artisans (35:31), and the command to fill the earth (Gen 1:28). The sense of divine presence continues to accompany divine commissioning and divine enabling. Fourth, even though it is difficult to pinpoint the precise moment of Joshua's initial filling, the author of the Pentateuch desires to show that Joshua's filling with the Spirit is comparable to Moses's filling. Practically speaking, the Israelites can know for certain that Joshua is God's choice (Josh 3:7), and miracles such as the parting of the Jordan (note the "dry ground"; Josh 3:17; cf. Exod 14:22) demonstrate that Joshua continues to function as a charismatic prophet in the tradition of Moses.⁵⁸ Fifth, despite the commonality between the two leaders, the recorder of Moses's death carefully preserves the uniqueness of Moses's leadership: "And there has not arisen a prophet since in Israel like Moses, whom the LORD knew face to face, none like him for all the signs and the wonders that the LORD sent him to do in the land of Egypt" (Deut 34:10–11a ESV). The author seems to suggest that Joshua was not the expected prophet like Moses (18:15, 18); therefore a greater fulfillment lay in the future.

Finally, the mention of Joshua's pneumatic empowerment occurs in conjunction with reminders of Moses's disobedience and approaching death (Num 27:12–18), or in the context of grief over his death (Deut 34:5–9). The Spirit acts as the divine agent who continues to move the plan of God forward. Disobedience and death will not stop the plan. The Spirit will use Joshua in place of Moses, but the plan will continue until a greater prophet rises in Israel (v. 10).

Balaam and the Spirit

Balaam seems like an even less likely candidate for the prophetic Spirit than Saul was after the Spirit departed from him and left him in the grips

---

57. Ashley notes how the shepherding terminology highlights the necessity of good leadership. Ashley, *Book of Numbers*, 551.

58. Hildebrandt notes several similarities between events under Moses's and Joshua's leadership. Hildebrandt, *Old Testament Theology*, 109.

of paranoia, yet Balaam's story testifies to the truth that the author of Numbers understood that a larger plan was in motion and God could sovereignly intervene to keep the plan on track. Balaam's oracles indicate that there is more at stake than just an individual nation's welfare; God's covenant blessings and promises are at issue (Num 23:10, 19–20; 24:9) as well as the very presence of God in Israel: "Yahweh his God is with him" (23:21b). In addition, the reader becomes cognizant of Yahweh's complete dominance over sorcery and every opposing spiritual power (23:23; 24:1; cf. Acts 13:42).

The text offers several pointers to the solemnity of Balaam's final oracles. The author specifically says that Balaam avoided using sorcery and that "the Spirit of God came upon him" (וַתְּהִי עָלָיו רוּחַ אֱלֹהִים; Num 24:2b). He also functions with an unusual degree of spiritual vision and revelation[59] and prostrates himself in humility (vv. 3–4, 15–16). His encounter with the Spirit is certainly not regenerational but is obviously prophetic, as indicated by the repetition of oracular terminology (מָשָׁל "oracle" and נְאֻם "utterance"),[60] visionary vocabulary (vv. 3–4, 15–16), insight into Israel's state of covenantal blessing (v. 9), and predictions of the future. Of particular interest is the way King David later repeats the terminology of 24:1–4 in 2 Sam 23:1–2. Both passages credit the Spirit for their utterances and attribute their oracles to God. Balaam claims his utterance is "the oracle of the man [וּנְאֻם הַגֶּבֶר] whose eye is opened" (Num 23:3b), and David's is "the oracle of the man [וּנְאֻם הַגֶּבֶר] who was raised on high" (2 Sam 23:1a ESV).[61] Balaam describes Jacob's dwelling places in Edenic terms (Num 24:5–7a) and then predicts that "his king shall be higher than Agag, and his kingdom shall be exalted" (v. 7b ESV).[62] This picture of Israel's king is consistent with previous predictions (Gen 17:6, 16; 35:11) and quite striking considering that the prediction predates the monarchy.[63] Cole notices the implications of David's borrowing from

---

59. Rea, *Holy Spirit in the Bible*, 48.

60. The noun מָשָׁל occurs in Num 23:7, 18; 24:3, 15, 20–21, 23 and נְאֻם in 24:3 (2x), 4, 15 (2x), 16.

61. I owe the observation of the Hebrew similarity to Cole, *Numbers*, 418.

62. For an overview of the issues involved in identifying "Agag," see Ashley, *Book of Numbers*, 492–93; Cole, *Numbers*, 420–21.

63. Even if one allows for later editing of Numbers or espouses some version of the documentary hypothesis, there is still evidence suggesting an early date for Balaam's oracles. "Several poetic passages (such as the utterances of Balaam in chs. 23–24) are written in very ancient Hebrew, i.e., thirteenth to tenth century B.C." LaSor et al., *Old Testament Survey*, 102.

this story and Balaam's royal prediction, as Balaam's words "provide a precursive pattern for the coming fulfillment of the anointed deliver [sic] for the kingdom."[64] Thus, Balaam's prophecies play an important role in raising expectations of a future king in Israel.

It is within the above context that the more familiar predictions of Balaam must be understood: "A star shall come out of Jacob, and a scepter shall rise out of Israel" (Num 24:17b ESV), and, "And one from Jacob shall rule and destroy the survivors of cities" (v. 19 ESV). The mention of a "scepter" confirms the royal allusion in the parallel "star" (v. 17b; cf. Gen 49:10). Scholars generally agree that the conquest of Agag, Moab, Edom, and various other hostile nations (Num 24:7–24) refers at least in part to the period of the early monarchy.[65] However, reference to the early monarchy fulfills neither the larger biblical expectation of a messianic figure nor that of the immediate context. Balaam speaks of what will transpire "in the days to come" (בְּאַחֲרִית הַיָּמִים; v. 14; cf. Gen 49:1; Isa 2:2; Dan 10:14; Hos 3:5), at a time in the distant future (Num 24:17a). David's conquest of Moab and Edom proved to be temporary, thus these two nations became typical of nations opposing Yahweh (Ezek 25:8–14).[66] One finds evidence of a later messianic understanding of the "star" (כּוֹכָב; Num 24:17) from the name of Bar-Kochba ("son of the star"),[67] the literature of Qumran (CD VII, 15–20), the New Testament (Matt 2:1–2, 9–12; Rev 22:16), and *Targum Onkelos*.[68] Conceptual parallels in Daniel and reference to risen and wise ones who will shine "like the stars forever and ever" (Dan 12:3) may build on Num 24. Daniel also depicts an anointed ruler (Dan 9:25) who smashes opposing kingdoms (2:34, 44–45) but whose own kingdom is exalted (7:13–14). The heavenly visitor in Daniel (10:14) and Balaam (Num 24:14) use identical terms to describe the future of Israel and Moab, that is, what will happen "to your people in the last days" (לְעַמְּךָ בְּאַחֲרִית הַיָּמִים). The imagery of a star as representative of a king seldom occurs in the Old Testament (Isa 14:13),[69]

---

64. Cole, *Numbers*, 418.

65. Wenham, *Numbers*, 179; Ashley, *Book of Numbers*, 502–3; Noth opines that "it is the historical emergence of David that forms the background of this discourse." Noth, *Numbers*, 192.

66. Ashley provides several supporting Scripture references. Ashley, *Book of Numbers*, 503 and notes.

67. Ashley, *Book of Numbers*, 503.

68. The *Targum Onkelos* substitutes "ruler" for "star."

69. The Hebrew term כּוֹכָב only occurs thirty-seven times in the Old Testament,

but this increases the likelihood that Daniel depends on Num 24:17 when he envisions the persecuted but faithful saints as sharing in the exalted status of their messianic star (Dan 8:10; 12:3). In the end, the stars will shine like their chief star.

The immediate function of the Spirit in Num 24 is to inspire a prophetic message as the means of saving Israel from a curse, but in the grand scheme of things the Spirit acts as the agent who advances the divine agenda to bring God's people into his presence and to introduce the eschatological king. Moses and Joshua lead in the power of the Spirit in anticipation of the king, but they are only pointers to a greater anointed one. The seventy elders typify the eschatological people of God who will one day act as God's Spirit-filled prophets, and a pagan diviner prophesies under the inspiration of the Spirit about an exalted king who will one day rise out of Israel and crush the enemies of God. These same emphases appear to converge in Luke's Pentecostal narrative. The Spirit anoints Jesus; he is raised to life and exalted to the right hand of the Father as Lord and Judge of all (Acts 2:36; 10:42); he shares his prophetic Spirit with his people in order to proclaim his kingdom; his people faithfully testify of the King through persecution; and this proclamation continues until his people "enter the kingdom of God" (14:22) and enjoy the final restoration of all things (3:21).

Summary

The opening verses of Genesis point to a fundamental relationship between eschatology, the Spirit's activity in creation, and the prophetic word (Gen 1:1-3). The prophetic aspect of the Spirit's work becomes more obvious in Joseph, Moses, the seventy elders, and even the pagan prophet Balaam. Luke's dependence on Num 11 and later texts, which build on the pneumatological emphases articulated there, make it evident that his pneumatology is not rooted primarily in later Judaism and does not derive from Greek influence. The account of the transfer of the Spirit from Moses to the seventy elders is particularly informative in understanding Luke's pneumatology, as it incorporates a concern for the divine presence, anticipates the Spirit's resting ultimately on Christ, connects the

---

and it is most commonly employed in reference to God's covenant with Abraham to multiply his descendants (e.g., Gen 15:5) or in reference to God as the Creator or as sovereign over his creation (e.g., Ps 8:3).

Spirit directly with prophetic speech, foreshadows the democratization of the Spirit in multiple ways, and suggests that charismatic experiences should also have an influence on personal morality. The emphasis on divine presence and morality suggests that a charismatic experience, which does not amount to admission into membership among God's covenant people, can involve more than empowerment for service and prophetic speech, even though those elements are central to the experience. Thus, Luke is consistent with the Pentateuch when his narrative also intimates that the Spirit directs the affairs of the early church and influences the behavior of the saints.

I have also argued that Luke's view of ecstasy follows the pattern of Num 11, although speaking in tongues, with its missiological symbolism, is reserved for the new era. The most important element of the Spirit's prophetic work in Num 11–12 and in Balaam's prophecies, however, is the eschatological element of messianic prediction and foreshadowing. Luke sees this in the person of Moses as a precursor to Christ and in his anticipation of a day of universal prophethood. Conceptually speaking, Luke's Christology also has affinities with Balaam's predictions of the coming of a royal personage. Chapters 6–8 focus on how Luke brings together the christocentric and pneumatic emphases found in the Pentateuch. For now, though, the discussion turns toward an investigation of the origins and development of the second major theme of this study, the resurrection from the dead.

4

From Death and Barrenness to the Resurrected King

IN THE PREVIOUS DISCUSSION I called attention to the role of the Spirit as an agent of eschatological renewal and placed the specific functions of the Spirit, such as inspiring prophecy, in that broader context. I also offered some preliminary implications of the Pentateuch's pneumatology to Luke's writings. Because Luke also focuses so heavily on the resurrection, the next two chapters investigate how emphases originating in the Pentateuch may have informed Luke's perspective on it. This chapter offers arguments that the foundational elements of a doctrine of resurrection lie in the Pentateuch, and that resurrection—as an eschatological reversal and exaltation—ultimately characterizes the messianic figure anticipated by Moses and David.

The discussion begins with an investigation of how the translations of Enoch and Elijah provide an eschatological perspective, bring a ray of hope in the shadow of the fall, and anticipate Christ's resurrection. The next segment draws attention to the concept of resurrection hope observed in miraculous births from the time of Abraham to John the Baptist. This leads to an exploration of the birth narratives to see if there is any evidence that Luke places them within a context of resurrection. An examination of the birth narratives quickly turns toward the dominant motif of Christ's lordship, which has strong associations with resurrection and exaltation. A comparison of the narratives of Hannah and Mary highlights how the miraculous births, reversals, royal emphases, and anointing of the Spirit anticipate Luke's presentation of Jesus as the risen and anointed one.

The Intrusion of Death and Hope for Life (Gen 1–11)

The early chapters of Genesis picture creation as teeming with life following the Spirit's hovering activity and the creative commands of Elohim. The author does not hesitate, however, to hint that it will soon rain on the parade, for the Garden contains not only a tree of life, but a tree of the knowledge of good and evil (Gen 2:9). Also, Adam receives the warning that if he partakes of the latter tree, he will not only die, but "surely die" (מוֹת תָּמוּת; v. 17). This consequence of disobedience becomes a central element in the dialogue between the woman and the serpent (3:3), who uses an unusual arrangement of Hebrew words to mirror but deny the efficacy of the earlier warning: "You will not surely die" (לֹא־מוֹת תְּמֻתוּן; 3:4).[1] In the wake of the first couple's disobedience, the reader discovers that the divine intention had been for humanity to experience eternal life (3:22). With the morpheme for death (מות) occurring seventy-nine times in Genesis, the plunging of humanity into continually greater depths of sin, and the not-so-subtle reminder of "and then he died" oft repeated in Gen 5, the reader wonders what kind of a redemption would be required to overcome the devastating effects of the fall, restore humanity to its original design, and regain access to the tree of life.

Enoch: Breaking the Pattern of Death

The announcement "to dust you will return" (Gen 3:19) is more than sufficiently well illustrated by the refrain "and then he died," which occurs eight times in Gen 5 and a ninth time after Noah's bout with drunkenness and his shameful nakedness.[2] The total number of occurrences of the death formula would have been a complete ten were it not for the shining ray of hope bursting through the clouds of death in the narrator's account of Enoch (5:21–24), for Enoch lives on as a testimony that death does not ultimately have a hermetic seal over all of life.

Some scholars have noticed parallels between the genealogy of Gen 5 and lists of Mesopotamian kings. The length of Enoch's life (365 years)

---

1. Wenham mentions that the "not" would usually be placed between the verb and infinitive absolute. He summarizes several different ways to understand this passage, but however one interprets it, it seems apparent that the verbal parallel between Gen 2:17 and 3:4 suggests the serpent's intentional denial of the warning. Wenham, *Genesis*, 1:74.

2. Gen 5:5, 8, 11, 14, 17, 20, 27, 31; 9:29.

is the same as a solar year, and both Enoch and the Sumerian king Enmeduranki occur seventh in the lists. The latter was "King of Sippar, city of the sun," and, in the view of Robert Martin-Achard, "Enoch was originally an astral divinity, a sun-god, but his presence in the list compiled by P gives him another significance."[3] The latter portion of the statement is correct—Enoch certainly has "another significance." As with other biblical parallels with ancient accounts, the nonbiblical accounts lack the eschatological and ethical significance built into the biblical context. The biblical author certainly used the literary structures of the day when he placed Enoch in the seventh position, but this was to call attention to the fact that he "walked with God" (Gen 5:22, 24). Although the line of Seth is full of godly men who live long lives, the generally positive appraisal of them gives way to the sobering words "and then he died" (vv. 5, 8, 11, 14, 17, 20, 27, 31). Even the favored line of Seth could not escape death, highlighting all the more the uniqueness of Enoch.

With regard to the statement that Enoch "was no more" (Gen 5:24), Nahum Sarna remarks, "The regular formula, 'then he died,' is replaced by a description of how he died."[4] Thus, "for God took him" (v. 24) is "a euphemism for death, as is clear from such passages as Ezekiel 24:16, 18 and Jonah 4:3 ... It was the narrative about Elijah's transference to heaven without dying, as told in 2 Kings 2, that gave rise to the popular legend that Enoch too underwent this experience of apotheosis."[5] Levenson is more cautious than Sarna, but he says there is "ambiguity" about the destination of Elijah and Enoch.[6]

---

3. Martin-Achard, *From Death to Life*, 69. For a brief overview of ancient parallels, see also Hamilton, *Book of Genesis*, 1:257-58. Martin-Achard observes the parallels but assumes that the biblical writer did the borrowing; it is also possible that the Mesopotamian accounts were embellished stories of an earlier tradition more akin to the account of Enoch. Many commentators who notice the parallels also recognize that the biblical account is much more reserved and contextually very different than its secular counterparts.

4. Sarna, *Genesis*, 43.

5. Sarna, *Genesis*, 43.

6. Levenson, *Resurrection and Restoration*, 104. The "ambiguity" regarding the destination of Enoch and Elijah does not come from the biblical texts but from Judaism. Jubilees places Enoch in the garden of Eden, a place untouched by the flood (4:23-24). Targum Ps.-J. on Gen 5:24 records him as withdrawn into the firmament. In *1 En.* 70:1-4 he disappears in a chariot of wind and then has heavenly visions in ch. 71. In *1 En.* 106:7-8 he is with the angels at "the ends of the earth." In a similar account, the *Genesis Apocryphon* locates Enoch in paradise (IQapGen 2:23). In *2 Enoch* he reaches the tenth heaven, where he receives clothes of glory (22:8) and becomes "like one of

The stark contrast between life and death in the Genesis context[7] and the sudden exception to "and then he died" in 5:24, however, surely suggest more than death as usual or an earthly relocation. Typically the name of each member of the genealogy occurs five times, two of which occur as subjects. In Enoch's case his name occurs a sixth time (vv. 18–24) and as the subject of the repeated and emphatic phrase "Enoch walked with God," to which the author adds "and he was not; for God took him" (v. 24). Sarna's certainty that Ezek 24:16, 18 (the taking of Ezekiel's wife in death) and Jon 4:3 (Jonah's request that God take his life) provide an explanation for Gen 5:24 on the basis of the common use of the verb לָקַח ("to take") seems ill-founded when one considers that the root of the word (לקח) occurs in the neighborhood of one thousand times in the Old Testament and with a variety of applications,[8] that the supposed parallels definitively state that death is in view when the Genesis text does not, and that there is no convincing contextual evidence linking these later texts to Enoch.[9]

Enoch, Elijah, and Jesus: Taken to Heaven

Surely the story of Elijah's ascension in 2 Kgs 2 serves as a better prospect for comparison than the story of Jonah's morbid prayer that Yahweh take his life (4:3) or the taking of the life of Ezekiel's wife. The verb לָקַח ("to take") occurs in reference to Elijah's departure four times (2 Kgs 2:3, 5, 9–10); the Septuagint employs the verb λαμβάνω ("to take") in 2:3, 5 and ἀναλαμβάνω ("to take up") in 2:9–10. The latter term, although not called for in the Hebrew text,[10] apparently conforms to the description of Elijah

---

his glorious ones" (v. 10). Generally speaking, the texts of Judaism view Enoch in some sort of celestial place. See also Vermes, *Resurrection*, 25–26.

7. E.g., note how the author places life and death in close proximity to one another in Gen 7:22: "All in whose nostrils *was* the breath of life (נִשְׁמַת־רוּחַ חַיִּים בְּאַפָּיו), of all that *was* in the dry *land*, died (מֵתוּ)" (KJV).

8. The count varies, but Els lists 866 occurrences, and a search in BibleWorks 10 lists 975. Els, "לקח," 813.

9. Levenson points out that Sarna's interpretation was also proffered in ibn Ezra to Gen 5:24 (twelfth century). Levenson, *Resurrection and Restoration*, 102. The similarity in terms could be significant if there was sufficient contextual evidence to point in that direction, as the ensuing discussion shows. Ezekiel contains no clear parallels, but one could argue that Ezekiel's visionary experience has a closer affinity to Gen 5:24 than does Ezek 24:16: "The Spirit lifted me up and took me away" (3:14).

10. That is, the identical Hebrew word is used until verse 11, but the Greek word

going up (וַיַּ֫עַל; ἀνελήμφθη) into heaven (εἰς τὸν οὐρανόν) in verse 11. The verb ἀναλαμβάνω ("to take up") although used only thirteen times in the New Testament, is Luke's term of choice for Christ's ascension in Acts 1:2, 11, 22 (cf. Mark 16:19; 1 Tim 3:16). The phrase "into heaven" (εἰς τὸν οὐρανόν) is also a favorite of his, and he uses it thirteen times, of which five refer directly to Christ's ascension (Luke 24:52; Acts 1:10, 11 [3x]; cf. 7:55). The record of Elijah's ascension looks remarkably similar to that of Jesus's ascension:

> καὶ ἀνελήμφθη Ηλιου ἐν συσσεισμῷ ὡς εἰς τὸν οὐρανόν (2 Kgs 2:11 LXX)
> "and Elijah was taken up in a whirlwind as into heaven"

> οὗτος ὁ Ἰησοῦς ὁ ἀναλημφθεὶς ἀφ' ὑμῶν εἰς τὸν οὐρανὸν (Acts 1:11)
> "This Jesus, who was taken up from you into heaven"

Luke clarifies the significance of "into heaven" when he also notes that the sound of a violent wind came "from heaven" (ἐκ τοῦ οὐρανοῦ; Acts 2:2), and Jews from every nation "under heaven" (ὑπὸ τὸν οὐρανόν; v. 5) heard the mighty deeds of God declared in their own tongues (v. 11). The one who ascended "into the heavens" (εἰς τοὺς οὐρανούς; v. 34) is Lord and Christ, and he has poured out the Holy Spirit to empower his followers to proclaim his majesty to people of every tongue. Thus, Christ ascended to heaven in fulfillment of the pattern established first in Enoch and then, particularly, in Elijah.

Enoch, Ethics, and Eschatology

The comparison between Enoch and Elijah is justified, and not only on the basis of the common use of a verb, but on larger contextual considerations—both texts describe the unusual departure of an unusually righteous servant of Yahweh in defiance of death. The hope for all the faithful inherent in these two stories seems also to be reflected in these two psalms: "But God will ransom my soul from the power of Sheol, for he will receive me [יִקָּחֵנִי]" (49:15 ESV); and "You guide me with your counsel, and afterward you will receive me [תִּקָּחֵנִי] to glory" (73:24 ESV).[11]

The author of Hebrews leaves no doubt about his position on the destiny of Enoch: "By faith Enoch was taken up [μετετέθη] so that he

---

switches in verses 9–10.

11. Various authors have noticed a verbal connection between Enoch's story and these psalms. E.g., see Gowan, *Bridge between the Testaments*, 376; Kidner, *Genesis*, 81.

should not see death, and he was not found, because God had taken him [μετέθηκεν]. Now before he was taken [μεταθέσεως] he was commended as having pleased God" (Heb 11:5). The Hebrews passage clearly follows the Septuagint, as both add the explanatory phrase "he was not found" before "God took him" (Heb 11:5: καὶ οὐχ ηὑρίσκετο διότι μετέθηκεν αὐτὸν ὁ θεός; Gen 5:24 LXX: καὶ οὐχ ηὑρίσκετο ὅτι μετέθηκεν αὐτὸν ὁ θεός). The use of μετατίθημι ("to transfer") in both texts also suggests that both authors viewed Enoch's experience as a major change in place. Johannes Louw and Eugene Nida concur that Heb 11:5 "is clearly a significant change of location from one place to another, that is to say, from earth to heaven,"[12] and Maurer speaks of Enoch's experience as a translation from earth.[13] Both biblical texts also view Enoch's translation as directly related to his character and employ εὐαρεστέω ("to please") to describe Enoch's relationship with God (Gen 5:22, 24; Heb 11:5, 6).[14] Death would hardly be a great reward for extraordinary character.

The ethical aspect of "walked with God" (Gen 5:22, 24) is fairly obvious in the Genesis context. Noah also "walked with God," which is directly associated with his "righteous" and "blameless" character (6:9). Later, God tells Abraham to "walk before me, and be blameless" (17:1), but relationality and intimacy are also implied in the description of Enoch when he not only walks "before" God but "with" him.[15] This aspect of "walk" (הלך) is clearly but tragically illustrated after the fall when God walks in the garden but Adam and Eve hide themselves "from before the presence of Yahweh" (מִפְּנֵי יְהוָה; Gen 3:8). Sailhamer rightly points out, however, that the biblical author includes the story of Enoch for a purpose beyond recording an unusual event; Enoch illustrates how the way to life is through an obedient relationship with God.[16] Even the outstanding example of Noah as a righteous man and recipient of grace (6:8-9) does not quite measure up to the precedent of Enoch. Although (as with Enoch) the story of Noah interrupts the genealogical pattern, the indecent behavior of Noah and his sons demonstrates the appropriateness

---

12. Louw and Nida, *Greek-English Lexicon*, 1:182.

13. Maurer, "Τίθημι," 161.

14. Phillips explains the substitution of "pleased" for "walked with" as an example of the tendency of the LXX translators to avoid the use of anthropomorphisms. Phillips, *Hebrews*, 417.

15. Hamilton, *Book of Genesis*, 1:258; Kidner also remarks on the intimacy implied in this statement. Kidner, *Genesis*, 81.

16. Sailhamer, "Genesis," 74.

of the all-too-familiar words "and then he died" (9:29);[17] but without those ominous words, Enoch becomes the prototype for Israelite faith and conduct. His continued life provides an enduring model to Israel, who must "choose life" (Deut 30:19) when Moses declares the options: "See, I have set before you today life and good, death and evil. If you obey the commandments of the LORD your God . . . by loving the LORD your God, by walking [לָלֶכֶת] in his ways, . . . then you shall live and multiply, and the LORD your God will bless you in the land that you are entering to take possession of it" (Deut 30:15–16 ESV).[18] Thus, Enoch's life not only has eschatological significance because it points to a potential embodied, lasting existence, but also because it sets forth the way (walking with God) that life can be experienced.

A fairly substantial amount of literature later developed around the account of Enoch in Gen 5,[19] but the noncanonical texts provide little assistance in understanding the perspective of ancient Israel. However, the most noteworthy Second Temple text, *1 Enoch*, assumes throughout that Enoch did not see death and also affirms the idea of a future resurrection of the righteous (e.g., 10:17–19; 62:15; 102:4; 103:2–4; 104:4; 108:11, 13).[20]

Enoch's translation serves as a model of what it means to live in relationship with God, that is, to live in his presence; the potency of his witness is all the more acute against a backdrop of exile from the garden and hope for a renewed dwelling place in the promised land. For ancient Israel, the path forward involves walking with God in intimate obedience.

The eschatological element of Enoch's story also gets traction when viewed in combination with God's gracious intervention in promising a seed and with the following story of Noah. By Gen 5 the reader has already been primed to hope for the future, but the story of Enoch arrests the reader's attention and inspires even greater reflection on the notion of the demise of death itself. The narrative simultaneously records the

17. Sailhamer, "Genesis," 75.
18. Sailhamer, "Genesis," 74.
19. Jude 14–15 draws from 1 En. 1:9. Green lists many relevant examples. See Green, *Jude and 2 Peter*, 102.
20. George Foot Moore captures both the difficulty in summarizing *1 Enoch*'s view of resurrection and the significance of its presence: "The several writings brought together in the book of Enoch are distributed over almost a century, and come not only from different authors but out of widely different historical situations. That the revivification of the righteous dead occurs in so many parts of the book, with one conception or another, is evidence of the currency of the idea in that age." Moore, *Judaism in the First Centuries*, 306–7.

harsh realities of a world immersed in sin and destruction and holds out hope for a new Eden. Even through the deluge, glimpses of a new creation catch the reader's eye, for the dry land emerges via the action of the רוּחַ ("wind," "spirit"; 8:1; cf. 1:2) and the divine blessing follows (9:1; cf. 1:28).[21] Although the term רוּחַ is properly translated as "wind" in 8:1, the choice of the term is certainly deliberate. It has been associated with life throughout the account (6:17; 7:15, 22), but Yahweh's Spirit (רוּחַ) "will not always strive with man" (6:3), and when he withdraws his Spirit creation plunges into chaos until the Spirit hovers over the waters once again (1:2).[22] In this way the narrator hints that the רוּחַ ("Spirit") is also the agent of re-creation who brings about a resurrection of sorts. For, although the specific vocabulary of resurrection is not yet employed, the concept of resurrection (restoration to life) is deeply embedded in the eschatological perspective of the Genesis narrative. This is so because it is also fundamental to the restorative nature of God himself.

That Enoch does not experience a corporal resurrection does not detract from the developing hope, for his experience provides the paradigm for a future ascension. Likewise, the resurrections in the ministries of Elijah and Elisha advance the story, although they are not permanent resurrections. These events anticipate a greater fulfillment in the corporal and permanent resurrection of Christ in combination with his ascension and session. Luke depicts Elijah as a model prophet who anticipates the coming of John the Baptist (1:17) and Christ (4:25–26; 9:30–33) and who provides the paradigm for performing resurrections (1 Kgs 17:17–24; Luke 7:11–17). The ascension of Jesus follows the pattern of Elijah's ascension (Acts 1:1–10; cf. 2 Kgs 2:11–12) as does the resulting transferal of pneumatic ministry (Acts 2; cf. 2 Kgs 2:15).[23] And although the brief mention of Enoch in Genesis does not provide much material from which Luke may draw, he is not ignorant of him, for Enoch appears in the genealogy (Luke 3:37).

One might object to viewing Enoch and Elijah as precursors to Christ's resurrection because they bypassed death altogether. However, it is important to remember that, although the death, resurrection, and ascension of Christ are chronologically distinct, for Luke these events function as parts of one theological motion culminating in the reign of

---

21. See Alexander for a comparison of the flood account with the creation account. Alexander, *From Paradise to the Promised Land*, 118–19.

22. Hamilton, *Book of Genesis*, 1:267.

23. Stronstad, *Charismatic Theology of St. Luke*, 24.

Christ as Lord (Acts 2:22–36). Luke employs the shorthand expression "the word" (e.g., 2:41; 4:4; 10:36, 44) for the resurrection of Christ, but the term incorporates both his death and ascension as well. Thus, the "word of the Lord" for Luke entails the various events of the gospel message and is the fulfillment of what has transpired in history in people such as Enoch and Elijah. Christ is like them but greater, for he is "the Holy and Righteous One" (3:14) who rose from the dead and ascended into heaven to reign as King on David's throne.

Glimpses of Resurrection: From Abraham to John the Baptist

Another powerful image that anticipates a full doctrine of resurrection is that of a barren woman miraculously experiencing life in her womb. The following discussion reviews some of the birth narratives from the time of Abraham to John the Baptist and highlights terminology and concepts related to national restoration and resurrection.

The Abrahamic Narrative and Resurrection

The word "death" does not occur throughout the story of the tower of Babel, nor through the genealogy from Shem to Abram (Gen 11:10–27), but it appears somewhat unexpectedly at the outset of the Abrahamic narrative. "Haran died in Ur" even before his father Terah, who "died in Haran" (11:28, 32). And between these deaths in Abraham's family the narrator notes another problematic reality along the same lines, that is, "Now Sarai was barren; she had no child" (v. 30).[24] It is within this context that the author records Yahweh's bold promise to Abram: "I will make you a great nation" (12:2a). And thus begins the repeated theme of barrenness threatening to derail the plan of redemption through a promised seed followed by the miraculous intervention of God overcoming the deadness of the womb to bring about salvation.

The potential derailment of the plan explains God's sending of "great plagues" on Pharaoh and his household after he took Sarai into his palace (Gen 12:17) and, similarly, God's warning to Abimelech in a dream: "Behold, you are a dead man [הִנְּךָ מֵת]" (20:3; cf. Rom 1:18).

---

24. Once again, as with Enoch and Noah, a genealogy is temporarily interrupted to make a significant point. Wenham also notes this. See Wenham, *Genesis*, vol. 1.

And if Abimelech does not return Sarah, God warns, "know that you will surely die [דַּעְ כִּי־מוֹת תָּמוּת], you and all who are yours" (Gen 20:7; cf. 2:17). At the end of the story the reader learns that Yahweh had closed the wombs of the women in Abimelech's household (20:18). Death looms over the characters in both stories, but in the latter story Abimelech experiences a foretaste of death through the inability of his wife and slave girls to have children. They return from the precipice of death only at the word of God's prophet (v. 7; cf. Ps 105:15). This association between death and barrenness supports one of Levenson's major arguments—that "childlessness is the equivalent of death" and "birth is the reversal of death and thus to a large degree the functional equivalent of resurrection."[25] Thus, the announcement that Eve will have children tempers the consequence of pain, for there is hope for rescue through the promised seed (Gen 3:15–16). Later in the narrative and immediately following the story of Abimelech, life comes to Sarah's barren womb in fulfillment of God's promise (21:2). The concept of life from death is inherent in the infertility stories of the Bible.

That Sarah's miracle is not merely an isolated tale intended primarily to entertain, to record the history of an ancient people, or to celebrate the continuation of a family is borne out by the numerous pointers in the immediate context and later biblical commentary. This occasion is surrounded with eschatological markers pointing to both a coming fulfillment in the promised land and a more distant and universal fulfillment. Regarding the anticipation of Canaan, Abram scouts out the land, receives a promise from God, and builds an altar as a first step in restoring proper worship in this land (Gen 12:7–8; cf. 13:4).[26] Abram's further scouting of the land and altar building anticipates the return from Egypt under Moses (13:14–18). In addition, the region of the Jordan was "like the garden of Yahweh" (v. 10),[27] but the narrator quickly digresses and

---

25. Levenson, *Resurrection and Restoration*, 115–16. Levenson uses the story of Naomi and Ruth to illustrate dying and rising again through the loss and acquisition of offspring. He also views the psalmists as experiencing Sheol prior to natural death in some cases (77–78). As is typical of the Jewish perspective, he also sees the future of biblical characters as bound up with the continuation of their offspring. However, the future life via the continuation of the natural line largely receives the accent in Levenson's work (83), rather than the eschatological hope of a Messiah coming through the biblical families and so necessitating the maintenance of the family line and blessing.

26. Beale sees a clear connection between the building of altars, worship in Eden, and the coming new sanctuaries in Canaan. Beale, *Temple and Mission*, 96–98.

27. Although Hamilton fixes Lot's territory outside the boundaries of Canaan, the

adds that this was before the destruction of Sodom and Gomorrah. Abraham's intercession and insistence that the Judge of all the earth distinguish between the righteous and the wicked (18:25) reminds the reader of the account of Noah. The decimation of Sodom and Gomorrah serves as another example of creation returning to chaos under the weight of sin and judgment, and the event serves as a warning to the Israelites of what can happen if they desecrate their new garden.

Even Ishmael's near death is practically a resurrection, and his life has long-term significance (Gen 21:16, 18–19).[28] The record of Sarah's death and burial takes a whole chapter, not so much to pay tribute to her as to describe how Abraham gained a foothold in the land and to provide the legal basis for Israel's claim to this piece of property (23:1–20).[29] Jacob's final instructions include orders to bury him in the same cave in the field of Machpelah along with Abraham, Sarah, Isaac, Rebekah, and Leah (49:29–32). Jacob's request could be understood as both a desire to maintain solidarity with his ancestors in burial and as faith in God to fulfill his promise regarding Canaan, but the author of Hebrews sees more, for "they desire a better country, that is, a heavenly one. Therefore God is not ashamed to be called their God, for he has prepared for them a city" (11:16 ESV). Out of a story of death and burial comes a strong eschatological note about the promises of God (cf. v. 21). This is consistent with Luke's development of an individual eschatology in relation to Christ, for Jesus fully expects death to lead into God's presence and to result in resurrection (Luke 9:22; 16:31; 23:43, 46; cf. Ps 31:5b).

There are other pointers to a more distant, future fulfillment of the story of Abraham and Sarah. In Gen 15:2 Abram expresses his concern over his childless state and God responds with a promise of countless offspring. Genesis records, "And he believed the LORD, and he counted it to him as righteousness" (15:6 ESV; cf. Rom 4:3). In Paul's discussion of Abraham in Romans 4, he argues that Abraham became the father of many nations (Gen 17:5) and serves as a model of faith in the God "who

---

reader observes that Eden has once again inserted itself into the narrative. Hamilton, *Book of Genesis*, 1:393.

28. Hermann Gunkel's loose rendering of Gen 21:18 highlights some significant points in the verse: "So hold the boy firmly; Do not cast him down again as though he were dedicated for death. He is destined for greatness." Gunkel, *Genesis*, 228.

29. Hamilton notes that Gen 23:20 is added for emphasis to show the author's central concern of Abraham as rightful owner of the property. Hamilton, *Book of Genesis*, 2:136.

gives life to the dead and calls into existence the things that do not exist" (Rom 4:17b). And Abraham "did not weaken in faith when he considered his own body, which was as good as dead [νενεκρωμένον] (since he was about a hundred years old), or when he considered the barrenness of Sarah's womb" (v. 19). Paul encourages the Romans to trust in this God "who raised Jesus our Lord from the dead" (v. 24b), the Lord who was "raised for our justification" (v. 25b). Paul is not taking liberties with the Genesis text and giving a forced, allegorical interpretation; he is drawing on a common understanding of the relationship between infertility and death, on the one hand, and miraculous childbirth and resurrection, on the other.

This perspective gains added support from Hebrews: "Therefore from one man, and him as good as dead [νενεκρωμένου], were born descendants as many as the stars of heaven and as many as the innumerable grains of sand by the seashore" (11:12 ESV). The verb νεκρόω ("to put to death") occurs only three times in the New Testament (Rom 4:19; Col 3:5) and not at all in the Septuagint, and Paul Ellingworth rightly calls the parallel between Rom 4:19 and Heb 11:12 "astonishingly close" and "suggesting common tradition."[30] Both passages view infertility as a kind of death and suggest that the miraculous demonstration of God's power to bring life is a sort of resurrection.

The author of Hebrews even goes so far as to inform the reader of Abraham's thought process when "he considered [λογισάμενος] that God is even able [δυνατὸς] to raise from the dead, therefore [ὅθεν] he received him back as a type [ἐν παραβολῇ]" (11:19).[31] Some might dismiss the reasoning of Abraham as merely the imposition of a later idea onto the text of the Old Testament,[32] but there are good reasons to believe that the author of Hebrews was simply a good, enlightened reader who understood the eschatological moorings of Genesis. First, many scholars

---

30. However, I would prefer the expression "common perspective" over "common tradition." Ellingworth, *Epistle to the Hebrews*, 590.

31. Cockerill is right to translate ὅθεν as "therefore" since this word has an inferential or consequential use elsewhere in Hebrews (2:17; 3:1; 7:25; 8:3; 9:18). Cockerill, *Epistle to the Hebrews*, 557. Likewise, based on usage in Heb 9:9, παραβολή means more than a figure of speech (ESV, RSV, NIV). See O'Brien, *Letter to the Hebrews*, 425; Ellingworth, *Epistle to the Hebrews*, 604; Lane, *Hebrews 9–13*, 362–63.

32. Ellingworth seems to lean in this direction; however, the employment of terminology reflecting the New Testament era is a separate matter from finding the conceptual source of the theology in the New Testament era. Ellingworth, *Epistle to the Hebrews*, 602.

have pointed to the apparent incongruence between God's command to Abraham to sacrifice Isaac and Abraham's statement that "we" will worship and return (Gen 22:2, 5) as implying Abraham's belief in resurrection.[33] The author of Hebrews follows similar reasoning when asserting that belief in resurrection resolves the conundrum of God's command to sacrifice Isaac in light of God's promise of offspring through Isaac (Heb 11:17–18). Second, some have correctly noted that the miraculous bringing of life to the "dead" bodies of Abraham and Sarah provided Abraham with a precedent for resurrection (vv. 11–12, 17–19).[34]

Third, Heb 11:19 refers to God's ability (δυνατὸς) to raise the dead. The author of Hebrews appears to tap the references to God's power (Gen 17:1) and character in the Abrahamic narrative. The story reveals the nature of God as provider (Gen 22:8, 14), but immediately prior to the testing of Abraham's faith, Abraham concludes a treaty with Abimelech and worships "Yahweh, the Everlasting God" (יְהוָה אֵל עוֹלָם; 21:33). The designation is appropriate as an indicator of God's faithfulness to his promises throughout all of Abraham's dealings, but, literally speaking, it is located at an extremely advantageous crossroads, for Abraham must trust the Everlasting God through an ordeal with the assumed death of the promised heir. The Everlasting God will not be limited by a moment of death. The nature of God serves as the foundation for belief in his promises and the possibility of a resurrection.

Conception and Resurrection in 2 Maccabees

The story of the martyrdom of seven brothers and their mother in 2 Macc 7 also references the power of God in resurrection and the analogous nature of conception to resurrection. The second brother defies King Antiochus IV when at his final breath he affirms, "The King of the universe will raise us up to an everlasting renewal of life" (v. 9b NRSV). The third son alludes to God's creation of his body when he raises his hands and retorts, "I got these from Heaven . . . and from him I hope to get them back" (v. 11 NRSV). The mother specifically draws a parallel between God's life-giving power in both creation and the womb and resurrection:

---

33. E.g., Bruce, *Epistle to the Hebrews*, 19; Hamilton, *Book of Genesis*, 2:108; O'Brien, *Letter to the Hebrews*, 424.

34. Cockerill, *Epistle to the Hebrews*, 557; Lane, *Hebrews 9–13*, 362; O'Brien, *Letter to the Hebrews*, 424.

"I do not know how you came into being in my womb. It was not I who gave you life and breath, nor I who set in order the elements within each of you. Therefore the Creator of the world, who shaped the beginning of humankind and devised the origin of all things, will in his mercy give life and breath back to you again" (vv. 22–23 NRSV; cf. Rom 4:17).[35] The mother again admonishes her last surviving son to observe creation and "recognize that God did not make them out of things that existed." She continues, "And in the same way the human race came into being" (2 Macc 7:28b NRSV). The rationale for resurrection in these passages is akin to the logic found in Gen 21–22, Rom 4, and Heb 11, but what the characters in Maccabees knew in principle Abraham knew experientially—the eternal God gives life to barren wombs and returns children who are as good as dead to life again.

Miraculous Births from Genesis to John the Baptist

The biblical stories of infertility repeatedly remind the Israelites that God's agenda advances not by human potency but by divine power. Rebekah remained childless for twenty years after marrying Isaac (Gen 25:19–21, 26). Rachel struggled with her barrenness until "God opened her womb" (30:22). Only after the angel of Yahweh prophesied a coming child did Manoah's wife conceive and give birth to Samson (Judg 13:2–5, 24). Hannah gave birth to Samuel after "Yahweh remembered her" (1 Sam 1:19). Isaiah likened Jerusalem to a barren woman who could sing because of the abundance of her children (ch. 54). The latter figure serves as a powerful and appropriate symbol of exile and national restoration. In the New Testament only Luke describes the miraculous arrival of John the Baptist and provides a detailed account of Mary's song of praise. While Paul and the author of Hebrews comment directly on the ancient origins of belief in resurrection, Luke first presents his case in narrative form by telling the stories of Elizabeth and Mary in light of previous miraculous births. Luke's birth narratives contain five main elements found in Old Testament birth announcements: (1) the appearance of an angel, (2) fear or perplexity at the angelophany, (3) a divine message, (4) the recipient's objection, and (5) a reassuring sign.[36] The story of Zechariah

---

35. Lane also notes this parallel. Lane, *Hebrews 9–13*, 362.

36. Bock, *Luke*, 1:73; Brown, *Birth of the Messiah*, 156; Fitzmyer, *Gospel According to Luke*, 1:335.

From Death and Barrenness to the Resurrected King 67

and Elizabeth has clear points of contact with the accounts of Abraham and Sarah, Rachel, and Samson's parents, while Mary's story most clearly parallels Hannah's.

Luke immediately signals the eschatological significance of his gospel when he refers to his work and that of his predecessors as a "narrative account of the events that have been fulfilled [πεπληροφορημένων] among us" (1:1). I. Howard Marshall notes how the perfect passive participle of the verb πληροφορέω ("to fulfill") suggests divine activity and the completion of promised events.[37] Because Luke writes to provide Theophilus with assurance regarding those events of which he already possesses some knowledge (vv. 3–4), it is evident that Luke is placing the life, death, resurrection, and ascension of Christ within an eschatological context and suggesting that God continues to act in power among his people as he has in the past. Thus, the way is prepared for an account of miraculous births.

The account of John's birth emphasizes the righteous character of Zechariah and Elizabeth (Luke 1:5–6), suggesting that their childless state was not the result of any moral deficiency.[38] The term "barren" (στεῖρα) describes Elizabeth (1:7, 36), just as the Septuagint used this term for Sarai (Gen 11:30), Rebekah (25:21), Rachel (29:31), Manoah's wife (Judg 13:2–3), and Hannah (1 Sam 2:5). Like Abraham and Sarah (Gen 17:17), Zechariah and Elizabeth face the hard reality of old age (Luke 1:7, 18). Abraham and Zechariah ask for a sign in practically identical terms: "How can I know that I will inherit it?" (κατὰ τί γνώσομαι ὅτι κληρονομήσω αὐτήν; Gen 15:8 LXX) and "How can I know this?" (κατὰ τί γνώσομαι τοῦτο; Luke 1:18). Both men question the message (Gen 15:2; 17:17–18; Luke 1:18). The promise of a son to Sarah is nearly identical to that to Elizabeth: "Yes, behold, Sarah your wife will bear you a son and you will call his name Isaac" (ναί ἰδοὺ Σαρρα ἡ γυνή σου τέξεταί σοι υἱόν καὶ καλέσεις τὸ ὄνομα αὐτοῦ Ισαακ; Gen 17:19 LXX); "And your wife Elizabeth will bear you a son and you will call his name John" (καὶ ἡ γυνή σου Ἐλισάβετ γεννήσει υἱόν σοι καὶ καλέσεις τὸ ὄνομα αὐτοῦ Ἰωάννην; Luke 1:13).[39] The verbal similarities extend beyond thematic parallels

---

37. Marshall, *Gospel of Luke*, 41; Also see Bock, *Luke*, 1:56–57.

38. Stronstad points out that Luke consistently informs the reader of the spiritual state of people before he records the event of their filling with the Spirit (e.g., Luke 1:41, 67). Stronstad, *Charismatic Theology of St. Luke*, 64.

39. Edwards also notices the similarity. Edwards, *Gospel According to Luke*, 36. The list of similarities mentioned here is not exhaustive. Other examples, such as the giving of thanks after the birth of the child (Gen 21:6; Luke 1:25), have been noted

and suggest that Luke knows the Genesis narrative well and intentionally draws attention to it in order to highlight the eschatological significance of the arrival of John.[40]

Although the story surrounding Samson's birth contains fewer verbal parallels with John's birth, there are a number of conceptual parallels. Manoah and his wife encounter the angel of Yahweh (Judg 13:3-23) just as Zechariah meets Gabriel (Luke 1:11-20). Both promised boys must avoid "wine and strong drink" (οἶνον καὶ σίκερα; Judg 13:14 LXX; Luke 1:15) because of their callings. Samson will be "a Nazarite of God from the womb and will begin to save Israel from the hand [σῶσαι τὸν Ισραηλ ἐκ χειρός] of the Philistines" (Judg 13:5). John's work has a different emphasis in that his calling involves turning hearts back to God and preparing for the Lord's coming (Luke 1:15-17, 76-77), yet his work involves giving the "knowledge of salvation [σωτηρίας]" (v. 77). In addition, Zechariah's prophecy follows hard on the heels of John's birth, yet the first eight verses of the prophecy (69-75) focus not on John but on how God "has raised up a horn of salvation for us in the house of his servant David" (ἤγειρεν κέρας σωτηρίας ἡμῖν ἐν οἴκῳ Δαυὶδ παιδὸς αὐτοῦ; v. 69). This salvation was proclaimed by the prophets (v. 70) as "salvation from our enemies and from the hand [ἐκ χειρός] of all those who hate us" (v. 71; cf. v. 74; Judg 13:5; Ps 105:10 LXX) and is God's remembrance of his covenant with Abraham (Luke 1:72-73).[41]

Other similarities between the stories exist, as Luke multiplies nearly too many Old Testament references to even count. In both stories the woman seems to outshine the man in simple faith and common sense. Manoah must "follow" his wife (Judg 13:10-11a)[42] and later receive her instruction (vv. 22-23).[43] Zechariah remains mute throughout Eliza-

---

by others. Bock, *Luke*, 1:98.

40. Although there are strong parallels between the two stories, the many unique features demonstrate that the Lukan stories are not contrived. The similarities primarily come from an organic relationship between the two divinely orchestrated events, and Luke uses terminology that highlights this relationship.

41. The phrase ἐκ χειρός occurs 172 times in the Old Testament and most commonly in 1 Samuel (20x), Psalms (16x), Judges (12x), and 2 Kings (12x).

42. Webb, *Book of Judges*, 354.

43. Manoah plays a secondary role in the story, and the reader never learns his wife's name. Perhaps the author purposely minimizes their agency in the story in order to highlight the divine initiative. Throughout Judges the Israelites call on God in their distress, but no such call precedes Samson's story (as noted by Webb, *Book of Judges*, 350). God acts out of his own mercy to raise up a deliverer through a barren woman

beth's pregnancy because of his questioning rooted in unbelief (Luke 1:20), but one of the most striking commonalities between the narratives is the male child's endowment with the Spirit. The angel instructs Samson's parents to raise the boy as a Nazirite, which includes abstention from contact with corpses (Num 6:1–12; Judg 13:5). The preceding stories have familiarized the reader with the tragedy of death in Israel, as Jephthah apparently sacrificed his own daughter (Judg 11:39)[44] and then led the Gileadites in slaughtering forty-two thousand Ephraimites, their own countrymen (12:4–6). Nevertheless, the Spirit intervened: "And the young man grew, and the LORD blessed him. And the Spirit of the LORD began to stir him in Mahaneh-dan, between Zorah and Eshtaol" (13:24b–25 ESV; cf. Luke 1:80).

It is less certain that John was a Nazirite, as Luke never explicitly says so,[45] yet his consecration is directly linked with the prophecy that "he will be filled with the Holy Spirit while still in his mother's womb" (Luke 1:15). Zechariah's prophesy that John will go before the Lord "to give light to those who sit in darkness and in the shadow of death" (Luke 1:79; cf. Isa 9:2) casts John in the role of one who delivers God's people from the infringement of death.[46] J. Alec Motyer notes that "the darkness-light motif points to a creative work of God."[47] As God brings light and life in creation through the activity of his Spirit (Gen 1:1–3), so he brings light and life through a miracle child who is endowed with his Spirit (Judg 13:25; Isa 9:2–7; 11:1–2; Luke 1:15). The consistent element in these accounts is that the Spirit, whether functioning directly or through human agency, is the one who brings light and life out of a setting of darkness and death. In addition, the type scene of a miraculous birth from a dead womb serves as an appropriate metaphor for national restoration and resurrection. Thus, the idea of a national resurrection is

---

for a compromising people who are not even calling on God.

44. Webb, *Book of Judges*, 333. Webb agrees that Jephthah did sacrifice his daughter, but see his notes for a list of scholars who take a different position.

45. Bock briefly names some leading scholars on both sides of the issue and then concludes that the main point is that John is an ascetic prophet. Bock *Luke*, 1:85.

46. Samson is a complex character, and he clearly does not live up to his calling to separation from uncleanness. John is clearly greater than Samson both in sanctity of lifestyle and in his position in redemptive history. Nonetheless, Samson's personal deficiencies do not detract from the greater point that God is acting in a miraculous way in history, bringing life from a dead womb, and empowering an individual by his Spirit to bring new life to a people living in the shadow of death.

47. Motyer, *Prophecy of Isaiah*, 100.

integral to the Scriptures and is not limited to Ezekiel or later Judaism. The Spirit is directly involved in the activity of dispelling the darkness directly in creation and through empowering human agents in restoration. Luke is familiar with these concepts, and he understands that John's miraculous birth and Spirit-filled ministry is grounded in an ancient pattern of life from death.

Resurrection as Integral to the Lukan Birth Narratives

The preponderance of references to resurrection in Luke-Acts as a whole causes one to wonder why Luke does not appear to mention resurrection in his prologue, birth narratives, or inauguration narratives. As the previous discussion has shown, though, the birth narratives themselves testify to Luke's awareness of the death-to-life concept. However, there are at least five other indicators that resurrection is central to Luke's thought from the outset.

First, as noted previously, Luke's "narrative account [διήγησιν] of the events that have been fulfilled among us" certainly includes Jesus's resurrection (Luke 1:1; cf. 24:44–46). Second, Luke takes care to demonstrate the reliability of his account by pointing out that those who handed it down were "from the beginning eyewitnesses and servants of the word" (οἱ ἀπ' ἀρχῆς αὐτόπται καὶ ὑπηρέται γενόμενοι τοῦ λόγου; 1:2).[48] Although αὐτόπτης is not Luke's usual word for "witness," still the emphasis Luke places on visual witnesses is obvious.[49] One calls to mind Peter's time stipulation for Judas's replacement (John's baptism until Jesus's

---

48. Green notes that the one article governs both the eyewitnesses and the servants of the word, indicating that they are the same group of people. Green, *Gospel of Luke*, 41n43.

49. The theme of witness is represented by eight different words sharing the same root in Luke-Acts, but the concept of witness is so pervasive that it is difficult to identify every occurrence. The gospel contains a total of nine occurrences of the various forms of "witness," and Acts has thirty-nine. They occur as follows: μάρτυς (Luke 2x; Acts 13x), μαρτυρέω (Luke 1x; Acts 11x), διαμαρτύρομαι (Luke 1x; Acts 9x), μαρτύριον (Luke 3x; Acts 2x), μαρτυρία (Luke 1x; Acts 1x), μαρτύρομαι (Acts 2x), ἀμάρτυρος (Acts 1x), and ψευδομαρτυρέω (Luke 1x). Luke uses the noun μάρτυς more often than the other terms, and it has a strong forensic sense in that the witness testifies to the facts he or she has seen or heard (22:15; 26:16). The term is most often used of the Twelve as witnesses of Christ's resurrection (Luke 24:48; Acts 1:8, 22; 2:32; 3:15; 5:32; 10:39, 41; 13:31). The word αὐτόπται occurs only here in the Greek Bible. Bauckham points out that it does not have a forensic meaning. Bauckham, *Jesus and the Eyewitnesses*, 117.

From Death and Barrenness to the Resurrected King   71

ascension) and the job description of the new disciple: "a witness to his resurrection" (Acts 1:22 ESV; cf. 10:36–42).

Luke explains his emphasis on eyewitnesses to Theophilus: "that you may know the certainty of the words [λόγων τὴν ἀσφάλειαν] you have been taught" (Luke 1:4). The eyewitnesses are "servants of the word," and Theophilus needs certainty regarding the "words" (1:2, 4). The "word" is a favorite expression of Luke's. Jesus spoke of the "word of God" (Luke 5:1; 8:11, 21; 11:28), Luke called his gospel his "first word" (Acts 1:1), and throughout Acts "the word" is a shorthand term for the message of the gospel.[50] In Luke 24:44–46 Luke gives the essence of Jesus's "words" (οἱ λόγοι; v. 44) in three infinitives: (1) "the Christ is to suffer [παθεῖν]," (2) "to rise [ἀναστῆναι] from the dead on the third day" (v. 46), and (3) "repentance for forgiveness of sins is to be preached [κηρυχθῆναι] in his name unto all nations, beginning at Jerusalem" (v. 47). Of these three, Jesus asserts, "You are witnesses of these things" (ὑμεῖς μάρτυρες τούτων; v. 48). At the center of Christ's words and "the word" (Acts 2:41) is the resurrection of Christ. Confirmation that Luke already has in mind the resurrection may be found in Acts 2:36, where the adverb ἀσφαλῶς ("certainly") occurs in the midst of Peter's sermon on the resurrection (cf. Luke 1:4). Luke is concerned to demonstrate to Theophilus the credibility of the identification of Jesus as the risen Lord. The Lukan prologue anticipates that the readers' knowledge of gospel events will inform their understanding of "fulfillment," "eyewitnesses," and "the word." Thus, Luke has immediately clued in the reader that he will buttress the case for Christ's resurrection with credible witnesses.

Third, Gabriel roots the births of John and Jesus in the miracle-working power of God, much as Paul (Rom 4:18–21), the author of Hebrews (11:11–12, 19), and the author of 2 Maccabees (ch. 7) root their resurrection comments in that same power. The angel declares to Mary, "The Holy Spirit will come upon you and the power [δύναμις] of the Most High will overshadow you" (1:35b). He also announces to her that barren Elizabeth is six months pregnant, "for no word will be impossible with God" (ὅτι οὐκ ἀδυνατήσει παρὰ τοῦ θεοῦ πᾶν ῥῆμα; 1:37). This is clearly a reference to God's question to Sarah: "Is any word impossible with God?" (μὴ ἀδυνατεῖ παρὰ τῷ θεῷ ῥῆμα; Gen 18:14 LXX).[51] The mention of Eliz-

50. Important examples include: Acts 2:41; 4:4, 29, 31; 6:2, 4, 7; 8:4, 14, 21, 25; 10:36, 44; 11:1, 19; 12:24; 13:5, 7, 26, 44, 46, 48–49; 14:3, 12, 25; 15:7, 35–36; 16:6, 32; 17:11, 13; 18:5, 11; 19:10, 20; 20:7, 32.

51. The verb ἀδυνατέω rarely occurs in the Greek Bible and not at all in Genesis

abeth is an aid to Mary's faith, and the reference to Sarah is a solicitation to respond in faith. The reliability of God's "word" (ῥῆμα) applies first to Elizabeth's miraculous pregnancy, but Mary's call to faith and the future tense "will be impossible" (ἀδυνατήσει; Mary's miracle is not yet evident) implies that the phrase equally applies to Mary.[52] The Spirit, the overshadowing, and the "word" (ῥῆμα) are reminiscent of God's creative power in Gen 1. This background, along with the tie to Sarah and the association of barrenness with death, suggests that Luke is presenting his miraculous birth stories with a similar understanding to the others mentioned above and that, for him, the stories are essentially life-from-death miracles or fresh creative acts of God necessary for advancing his plan.

Fourth, Luke may be hinting at his interest in resurrection and employing somewhat of a double entendre when he records Simeon's prophecy that Jesus was "appointed for the fall and resurrection of many in Israel" (κεῖται εἰς πτῶσιν καὶ ἀνάστασιν πολλῶν ἐν τῷ Ἰσραὴλ; Luke 2:34). To be sure, the stumbling stone passages provide part of the conceptual background for the falling and rising (Isa 8:14-15; 28:13-16; Luke 20:17-18), even if the verbal links are limited, but there are good reasons to believe Luke is driving at something more. He uses the noun ἀνάστασις ("resurrection") only in reference to resurrection from the dead in the sixteen other places it occurs in Luke-Acts.[53] In addition, one of the twenty-two verses in the Old Testament where the combination of the verbs "to fall" (πίπτω) and "to rise" (ἀνίστημι) occurs is a key resurrection passage.[54] "The dead will rise [ἀναστήσονται], and those in the tombs will be raised, and those in the earth will be glad; for the dew from you is healing to them, but the land of the ungodly will fall [πεσεῖται]" (Isa 26:19). The rising and falling theme is an important concept to Luke, and Luke 2:34 will receive more attention later. For the moment, it is worth noting that Luke appears to lay a foundation for his resurrection emphasis early in his account.

---

or in Luke-Acts outside of the texts under consideration.

52. Green also sees the phrase as applying to both Elizabeth and Mary. Green, *Gospel of Luke*, 92.

53. Luke 14:14; 20:27, 33, 35-36; Acts 1:22; 2:31; 4:2, 33; 17:18, 32; 23:6, 8; 24:15, 21; 26:23.

54. The falling and rising expression carries the notion of a reversal or contrast of positions, but there is no singular application of the expression in the Old Testament. However, the falling is often connected with judgment. See especially Isa 51:17, which uses a form of the verb ἀνίστημι ('to rise') and a form of the noun πτῶσις ("fall").

Finally, the Christology of the birth narratives reflects the resurrection and ascension Christology of the end of Luke's gospel and the sermons in Acts. This suggests that Luke already had the resurrection clearly in view when he penned the birth narratives. The various points mentioned above in combination with Luke's perspective on miraculous, death-to-life births demonstrate that the thought of resurrection was integral to Luke's birth narratives.

Luke's Christological Birth Narratives, Resurrection, and Spirit

Raymond Brown notices the parallel Christology between the Lukan birth narratives and Acts and accounts for its presence in the birth narratives by appealing to the early church's post-resurrection theological reflection and Luke's use of prosopopoeia:

> The same combined ideas that early Christian preaching had once applied to the resurrection (i.e., a divine proclamation, the begetting of God's Son, the agency of the Holy Spirit), and which Mark had applied to the baptism, are now applied to the conception of Jesus in the words of an angel's message to Joseph and to Mary (respectively, in Matthew and in Luke). And once the conception of Jesus has become the christological moment, the revelation of who Jesus is begins to be proclaimed to an audience who come and worship . . . And thus the infancy stories have become truly an infancy gospel.[55]

Brown rightly notices the parallel, but it is not necessary to resort to speculative source-critical methods to account for it. Luke certainly planned the "infancy gospel" and intentionally employed certain theological terms to evoke images of the later resurrection speeches, but his selectivity of material does not preclude the historicity of the birth narratives nor justify assumptions about what sources Luke did or did not have available.[56]

---

55. Brown, *Birth of the Messiah*, 31.

56. Brown suggests that Luke simply borrowed from the story of Abraham and Sarah to construct the story of Zechariah and Elizabeth. He also claims that this was a "Lucan technique." Brown, *Birth of the Messiah*, 316, especially note 57.

Jesus as "Lord" in Lukan Christology

The christologically loaded announcement of the angel in Luke 2:11 is not an imposition from a later idea into the story; it is the truth that the disciples and others should have known all along but struggled to realize. "For a Savior who is Christ the Lord was born to you today in the city of David" (ὅτι ἐτέχθη ὑμῖν σήμερον σωτὴρ ὅς ἐστιν χριστὸς κύριος ἐν πόλει Δαυίδ). Luke alerts the reader at the outset of his narrative of what is commonly known among Christians—the risen Jesus is a descendant of David and is Lord of all. However, he uses the difficulty of the characters in the story as a literary strategy both to record his history and to evangelize the reader. The omniscient narrator already knows the outcome, but the reader, in identifying with the characters, is confronted with the same decision as the disciples. Will the reader realize the truth and call him "Lord"? He was Lord at birth and proclaimed by Peter as Lord at Pentecost: "Therefore let all the house of Israel know for certain that God has made him both Lord and Christ, this Jesus whom you crucified" (Acts 2:36).

Luke's careful use of "Lord" (κύριος) throughout Luke-Acts demonstrates that he intends the reader to connect Luke 2:11 with the resurrection. He employs the term 104 times in the gospel and 107 times in Acts. In the birth narratives "Lord" occurs 27 times, and nearly every occurrence refers to the Lord God. Luke 1:43 and 2:11 arrest the reader's attention, however, because they clearly refer to Jesus. Elizabeth's prophetic query in 1:43 stands out: "And how has this happened to me that the mother of my Lord should come to me?" This is all the more astounding in light of the fact that Elizabeth then blesses Mary for believing the words spoken to her by "the Lord" God (1:45). And the angel's announcement that the Savior has been born "today" (a favorite term of Luke's to describe the arrival of eschatological salvation)[57] and that this Savior's identity is none other than "Christ the Lord" (χριστὸς κύριος) provides an interpretive lens for the rest of Luke's two volumes (2:11). References to the Lord God continue throughout Luke's works, but in the gospel narrative the disciples and other characters refer to Jesus as κύριος ("lord," "master," "sir"), but, ironically, as a term of respect and not with the full implications of the term as used in 2:11 and Acts 2:36. Meanwhile Jesus hints at the full implications of the term, such as when he says he is "the Lord of the Sabbath" (6:5; cf. v. 46; 20:42, 44), and the narrator of the gospel begins describing Jesus as Lord in the full sense in 7:13 (cf. 11:39; 13:15).

---

57. E.g., see Luke 4:21; 19:5, 9; Acts 13:33. Bock, *Theology of Luke and Acts*, 135.

The characters grapple with understanding what the narrator and reader are privy to in the story, but the revelation of Jesus's lordship reaches a new height in Luke 24:3, when the women enter the tomb on resurrection day and do "not find the body of the Lord Jesus." Luke has reserved the phrase "Lord Jesus" for the occasion of the resurrection, and Peter becomes the first disciple to use this appellation in Acts (1:21), but it serves as the common title for Jesus in Acts (e.g., 4:33; 7:59; 8:16; 16:31) along with the shorter "Lord." So, although the characters in the story do not fully realize the import of the angel's announcement until the resurrection, the reader knows that the resurrection marks the unveiling of Jesus's exalted status and that the term "Lord" is theologically saturated with the resurrection motif throughout the narrative.

The angel's announcement to Mary that her child will have "the throne of his father David" (Luke 1:32) and that "he will reign over the house of Jacob forever and of his kingdom there will be no end" builds on the promises of 2 Sam 7 and previews the exaltation of Christ expounded on by Peter in Acts 2:22–36. Peter's sermon explicitly mentions David three times (vv. 25, 29, 34), extensively quotes a Davidic psalm in support of the resurrection (Ps 15:8–11 LXX; Acts 2:25–28), quotes Ps 132:11 (Acts 2:30) about the promise to David of an enthroned descendent (2 Sam 7:11, 13, 16), and cites Ps 110:1 as evidence that God made Jesus "Lord and Christ" through the resurrection and exaltation (Acts 2:34–36). Luke's specific reference to Joseph as "from the house of David" (Luke 1:27), the angel's reference to "the throne of David" (v. 32), and the promise of an everlasting kingdom (v. 33) anticipate the resurrection and Peter's christological sermon at Pentecost.

Hannah and Mary in Luke's Resurrection Christology

The similarities between the stories of Mary and Hannah, and especially between the Magnificat (Luke 1:46–55) and Hannah's prayer (1 Sam 2:1–10), deepen the association between Luke's Christology and 2 Sam 7. Besides the obvious relationship between two stories featuring the miraculous birth of an important male child, both stories include a "handmaid" who receives favor from the Lord (1 Sam 1:18; Luke 1:30, 38),[58] a woman who believes a prophetic word (1 Sam 1:17–18; Luke 1:38), and a prophetic psalm of praise (1 Sam 2:1–10; Luke 2:46–55). In both cases

---

58. Brown, *Birth of the Messiah*, 319.

the prophetic psalm includes an emphasis on reversal of status, a heavy theocentricity,[59] an eschatological perspective,[60] and a broader concern for the nation beyond the plight of the individual (1 Sam 2:10; Luke 1:54–55). The prominence of both songs, by virtue of their location in the narratives, calls attention to them, and the significance of Hannah's song particularly stands out because, along with the songs of David in 2 Sam 22–23, it forms an inclusio around the entire narrative of 1–2 Samuel.[61]

However, many scholars have concluded that Hannah's song was later imported into the narrative. Randall Bailey, governed by source-critical presuppositions, rejects the attribution of the song to Hannah because (1) only verse 5 fits Hannah's life setting and the barren woman mentioned there has seven children rather than Hannah's six, (2) verse 10 anachronistically mentions a king, and (3) the war imagery in verse 4 does not seem to fit.[62] The experience of Hannah fits very well, however, with a reversal of status theme and as a basis for inductive reasoning about the character of God. The symbolism of seven children is apparent, and the Lord's breaking of the bows of warriors would not be foreign terminology to a woman living at the end of the period of the judges. More to the point, though, to deny Hannah her song and her king implies that Mary should equally be denied her song and her King. It is no less likely that Hannah prophesied of a coming anointed king than Mary heard an angelic announcement of such and prophesied God's victory through her promised child.[63] Bergen captures Luke's sentiments on the issue: "The close parallels between Hannah's Prayer and Mary's Song (Luke 1:46–55) suggest that the first-century Christian community considered the entire passage, and especially the phrases 'his king' and 'his anointed,' to be prophetic references to Jesus Christ and his ministry."[64] Neither Han-

---

59. Regarding Hannah's song, Bergen observes, "Linguistic marking is seen in the employment of a divine figure, in this case Yahweh, as the subject of eighteen different verbs in a section containing only fifty-eight words." Bergen, *1, 2 Samuel*, 76n35.

60. Hannah incorporates creation (2 Sam 2:8), judgment (v. 10), and an anointed king (v. 10), while Mary speaks of what will happen "from now on" (Luke 1:48), mercy extending "from generation to generation" (v. 50), and God's faithfulness to "Abraham and his seed forever" (vv. 54–55). See Bock's comments on the phrase "from now on" in Luke. Bock, *Luke*, 1:151.

61. Tsumura, *First Book of Samuel*, 135.

62. Bailey, "Redemption of YHWH," 214.

63. See Bock's discussion of the various views of the six prophetic aorists used by Mary in Luke 1:51–53. Bock, *Luke*, 1:154–56.

64. Bergen, *1, 2 Samuel*, 77.

nah's song nor Mary's song presents a problem for those who embrace a prophetic worldview.

There are several indicators that the author of Samuel used the inclusio to draw attention to important themes in the narrative, such as the fall of Saul and the rise of David, the significance of an anointed king, and the covenantal promises to David of an everlasting throne. Hannah speaks of salvation from enemies (1 Sam 2:1) and, after a final summary of events in which God rescues David in various ways (2 Sam 21), David's song of praise commences with an acknowledgement of such: "And David spoke to the LORD the words of this song on the day when the LORD delivered him from the hand of all his enemies, and from the hand of Saul" (2 Sam 22:1 ESV). Both ends of the frame feature a "horn" (1 Sam 2:1, 10; 2 Sam 22:3), God as "Rock" (1 Sam 2:2; 2 Sam 22:2, 3, 32, 47; 23:3), a reversal of fortunes for the arrogant (1 Sam 2:3–5; 2 Sam 22:28), a bow (1 Sam 2:4; 2 Sam 22:35), mention of "the foundations of the earth" (1 Sam 2:8; 2 Sam 22:16), thunder from heaven (1 Sam 2:10; 2 Sam 22:14), and the language of rescue from death (1 Sam 2:6; 2 Sam 22:5–7).[65]

Hannah prophesies the coming of an anointed king: "The LORD will judge the ends of the earth; he will give strength to his king and exalt the horn of his anointed" (1 Sam 2:10b ESV; cf. v. 35); David acknowledges God's kindness to him as the anointed king: "Great salvation he brings to his king, and shows steadfast love to his anointed, to David and his offspring forever" (2 Sam 22:51 ESV). That the covenant of 2 Sam 7 remains in view is evident from David's reference to an "everlasting covenant" (23:5; cf. 1 Sam 25:28). What Hannah has prophetically uttered about an anointed king has begun to transpire in David, the king anointed by God and who speaks by the Spirit of an everlasting covenant (2 Sam 23:2). Between the bookends of an anointed king, the narrative delineates what that encompasses.

The Spirit-Anointed King

For both Saul and David a physical anointing with oil represents God's choice of king, involves a commissioning, and is closely associated with the empowering of the Spirit.[66] The sixteen occurrences of the verb

---

65. Childs also notices several of the similarities noted here. See his treatment of the matter. Childs, *Introduction to the Old Testament*, 272–78.

66. Hildebrandt, *Old Testament Theology*, 125.

"anoint" (מׁשח) and the fifteen occurrences of the noun "anointed" (מָׁשִיחַ) in 1 and 2 Samuel largely focus on the identity of the king as the one especially elected for the royal office. At the same time the author draws attention to Saul's charismatic reception of the Spirit by omitting the details of the fulfillment of signs predicted by Samuel and recounting only Saul's filling with the Spirit (1 Sam 10:1-13).[67] The author clearly connects the anointing and coming of the Spirit upon David: "Then Samuel took the horn of oil and anointed him in the midst of his brothers. And the Spirit of the LORD rushed upon David from that day forward" (1 Sam 16:13 ESV). As with Saul (10:10; 11:6-11), the Spirit not only confirms God's selection of David by the Spirit, but the Spirit empowers him to lead and enables him to prophesy, for the "oracle" inspired by the Spirit (2 Sam 23:1-2) at the end of David's career was not unique, as the first portrait painted of David after his filling pictures him driving away the evil spirit with music inspired by the Spirit.[68]

Despite the fact that on eight occasions David refers to the backslidden Saul as "Yahweh's anointed," it is clear that David is rising, Saul is falling, and Saul's anointing has become a temporary matter of formal position, not divine blessing.[69] Several pointers in the narrative indicate David's rise and God's choice of him as the one for an everlasting covenant. First, the juxtaposition of the Spirit's arrival upon David and his departure from Saul confirms that Samuel's predictions are coming true (1 Sam 15:23; 16:13-14). Second, "the Spirit of the Lord rushed upon David from that day upward [מֵהַיֹּום הַהוּא וָמָעְלָה]" (1 Sam 16:13), and the context suggests that this ingressive and continual experience directly contrasts with the departure of the Spirit from Saul (v. 14; cf. Ps 51:11).[70] Taking 1 Sam 16:13 with 2 Sam 23:2, "the whole of David's reign is bracketed

---

67. Firth, "Historical Books," 19; Bergen, *1, 2 Samuel*, 129.

68. Firth views the Spirit's coming on David as primarily demonstrating God's choice of David, and he sees prophecy emphasized at the end of 2 Samuel. Firth, "Historical Books," 14. Neve views David's final oracle as "poetic inspiration" rather than "prophetic inspiration." Neve, *Spirit of God in the Old Testament*, 27.

69. 1 Sam 24:6, 10; 26:9, 11, 16, 23; 2 Sam 1:14, 16.

70. The "rush upon" terminology similar to that in Judges makes it easy to see why Neve suggests that the continuous presence of the Spirit with David is in contrast to the period of the Judges, but the contrast with Saul better explains the author's comment about the permanence of the Spirit, for he pictures David as God's enduring choice to receive royal and covenantal promises. See Judges 14:6, 19; 15:14; 1 Sam 10:6, 10; 11:6. Neve, *Spirit of God in the Old Testament*, 22.

by references to the Spirit."[71] Third, after the description of the Spirit's coming to David and departing from Saul, one of Saul's servants cites this qualification for the music ministry from David's résumé: "Yahweh is with him" (1 Sam 16:18). Yahweh is present with David by the Spirit, and three more similar statements confirm the importance of the matter to the narrator (18:12, 14, 28).[72] Fourth, the author appears to create a bit of covenant distance between Saul and Yahweh by using a subtle change in language. Samuel prophesies that "the Spirit of Yahweh" will come upon Saul (10:6), and the narrator later reports that "the Spirit of Yahweh" left Saul (16:14), but the description of Saul's actual experience of the Spirit refers to the Spirit as "the Spirit of Elohim" (10:10; 11:6; 19:23). Saul receives the same Spirit, but the language substitution lacks the forcefulness and covenantal dimensions of "the Spirit of Yahweh" coming upon David, and the writer of 1 and 2 Samuel never applies the phrase "Spirit of Elohim" to David.[73]

Fifth, the author portrays David as one who is generally well suited to bear the prophetic Spirit, while Saul appears no more fit to bear the Spirit than David was to wear Saul's armor. Saul requires a change in heart to receive the Spirit (1 Sam 10:9), and observers comment on the apparent dissonance between Saul's station in life and his prophetic experience at both the outset of his kingship (10:9–13) and during the waning days of his reign (19:23–24). The incompatibility of Saul and the Spirit is highlighted in the latter passage, where the Spirit prevents him from killing David and renders Saul powerless and stripped of his royal robes. The kingship will instead go to the one who willingly and in humility disrobes in worship to God (2 Sam 6:20–23).

Thus, the inclusio beginning with Hannah's praise pictures a reversal in which God exalts a shepherd boy who, though persecuted by a powerful king, becomes heir to the promises of an eternal kingdom. He is anointed with oil as well as the accompanying Spirit, and the Spirit

---

71. Firth, "Historical Books," 20.

72. Bergen views the presence of Yahweh as the theme of this section of 1 Samuel. Bergen, *1, 2 Samuel*, 181.

73. Bergen remarks, "Five Israelites are mentioned as having 'the Spirit of the LORD' come over them, but in Genesis to 2 Kings the only other person said to have 'the Spirit of God' come over him is Balaam, a non-Israelite (cf. Num 24:2) who ultimately brought harm to Israel (Num 31:16)." Bergen, *1, 2 Samuel*, 136. One could argue that the distinction in the titles for God are only stylistic, but given the author's careful treatment of the Spirit in relation to both kings, the change in title seems more than incidental. See also Hildebrandt, *Old Testament Theology*, 172.

confirms that he is God's choice, empowers him to lead, imparts prophetic gifts of song, and continually abides with the king. With the addition of one other significant element of the inclusio, an important pattern emerges which more fully explains the import of Mary's allusions to Hannah's song of praise.

The Reversal in 1 and 2 Samuel: Resurrection from Sheol

The Hebrew term "Sheol" (שְׁאוֹל) occurs sixty-five times in the Old Testament but never in either volume of Samuel—except for one time at each end of the inclusio (1 Sam 2:6; 2 Sam 22:6). This observation further supports the argument for an intentional frame in the book, and it adds particularly significant theological commentary on the extent of God's reversals in raising up a shepherd to be his anointed king. Hannah exclaims, "Yahweh puts to death and makes alive; He brings down to Sheol and raises up" (1 Sam 2:6). And David praises God for deliverance from death: "The cords of Sheol entangled me; the snares of death confronted me" (2 Sam 22:6). The first passage so emphatically affirms God's sovereignty over death that it is difficult to imagine that resurrection could be excluded. The raising up from Sheol in the latter portion of the verse makes one even more cognizant of the possibility of resurrection than the similar statement of God's all-encompassing power in Deut 32:39. But what is particularly striking is how the raising up from Sheol follows hard on the heels of Hannah's poetic expression of her own reversal of fortunes: "She who was barren has borne seven children, but she who has had many sons pines away" (1 Sam 2:5b NIV).[74] Thus, an amazing convergence of important biblical and Lukan themes takes place in the frame of Hannah's praise and David's praise. Another barren woman serves as the real-life illustration of God's power to overcome death and

---

74. Levenson notes this connection, viewing childlessness as the "functional equivalent" of death and childbirth as the "functional equivalent of resurrection." He cites the story of Ruth and Naomi in support of his thesis, and his emphasis on the future life as realized through one's offspring is formative in his thinking on this. However, he pushes the argument too far when he says, "Nonetheless, and despite a long tradition of viewing the sin of Adam and Eve (and the mortality thought to go with it) as the most memorable event in Genesis, the great enemy in that book is not death as we think of it at all (still less is it sin) but death in the twin forms of barrenness and the loss of children." Nonetheless, he is right to note the profound connection between the barren woman's reversal and the death to life reversal of resurrection. Levenson, *Resurrection and Restoration*, 115–16, 120.

the grave, to fulfill his purposes, and to advance his plan. The Creator creates a miracle in Hannah's womb and overcomes the power of death. Out of this comes an announcement of an anointed king who rises to power from humble circumstances and endures the threat of death on his way to exaltation. This king is anointed not only with oil but with God's Spirit, and through his seed will come an eternal kingdom. The rescue from death of God's anointed servant becomes an oft-repeated theme in the Psalms (e.g., Ps 2). For David, existence on the verge of death is essentially a participation in it (Ps 22:14–18). However, his cry for help (v. 24) and his deliverance portend the reversal experienced by the Messiah, who, despite the cross, will "be seated at the right hand of the power of God" (Luke 22:69). The psalmist can confidently say, "But God will ransom my soul from the hand of Sheol, for he will take me [יִקָּחֵנִי]" (Ps 49:14–15). David's Lord will sit at God's right hand until his enemies become his footstool (110:1). The rejected stone will become the capstone (118:22) on the day of salvation, and God will not abandon his servant to Sheol (16:10; Acts 2:31).

The Lukan Depiction of a Risen and Anointed One

This ancient pattern of God rescuing his anointed from death is a specific application of the reversal theme and the stream that Luke drinks from throughout his two volumes. Thus, from the barrenness and reversals in the birth narratives (Luke 1:5–17, 46–56, 67–75; 2:29–35) forward, Luke narrates the unique anointing of Jesus, the accompanying opposition to him, his triumph over death, and the similar pattern experienced in his disciples.[75] The Savior born is the Christ (Χριστός; "anointed one"; 2:11),[76] and the direct connection Luke makes between this term and the Spirit demonstrates that, to him, the word is heavily pneumatological and a highly significant title. Only with this understanding does one feel the full force of the three references to the Holy Spirit operating in Simeon (vv. 25–27), for it was the Spirit himself who revealed to Simeon that he would see the Lord's anointed one. The people's wondering about the possibility of John as Christ (3:15) prompted his identification of

---

75. See the full discussion of the relationship between the Spirit and suffering in Luke-Acts in Mittelstadt, *Spirit and Suffering in Luke-Acts*.

76. The following discussion often substitutes the translation "anointed one" for "Christ" in order to emphasize the pneumatological dimensions of the title.

the coming one as a baptizer in the Holy Spirit (v. 16). This leads to the record of Jesus's reception of the Spirit and the Father's recognition of him (3:21–22) based on Isa 42:1 (cf. Luke 23:35), which emphasizes both God's election of the servant and God's action in putting the Spirit upon him. Jesus himself identifies the Spirit's presence as the Lord's anointing: "The Spirit of the Lord is on me, because he has anointed (ἔχρισέν) me to proclaim good news to the poor" (Isa 61:1a; Luke 4:18a).

On resurrection Sunday, Jesus rebukes the two on the road to Emmaus for failing to understand from the Scriptures the divine necessity (ἔδει) of the anointed one's suffering and entrance into glory (Luke 24:25–27). The same idea is repeated to the disciples when Jesus cites the Scriptures as prophesying the suffering and resurrection of the anointed one (24:44–46). He follows this with the promise of "power from on high" (v. 49). Peter's entire Pentecostal sermon is based on the premise that the glossolalia indicates that Jesus is the anointed one who exercises the divine prerogative of pouring out the eschatological Spirit (Acts 2:33). The crowd at Pentecost, through the assistance of lawless men, put Jesus to death, but God raised him up (vv. 23–24). Peter credits David with the authorship of Ps 16:10 and says that David "spoke about the resurrection of the Christ" (Acts 2:29–31). And "God made this Jesus whom you crucified both Lord and Christ" (v. 36). Repentance based on Jesus's identity as Christ secures forgiveness of sins and a position of eligibility to receive the promised Spirit (vv. 38–39). In short, hunting for the term "Spirit" (πνεῦμα) while failing to note the pneumatological dimensions of Jesus as Christ (Χριστός) results in both a truncated pneumatology and Christology.[77]

The occurrence of the threefold designation of Jesus as Lord and Christ at key junctures in the narrative of Luke-Acts (birth of Jesus, Pentecost, Cornelius's household, conclusion) confirms the previous observations and demonstrates the centrality of Jesus as Lord and Christ ("anointed one").[78] The angel refers to Jesus as "a Savior who is Christ the

---

77. Χριστός occurs twelve times in Luke and twenty-five times in Acts. Often the sermons in Acts center on the identity of Jesus as the Christ (5:42; 9:22; 17:3; 18:5, 28). The title has become so familiar to Christians that the pneumatological, eschatological, and royal implications of the term are often overlooked. I agree with Menzies (against James Dunn) that Jesus's anointing with the Spirit was not primarily to "initiate him into the new age," and that one must also avoid an adoptionistic view of Jesus's Jordan experience. At the same time, making the prophetic ministry aspect of Jesus's anointing the central element does not do justice to the identification aspect of Jesus as the Christ, the anointed one. Menzies, *Empowered for Witness*, 132–56.

78. Only two other verses in Luke-Acts contain this combination of terms. Acts

Lord" (σωτὴρ ὅς ἐστιν χριστὸς κύριος; 2:11); at Pentecost Peter declares that "God made him both Lord and Christ, this Jesus" (κύριον αὐτὸν καὶ χριστὸν ἐποίησεν ὁ θεός, τοῦτον τὸν Ἰησοῦν; Acts 2:36); at Caesarea Peter proclaims peace "through Jesus Christ—he is Lord of all" (διὰ Ἰησοῦ Χριστοῦ, οὗτός ἐστιν πάντων κύριος; Acts 10:36); and Luke concludes Acts with Paul "teaching the things concerning the Lord Jesus Christ" (διδάσκων τὰ περὶ τοῦ κυρίου Ἰησοῦ Χριστοῦ; Acts 28:31). All four passages refer to Jesus as both Lord and Christ, and only Luke 2:11 has "Savior" instead of "Jesus," though the two terms have essentially identical meanings. What Childs says of 1 Sam 2 is true of Luke 2:11: "The focus on God's chosen king, his anointed one, David, appears right at the outset, and reveals the stance from which the whole narrative is being viewed."[79] The first and last passages frame Luke's entire enterprise in Christology, just as the anointed king frames 1 and 2 Samuel. The cotexts of each passage emphasize the universal implications of Christ as Lord. The gospel is "joy for all people" (Luke 2:10); the Pentecostal tongues are the languages of the nations (Acts 2:4–12); Peter's sermon at Cornelius's household begins with God's acceptance of "men from every nation" (10:35); and Paul preaches the "kingdom of God" (28:31) to the Gentiles (v. 29). The emphasis on the expanding kingdom of the anointed Lord is entirely consistent with promises made to David.

Luke reveals his indebtedness to the Old Testament when he uses its patterns to articulate the story of Jesus, but his indebtedness to the pattern of 1 and 2 Samuel is particularly impressive. Both stories begin with barrenness, which in Hebrew thought is closely identified with death. A prophetic word from God announces life and, in the case of Jesus, the birth miracle surpasses even that of John and Samuel in accordance with his superior identity. Mary and Hannah announce reversals, and both stories speak of an anointed king, whom the authors use as a lens for their narratives. Both narratives feature a uniquely Spirit-anointed king who experiences suffering, rejection, and death (or death in principle). Despite opposition to these kings, the authors reaffirm throughout their narratives the special standing of these kings and the divine favor on

---

11:17 alludes to the Cornelius episode via Pentecost, and Acts 15:26 refers to Paul's and Silas's risks on behalf of the "Lord Jesus Christ." These will be discussed in chapter 6. There is a textual variant in Acts 20:21 that includes "Christ" after "our Lord Jesus." However, scribal expansion most likely accounts for the variant. See Metzger, *Textual Commentary*, 479.

79. Childs, *Introduction to the Old Testament*, 273.

them. From humble beginnings, debasement, and death, both kings experience a reversal and both narratives emphasize a falling and rising.[80] Both kings experience exaltation, but Christ, as the superior King, also experiences a physical resurrection and takes a seat at God's right hand. Nonetheless, the comparison with David still works because the ancient concept of death to life was inherent in 1 Samuel from the beginning. A reaffirmation of the exalted status of both kings concludes each book.

Death, resurrection, exaltation, and enthronement are all conceptually present in 1 and 2 Samuel. Of course the comparison has obvious redemptive-historical limitations, as Christ is the superior fulfillment. It is his superior status as even David's Lord that explains his exercising of the divine prerogative to pour out the Spirit on others at Pentecost. Because of the limitations of any individual pattern to describe all that Christ accomplishes, Luke also draws from Num 11 to explain how the Spirit is transferred from a uniquely anointed leader to others who will carry on the anointed ministry. However, the primary emphasis is on the identification of the Christ (anointed one), who is King. The secondary emphasis is on the charismatic aspects of that anointing which point to that identity.

Summary

The above discussion has pointed out the essentially eschatological orientation of the translations of Enoch and Elijah. Genesis provides a ray of hope for restoration in the midst of the effects of the fall, and Enoch's lifestyle and translation illustrate the way to life and the reality of future life. Together the stories of Enoch and Elijah provide a conceptual basis for Luke's theology of resurrection, and he directly draws on terminology from Elijah's translation to present Christ as the resurrected and exalted Lord.

Both Paul and the author of Hebrews find grounds for the hope of resurrection in the Abrahamic narratives. Luke's mirroring of elements from the story of Abraham and Sarah in his own birth narratives points to his familiarity with the concept of barrenness as death and birth as life. This ancient idea of miraculous birth and resurrection by the power of God is reflected in 2 Maccabees. Luke is familiar with

---

80. Arlandson does an in-depth survey of the falling and rising theme in Luke-Acts. See Arlandson, *Women, Class, and Society*.

these concepts, and he presents John the Baptist's miraculous birth and Spirit-filled ministry as grounded in this ancient pattern exhibited in the various biblical accounts such as that of Samson's birth. An examination of Luke's birth narratives reveals that the concept of resurrection is integral to his birth narratives.

The announcement of Jesus's identity as "Christ the Lord" (Luke 2:11) in the birth narratives draws attention to Luke's central interest in writing. The threefold title of Jesus occurs in the most important places in the narrative of Luke-Acts. The title unites the concepts of anointing by the Spirit and resurrection/exaltation as anticipated in the songs of Hannah and Mary and in the broader narrative of 1–2 Samuel. The reversal of humiliation to royal exaltation in the life of David prefigures the humiliation of Christ and his resurrection/ascension/exaltation. The Lukan birth narratives prepare the way for Luke's presentation of Jesus as the risen and anointed one, Lord and Christ.

5

Beyond Grave Expectations
Moses, the Prophets, and Luke

LUKE'S EMPHASIS ON THE resurrection of Jesus carries with it a number of presuppositions about the nature of the afterlife and individual destinies. This chapter explores the perspective of the Pentateuch and related texts on individual eschatology and demonstrates the formative influence of this perspective on Luke and his record of Christ's resurrection. In addition, there is an examination of how the prophets Hosea, Isaiah, Ezekiel, and Daniel shape Luke's thinking about eschatology and provide a conceptual and even linguistic foundation for his doctrine of Messiah's resurrection.

Individual Eschatology from Moses to Luke

"Gathered to His People"

Genesis 25:8 records that "Abraham breathed his last and died in a good old age, an old man and full of years, and was gathered to his people." The latter phrase occurs (sometimes with minor variations) ten times in the Pentateuch.[1] The question is whether the expression points to existence beyond the grave or is simply a euphemism for death or burial.[2]

---

1. Gen 25:8, 17; 35:29; 49:29, 33; Num 20:24, 26; 27:13; 31:2; Deut 32:50. The phrase occurs nowhere else in the Old Testament, but similar phrases do occur in Gen 15:15; 47:30; Judg 2:10; 2 Kgs 22:20; and 2 Chr 34:28.

2. For a brief overview of various interpretations of the phrase, see Cornelius et al., "אסף‎," 470.

Some scholars point to the parallel passages 2 Kgs 22:20 and 2 Chr 34:28 as favoring an identification of "your fathers" with "your grave": "I will gather you [אֹסִפְךָ] to your fathers, and you shall be gathered [וְנֶאֱסַפְתָּ] to your grave in peace" (ESV).[3] Certainly the close association of the gathering terminology with death can make it difficult to discern any possible distinction in destinations, but this passage does not decisively answer the question. It does, however, reflect some of the same associations as are found in the Pentateuch, such as solidarity with one's people and dying in a blessed or peaceful state (Gen 15:15), and the record of Abraham's death does hint at an existence beyond the grave.

That "gathered to his people" is not satisfied by reference to the grave alone is indicated by the fact that Abraham (25:8), Ishmael (v. 17), Aaron (Num 20:24; Deut 32:50), and Moses (Num 27:13; Deut 32:50) "were not buried in an ancestral grave."[4] Wenham notices the distinction between Abraham being gathered to his people and his burial by Isaac and Ishmael (Gen 25:8–9) and concludes that the gathering likely refers "to the soul of Abraham being reunited with his dead relatives in the afterlife."[5] Still, one could argue that the phrase is merely a euphemism for death, but Hamilton points out that verse 8 contains four stages in Abraham's departure. He breathed his last, died, was gathered to his people, and was buried. There appears to be a sequence of events in which death is distinguished from the gathering and the burial.[6] Levenson also sees a continued "existence" beyond death but explains it differently: "Abraham, Isaac, and Jacob continue to exist after they have died, not, it should be underscored, as disembodied spirits but as the people whose fathers they will always be … In biblical thinking, it is possible to continue even after death, and without either resurrection or immortality in the sense of survival as a bodiless soul."[7] For Levenson, "The prolongation of those who die fulfilled comes, rather, not in the form of residence in a place, the

---

3. Cornelius et al., "אסף," 470.

4. Hamilton, *Book of Genesis*, 2:168. "People" is a plural noun, so Abraham's burial with Sarah (Gen 25:10) does not fulfill the gathering expectation. Kidner also notes the time lapse between Jacob's resting with his fathers and his burial in the family tomb (Gen 49:29–33). Kidner, *Genesis*, 150, 212.

5. Wenham, *Genesis* 2:160.

6. Hamilton, *Genesis*, 2:168.

7. Levenson, *Resurrection and Restoration*, 30.

joyful antipode to the miserable Sheol, but in the form of descendants . . . It also comes in the form of the survival of the decedent's 'name' (*šēm*)."[8]

While Levenson correctly observes that the grave is not the end, and the Hebrews certainly placed a premium on descendants, it is difficult to see how his view adequately explains the patriarchs' gathering with their ancestors as well as their descendants. In other words, it is easier to account for continued existence through one's offspring than it is to explain how the deceased's existence relates in any significant way to those who have already died. Nor can he appeal to a biblical-theological connection between the saints of old, for his theologies approach does not allow for it.[9] However, Jacob's death provides a biblical portrait of a robust solidarity among God's people that extends to both the past and future, for he is "gathered" to his people (Gen 49:29, 33) after predicting the future of his children and the coming of a messianic figure, a ruler from Judah (vv. 10–11).

Sheol and the Future of the Righteous

It is true that the Pentateuch does not provide a detailed description of the afterlife, but the reality of it is suggested not only by the "gathering" terminology but by the descriptions of those who are not gathered. "Gathered to his people" is generally reserved for those who die in a proper relationship with God, and often in favorable circumstances. This is certainly the case for Abraham, Isaac, and Jacob. The narrator quickly sidelines the story of Ishmael, so the reader learns little of his death other than his lifespan of 137 years (Gen 25:17). Aaron and Moses do not see the promised land, yet they die as heroes of the faith. God allows Moses to see the land (Deut 34:4) and gives him a private burial (34:6). The narrator describes Moses at death: "Moses was 120 years old when he died. His eye was undimmed, and his vigor unabated" (34:7 ESV). In contrast to this, Jacob speaks of going down to Sheol in sorrow over the loss of Joseph (Gen 37:35) and potential loss of Benjamin (42:38; cf. 44:29, 31), but the term "Sheol" disappears from the narrative again once Jacob's family is safe. Thus, Jacob is "gathered to his people" (49:33). When Jacob does "go down," it is to Egypt to see Joseph and not to Sheol (37:35;

---

8. Levenson, *Resurrection and Restoration*, 78.

9. For example, one sees this approach in his reference to "two competing theologies" regarding Sheol. Levenson, *Resurrection and Restoration*, 75.

46:3–4; cf. 42:38).[10] The narrative highlights the contrasting picture when it describes the reviving of Jacob's spirit (45:27) and his determination to see Joseph (in Israel's words) "before I die" (v. 28). Hamilton sees a "parallel to the response of the disciples when they were told that Jesus was alive—shock, unbelief, which eventually turns to uncontrollable joy."[11] The Lukan narrative records such a pattern of unbelief, physical evidence of life, and ensuing joy (Luke 24:11–12, 37, 41). Jacob became "numb in heart" and did not believe the report, and the disciples disbelieved the women whose report seemed like "nonsense" (Gen 45:26; Luke 24:11).

Apart from Jacob's story, Sheol only occurs in the Pentateuch in reference to the earth swallowing Korah's household (Num 16:30, 33) and in reference to God's anger against idolatry burning to the depths of Sheol (Deut 32:22). The connotation of Sheol in the Pentateuch is decidedly negative, and Sheol does not seem to be an appropriate term to use in association with people who live and die under divine favor.

Douglas Stuart rightly notes that the meaning of Sheol in the Old Testament is "multifaceted but not contradictory."[12] The difficulty in defining its precise meaning is exacerbated by the fact that many of its occurrences are in poetic passages. Sheol is often associated with grief and lamentation (Job 7:9; 14:13; 17:13, 16; Ps 6:5) or judgment on the wicked (Num 16:30, 33; Job 24:9; Ps 9:17; 49:14; Prov 7:27; Isa 14:9; Ezek 31:16). It is a figure for the deepest place (Deut 32:22; Job 11:8; Isa 7:11; Amos 9:2) but it is a place over which God is sovereign (1 Sam 2:6; Job 26:6; Ps 139:8; Prov 15:11). At times it is simply the grave or the destination of all humanity (2 Sam 22:6; Job 21:13; Ps 16:10; 18:5; Prov 27:20; 30:16; Hab 2:5). Whether the term depicts a near-death experience, describes the grave, or intimates an afterlife, the term never rests comfortably with the righteous. Sheol is something from which the righteous are rescued. "The cords of Sheol entangled me; the snares of death confronted me. In my distress I called upon the LORD; to my God I called. From his temple he heard my voice, and my cry came to his ears" (2 Sam 22:6–7 ESV; cf. Jonah 2:2; Ps 116:3–4). "O LORD, you have brought up my soul from Sheol; you restored me to life from among those who go down to the pit" (Ps 30:3 ESV). "But God will ransom my soul from the power of Sheol, for he will receive me" (49:15 ESV). "For great is your steadfast love toward

---

10. Hamilton, *Book of Genesis*, 2:428.
11. Hamilton, *Book of Genesis*, 2:587.
12. Stuart, "Sheol," 472.

me; you have delivered my soul from the depths of Sheol" (86:18 ESV). "'I shall ransom them from the power of Sheol; I shall redeem them from Death. O Death, where are your plagues? O Sheol, where is your sting?'" (Hos 13:14 ESV).

"Sheol, Where Is Your Sting?"

Gordon Fee highlights a few alterations the apostle Paul makes in Hos 13:14 in order to make it a "powerful taunt of death" (1 Cor 15:55).[13] Douglas Stuart views Hosea's first two clauses as interrogatives, suggesting that the entire verse is one of judgment without hope of rescue.[14] Based on the judgment context, Stuart's position is understandable, but Thomas McComiskey correctly notes that "there is no grammatical indication that we have a question here."[15] In the midst of warnings of national judgment, Hosea inserts a reversal and holds out the hope for an eventual national restoration. It is a reversal similar to those in Hos 1:10–11; 2:14–23; and 14:4–7 (cf. Amos 9:11–15). Paul can allude to this passage in reference to physical resurrection because the resurrection described in Hos 13 is of the same eschatological stock as the passages previously discussed.

Two considerations particularly bear this out. First, Hos 13 shows dependence on Deut 32, where God acts independently to put to death and make alive (v. 39). Both passages warn of judgment due to idolatry and address Israel as an "unwise" (לֹא חָכָם) offspring (Hos 13:13; cf. 14:9; Deut 32:6; cf. vv. 28–29).[16] They abandoned their "Father," who created and formed them (Deut 32:6); they "deserted the Rock that fathered" them "and forgot the God" who gave them birth (v. 18). According to Hos 13:13, Ephraim does not even have the sense to be born at the proper time: "The pangs of childbirth come for him, but he is an unwise son, for at the right time he does not present himself at the opening of the

---

13. Fee, *First Epistle to the Corinthians*, 804.

14. Stuart, *Hosea–Jonah*, 207. Martin-Achard also views this as strictly a judgment text. "The prophet has to announce not an extraordinary deliverance, but an unprecedented calamity." He also rejects an eschatological interpretation of Hos 6:2. Martin-Achard, *From Death to Life*, 86, 91.

15. McComiskey, "Hosea," 223. So also, Hubbard, *Hosea*, 221. The Septuagint translates the phrases as future promises: ἐκ χειρὸς ᾅδου ῥύσομαι αὐτοὺς καὶ ἐκ θανάτου λυτρώσομαι αὐτούς (Hos 13:14a).

16. McComiskey, "Hosea," 223.

womb" (ESV). Both chapters use a word rarely found in the Hebrew text to describe a plague or destruction (קֶטֶב; Deut 32:24; Ps 91:6; Isa 28:2; Hos 13:14). Both chapters also feature a reversal in which God himself must act, rescuing his people and overcoming the power of death (Deut 32:36–43; Hos 13:14). Given the absolute affirmation of the defeat of death, the necessity of divine action to accomplish this defeat, the context of eschatological promises made to Israel, and the continuity of thought among biblical authors in describing God's sovereignty over death, it is not difficult to see how Paul saw in this passage the final resurrection of God's people through Jesus Christ.

Second, it is fascinating to note that Hos 13:13–14 exhibits yet one more strong association between the womb and death. The analogy has changed a bit in order to emphasize the stupidity of the child Israel, for this child will die in the womb due to its own lack of sense. The womb will serve as this child's grave. But Sheol will not have the final say, for God promises, "I will ransom" and "I will redeem." Once again the divine initiative solves the problem of death in the womb.

Sheol and the Righteous One (Psalm 16)

In Hos 13:14 Sheol is parallel to death, and in Ps 16:10 the parallel between Sheol and corruption suggests that the grave is in view: "For you will not abandon my soul to Sheol, or let your holy one see corruption" (ESV). The latter passage is of particular importance to Luke, as he quotes it three times (Acts 2:27, 31; 13:35). Peter quotes Ps 15:8–11 (LXX) verbatim in his Pentecostal sermon (Acts 2:25–28), except that he omits the final phrase, "in your right hand are pleasures forever." Luke cites the psalm not as a proof of the resurrection but as evidence that Jesus is the risen and anointed one about whom David prophesied.[17] Scholars have debated whether the original psalm supports Luke's understanding or an interpretation involving resurrection only results from alterations made by the Septuagint.[18] Hans-Joachim Kraus expresses the opinion of those who hold that "Psalm 16 does not deal with resurrection, or even immortality, but with the rescue from an acute mortal danger."[19] Kraus bases

---

17. Dupont is correct that the primary point is not to prove the resurrection, but that Jesus is the resurrected one. Dupont, *Salvation of the Gentiles*, 109.

18. Marshall, "Acts," 536–39.

19. Kraus, *Psalms 1–59*, 240.

this opinion on the notion that 16:1 focuses on protection from "the danger of death" and that "the assertions about the rescue from death in verses 9–10 do not materially differ from the corresponding descriptions in other psalms."[20]

Psalm 16:1 immediately strikes the note of security, but the security is of a rather general nature and the psalmist does not depict any particular threat.[21] Neither does the context provide any clear indicator of premature death.[22] Even if some unarticulated circumstance provided the impetus for the psalmist's rejoicing in temporal security, though, that would only serve as the starting point for a natural progression that leads to the psalmist's declaration of security even after death. The psalm begins with a general statement of security in God (16:1), describes that security metaphorically in terms of a cup and an inheritance in the land (vv. 5–6), and arrives at the ultimate expression of that security as a postmortem rescue from the grave itself (vv. 9–11).

Kraus's comparison with other psalms does not damage this argument but supports it, for the psalmists often attribute their rescue to the faithful character of God, which is not limited by circumstances or time. Thus, Jesus can quote Ps 22:1a on the cross ("My God, my God, why have you forsaken me?"; Matt 27:46) in identification with the righteous sufferer but with the full knowledge that God would rescue him: "For he has not despised or abhorred the affliction of the afflicted, and he has not hidden his face from him, but has heard, when he cried to him" (Ps 22:24 ESV; cf. Matt 20:18–19). Likewise, the psalmist places his confidence in the "steadfast love" (Ps 17:7) of God to rescue him from wicked men "whose portion is in this life" (v. 14a). In contrast to them, the psalmist asserts, "As for me, I shall behold your face in righteousness; when I awake, I shall be satisfied with your likeness" (v. 15 ESV). The psalmist will "awake" from more than mere sleep to see God in this way (cf. Isa 26:19; Dan 12:2).[23]

In Ps 49 those who trust in their riches and foolishly put confidence in themselves (vv. 12–13) are destined "for Sheol," and the psalmist continues, "Death shall be their shepherd, and the upright shall rule over them in the morning. Their form shall be consumed in Sheol, with no

---

20. Kraus, *Psalms 1–59*, 240.
21. deClaissé-Walford et al., *Book of Psalms*, 178.
22. Grogan, *Psalms*, 63.
23. Kidner, *Psalms 1–72*, 90.

place to dwell. But God will ransom my soul from the power of Sheol, for he will receive me [יִקָּחֵנִי]" (vv. 14–15 ESV). The word לקח ("to take") may reflect the taking of Enoch (Gen 5:24) and Elijah (2 Kgs 2:3, 5, 9, 10), and it forms a play on words with the inability of the rich man to "take" anything with him at death (Ps 49:17).[24] The psalmist trusts in the just character of God to ultimately resolve the problem of the prosperity of the wicked and to make a distinction between the righteous and wicked after death. Likewise, Ps 73 is also a theodicy in which the psalmist comes to understand the distinction between the end (אַחֲרִית) of the wealthy wicked (v. 17) and that of the righteous. The continual relationship with God results in the psalmist's confidence: "You guide me with your counsel, and afterward [אַחַר] you will receive me [תִּקָּחֵנִי] to glory" (v. 24 ESV; cf. Rom 8:29). God is the psalmist's "portion forever" (Ps 73:26). As with Ps 49, this psalm uses a play on words to contrast the two destinies and uses לקח ("to take") in a manner similar to that used of Enoch and Elijah. Although the examples of theodicy and of a vindicated afflicted one do not compare exactly with the context of Ps 16, still the foundational elements behind a doctrine of rescue from the grave are consistent. Death is no barrier to a relationship with God, for he has both the power to rescue out of the grave and the faithful character to continue the relationship beyond death.

Some of the specific language in Ps 16 also gives one pause before concluding that the final verses "should not be interpreted either messianically or in terms of individual eschatology," and that there has been a "new meaning imparted to the text" by the New Testament.[25] The psalmist rejoices over "the saints" (לִקְדוֹשִׁים; v. 3) but then uses a cognate of חֶסֶד ("faithfulness") to describe the "holy one" (חָסִיד) who will not see corruption (v. 10). The "body" or "flesh" (בָּשָׂר; σάρξ, LXX; v. 9; cf. Acts 2:26) of a specific holy one who lives "in accordance with the principles"[26] of חֶסֶד ("faithfulness") will not be abandoned to Sheol (ᾅδην, LXX). Darrell Bock notes how Peter emphasizes the physicality of Jesus's resurrection when he explains that David's body remains in the tomb. Peter quotes the Septuagint exactly the first time (οὐδὲ δώσεις τὸν ὅσιόν σου ἰδεῖν διαφθοράν; "nor will you allow your holy one to see corruption"; Acts 2:27b; Ps 15:10) but alters it to emphasize a fleshly, physical resurrection the second time

---

24. Crenshaw, "Love Is Stronger than Death," 60; See also Gowan, *Bridge between the Testaments*, 376.

25. Craigie and Tate, *Psalms 1–50*, 158.

26. Baer and Gordon, "חסד," 213.

(οὔτε ἡ σάρξ αὐτοῦ εἶδεν διαφθοράν; "nor did his flesh see corruption"; Acts 2:31c).[27] Thus, it is the "flesh" of the "holy one" that will not decay.

There are other reasons to think that both Peter (Acts 2) and Paul (Acts 13) have properly understood Ps 16. Scholars commonly conclude that the Septuagint translators, followed by Luke, have mistakenly translated the Hebrew noun שַׁחַת ("pit") as διαφθοράν ("corruption"; 15:10 LXX). The supposed error resulted from confusion with the similar Hebrew verb שָׁחַת, which means "to ruin" or "to corrupt." Bock, though, suggests that the Septuagint uses a wordplay so that "the rendering διαφθοράν would emphasize concretely the results of being abandoned in Sheol, that is bodily corruption."[28] Bock is right that abandonment to the pit implies the corruption of the body, thus the principle idea of the psalm is preserved.

The strong emphasis on Davidic fulfillment in Acts 2 fits very well with Ps 16, as it is entitled "A *miktam* of David." Bock observes that the inheritance language of verses 5–6 may suggest that the Davidic covenant provides some of the backdrop for the psalm and lends itself to a messianic interpretation.[29] The Septuagint also speaks of a restoration of the psalmist's inheritance (ἀποκαθιστῶν τὴν κληρονομίαν μου ἐμοί; Ps 15:5b), which seems to imply an eschatological aspect to it. The verb ἀποκαθιστάνω ("to restore") occurs only eight times in the New Testament, including one time in Luke (6:10) and one time in Acts (1:6). The cognate noun ἀποκατάστασις ("restoration") occurs only once in the entire Greek Bible—when Peter announces the coming restoration at Christ's return (Acts 3:21). The disciples employ the verb when they inquire about the timing of the kingdom's restoration (1:6). The restoration terminology is quite appropriate in the Lukan context, where the risen Christ has inaugurated a kingdom, reigns on David's throne, and awaits the full consummation of that kingdom.

As mentioned earlier, Peter's heavy emphasis on the resurrection does not serve primarily as an apology establishing the factuality of the event; rather the preaching of Jesus's resurrection demonstrates his identity as the long-expected Davidite whom God has made "both Lord [κύριον] and Christ [χριστὸν]" (Acts 2:36). In the Pentecostal context, then, the resurrection fulfills Old Testament expectations of a coming holy one and

---

27. Bock, *Proclamation*, 178.
28. Bock, *Proclamation*, 175; So also, Kidner, *Psalms 1–72*, 86n1.
29. Bock, *Proclamation*, 178.

is a key eschatological event among the complex of events associated with Jesus's exaltation. Through resurrection Jesus is recognized as Lord, and the outpouring of the Spirit is the consequence of his lordship. Thus, the resurrection and the outpouring of the Spirit are alike in that they are both eschatological events anticipated by the Old Testament and confirming Christ's identity as Lord: the one is a stage in his enthronement and the other the exercise of a divine prerogative of the recently enthroned King. Thus, resurrection and Spirit travel together in Acts, for the preaching of the resurrection is the preaching of Christ's lordship, and the Spirit advances the breadth of Christ's reign over the nations.

Cut Off from One's People

The Pentateuch prefers to describe those who die under divine favor as gathered to their people and avoids depicting them in Sheol. Later biblical texts more clearly identify Sheol as the grave, yet Sheol is not the ultimate destination of the righteous. Just as the righteous continue to experience solidarity with their people in death, so the phrase "cut off from his people" describes the opposite set of circumstances, somewhat like Sheol does, but in even stronger terms.[30] The phrase "he shall be cut off from his people" (וְנִכְרְתָה מֵעַמָּיו) occurs as a warning of the consequences for violations of the covenant, especially concerning proper observance of worship guidelines and rituals. Thus, the cutting off will occur to the one who: fails to observe circumcision (Gen 17:4), eats yeast during the Passover (Exod 12:15, 19), misuses the sacred anointing oil (30:33, 38), desecrates the Sabbath (31:14), approaches the sacred offerings in an unclean state (Lev 7:20, 21; 22:3; cf. 7:25, 19:8), eats blood (7:27; 17:10, 14), sacrifices outside the tent of meeting (17:4, 9), works on the Day of Atonement (23:29), ignores the Passover celebration (Num 9:13), or fails to purify himself after touching a dead body (19:13, 20). The same judgment applies to those who: commit any of the sexual sins itemized in Lev 18 (see v. 19; cf. 20:17–18), sacrifice their children to Molech (Lev 20:3, 5), turn to mediums and spiritists (v. 6), or blaspheme God (Num 15:30–31).

Scholars have debated whether the "cutting off" refers to banishment, capital punishment, loss of descendants, premature death at the

---

30. Pentateuchal passages using the verb כרת ("to cut") that are pertinent to this study include: Gen 9:11; 17:14; Exod 4:25; 8:9; 12:15, 19; 30:33, 38; 31:14; Lev 7:20–21, 25, 27; 17:4, 9–10, 14; 18:29; 19:8; 20:3, 5–6, 17–18; 22:3; 23:29; Num 4:18; 9:13; 15:30, 31; 19:13, 20; Deut 12:29; 19:1; 23:1.

hand of God, or eternal separation from God and the community.[31] Genesis 17:14 emphasizes that failure to observe circumcision is a breaking of the covenant and results in exclusion from the covenant people. Likewise, improper observance of the Passover results in being cut off from "Israel" (Exod 12:15) and "the congregation of Israel" (12:19). Inherent in the "cutting off" terminology is exclusion from membership in the covenant community. Sometimes the Law mandates judicial execution (Exod 31:14; Lev 20:3; Num 15:30–36) and at times God sets his face against the guilty and performs the cutting off without human agency (Lev 17:10; 20:5, 6; 23:9). All of the various elements listed above play a role in defining what it means for someone to be "cut off from his people."[32] But of particular concern in the various passages is the notion of removal from God's "presence" or "face" (Lev 22:3), the continually remaining guilt of sin (Lev 17:4; Num 9:13; 15:31), and the broken solidarity with God's covenant people, which amounts to exclusion from the covenant. Behind all of the regulations is the overarching concern that God's people properly worship him and host his presence in their midst: "'You must keep the Israelites separate from things that make them unclean, so they will not die in their uncleanness for defiling my dwelling place, which is among them'" (Lev 15:31 NIV). It is this separation from God—reminiscent of the fall—that suggests more than a temporal consequence in at least some of the passages cited above. The stark contrast between being gathered to one's people and being cut off from them suggests a distinction that goes beyond death. Wenham notes that "offenders will be cut off from their people forever."[33] For the one cut off, judgment spills over into the afterlife.

The Septuagint commonly employs the term ἐξολεθρεύω ("to destroy utterly," "to be completely cut off") for כרת ("to cut off"), but the term only occurs in Acts 3:23 in the New Testament: "Moses said, 'The Lord your God will raise up [ἀναστήσει] for you a prophet like me from your brothers; you will listen to everything he says to you. And it will be that every person who does not listen to that prophet will be cut off from the people [ἐξολεθρευθήσεται ἐκ τοῦ λαοῦ]'" (vv. 22–23). This is a rather loose quotation of Deut 18:15–19, with the bulk of the terminology originating from

---

31. For a summary of various views, see Wenham, *Book of Leviticus*, 241–42; Hamilton, *Exodus*, 188.

32. Ashley also takes a broad approach to defining the phrase. Ashley, *Book of Numbers*, 180–81.

33. Wenham, *Book of Leviticus*, 242.

verse 15 and a few phrases coming from verses 16 and 19. The "cutting off from the people" expression does not occur in the Deuteronomy passage and could potentially come from any number of Old Testament references, but the phrase "every person who" (πᾶσα ψυχὴ ἥτις) narrows the quotation to Lev 23:29. The unusual combination of texts has prompted some scholars to speculate that a *testimonia* source lies behind the quotation, although the evidence is neither compelling nor particularly helpful in explaining Luke's intentions.[34] Of the numerous passages in the Old Testament that Peter could have selected (there are about thirty "cut off from" passages in the Pentateuch alone), it seems too coincidental that he chose the one that focuses on failure to properly observe the Day of Atonement (Lev 23:26–32). This fits well with the numerous themes woven together in Acts 3 that emphasize the centrality of Christ and his work in defining what constitutes membership in God's family.[35]

Other elements in the context demonstrate how the qualification to be cut off revolves around one's response to Christ. The lame man rises "in the name of Jesus Christ" (Acts 3:6; cf. v. 16; 4:7, 10), and this illustrates what "times of refreshing" look like under "Christ Jesus" (3:20) and anticipates the "times of restoration" (v. 21) at the Parousia. Peter rehearses elements of Jesus's trial and presents him as an innocent sufferer (vv. 13–14, 18) "whom God raised from the dead" (v. 14). God is "the God of Abraham and the God of Isaac and the God of Jacob, the God of our fathers" (v. 13). That is, the same living God that Jesus already referred to as the guarantor of resurrection (Exod 3:6; Luke 20:37) has now "glorified" (Acts 3:13) Jesus—only the added phrase "the God of our fathers" (cf. Acts 3:15) invites the Jewish audience to accept the fulfillment of its own Scriptures. Not only will God "raise up" (ἀναστήσει) a prophet like Moses on the stage of history, but the wordplay on resurrection informs the audience that God has already raised up Jesus from the dead as the one who fulfills the Mosaic expectation (Acts 3:22; cf. v. 26). The annoyance of the Jewish officials over the disciples' proclaiming "in

---

34. For an overview of the subject, see Marshall, "Acts," 547–48; Barrett entertains the possibility of a *testimonia* source. Barrett, *Acts of the Apostles*, 1:209–10.

35. Bock also notices the atonement context in Leviticus but is cautious in deriving any Lukan significance from it. Bock, *Proclamation*, 193. However, Luke emphasizes the atoning work of Christ in various ways. For example, he emphasizes the necessity of his suffering (Luke 9:22; 24:44–49); the innocence of the suffering Christ (23:4, 14–15, 20, 22, 41, 47); Christ as Passover Lamb (22:7–22); and Christ as Servant from Isaiah (Isa 53:7–8, 12; Luke 22:37; 23:34; Acts 8:32–33). For a good discussion on the atonement in Luke-Acts, see Moessner, "Reading Luke's Gospel," 125–54.

Jesus the resurrection of the dead" (4:2) suggests that they understood the apostolic message as not only claiming Jesus's individual resurrection but also as affirming the Pharisaic teaching of an eschatological resurrection of the people of God with its accompanying period of restoration. Thus, the Jewish leaders correctly understood the disciples' teaching that all eschatological fulfillment and every eschatological blessing hinges upon recognition of the lordship of Christ Jesus. Peter employs exalted messianic language when he depicts Jesus as "the Christ" (Acts 3:18, 20), "his servant Jesus" (v. 13; cf. Isa 52:13), "the Holy and Righteous One" (Acts 3:14), and "the Originator of Life" (v. 15).

A few more terms that heighten the urgency of listening to God's prophet deserve mention. First, aside from the direct quotations of Old Testament fulfillment (Acts 3:25b; cf. Gen 22:18), one of Luke's favorite terms, δεῖ ("it is necessary"), appears in the middle of his discussion of Christ's time in heaven until the restoration (Acts 3:21). This term along with προκαταγγέλλω ("announce beforehand"; v. 18) and προχειρίζομαι ("choose in advance," "appoint"; v. 20) heavily emphasizes the divine plan,[36] history's divine metanarrative, implying in a not-so-subtle manner that rejection of Christ amounts to rejection of God's redemptive plan set in motion in ages past. Second, the use of λαός ("people"; 3:23) in describing the people from whom one will be cut off is not merely a serendipitous quotation of another favorite Lukan term.[37] The term occurs thirteen times in Acts 2–4 alone, and its inclusion at this point begs a response to the question: What constitutes membership in the people of God?[38] Peter's answer is that the "first" opportunity to enter the family of forgiven sins belongs to the Jewish people (3:26), but the membership requirement "for all the families on earth" (v. 25) is repentance from rejecting Christ (v. 19) and submission to his name (4:12). Thus, the λαός in this passage is a christocentric people and not limited to a specific race of people (3:25; cf. 15:14). Third, the "and it will be [ἔσται δὲ] that every person who does not listen" of 3:23 reflects this statement in 2:21: "And it will be [καὶ ἔσται] that everyone who calls on the name of the Lord will be saved."[39] The emphasis on the "name" and the "Lord" in Acts

---

36. Conzelmann notes how Luke uses various compounds beginning with πρό to emphasize God's plan. Conzelmann, *Theology of St. Luke*, 151.

37. The word λαός occurs forty-eight times in Acts and thirty-six times in Luke.

38. Tannehill and Barrett have also recognized the significance of the λαός in this context. Tannehill, *Narrative Unity*, 2:59–60; Barrett, *Acts of the Apostles*, 1:210.

39. Marshall and others have also noted the similarity. Marshall, "Acts," 548. The

2 fits well with Peter's speech in Acts 3 and makes it all the more likely that Luke intends the reader to see submission to Christ's lordship as the determining factor between the contrasting outcomes of salvation and being cut off.

Given the events of Pentecost and the Jewish understanding of the relationship between the outpouring of the Spirit and the eschaton, the reader would likely assume the refreshing of Acts 3 includes the eschatological blessing of the Spirit. Alienation from God and his people, then, also involves resistance to and forfeiture of the eschatological Spirit, whose presence is both the unique gift from the exalted Lord and a unique witness to his exaltation.

Luke has understood the serious and potentially eternal implications of what it means to be cut off from one's people. He has followed this idea to its logical conclusion in redemptive history by observing how everything hinges on one's acceptance of a prophet like Moses from Abraham's seed (Acts 3:25). Rejection of his atoning work, resurrection, and exaltation as Lord results in "cutting off," which in turn means exclusion from the eschatological blessings of forgiveness, membership in God's people, times of refreshing, the experience of the Spirit, and participation in the coming age of restoration. To be cut off from God's people has both immediate and ultimate eschatological implications. It is to forfeit God's presence both in this age and in the age to come by rejecting God's Spirit and his Son.

The God of Abraham, Isaac, and Jacob

The previous discussion included mention of Luke's quotation of Exod 3:6 during his encounter with the Sadducees. Luke says that Moses called "the Lord 'the God of Abraham and the God of Isaac and the God of Jacob'" (Luke 20:37b). All three Synoptics include the pericope with the quotation (Matt 22:23–33; Mark 12:18–27; Luke 20:27–40) and all of them make minor alterations to the Septuagint.[40] But Luke shows his es-

---

Greek phrase is not found in the Septuagint of Deut 18:19, but Luke's use of it in Acts 3:23 may originate from the Hebrew text's וְהָיָה ("and it will be").

40. Matthew and Mark preserve the predicate nominative of the Septuagint (ἐγώ εἰμι ὁ θεός; "I am the God") but add articles before "God of" each time. Luke uses the accusative case but does not add articles. The textual problem with articles in Mark is not surprising, given the difficulty with expressing the Hebrew and the lack of articles in the Septuagint.

chatological interests when he also cites Jesus as distinguishing between "this age" when people marry and "that age" when they do not (20:34–35). Luke also includes Jesus's explanatory comment, "for all are alive to him" (v. 38), whereas Matthew stops with "He is not the God of the dead but of the living" (Matt 22:32b) and Mark adds, "you are much deceived" (12:27b). Luke makes explicit the same thoughts that the Old Testament has often expressed: death is no barrier to God, and his relationship with his children continues beyond death.[41]

The next chapter adds more details to the above argument, but for now it is important to note how consistent Jesus's comments are with the overall view of the Pentateuch. His interpretation is neither idiosyncratic nor a new idea formulated during the intertestamental period; rather it accurately captures the essence of what the Pentateuch has assumed all along about God's relationship with his people. It also demonstrates that the doctrine of resurrection derives from the reality of God's solidarity with his people.

Abraham's Bosom and Hades (Luke 16:19–31)

The parable of the rich man and Lazarus reinforces the Old Testament notion that there is a division between the righteous and ungodly at death.[42] Leading up to this parable Luke records the reaction of the Pharisees to the parable of the shrewd manager: they sneer at Jesus because, in their hearts, they love and excessively value money (Luke 16:14–15). The following few verses speak of the fulfillment of Scripture and the eager response to the preaching of the kingdom (16:16–18). The parable of the rich man and Lazarus encompasses these emphases by contrasting the financial statuses of the two men and demonstrating the continuity between one's response to "Moses and the Prophets" (v. 31) and to a resurrected person.[43] Thus, the contextual emphasis on the heart condition,

---

41. France is correct when he notes that the argument is not linguistic, based on the "I am" (ἐγώ εἰμι) of the Septuagint, but "rather on the nature of God's relationship with his human followers." These comments are made regarding Matthew's account, but they apply even more readily to Luke's. France, *Gospel of Matthew*, 840.

42. Although some scholars refer to this pericope as an "example story" or similar, Snodgrass points to the introductory formula and other elements in Luke's narrative that convince him that it is a parable. Snodgrass, *Stories with Intent*, 419, 426. See also Stein, *Luke*, 422–23.

43. Bock also emphasizes this continuity in revelation. Bock, *Luke*, 2:1376–77.

especially with regard to wealth, the rich man's neglect of the beggar at his gate, and the disregard for God's Law make it unnecessary to claim that any moral motivation is lacking in the text or must be assumed from Greco-Roman parallels.[44]

The parable anticipates Jesus's resurrection and the unbelieving response to it, but it is unnecessary to assume that Luke added this element to Jesus's parable, unless one is willing to artificially break up the conversation between the rich man and Abraham (thereby disrupting the narrative unity of the parable)[45] and reject the notion that Jesus actually predicted his own death and resurrection (Luke 9:22; 18:33). The reader of Luke-Acts will soon see how the resurrection of Jesus becomes the watershed event that causes one's attitude toward revelation to emerge in bold relief and identifies the true children of Abraham.

The Jewish nature of the parable is evident in that it names Moses twice and Abraham six times and builds on the reversal of Luke 13:28–30, where people who expect to attend the eschatological banquet with Abraham are thrown out and others attend instead. So also Lazarus finds himself in "Abraham's bosom" (εἰς τὸν κόλπον Ἀβραάμ) and the rich man "in Hades" (ἐν τῷ ᾅδῃ; 16:22–23).[46] There is neither an exact parallel to this parable in ancient literature nor another known occurrence of "Abraham's bosom" from Judaism in the first century, but there are a number of stories with similar themes and concepts.[47] The closest parallel to "Abraham's bosom" in the Bible is found in Gen 16:5 (LXX), where Sarah complains to Abraham, "I have given my maid into your bosom [εἰς τὸν κόλπον σου]." This passage obviously involves marital relations, but the intimacy of the phrase is consistent with many other applications in the Old Testament as well as with the close relationship between Jesus and

---

44. Based on Greco-Roman parallels, Hock sees the rich man as hedonistic and morally degraded in a variety of ways. Hock, "Lazarus and Micyllus," 459–62; Snodgrass rejects Hock's thesis and finds the main problem with the rich man in his neglect of the poor. Snodgrass, *Stories with Intent*, 429–30.

45. Snodgrass, *Stories with Intent*, 428.

46. Bock refers to the plural expression ἐν τοῖς κόλποις αὐτοῦ (v. 23) as a "classical plural" and says it does not affect the meaning. Bock, *Luke*, 2:1369.

47. Stein, *Luke*, 424. Snodgrass lists numerous ancient references. Snodgrass, *Stories with Intent*, 419–23. A few important extrabiblical references to note include *1 En*. 103–4; *4 Ezra* 7:36, 75–99; *4 Macc* 13:17; Lucian's *Cataplus*; *Exod. Rab.* 31:5; *Pesiq. Rab.* 43.4. The Greek word κόλπος is a fitting word to use in the parable, as it was used in Greco-Roman epitaphs, but, conceptually and contextually, the notion is very Jewish in Luke 16. See Hock, "Lazarus and Micyllus," 456.

John (John 1:18; 13:23). Combining this thought with the reward element of Luke 13:28–29, the parable pictures Lazarus enjoying the reward of a safe and secure relationship with his father Abraham in the eternal kingdom. He has been "gathered to his fathers" (Gen 15:15; Deut 31:16; Judg 2:10).[48]

Scholars justifiably use caution in drawing too many conclusions about the afterlife from this parable. The juxtaposition of Lazarus and the rich man in Abraham's bosom and Hades is more of a folkloric literary device used to make the parable work than a statement about the geography of the afterlife.[49] Nevertheless, the principles operating in the parable remain valid. A divine judgment will occur; death will separate the righteous from the wicked; the dead continue to exist but are powerless to change their fate; and the nature of the hereafter is one of blessing with the saints of old for the righteous but torment for the wicked. While the language has changed from Hebrew (Sheol) to Greek (Hades) and the portrayal of the hereafter is more vivid in the New Testament, Luke continues to follow the concepts of the afterlife set forth in Genesis.

The Prophets and Resurrection— Preparing the Way for Luke's Eschatology

Several passages in the prophetic writings continue to build and expand on resurrection themes established earlier in the Old Testament. Key texts include Isa 26:19; 53:10–12; Ezek 37:1–14; Dan 12:1–3, 13; and Hos 6:2. While all of these texts contribute to the eschatological atmosphere of Luke's theology, he does not overtly incorporate all of them into his writing. One might assume that the preponderance of allusions to the Spirit along with the resurrection terminology in Ezekiel would make it a primary reference point for Luke, but this is not the case. Given the clarity of Daniel's resurrection passage, it is also surprising that Luke does not directly quote Dan 12. Luke's use of the Hosea and Isaiah texts is complex, but he does allude to them more directly. The following discussion concentrates on the themes that these passages develop and share with one another as a backdrop for Luke-Acts.

---

48. Bock, *Luke*, 2:1368; Leaney, *Gospel According to St. Luke*, 225–26.
49. So also Snodgrass, *Stories with Intent*, 430; Bock, *Luke*, 2:1363.

Hosea 6:1–3

In Hos 5 Yahweh warns Ephraim of approaching judgment, condemns Ephraim's turning to the king of Assyria for help (v. 13), uses the graphic imagery of a vicious lion to describe his posture toward Ephraim and Judah (v. 14), and awaits their repentance (v. 15). The prophet then extends this invitation to the people: "Come, let us return to the LORD; for he has torn us, that he may heal us; he has struck us down, and he will bind us up. After two days he will revive us; on the third day he will raise us up, that we may live before him. Let us know; let us press on to know the LORD; his going out is sure as the dawn; he will come to us as the showers, as the spring rains that water the earth" (6:1–3 ESV). However, Ephraim and Judah will not accept the invitation (v. 4), and restoration awaits a future day. Controversy surrounds this passage, especially concerning its origin, the identification of the speaker, the nature of the repentance (Are the Israelites enacting a superficial repentance?), the meaning of the expression "after two days . . . on the third," and whether or not a resurrection of any kind is suggested in this text.

Although this passage is an abrupt reversal from the preceding context, it is typical of Hosea's style (1:10–11; 2:14–15; 11:8–11; 13:14; 14:1–9) and that of other Hebrew prophets (e.g., Amos 9:11–12; Mic 2:12–13).[50] The reversal in Hos 14:1–9 is similar to 6:1–3 in that it also begins with an admonishment to "return" (שׁוּב; 14:2 MT) to Yahweh, recites the proper words of repentance (14:1–3), has Assyria in view (5:13; 14:3), records God's response (6:4—7:16; 14:4–9), and mentions healing (6:1; 14:4) and dew (6:4; 14:5). "Dew" is used in a positive sense and signifies blessing in 14:5 because Israel finally heeds the repentance call in a future day.[51] That true healing does come in a future day (14:4–9) and 6:1–3 seems to anticipate it suggests that Hosea has an eschatological orientation. The reunification of Israel envisioned in the reversal in 1:11 confirms this notion: "And the children of Judah and the children of Israel shall be gathered together, and they shall appoint for themselves one head. And

---

50. Wolff speculates that the passage is a priestly penitential song added to the sayings of Hosea by "the traditionalists," but the passage makes adequate sense without resorting to such reconstructions. Wolff, *Hosea*, 117; For a summary of various views, see Stuart, *Hosea–Jonah*, 107.

51. Garrett reinforces the case for the logic of Hos 6:1–3 when he notes that the specific judgments announced in the preceding context are reversed in 6:1–3. Garrett, *Hosea, Joel*, 160. Key Hoseanic themes are also found in 6:1–3, as one would expect. So also Stuart, *Hosea–Jonah*, 107.

they shall go up from the land, for great shall be the day of Jezreel" (ESV). Likewise, the promise of a Davidic king reinforces this position: "And afterward [μετὰ ταῦτα] the sons of Israel shall return and seek the Lord their God, and David their king, and they shall be amazed at the Lord and his good things in the last days [ἐπ' ἐσχάτων τῶν ἡμερῶν]" (3:5 LXX). One wonders if this passage was not formative in Peter's argument in Acts 2:17 when he equates Joel's "afterward" (μετὰ ταῦτα; 3:1 LXX) with "the last days" (ταῖς ἐσχάταις ἡμέραις).[52]

The reversal of Hos 13:14, where Israel is ransomed from the grave and redeemed from death (cf. v. 1), also points to the strong eschatological orientation of Hosea's prophecy. Thus, although it is true that Hosea has a national restoration in view in 6:1–3, Martin-Achard goes too far when he both denies that 13:14 is a reversal and claims that 6:2 is political only and "has no eschatological character."[53] In addition, Wolff's assertion that 6:1–3 speaks of healing alone fails to see the close tie between healing and resurrection in the Hebrew perspective.[54] Healing and resurrection terminology are compatible, and the one does not negate the possibility of the other. The story of the lost son makes this connection with restoration when the father insists on a celebration "because this brother of yours was dead and is now alive; he was lost and is found" (Luke 15:31). Once again Deut 32:39 comes to mind: "I kill and I make alive; I wound and I heal."

Michael Barré views the parallel Hebrew verbs חיה ("revive") and קום ("rise," "stand") in Hos 6:2 as a "fixed formulaic pair."[55] Only a handful of biblical passages contain the two verbs in close proximity,[56] but the repeated resurrection contexts among them is remarkable. When a dead man was hurriedly thrown into Elisha's grave and came in contact with his bones, "he revived and stood on his feet" (וַיְחִי וַיָּקָם עַל־רַגְלָיו; 2

---

52. Although Isa 2:2 has a closer verbal affinity with Peter's phrase, the equation of "afterward" and "last days" in Hos 3:5 and the Davidic context of Acts 2 is quite provocative, perhaps suggesting that Luke's record also shows an awareness of Hosea's equation.

53. Martin-Achard, *From Death to Life*, 86, 91.

54. Wolff, *Hosea*, 117; Martin-Achard, *From Death to Life*, 81; Dearman, *Book of Hosea*, 192.

55. Barré, "New Light," 130. He correctly notes the recurring combination of these verbs particularly in passages where resurrection language is used, but, based on how Semitic languages use "after two days" and "on the third day," he ultimately concludes that the language of Hos 6:2 refers to recovery from illness and not resurrection.

56. Gen 43:8; 2 Kgs 8:1; 13:21; Job 19:25; Isa 26:14, 19; Hos 6:2.

Kgs 13:21). The pair is also used in Job: "For I know that my Redeemer lives [חָי], and at the last he will stand [יָקוּם] upon the earth. And after my skin has been thus destroyed, yet in my flesh I shall see God" (19:25–26 ESV). Perhaps the occurrence of the verbs in this text should give one pause before too easily dismissing the possible resurrection implications of the passage.[57] However, a closer parallel occurs when Isaiah contrasts the expanding borders of the nation and glorification of God (26:15) with the other lords who have ruled Israel: "They are dead, they will not live [בַּל־יִחְיוּ]; they are shades, they will not arise [בַּל־יָקֻמוּ]; to that end you have visited them with destruction and wiped out all remembrance of them" (v. 14 ESV). The same verb pair occurs in a reversal a few verses later when, despite the failure of Israel to fulfill the mission, God brings resurrection anyway: "Your dead shall live [יִחְיוּ]; their bodies shall rise [יְקוּמוּן]. You who dwell in the dust, awake and sing for joy! For your dew is a dew of light, and the earth will give birth to the dead" (v. 19 ESV). The occurrence of the verb pair in a story that clearly refers to a physical resurrection (2 Kgs 13:21) and in a reversal passage that heavily emphasizes a corporeal resurrection (Isa 26:19) strongly suggests that Hosea intentionally employs the verb pair to invoke an image of resurrection.[58] The application of the pair to the physical resurrection of an individual, to the corporeal resurrection of many, and to the restoration of national Israel also suggests that physical resurrection and figurative resurrection are not conceptually far apart in the Hebrew perspective.

Thus, the rigid distinction between individual resurrection and national restoration is somewhat artificial, for the same powerful, living, sovereign, and restorative God stands behind both. As the Old Testament story progresses, the reader sees various applications of the resurrection/

57. Statements such as "He who goes down to Sheol does not come up" (Job 7:9; cf. 14:7–14) have prevented many recent scholars from interpreting Job 19:25–26 as a resurrection passage. However, it is the genius of the biblical poets to elaborate on the hopelessness of death and the vanity of life only to punctuate these diatribes with the truth of an afterlife, a resurrection, and a day of judgment (cf. Eccl 3:16–17; 12:14).

58. Wijngaards argues that Hosea's language is drawn from ancient covenantal pacts where vassals were dethroned (killed) if they violated the covenant or enthroned (raised up) by the overlord when they were restored to their position. While the covenantal context of Hosea is evident, Barré is right to point out that he fails to see the importance of the word pairs. The biblical associations in the word pairs take precedence over the parallels in ancient literature, which lack the eschatological perspective of the Scriptures. Wijngaards, "Death and Resurrection," 226–39. Barré ultimately gives too much credence to Semitic parallels and overlooks the importance of the biblical texts he uses in his article. Barré "New Light," 129.

restoration principle. It is applied to the deaths of individuals (the Elijah/ Elisha episodes), to the coming Messiah (Isa 53:10–12), to the nation of Israel (Ezek 37), and to the physical resurrection of the multitudes in Dan 12:2. Therefore resurrection is not a notion birthed during the period of the Maccabees, and it is simply circular reasoning to conclude that the ancient Israelites could not have entertained the concept of a resurrection because resurrection ideas did not exist until the period of the Maccabees.

Scholars differ on the origin and meaning of Hosea's mysterious "after two days . . . on the third day" expression,[59] but if the above analysis is correct then it should not be too surprising if the New Testament authors tap into the resurrection principle found in this verse.[60] As F. Nötscher affirms, Hosea's saying provides the prophetic foundation for the resurrection of Christ.[61] The New Testament records numerous references to a resurrection on the third day,[62] and Paul writes that Jesus "was raised on the third day according to the Scriptures" (ἐγήγερται τῇ ἡμέρᾳ τῇ τρίτῃ κατὰ τὰς γραφάς; 1 Cor 15:4).[63] The Septuagint translates Hos 6:2 employing the double use of the article with the attributive adjective (ἐν τῇ ἡμέρᾳ τῇ τρίτῃ ἀναστησόμεθα; "on the third day we will rise"). Paul shares this construction but does not share the same verb for resurrection (Paul uses ἐγείρω; "to rise").[64] Three times Matthew uses the simpler

---

59. Martin-Achard sees the expression as "proverbial" and "cultic in origin." Martin-Achard, *From Death to Life*, 82–83. Wijngaards finds a reference to a covenantal pact in it. Wijngaards, "Death and Resurrection," 237. Barré finds its life situation in medical terminology. Barré, "New Light," 140. Many scholars assume the reference is to a short period of time, but Stuart says, "It should not be taken literalistically" and probably refers to a time when God would "again visit his people in mercy." Stuart, *Hosea–Jonah*, 108.

60. McCasland is so certain that the New Testament authors do not use Hos 6:2 that he claims, "Our conclusion is, therefore, that 'on the third day' did not have its origin in some Old Testament scripture, although Paul, Luke and John refer to scripture as the basis of their tradition. It seems more probable that the tradition arose on other grounds and was then attributed to scripture." McCasland, " Scripture Basis," 135.

61. "Das ist offenbar die prophetische Begründung der Auferstehung Christi." He also surveys various possible backgrounds for the third day sayings in the ancient world. Nötscher, "Zur Auferstehung Nach Drei Tagen," 314.

62. Matt 16:21; 17:23; 20:19; 27:63, 64; Mark 8:31; 9:31; 10:34; Luke 9:22; 18:33; 24:7, 21, 46; Acts 10:40; 1 Cor 15:4. Cf. Matt 12:40 (Jonah); Matt 26:61; 27:40; Mark 14:58; 15:29; John 20:19, 20 (rebuilding/raising the temple); Luke 13:32 (completion of Jesus's ministry).

63. See Sellin's monograph for a detailed discussion of resurrection in 1 Cor 15. Sellin, *Streit um die Auferstehung der Toten*, 237–39.

64. Stuart holds that Paul's "according to the Scriptures" is analogical and not

attributive adjective (τῇ τρίτῃ ἡμέρᾳ; "on the third day") with a form of the verb ἐγείρω (16:21; 17:23; 20:19). Mark consistently uses a form of ἀνίστημι ("to rise") following "after three days" (μετὰ τρεῖς ἡμέρας; 8:31; 9:31; 10:34). Luke uses τῇ τρίτῃ ἡμέρᾳ ("on the third day") four times (Luke 9:22; 24:7, 46; Acts 10:44), and on one of those occasions (9:22) he follows it with ἐγερθῆναι ("to be raised") in conformity to the parallel passage in Matt 16:21. More often Luke uses the third-day expression in combination with the verb ἀνίστημι (24:7, 46), bringing him closer to the Septuagint's rendering of Hos 6:2 than any other New Testament author.

One Lukan text stands out, however, as potentially demonstrating dependence on Hosea 6:2. There are several good reasons to suspect that Luke 18:33c (τῇ ἡμέρᾳ τῇ τρίτῃ ἀναστήσεται; "on the third day he will rise") intentionally mirrors Hos 6:2 (τῇ ἡμέρᾳ τῇ τρίτῃ ἀναστησόμεθα; "on the third day we will rise"). First, this is the only New Testament third-day-resurrection text apart from 1 Cor 15:4 to use the article twice with the attributive adjective. Second, only Luke follows "the third day" with the verb ἀνίστημι rather than ἐγείρω.[65] Thus, Luke's phrase is identical to Hosea's except for the form of the verb ἀνίστημι. Third, the Matthean parallel and Markan parallel passages differ from Luke 18:33, making it appear that Luke is purposely conforming to Hosea's text:

Hos 6:2b
τῇ ἡμέρᾳ τῇ τρίτῃ ἀναστησόμεθα
"on the third day we will rise"

Luke 18:33c
τῇ ἡμέρᾳ τῇ τρίτῃ ἀναστήσεται
"on the third day he will rise"

Matt 20:19c
τῇ τρίτῃ ἡμέρᾳ ἐγερθήσεται
"on the third day he will be raised"

Mark 10:34c
μετὰ τρεῖς ἡμέρας ἀναστήσεται
"after three days he will rise"

---

necessarily referring to Hos 6:2 as a clear prediction of Jesus's resurrection. Stuart, *Hosea-Jonah*, 108.

65. Mark has "after three days" rather than "third day" and Matthew uses ἐγείρω.

Fourth, Luke contains a significant note not found in the parallel passages: "Behold we are going up to Jerusalem, and everything that has been *written by the prophets* about the Son of Man will be fulfilled [τελεσθήσεται]" (18:31b). This statement fits well with Luke's eschatological perspective and fulfillment theme, and it also narrows the field of choices to the prophets for identifying the Old Testament expectation of Jesus's betrayal, suffering, death, and resurrection on the third day (18:32–33).[66]

In addition to this, it may not be coincidental that the two passages with similarities to Hos 6:2 also mention the biblical precedent for the third day (Luke 18:33; 1 Cor. 15:4).[67] Perhaps it is saying too much to suggest that Hosea directly and clearly predicts the resurrection of Jesus in three days, but one can make a good case that Hosea establishes a third-day resurrection principle and pattern that the New Testament authors view as finding ultimate fulfillment in Christ. The picture that emerges in Hosea is that of a backslidden nation that refuses to repent and is incapable of saving itself. Thus, God himself will act to restore the nation, introduce a Davidic king, accomplish a resurrection on the third day, and ransom his people from the grave.

Isaiah 25:7–8; 26:13–19; 53:10–12

As discussed above, Hos 6:1–3 shares with Isa 26:19 the verb pair חיה ("revive") and קום ("rise," "stand") as well as a sudden reversal of topic from gloom to hope. Other important themes associated with resurrection also appear in the broader context of Isaiah, and some of these parallel emphases are found not only in Hosea but also in Ezek 37 and Dan 12. Isaiah 25:6–7 envisions the Lord preparing a great banquet "for all peoples" (v. 6) and swallowing up the "veil" (by implication, "shroud") that covers "all peoples" (v. 7). Paul alludes to the second mention of swallowing in verse 8a ("He will swallow up death forever"), at the pinnacle of his lengthy resurrection monologue (1 Cor 15:54). Motyer calls attention to the universality of Isa 25:6–8, pointing to the repetition of "peoples" as well as the "nations" and "faces" and noticing that they become "his

---

66. One could posit that Jonah serves as the pattern for a third day resurrection, but Luke steers away from this notion (11:30; cf. Matt 12:40), and the language in his third day passages does not fit.

67. The case for Paul's allusion to Hos 6:2 may be strengthened by the observation that he draws from Hos 13:14 in 1 Cor 15:55.

people" in verse 8c.[68] The banquet depicted here could be that of a wedding or, more likely, a celebration of Yahweh's coronation.[69] While the complete swallowing of death and the wiping away of tears from the eyes (v. 8b; cf. Rev 21:4) awaits the consummation, one cannot help but ponder how Christ's vanquishing of death in his resurrection was followed by his enthronement and the securing of blessing for his disciples (Acts 2).

In contrast to Yahweh's removal of tears and disgrace from his people, he will trample Moab because of their pride and "bring them down to the ground, to the dust [עַד־עָפָר]" (Isa 25:12; cf. 26:5; Gen 2:7). Based on 1 Kgs 2, Walter Brueggemann argues that the antithesis of "dust" is kingship and that this understanding sheds light on the meaning of the J passages such as Gen 2:7 and 3:19.[70] Although his dependence on the Documentary Hypothesis to read into Genesis from 1 Kings is questionable, his point is well taken that arising from the dust can have royal associations (1 Sam 2:6–8).[71] Isaiah depicts the dethroning of "other lords" who had ruled Israel (26:13). "They are dead, they will not live; they are shades, they will not arise" (מֵתִים בַּל־יִחְיוּ רְפָאִים בַּל־יָקֻמוּ; v. 14a). Here the word pair is negated (in contrast to Yahweh's dead in verse 19), for the lot of the arrogant is humiliation, just as the king of Babylon is dethroned and greeted by the רְפָאִים ("shades," "spirits") in Sheol (14:9).[72] In contrast, Yahweh is honored (26:13) and glorified (v. 15) and those who belong to him find hope, for those "who dwell in the dust" will awaken (v. 19a), just as Daniel says that "multitudes who sleep in the dust of the earth will awake" (12:2 NIV). Thus, the primary issue is the glory and reign of King Yahweh, yet Yahweh's "dead will live" to rejoice and share in his triumph.[73]

---

68. Motyer, *Prophecy of Isaiah*, 209.

69. Childs, *Introduction to the Old Testament*, 184; Oswalt, *Book of Isaiah*, 1:462–63.

70. Brueggemann, "From Dust to Kingship," 2.

71. Brueggemann also sees the dust and enthronement concept as inherently covenantal, and while the covenantal implications are present in some contexts, I am less enthusiastic than he is regarding the extent of the relationship. Brueggemann, "From Dust to Kingship," 2–3.

72. The Hebrew רְפָאִים rarely occurs in the Old Testament and only three times in Isaiah (14:9; 26:14, 19).

73. Oswalt, *Book of Isaiah*, 1:485. The vivid, corporeal language of Isa 26:19 indicates more than a metaphorical application to the restoration of national Israel. The language is also more universal in scope and points to a greater restoration that fulfills all other temporal reversals. For additional support for this position, see Hasel, "Resurrection," 275.

Not only the righteous in general participate in a grand reversal via resurrection, but the suffering servant "shall be high and lifted up, and shall be exalted" (52:13b ESV) and Yahweh "will give him a portion among the great, and he will divide the spoils with the strong" (53:12a NIV). Motyer describes how "death ushers him into sovereign dignity and power, with his own hand administering the saving purposes of the Lord, and as victor taking the spoil."[74] Thus, the nations see the glory of King Yahweh through the resurrection and exaltation of a particular servant as well as through a grand reversal in the resurrection of his people.

The language of childbirth, so commonly associated with matters of life and death, serves to illustrate Israel's inability to fulfill God's mission. "We were pregnant, we writhed, but we have given birth to wind. We have accomplished no deliverance in the earth, and the inhabitants of the world have not fallen [וּבַל־יִפְּלוּ יֹשְׁבֵי תֵבֵל]" (26:18 ESV). Although the meaning of "fallen" is difficult, the main idea in this verse is that God must act alone to bring salvation because Israel has been ineffective. The Hebrew term נפל ("to fall") also occurs at the end of verse 19 and seems to have a more positive connotation as the earth releases its dead.[75] Just as God alone could swallow death (25:8),[76] only God can bring salvation

---

74. Motyer, *Prophecy of Isaiah*, 40–41; Grogan notices the contrast between verse 8 and the prolongation of days in verse 11 and the parallel with Ps 22, "which has so much in common with this passage, where a sufferer now vindicated declares, 'Posterity will serve him' (Ps 22:30)." Grogan, "Isaiah," 304.

75. The final phrases in verses 18–19 contain the verb נפל and are difficult to translate. This verb has a variety of meanings, but more than a quarter of its occurrences are in reference to falling in death. Seebass, "נָפַל," 499. Several versions employ an idiosyncratic translation of "give birth" in both verses based on the associations with birth in the noun נֶפֶל, the childbirth language in verse 18, and the use of a similar Aramaic term for "miscarriage." However, "miscarriage" does not make sense in this context. Seebass, "נָפַל," 496. The Septuagint clearly understands the first half of verse 19 as a physical resurrection: "The dead will rise and those in the tombs will be raised [ἀναστήσονται οἱ νεκροί καὶ ἐγερθήσονται οἱ ἐν τοῖς μνημείοις]," but the second part contrasts with this and translates, "But the land of the ungodly will fall [ἡ δὲ γῆ τῶν ἀσεβῶν πεσεῖται]." In conformity with this, the Septuagint omits the Hebrew negation (וּבַל) at the end of verse 18 and translates, "but those who dwell on the earth will fall [πεσοῦνται οἱ ἐνοικοῦντες ἐπὶ τῆς γῆς]." The Septuagint makes a clear contrast between the righteous and unrighteous in both verses and also gives the godly credit for bringing salvation to the earth. See Seebass, "נָפַל," 496. Also see Harman, "נפל," 129–31. Oswalt believes the verb means "to fall in battle" in verse 18. Thus, Israel has been unable to defeat the oppressive world powers, and they "do not fall." The term has a more positive meaning in verse 19 and is a reference to a devourer having to drop its prey ("let it fall") because of death's defeat. Oswalt, *Book of Isaiah*, 1:485, 476, 476n22.

76. Oswalt, *Book of Isaiah*, 1:463, 465.

and raise the dead (26:19), and the means by which he accomplishes all this is through a servant from David's line (Isa 55:3; Acts 13:34) who becomes a guilt offering (53:10), bears the sin of "many" (רַבִּים; 53:12; cf. v. 11; 52:14, 15), and yet sees his offspring and has prolonged days (53:10). Because of the close identification between national Israel as a servant and the Messiah as the servant, some scholars have failed to make any distinction between the two, but the failure of one and the success of the other, along with the Davidic descent of the one, clarifies the distinction. Nonetheless, the relationship between the two allows Luke to develop a picture of recapitulation in which the Messiah succeeds where humankind in general and Israel in particular failed (Luke 3:37—4:15).

Isaiah forms a foundational part of this study because Luke relies heavily on it for his pneumatology (e.g., Luke 4:18–19); his emphasis on a Davidic, suffering, and exalted (resurrected) servant; and his eschatological worldview. As Brevard Childs notes, Isaiah climaxes with the new heavens and new earth in 65:17–25, "but the hope of a radical new world order apart from evil and sickness has been adumbrated throughout the entire Isaianic corpus."[77] Eschatology, resurrection, and Spirit come together in Isaiah, and Luke recognizes the connections. This thought receives further treatment in chapter 8.

Ezekiel 37:1–14

A review of the Old Testament quotations in Luke-Acts shows that Luke often quotes the Pentateuch, Psalms, and Isaiah. He also quotes other books less frequently (especially the Prophets), but never directly quotes Ezekiel.[78] Neither his pneumatology nor his doctrine of the resurrection appears to find its primary footing in Ezekiel, yet Ezekiel provides important pneumatic language for personal and eschatological

---

77. Childs, *Isaiah*, 185.

78. About the closest Luke comes to direct dependence on Ezekiel is in his use of the phrase "house of Israel." Luke uses this expression in Acts 2:36 (ἀσφαλῶς οὖν γινωσκέτω πᾶς οἶκος Ἰσραὴλ ὅτι καὶ κύριον αὐτὸν καὶ χριστὸν ἐποίησεν ὁ θεός), and it sounds very similar to Ezek 39:22 (καὶ γνώσονται οἶκος Ισραηλ ὅτι ἐγώ εἰμι κύριος ὁ θεὸς αὐτῶν; LXX). Luke's employment of the term seems to fit the confrontational/prophetic tone of Peter's Pentecostal sermon, and it also draws attention to the exalted status of Jesus. This is probably the reason it is used, but it does not seem to be an indicator that Luke is building his pneumatology primarily from Ezekiel. For a discussion of this see Dunn, *Baptism in the Holy Spirit*, 46–49; Thompson, *Acts of the Risen Lord Jesus*, 128–29; Turner, *Power from on High*, 48–53.

transformation as well as language later used for articulation of the doctrine of resurrection (e.g., 4Q385psEzek 2). The Septuagint of Ezekiel also uses several verbs for the activity of the Spirit that have parallels in Luke-Acts.[79] Ezekiel uses the word "spirit" (רוּחַ) fifty-two times, and his pneumatology is multifaceted. The רוּחַ occurs in relation to God's chariot throne (*merkābāh*) in the opening chapter, refers to the wind on several occasions, enters and transports Ezekiel in visionary experiences, enables him to receive revelation, falls upon him in prophetic inspiration, describes the breath or animating life principle, causes a transformation in the hearts of the people, and represents Yahweh's favor and presence when poured out on Israel. Ezekiel's vision of the valley of dry bones also begins with parallel references to "the hand of Yahweh" and the "Spirit of Yahweh" (37:1), which illustrate the close association of the former expression with the Spirit in Ezekiel (1:3; 3:22; 8:1; 33:22; 40:1).[80] Thus, Ezekiel attributes his travel to the valley and his visionary experience to the Spirit.

Ezekiel's visionary passage (37:1-14) contains ten occurrences of רוּחַ and, in addition to the attribution in verse 1, the רוּחַ refers to the breath of life (vv. 5, 6, 8, 9 (3x), 10), the wind or direction (v. 9), and God's indwelling and life-giving Spirit (v. 14). However, the explanation in verse 14 suggests that the breath entering the dry bones symbolizes the revitalization of Israel by the Spirit. The Spirit plays an essential role in effecting obedience to God's laws (36:27) and restoring life. Ezekiel's vision also depicts the breath entering the bones in a manner reminiscent of the two-stage process of Adam's creation and subsequent insufflation (vv. 4-10; Gen 2:7).[81]

---

79. Common verbs of which the Spirit is the subject or means by which the action takes place include: ἔρχομαι (Ezek 2:2; 3:24; Acts 19:6) or ἐπέρχομαι (Acts 1:8); λαλέω (Ezek 3:24; Acts 28:25); λέγω (Ezek 3:24; 11:5; Acts 4:25; 8:29; 11:12; 13:2; 21:11); ἄγω and cognates (Ezek 8:3; 11:1, 24; 37:1; 43:5; Luke 4:1); and πίπτω (Ezek 11:5) or ἐπιπίπτω (Acts 10:44; 11:15). God also gives (δίδωμι) the πνεῦμα in the following passages: Ezek 11:19; 36:26, 27; 37:6, 14; Luke 11:13; Acts 5:32; 15:8. Ezekiel often uses ἀναλαμβάνω with the Spirit as the subject and Luke often uses λαμβάνω with the Spirit as the direct object; the meaning of the cognates is quite different.

80. Note the same expression found in conjunction with the phrase "your bones will flourish like the grass" in Isa 66:14.

81. The rare occurrence of the verb ἐμφυσάω ("to breath on") in Ezek 37:9 (LXX) reflects dependence on Gen 2:7. John 20:22 draws on Gen 2:7 as well, but perhaps John is also aware that this verb has been used in resurrection contexts such as 1 Kgs 17:21 and Ezek 37:9.

There is a general consensus among scholars that Ezek 37 does not directly prophesy a physical, eschatological resurrection, but there are elements in the vision that fit well with the Israelite preunderstanding discussed previously. First, when Ezekiel alters the metaphor to describe a cemetery, his vivid portrayal of graves opening employs resurrection terminology in an unmistakable manner. Second, Ezekiel's use of the resurrection metaphors implies a certain familiarity with the concept among his audience.[82] Third, although the exact Hebrew word pair found in Hos 6:2 and Isa 26:19 (חיה and קום) does not occur in Ezek 37, a similar combination does occur: וַיִּחְיוּ וַיַּעַמְדוּ עַל־רַגְלֵיהֶם ("and they lived and stood on their feet;" v. 10b).[83] Fourth, both Isaiah and Ezekiel employ the relatively uncommon term גזר ("cut off") in resurrection contexts. The servant of Isa 53:8 was "cut off from the land of the living" prior to exaltation and Israel despaired, saying, "We are cut off" (Ezek 37:11b) prior to the opening of their graves.[84] Fifth, the reversal of circumstances typical of resurrection passages is evident in Ezek 37. Finally, Israel's utter inability to rescue itself from the exilic predicament requires the sovereign intervention of Yahweh, who closes out the vision with this assurance: "Then you shall know that I am the LORD; I have spoken, and I will do it, declares the LORD" (37:14b ESV; cf. Isa 26:18–19).

Although Ezekiel's vision describes a national restoration, his resurrection metaphor fits comfortably with other resurrection passages. However, his combination of resurrection and "spirit" (רוּחַ) does not appear to be significantly formative in Luke's theology of resurrection and Spirit. Ezekiel's version of these motifs seems more at home in Matthew (27:51–54), John (20:22), the Apocalypse (Rev 11:1), and perhaps Paul (Rom 8:11). However, Ezekiel shares with Luke an emphasis on "my servant David" (34:23, 24; 37:24, 25) and an eschatological perspective that is consistent with resurrection language and the activity of the Holy Spirit.

Daniel 12:1–3, 13

Daniel 12:1–3 is well-known for its clear reference to a resurrection of both the righteous and the wicked, and, despite the discovery of the Dead Sea

---

82. Anderson, *"But God Raised"*, 55.

83. Block, *Book of Ezekiel*, 2:387n97.

84. Allen also notices the similar terminology in Isa 53:8. Allen, *Ezekiel 20–48*, 185.

Scrolls, many scholars continue to date Daniel to the Maccabean period, around 165 BC.[85] However, given the expectation of a divine reversal, the understanding of God's persistent loyalty, and the eschatological outlook of the Hebrew Scriptures from Gen 1:1 forward, this late date is unnecessary and unhelpful.[86] Daniel's resurrection text has strong affinities with earlier texts, especially Isaiah, and this is evident in Dan 12:2 (NIV): "Multitudes who sleep in the dust of the earth will awake: some to everlasting life, others to shame and everlasting contempt." Daniel has sleepers in the "dust" (עָפָר), and Isa 26:19 has dwellers in the "dust" (עָפָר; cf. Gen 3:19). Both texts also use the verb קיץ ("to awake") (cf. 2 Kgs 4:31; Ps 17:15), and Gerhard Hasel argues for a strong link between the two texts on the basis of their common apocalyptic eschatology.[87] The new element in Dan 12:2 is the resurrection of both the righteous and the ungodly, but the clear differentiation in their final destinies is certainly not new.

Similarities with the suffering servant passage of Isa 52–53 are also instructive. "Those who are wise [וְהַמַּשְׂכִּלִים] will shine like the brightness of the heavens, and those who lead many [הָרַבִּים] to righteousness [וּמַצְדִּיקֵי], like the stars for ever and ever" (Dan 12:3 NIV). The wise ones (from the verb שׂכל) will rise and "shine" (12:2–3), including the persecuted faithful (11:33, 35) and Daniel himself (1:4, 17; 9:22, 25; 12:13).[88] Likewise the suffering servant "will act wisely [יַשְׂכִּיל]" and "be exalted" (Isa 52:13).[89] And "by his knowledge the righteous one [צַדִּיק], my servant, will justify [יַצְדִּיק] many [לָרַבִּים]" (53:11b). Various scholars have noted the common justification theme and how Daniel casts his righteous sufferers in a manner similar to the suffering servant.[90] However, a great deal of controversy exists over whether the "many" in Dan 12:2 refers to "multitudes" (NIV) that rise or to a partial resurrection, particularly of

---

85. Relevant texts include 1QDana, 1QDanb, 4QDana, 4QDanb, 4QDand, 4QDane, 4QFlor, 6QDan and especially 4QDanc. See the discussion in Hasel, "New Light on the Book of Daniel," 45–53; Baldwin, *Daniel*, 35–46.

86. It appears that the anti-supernatural bias against prophetic revelation continues to provide the impetus for adherence to such a late date. The problem with such a late date is that it creates an artificial *Sitz im Leben* for Daniel.

87. Hasel, "Resurrection," 276–81.

88. Goldingay also recognizes that the resurrection includes more than the Maccabean martyrs but then dismisses the implications pointing to a general resurrection. Goldingay, *Daniel*, 308.

89. The verb שׂכל is relatively uncommon in the Old Testament, and Isaiah uses it only three times. Thus, Daniel likely intends a link via terminology.

90. Anderson, "But God Raised," 60; Wright, *The Resurrection*, 115.

the Maccabean martyrs.[91] The latter argument depends on a reconstruction of Daniel based on a late date and the common partitive use of רַב ("many," but not "all"), but Joyce Baldwin has argued that the term can mean "all" in some contexts and seems to have a more "inclusive significance" in its five occurrences in Isa 52:14–15; 53:11–12.[92] Given the inclusion of Daniel in the resurrection (12:13), Daniel's overall concern for the universal dominion of God, and the New Testament hope "that there will be a resurrection of both the just and the unjust" (Acts 24:15b), it seems more likely that Daniel does not intend to limit the resurrection but is more concerned with mirroring the themes developed in Isa 52–53.

Daniel employs astral imagery to describe the glorification of the righteous (12:3b). This too is akin to the suffering servant's exaltation after his humiliation (Isa 52:13; 53:12). N. T. Wright correctly observes that Dan 12:3 has a "royal connotation" and that "this appears to be, in line with other ideas in Daniel, a kind of democratization of earlier royal traditions: it belongs with the idea that 'the saints of the Most High' will receive the kingdom (7.18, 22, 27)."[93] This pattern of resurrection and exaltation provides a foundation for Luke's presentation of Christ's resurrection, ascension, and exaltation at God's right hand as a single theological motion. Similarly, the goal of resurrection for the righteous is not only renewed bodily existence but a glorification and sharing in the royal rule of Christ.

Daniel has several touch points with Luke that affirm and build on emphases from other parts of the Old Testament. Daniel heavily emphasizes the kingdom of God, especially an enduring "kingdom that will never be destroyed" (2:44; cf. 4:3, 34; 7:13–14). This prophecy is similar to the Davidic promises as well as to Gabriel's announcement to Mary (Luke 1:32–33). Only Luke pictures Christ as the stone that "will crush" (λικμήσει) those it falls on (20:18) just as the stone cut out by God "will crush" the kingdoms of the world (Dan 2:44).[94] And the arrival of Gabriel

---

91. Elledge is among those who hold the latter view. Elledge, "Resurrection of the Dead," 27.

92. Baldwin, *Daniel*, 204.

93. Wright, *Resurrection*, 112–13.

94. The Greek term λικμάω occurs only in Luke 20:18 in the New Testament except for the parallel text in Matt 21:44, but there is a textual problem in the latter passage. The term only occurs eighteen times in the Septuagint and only once in Daniel (2:44, TH). The Septuagint of 2:44 uses ἀφανίζω, but this is still conceptually the same as in Luke.

at "the time of the evening sacrifice" (9:21) in Luke 1:8–11 signals the fulfillment of prophecies related to "an anointed one" (Dan 9:25).[95] Gabriel's prophecy about John's empowerment (Luke 1:17) combines elements of Elijah's ministry, Malachi's turning of hearts (4:5–6), and language ("the wisdom of the just") that sounds very much like Dan 12:3. And just as Gabriel announces to Daniel that he is "treasured" by God (9:23), so he also announces to Mary that she is "highly favored" (Luke 1:28). Gabriel follows this address with prophecies about the coming ruler, "an anointed one" (Dan 12:25), the "Son of the Most High" (Luke 1:32).

Although Daniel never directly mentions the divine Spirit, his repeated reference to "an anointed one, a prince" (9:25–26) certainly reminds the reader of David (2 Sam 23:1–2).[96] Atonement takes place through an anointed one (Dan 9:24) who "will be cut off" (יִכָּרֵת; v. 26)—concepts that once again place the reader of Scripture squarely in Isa 53 (especially v. 8) as well as in Acts 8:32–33.

Thus, Daniel demonstrates continuity with the Hebrew Scriptures and builds on themes that come to greater fruition in the New Testament and Luke in particular. Daniel's view is heavily eschatological, clearly anticipates a physical resurrection, draws on the creation story ("dust"), speaks of the cutting off of an anointed one who atones for sin, envisions a reversal of fortunes and exaltation of the righteous, and proclaims the final triumph of God's everlasting kingdom. These are all concepts right at home with Luke.

Summary

Elements of Luke's eschatology are obvious even to the most casual reader. One can hardly miss his emphasis on fulfillment, and some will notice the pointers toward new creation. What receives less attention is the extent of Luke's individual eschatology and its consistency with concepts articulated in the Pentateuch. This eschatology directly results from Luke's focus on Jesus's resurrection, for a highly developed reflection on resurrection necessitates the presence of an advanced perspective on

---

95. Goldingay points out the timing of Gabriel's arrival in both passages, although it is not certain whether the morning or evening offering is intended in Luke. Bock favors the evening sacrifice because of the large attendance. Goldingay, *Daniel*, xxviii–xxix; Bock, *Luke*, 1:79–80.

96. The adjective מָשִׁיחַ ("messiah") only occurs eleven times in the Old Testament, but seven of those refer to either Saul or David.

individual destinies. Thus, Luke alludes to the judgment of the wicked as being cut off; however, the christocentric nature of the judgment becomes evident when the punishment results from one's failure to repent and submit to the Lord Jesus. Likewise, one can enter Abraham's bosom (i.e., be gathered to one's people) based on the faithfulness of God that extends beyond death and one's response to Jesus's resurrection from the dead. Sheol and Hades have no hold on Christ or his followers.

The prophets Hosea, Isaiah, Ezekiel, and Daniel build on the resurrection principles rooted in the Pentateuch. They flesh out the picture by further clarifying the reality of resurrection and developing the centrality of Christ as one who both experiences this great reversal of death and brings reversal for those who live under his royal rule. The prophets provide third-day language, add details on the suffering and rising of the servant, and forecast the bright future of the righteous. In Luke and his predecessors, Theophilus sees that resurrection is an ancient and central element of God's eschatological plan to bring restoration to those under the curse of death.

The above picture also reveals an aspect of Lukan pneumatology that is more fundamental than the Pentecostal outpouring. The Christ (anointed one) who is anticipated by the prophets is primary to Luke, and it is only when his identity as the one anointed with the Spirit receives due attention that one can understand the charismatic elements in the story. Everything depends on Jesus's identity as the anointed and exalted King, and the Spirit who moves the story toward its eschatological goal keeps an uncompromising focus on Jesus. Chapter 6 develops this idea in greater detail.

6

The Center of Luke-Acts
Lord and Christ

It is imperative to identify Luke's central interest in his two volumes, as one's understanding of this provides the context for how the important themes of resurrection and Spirit relate to one another. This chapter highlights Luke's emphasis on Jesus as Lord and Christ. The argument develops by first examining how Luke structures his narrative and uses Jesus's messianic titles to focus on his royal identity. A review of Luke's incorporation of the concept of the kingdom, then, provides support for the notion that Luke's central interest concerns Jesus's royal identity. A look at the content of the preaching in Luke-Acts further demonstrates Luke's royal and christocentric interests.

The Purpose of Luke-Acts

There are often as many proposals for the purpose or central message of any given biblical book as there are commentators on the book. Luke-Acts is no exception, and the task of locating a center is complicated by the addition of a second volume. Henry Cadbury recognizes the possibility of "a variety of motives"[1] and notes important elements such as the christocentric nature of Luke-Acts, the progress of the divine agenda with its future orientation, and the role of the Spirit in guiding God's plan.[2] In

---

1. Cadbury, *The Making of Luke-Acts*, 302.
2. Cadbury, *The Making of Luke-Acts*, 300–305.

the end, he most heavily emphasizes the apologetic nature of Luke's two volumes in defending Christianity against misinformation and criticism from both Jews and Gentiles.[3]

In the eyes of Hans Conzelmann, Luke's primary concern is to explain the delay of the Parousia.[4] Robert Maddox notes how various scholars have emphasized Luke's themes of ecclesiology and eschatology, but he rightly eschews Conzelmann's artificial reconstruction of eschatology and highlight's the fulfillment of God's plan in Christ, the giving of the Spirit, and a continued expectation of the Parousia.[5] Maddox concludes that Luke "writes to reassure the Christians of his day that their faith in Jesus is no aberration, but the authentic goal towards which God's ancient dealings with Israel were driving."[6] Alfred Plummer sees Luke as concerned with establishing the factual basis of the gospel as a foundation for the salvation of all people, particularly Gentiles.[7] The title of Jacques Dupont's book expresses the sentiment of many scholars: *The Salvation of the Gentiles*, although some would prefer to place the accent more on "inclusive" or universal salvation.[8]

David Pao attempts to move beyond christological concerns alone and to highlight ecclesiology, that is, how the Christian community is "the true extension of the people of God."[9] Darrell Bock views Luke's interests as encompassing both God's agenda to bring salvation and the new community.[10] Craig Keener entertains the possibility of multiple purposes but emphasizes Luke's apologetic interest in relation to missions.[11]

One can only affirm that many of the emphases highlighted above are incorporated in Luke's statement of intention when he writes in order that Theophilus "might know the certainty [ἀσφάλειαν] of the words concerning which" he was informed (Luke 1:4). The noun ἀσφάλεια occurs

---

3. Cadbury, *The Making of Luke-Acts*, 306–15.

4. Conzelmann, *Theology of St. Luke*, 95–97.

5. Maddox, *The Purpose of Luke-Acts*, 182–83.

6. Maddox, *The Purpose of Luke-Acts*, 187.

7. Plummer, *Gospel According to S. Luke*, xxxvi.

8. Tannehill speaks of "God's purpose of inclusive salvation." *Narrative Unity*, 1:12; Marshall emphasizes salvation for all. *Gospel of Luke*, 35–36.

9. Pao, *Acts and the Isaianic New Exodus*, 143.

10. See his list of various suggestions for Luke's primary purpose. Bock, *Luke*, 1:14.

11. Keener also surveys various views on Luke's purpose. Keener, *Acts: An Exegetical Commentary*, 1:435–58.

elsewhere in the New Testament only in 1 Thess 5:3 and Acts 5:23, and neither text has any theological bearing on Luke's prologue. However, Luke employs the equally rare cognate adverb ἀσφαλῶς ("certainly"; Mark 14:44; Acts 16:23) in Acts 2:36, clarifying the object of assurance: "Let all the house of Israel therefore know for certain [ἀσφαλῶς] that God has made him both Lord [κύριον] and Christ [χριστὸν], this Jesus whom you crucified." Therefore any purpose statement of Luke-Acts must incorporate Christology into it, that is, that Jesus is Lord and Christ. Ironically, Cadbury dismisses such texts as signifying Luke's intent when he posits, "We may choose our own 'golden texts' for these volumes—compendiums of theology or history—like the angels' triad formula for Jesus, 'a Savior, Christ, the Lord,' and the geographical scheme of Acts . . . , but I suspect the author's motive is more faithfully represented by" texts related to the emphasis on apology.[12] Without the primacy of Christology, the many derivative themes of Acts are groundless. The eschatological plan moves toward fulfillment in and through Christ; the Scriptures testify to Christ; salvation is available in the name of Christ; the new community forms around Christ; Gentiles and those on the fringes of society comprise the kingdom of Christ; and the disciples testify to Christ. All of this presupposes Luke's identification of Jesus as Christ and his development of the thought of his universal reign as Lord. Thus, it is accurate to speak of Luke's primary purpose in establishing that Jesus is Lord and Christ and his related purpose of teasing out the implications of that central truth, especially salvation for all peoples.

It is important to also recognize the Trinitarian implications of Luke's lofty Christology. After all, Luke attributes the resurrection and titles of Christ to the activity of God the Father, who "made him both Lord and Christ" (Acts 2:36). At the same time, recognition of Luke's christological focus is essential for a proper understanding of the relationship between Luke's doctrine of the resurrection and his pneumatology, because the acceptance of the theological notion of Jesus as Lord and Christ contextualizes all other themes, provides the key point at which the resurrection and Spirit converge, and enables the reader to ask the right question: How do Luke's resurrection and Spirit themes relate to Jesus as Lord and Christ?

The discussion in chapter 4 pointed out the significance of Luke's threefold formula, which identifies Jesus as Lord and Christ at his birth,

---

12. Cadbury, *The Making of Luke-Acts*, 316.

The Center of Luke-Acts

Pentecost, Cornelius's home, and the ending of Acts (Luke 2:11; Acts 2:36; 10:36; 28:31). Two other occurrences of the triad (including Peter's defense of the Caesarean Pentecost and the Jerusalem Council letter) reinforce the previous conclusions about the importance of this designation. A comparison of the six occurrences of the triad is recorded below.

<u>σωτὴρ</u> ὅς ἐστιν <u>χριστὸς</u> <u>κύριος</u> (Luke 2:11)
<u>κύριον</u> αὐτὸν καὶ <u>χριστὸν</u> ἐποίησεν ὁ θεός, τοῦτον τὸν <u>Ἰησοῦν</u> (Acts 2:36)
διὰ <u>Ἰησοῦ</u> <u>Χριστοῦ</u>, οὗτός ἐστιν πάντων <u>κύριος</u> (Acts 10:36)
πιστεύσασιν ἐπὶ τὸν <u>κύριον</u> <u>Ἰησοῦν</u> <u>Χριστόν</u> (Acts 11:17)
ὑπὲρ τοῦ ὀνόματος τοῦ <u>κυρίου</u> ἡμῶν <u>Ἰησοῦ</u> <u>Χριστου</u> (Acts 15:26)
τὰ περὶ τοῦ <u>κυρίου</u> <u>Ἰησοῦ</u> <u>Χριστοῦ</u> (Acts 28:31)

"a Savior who is Christ the Lord" (Luke 2:11)
"God made him both Lord and Christ, this Jesus" (Acts 2:36)
"through Jesus Christ—he is Lord of all" (Acts 10:36)
"who believed on the Lord Jesus Christ" (Acts 11:17)
"for the name of our Lord Jesus Christ" (Acts 15:26)
"the things concerning the Lord Jesus Christ" (Acts 28:31)

These are the only places in Luke-Acts where the threefold title of Jesus occurs, and their locations at such significant moments in the narrative points to intentionality in emphasis and structure.

In the first of the two additional texts under discussion (Acts 11:17), Peter defends his actions at Cornelius's home by appealing to divine activity in giving the "same gift" to the Gentiles as God had given "to us who believed on the Lord Jesus Christ." It is rather striking that the triad occurs directly in reference to both Pentecost and Cornelius's household, so that the two events are joined not only by the similar outpouring of the Spirit but by the central christological point that Jesus is Lord and Christ.

The remaining triad occurs in Acts 15:26, where the Council affirms Barnabas and Paul as reliable messengers who have laid down their lives "for the name of our Lord Jesus Christ." The triad is significant here because it occurs at the Jerusalem Council in the middle of the debate about what Jewish regulations are necessary (δεῖ) for Gentiles to observe (v. 5).[13] The plural "our" indicates that the same Lord Jesus Christ in whose "name" Barnabas and Paul suffer is also Lord of the Jews in Jerusalem and the Lord of the Gentiles upon whom God has "called" his "name"

---

13. Luke may have used one of his favorite terms here to emphasize that these regulations are absolutely not necessary and not part of the divine plan for Gentiles at this stage in God's redemptive plan.

(v. 17; Amos 9:12). The employment of "our Lord Jesus Christ" therefore becomes a phrase of solidarity, bringing believers from every ethnicity under the umbrella of one "Lord of all" (Acts 10:36). Peter argues that it is "through the grace of the Lord Jesus" that both Jew and Gentile are saved (15:11). His first and primary argument for defending the liberty of the Gentiles is the divine initiative in "giving to them the Holy Spirit just as he gave us" (v. 8). Additional evidence in the argument comes from God's initiative in performing signs and wonders among the Gentiles through Barnabas and Saul (v. 12) and then from Israel's Scriptures (vv. 16–17; Amos 9:11–12). The evidence supports the inclusive claim that Jesus is "our Lord Jesus Christ" (Acts 15:26).

The Council decides not to burden the Gentiles with excessive regulations but to caution them to avoid idolatrous worship practices (Acts 15:28–29),[14] for this plan "seemed good to the Holy Spirit and to us" (v. 28). Scholars commonly view this passage as a reference to the Spirit's supervisorial role in church affairs, but this is more than "the Lucan emphasis on the Spirit-guided institutional church in Jerusalem guiding like a mother its daughter churches."[15] As Peter points out (v. 8), the Spirit had already expressed his opinion at Cornelius's house, not to mention his repeated affirmations of the Gentiles through miraculous signs and the inspired Scriptures. This is more than a spontaneous gift of wisdom; this is a decision grounded in previous revelation.

The placement of the threefold identification of God's Son as "Lord," "Jesus," and "Christ" in Luke-Acts demonstrates that Luke attributes substantial theological import to the triad. The first (Luke 2:11) and last (Acts 28:31) form a theological frame around the narrative, emphasizing Jesus's identity as the Savior, Jewish Messiah (anointed one), and Lord of all. The first announces good news "for all people" (Luke 2:10) and the last emphasizes the preaching of the kingdom to the Gentiles (Acts 28:28–31). The four other occurrences are all directly related to Luke's most pivotal events in the narrative of Acts: Pentecost (2:36), the Caesarean Pentecost (10:36; 11:17), and the Jerusalem Council (15:26). The latter passage draws together the previous two so that the outpouring of the Spirit becomes the evidence that God's saving activity has swept away all ethnic barriers to salvation and that Christ's lordship is expanding over

---

14. Witherington argues that all four restrictions relate directly to pagan temple practices, but Bock leaves some room for the influence of the Noahic law regarding bloodshed. Witherington, *Acts of the Apostles*, 462–66; Bock, *Acts*, 506.

15. Fitzmyer, *Acts of the Apostles*, 563; See also Barrett, *Acts of the Apostles*, 2:744.

the globe. The outpouring of the Spirit at once confirms God's acceptance of those whom he has saved and the exalted position and identity of Jesus as Lord. A closer look at Luke's kingdom context and his use of "Lord" (κύριος) and "Christ" (Χριστός) in the narrative reveal associations between his doctrine of the Spirit and of the resurrection.

The Kingdom Context of Luke-Acts

In chapter 4 I argued that there are several significant parallels between Luke-Acts and 1 and 2 Samuel. Those parallels begin in the birth narratives of each book and include important theological themes such as the concept of kingdom, anointing as confirmation of God's choice of leader, anointing as the symbol of empowerment with the Spirit, the suffering of the one anointed, the reversal from mistreatment to enthronement, and the related concept of death to life. Before continuing with the specifics of Jesus's identity as Lord and Christ and the implication of those terms for this study, an overview of the kingdom context of Luke-Acts first sets the stage for the discussion.

Luke has skillfully frontloaded his narrative with numerous references to Jesus's Davidic descent and has incorporated the covenant with Abraham (Luke 1:72–73) into his narrative. David is mentioned by name six times in the first two chapters of Luke and four times in the first two chapters of Acts.[16] The early concentration on David in both books is highly suggestive for Luke's theology: he views Jesus as the fulfillment of the Davidic promises and the King who reigns eternally on the Davidic throne. What is primary for Luke is his presentation of Jesus as the fulfillment of God's promise to David (2 Sam 7:12–16). God will give Jesus "the throne of his father David" (Luke 1:32). "And he will reign [βασιλεύσει] over the house of Jacob forever, and of his kingdom [βασιλείας] there will be no end" (v. 33). Matthew and Luke are the only gospel writers who use the verb βασιλεύω ("to reign"; Matthew uses it of Archelaus; 2:22), and Luke alone employs it to describe the reign of Christ (1:33; cf. 19:14, 27). Although Matthew heavily emphasizes Jesus as "the son of David" (1:1; 9:27; 12:23; 15:22; 20:30, 31; 21:9, 15; 22:42), only Luke has "the house of David" (1:69; cf. v. 27), "the throne of David" (1:32), and Christ's eternal

---

16. Luke 1:27, 32, 69; 2:4 (2x), 11; Acts 1:16; 2:25, 29, 34. David is named a total of 13 times in Luke and 11 times in Acts. See Luke 3:31; 6:3; 18:38–39; 20:41, 42, 44; Acts 4:25; 7:45; 13:22 (2x), 34, 36; 15:16.

reign in fulfillment of the promise to David.[17] Through the prophet Nathan and in keeping with a long history of "seed" promises (e.g., Gen 3:15; 17:6; 35:11; 49:8–12), God promised David, "I will raise up your seed after you" (ἀναστήσω τὸ σπέρμα σου μετὰ σέ; 2 Sam 7:12 LXX; cf. Ps 132:11–12). God further promised an eternal house, kingdom, and throne (2 Sam 7:16).

Luke also ties this picture of Christ as a Davidite to the covenant with Abraham.[18] The "God of Israel . . . raised up a horn of salvation for us in the house of his servant David . . . to show mercy to our fathers and to remember his holy covenant, the oath he swore to our father Abraham" (Luke 1:68–73 NIV). The "horn of salvation" refers to Christ (cf. Ps 132:17). This same mercy (ἔλεος; 1:72) is found in the Magnificat when Mary prophesies, "He has helped his servant Israel, in remembrance of his mercy [ἐλέους], as he spoke to our fathers, to Abraham and to his offspring [τῷ σπέρματι αὐτου] forever" (Luke 1:54–55 ESV). These early references to David and Abraham provide an interpretive lens through which Luke's readers must view his narrative.

The frequency, location, and general use of βασιλεία ("kingdom") throughout Luke-Acts reinforce the observation that Jesus's Davidic reign is a central interest of Luke's. "Kingdom" and its cognates occur in reference to God or Christ about fifty times in Luke and about ten times in Acts, but the numerical count is not as significant as the location of the occurrences. In addition to the important reference in Luke 1:33, there is also a cluster of kingdom terms surrounding the passion narrative (22:16, 18, 29–30; 23:42, 51). Several passages focus particularly on the question of Jesus's identity as Christ and King (23:2–3, 37–38). Although "kingdom" occurs less frequently in Acts than in Luke's gospel, the double occurrence of the term in both Acts 1 (vv. 3, 6) and Acts 28 (vv. 28, 31) forms an inclusio around Acts, as various scholars have noted.[19] This strongly suggests that Luke purposely fashioned the narrative of Acts in such a way as to place the entire story within the context of the establishment of God's kingdom through Christ. This fits well with the emphasis on David.

---

17. Matthew mentions David seventeen times (more than the thirteen times in the Gospel of Luke and the seven times in Mark), but more than half of the occurrences are in reference to "the son of David."

18. O'Toole, "Acts 2:30 and the Davidic Covenant," 252.

19. E.g., Thompson, *Acts of the Risen Lord Jesus*, 44; Keener, *Acts: An Exegetical Commentary*, 1:670; Fitzmyer, *Acts of the Apostles*, 203n3.

The Center of Luke-Acts

Most of Mark's twenty references to the kingdom refer to "the kingdom of God." Both Luke and Matthew generally include Mark's kingdom themes, but they add numerous other kingdom sayings.[20] Although Luke shares with Matthew and Mark important scenes such as the mocking of Jesus as the king of the Jews (23:3, 37–38; cf. v. 2), he also emphasizes the royalty of Jesus in unique ways. His parable of the ten minas (19:11–27) differs from Matthew's parable of the talents in that the Lukan story depicts the enthronement of a king and the judgment on those who reject his reign, while Matthew's stewardship parable lacks the royal theme (25:14–30). Luke also uses a scene imbued with eschatological significance to cast Jesus in the role of one who confers a kingdom (22:29; cf. Matt 25:31–46). In Luke's narrative Jesus promises the disciples a kingdom and royal rule over Israel and that they may "eat and drink at my [μου] table in my [μου] kingdom" (Luke 22:30). This is the only place in the gospels where the possessive pronoun "my" is used with reference to Jesus's kingdom, and the only other similar occurrence is when the criminal crucified next to Jesus implores him: "Jesus, remember me when you come into your [σου] kingdom" (23:42). Jesus does not fully arrive in his kingdom until experiencing death, resurrection, and ascension, but he "is already granting royal clemency" to the penitent criminal (v. 43).[21]

All four gospels present Jesus as a king and record the epigraph on the cross, "the king of the Jews" (Matt 27:37b; Mark 15:26b; Luke 23:38b; John 19:19b), but Matthew twice records unique statements about Jesus as the "Son of God" in the account of the crucifixion (27:40, 43). This is consistent with his record of Peter's confession, which is also unique to

---

20. Both writers take an interest in the character of those who belong to the kingdom (Matt 5:3, 10; 8:11–12; 11:12; 13:38, 43; 19:14; 21:43; Luke 6:20; 12:32; 13:28–29; 14:15; 18:16–17), although Matthew says a little more about the least and greatest in it (Matt 5:19; 11:11; 18:1, 4; Luke 7:28). Both authors comment on the proximity of the kingdom, but Luke seems to take more interest in the timing of its arrival (Matt 3:2; 4:17; 6:10; 10:7; Luke 10:9, 11; 11:2, 20; 17:20–21; 19:11; 21:31; 23:51). Matthew and Luke share a concern with entrance into the kingdom (Matt 5:20; 7:21; 18:3; 19:23–24; 21:31; 23:13; Luke 16:16; 18:17, 24–25; 23:42), but Matthew especially incorporates kingdom similes (Matt 13:24, 31, 33, 44–45, 47; 18:23; 20:1; 22:2; 25:1; Luke 13:18, 20). Mark repeatedly emphasizes the labelling of Jesus as "the king of the Jews" (ὁ βασιλεὺς τῶν Ἰουδαίων; 15:2, 9, 12, 18, 26; cf. v. 32) during his trials. Matthew includes this element (27:11, 29, 37; cf. v. 42) but also clarifies Jesus's identity from the outset by citing the words of the would-be worshipers who sought the one "born king of the Jews" (2:2). Matthew also depicts Jesus as the King on the throne who gives a kingdom to his sheep (25:31–46).

21. Nolland, *Luke 18:35—24:53*, 1152.

Matthew: "You are the Christ, the Son of the Living God" (16:16). It is also consistent with his account of the voice from heaven at the transfiguration: "This is my beloved Son in whom I am well pleased, hear him" (17:5; cf. 3:17). In Matthew's crucifixion account Jesus is "the king of the Jews" (27:37), "the Son of God" (v. 40), "the king of Israel" (v. 42), and the "Son of God" again (v. 43).

Likewise, Luke tailors his account to draw attention to Jesus as the royal and exalted Christ. Luke adds new statements, the voice of the soldiers, and that of the dying criminals to present Jesus as "the Christ of God, the Chosen One" (23:35), "the king of the Jews" (v. 37), "the king of the Jews" again (v. 38), "the Christ" (v. 39), and one who has a "kingdom" (v. 42). While the notion of a royal Christ is not unique to Luke, it is particularly evident in his alternating of terms that the term "Christ" (χριστός) has inherent royal associations to Luke, even though, ironically, the characters express the thought in mockery and disdain. As in Matthew's gospel, the titles in the Third Gospel build on earlier statements. Only in Luke does Peter confess that Jesus is "the Christ of God" (9:20) and does the heavenly voice declare that "this is my Son, the Chosen One [ὁ ἐκλελεγμένος]" (v. 35).[22] The allusion to these texts at the crucifixion is significant because it places the events of the crucifixion within the framework of Jesus's prediction of his passion, resurrection, and transfiguration. Upon Peter's confession, Jesus insists, "It is necessary [δεῖ] for the Son of Man to suffer much, and to be rejected by the elders and chief priests and scribes, and to be killed, and on the third day to be raised" (9:22). Jesus then speaks of how he will respond to those who are ashamed of him "when he comes in his glory [ἐν τῇ δόξῃ αὐτου] and that of the Father and of the holy angels" (v. 26). Luke alone has "his glory" in reference to Jesus, while Matthew and Mark have "in the glory of his Father" (ἐν τῇ δόξῃ τοῦ πατρὸς αὐτου; Matt 16:27; Mark 8:38). The emphasis on "his glory" ties the narrative of Peter's confession to the transfiguration, where the disciples see "his glory" (Luke 9:32). Between the references to "glory," Jesus promises that some will "see the kingdom of God" (v. 27) and, given Luke's emphasis on "words" as a connection between the transfiguration (μετὰ τοὺς λόγους τούτους; v. 28) and the account of

---

22. Nolland, *Luke 18:35—24:53*, 1146.

Peter's confession (τοὺς ἐμοὺς λόγους; v. 26),[23] the disciples do become witnesses to the kingdom of God, "albeit in a proleptic way."[24]

Jesus asks the two on the road to Emmaus, "Was it not necessary [ἔδει] for the Christ to suffer these things and to enter into his glory [δόξαν αὐτοῦ]?" (Luke 24:26). He continues, "And beginning with Moses and with all the Prophets he interpreted to them in all the Scriptures the things concerning himself [περὶ ἑαυτου]" (v. 27). In a resurrection account unique to Luke, he implies the royal status of the Christ, associates resurrection with exaltation/glory, delineates the pathway to glory as suffering, and affirms the christocentric nature of all of Scripture. The latter point confirms that the multiple references to the Hebrew Scriptures in the transfiguration and crucifixion accounts are not accidental. Jesus is the Chosen One of Isa 42:1 (Luke 9:35); he is the fulfillment of the eschatological plan anticipated in Moses and Elijah (9:30); he has an "exodus" (ἔξοδον; v. 31), an experience on a mountain, a change in countenance, and an overshadowing cloud (vv. 28–36); and he must be heard (v. 35; cf. Deut 19:15).[25] Similarly, Peter expounds on how "the God of Abraham, and the God of Isaac, and the God of Jacob, the God of our fathers, glorified his servant [ἐδόξασεν τὸν παῖδα αὐτοῦ] Jesus" (Acts 3:13a). As Peter continues, it becomes evident that this glorification is parallel to Jesus's resurrection: "And you killed the Originator of Life [ἀρχηγὸν τῆς ζωῆς], whom God raised from the dead; we are witness of this" (v. 15; cf. 5:31).[26] Thus, the various royal terms and concepts evident in the high points of Luke's gospel come into full view in the early sermons of Peter, who declares that the risen Davidite is Lord and Christ (2:36).

---

23. Green, *Gospel of Luke*, 377. Marshall acknowledges both the kingdom's presence at the transfiguration and at the resurrection and Pentecost, but he is less enthusiastic about seeing the fulfilment of Jesus's kingdom promise at the transfiguration. Marshall, *Gospel of Luke*, 378–79.

24. Green, *Gospel of Luke*, 376.

25. See Green for these and other parallels between the transfiguration and the exodus. Green, *Gospel of Luke*, 377–78.

26. The term ἀρχηγός occurs only four times in the New Testament and is notoriously difficult to define. Müller notes that it is used exclusively of the exalted Christ. He translates Acts 3:15 as "one who leads the way into life" and places the emphasis on Jesus as leading the way to resurrection life. Müller, "Ἀρχηγός," 163. Anderson argues that "Originator" is a better fit with the genitive case, but Jesus as Originator guarantees the resurrection of his followers. It seems that some combination of Originator and Leader is in order. Anderson, *"But God Raised,"* 224–25; See also Keener, *Acts: An Exegetical Commentary*, 2:1096–99.

The Proclamation of the Kingdom in the Third Gospel

"Kingdom" occurs in the phrase "the kingdom of God" (ἡ βασιλεία τοῦ θεοῦ) thirty-eight times in Luke-Acts, and this phrase is often used as the object of proclamation. Luke places more emphasis on the proclamation of the kingdom than Matthew does (Matt 4:23; 9:35; 10:7; 24:14; Luke 4:43; 8:1; 9:2, 11, 60; 10:9, 11; 16:16). The kingdom is never the direct object of preaching in Mark, and only once is the nearness of it preached (1:15), but he frequently employs the noun "gospel" (εὐαγγέλιον; 1:1, 14–15; 8:35; 10:29; 13:10; 14:9; 16:15) and sometimes uses it as the object of preaching. Luke seldom uses the noun (Acts 15:7; 20:24) but engages the verb εὐαγγελίζω ("to preach good news") twenty-five times in Luke-Acts in keeping with Isaiah's use in the Septuagint (Isa 40:9 [2x]; 57:7 [2x]; 60:6; 61:1). Luke uses the combination of εὐαγγελίζω and the kingdom of God on four occasions (Luke 4:43; 8:1; 16:16; Acts 8:12). The first occurrence of this combination is revealing, for it follows shortly after Jesus's quotation of Isa 61:1 in the synagogue of Nazareth: "The Spirit of the Lord is on me because he has anointed me to preach good news [εὐαγγελίσασθαι] to the poor" (Luke 4:18a). Jesus states in 4:43, "Also in other cities it is necessary for me to preach the good news of the kingdom of God [εὐαγγελίσασθαί με δεῖ τὴν βασιλείαν τοῦ θεοῦ], because I was sent for this purpose." Both texts express the reason Jesus was "sent" (ἀπέσταλκέν, v. 18; ἀπεστάλην, v. 43). In fulfillment of the Isaianic expectation, Jesus preaches the good news, and the latter passage expresses the divine motivation with δεῖ ("it is necessary") while the former expresses it with the anointing of the Spirit. In this manner Luke associates the progression of the divine plan with the impetus of the Spirit. In addition, the content of the preaching is release and healing, summed up in a new Jubilee (4:18b, 19), and this parallels the kingdom of God in verse 43.[27] The conceptual parallel between Luke 4:18–19 and 43 also implies that the Spirit of the Lord has anointed Jesus to preach the kingdom of God.

The kingdom of God or its nearness is the object of speaking or preaching seven times in the Third Gospel (4:43; 8:1; 9:2, 11, 60; 10:9; 16:16) and it is sometimes directly associated with healing. When Jesus

---

27. Pao notes the rare Lukan term δεκτός ("acceptable") in 4:19, 24 and Acts 10:35. The occurrence in the latter text implies that the Gentiles will also experience this Jubilee. Pao, *Acts and the Isaianic New Exodus*, 71–75, 81; Tannehill also notices the parallelism between Luke 4:18–19 and the proclamation of the kingdom in 4:43. Tannehill, *Narrative Unity*, 1:68.

sends out the Twelve, two infinitives express their purpose: κηρύσσειν τὴν βασιλείαν τοῦ θεοῦ καὶ ἰᾶσθαι ("to preach the kingdom of God and to heal"; 9:2).[28] In 9:11 Jesus "was speaking to them concerning [περὶ] the kingdom of God, and he was healing those who needed healing."[29] Luke 10:9 also directly associates healing with the proclamation of the kingdom. If the earlier observation that the kingdom and healing are closely related and are both proclaimed through the anointing of the Spirit, then it is not likely that Luke omits the mention of the Spirit in the Beelzebub passage because he is consciously avoiding connecting the Spirit to the miraculous or to exorcism (11:20).[30] Neither does the absence of "to heal the brokenhearted" (ἰάσασθαι τοὺς συντετριμμένους τῇ καρδίᾳ; Isa 61:1b LXX) in Luke 4:18 signal an attempt to excise from Luke all attributions of healing to the Spirit.[31] The reason for the omission may be found in the addition of the phrase "to send away the oppressed in release" (ἀποστεῖλαι τεθραυσμένους ἐν ἀφέσει; Luke 4:18c; cf. Isa 58:6c).[32] Several scholars have noticed how the addition of this phrase results in two occurrences of ἄφεσις ("release") and thereby emphasizes Jesus's role in bringing release.[33] But at the same time the addition of θραύω ("to break in pieces")[34] has nearly the identical definition as συντρίβω ("to break into pieces, to shatter, to crush, to bruise"),[35] with both terms figuratively meaning "oppress." Thus, the similar concept of deliverance from oppression is contained in the additional quotation, so Luke may simply have left out the one phrase knowing that the addition of the other would cover similar ground. When Luke says Jesus was "anointed with the

---

28. The Markan parallel omits mention of the kingdom (6:7–11), and the Matthean parallel has the disciples preach the nearness of the kingdom rather than the kingdom itself (10:7), which is closer to Luke 10:9.

29. The use of περὶ ("concerning") is important to note in conjunction with the kingdom, as will be demonstrated shortly.

30. Menzies follows Schweizer in his interpretation of Lukan pneumatology as strictly prophetic. Menzies, *Empowered for Witness*, 112–16, 161–68; Schweizer, "Πνεῦμα, Πνευματικός," 407.

31. Contra Menzies, *Empowered for Witness*, 112; Rese also believes Luke omits the phrase in order to emphasize prophecy. *Alttestamentliche Motive*, 145.

32. The only change Luke makes to Isaiah's phrase is to change the form of the verb ἀποστέλλω from an imperative to an infinitive. The latter conforms better to Luke's list of infinitives.

33. See especially the discussion in Tannehill, *Narrative Unity*, 1:60–68.

34. Bauer, et al., *Greek-English Lexicon*, 363.

35. Louw and Nida, *Greek-English Lexicon*, 226, 227 (see sections 19.39, 46).

Holy Spirit and power" and was "healing all those who were oppressed [καταδυναστευομένους] by the devil" (Acts 10:38), he uses yet another term for oppression which has conceptual ties with θραύω.[36] Not surprisingly, καταδυναστεύω ("to oppress") has a direct link with the exodus (Exod 1:13 LXX; cf. 6:7). Luke seems to have no problem crediting the Holy Spirit as the source of power behind the deliverance from all forms of oppression.[37] This does not detract from Luke's obvious emphasis on prophetic proclamation, for what appears to be a Lukan redaction of Isa 61:1-2 does not omit healing altogether but leaves intact the proclamation of healing (κηρύξαι αἰχμαλώτοις ἄφεσιν καὶ τυφλοῖς ἀνάβλεψιν; Luke 4:18b; cf. 7:22) and emphasizes the preaching of a new Jubilee or new exodus by repeating the word κηρύξαι ("to proclaim") (instead of καλέσαι; "to call"; Isa 61:2a) in Luke 4:19 (κηρύξαι ἐνιαυτὸν κυρίου δεκτόν).

Much discussion surrounds the difference between Matthew's record of driving out demons "by the Spirit of God" (12:28) and Luke's version of exorcism "by the finger of God" (11:20). Opinions also divide over which author alters Q.[38] Matthew's reading may very well reflect the more original reading, but the reason for Lukan redaction is to emphasize Jesus's activity as a fulfillment of the expectation of a prophet like Moses. Edward Woods points out the connections between the transfiguration account, with its anticipation of an ἔξοδος ("exodus"; Luke 9:31) and a prophet like Moses who must be heard (αὐτοῦ ἀκούετε; 9:35c; Deut 18:15c LXX), and the following exorcism account (Luke 9:37-45), exorcism ministry of the seventy (10:10-24), and reference to "the finger of God" (11:20).[39] The most natural referent of the phrase occurs in Deut 8:15, where Pharaoh's magicians attribute the plague of gnats to "the finger of God." Various scholars have also argued that Luke's phrase no less refers to the Spirit of God than does Matthew's direct mention of the Spirit. While this may be true, a narrative reading of the text suggests that

---

36. Louw and Nida, *Greek-English Lexicon*, 245.

37. Hildebrandt is probably correct to suggest that Exod 15:8 and 10 refer to the Spirit of God rather than the wind (cf. Isa 63:11-12). Hildebrandt emphasizes God's Spirit as active in establishing the nation, but one can also see the Spirit as active in bringing deliverance to Israel. Hildebrandt, *Old Testament Theology*, 69-71.

38. E.g., these scholars hold that Luke retains the Q tradition: Fitzmyer, *Gospel According to Luke (X-XXIV)*, 918; Marshall, *Gospel of Luke*, 475-76; Haya-Prats, *Empowered Believers*, 10n16. Recent scholarship generally attributes "the finger of God" to Lukan redaction: Turner, *Power from on High*, 255-59; Menzies, *Empowered for Witness*, 161-63; Nolland, *Luke 9:21—18:34*, 639-40.

39. Woods, "Finger of God", 242-43.

Luke has not altogether removed πνεῦμα from the equation anyway. His substitution of "the Holy Spirit" (11:13) for Matthew's "good gifts" (7:11) not only concludes the discussion on prayer for the kingdom to come (Luke 11:2), but also forms a bridge to Jesus's claims about the arrival of the kingdom. Matthew's potential petitioners ask for bread/fish and do not receive a stone/snake (7:9–10), but Luke's ask for a fish/egg and do not receive a snake/scorpion (11:11–12). Jesus has just equated the exorcism ministry of the seventy to "authority to trample on snakes and scorpions" in 10:19, thus implying a clear contrast between the citizens of the kingdom who are graced with the Spirit and the kingdom of Beelzebub. Thus, Jesus's exorcism ministry manifests the gift of the Holy Spirit and signals the arrival of the kingdom. The position of the Spirit's mention in the narrative both anticipates how the disciples will overcome spiritual opposition in the future and reveals the empowering source behind the arrival of the kingdom in Christ's ministry.[40]

The Proclamation of the Kingdom in Acts

In Acts, all seven occurrences of the "kingdom of God" relate to its proclamation or teaching.[41] Luke's summary of Jesus's teaching during the forty days prior to his ascension as a time of "speaking the things concerning the kingdom of God" (1:3) reveals something of Luke's agenda. The parallel between Acts 1:3 and Luke 24:19 alerts the reader that the central message of the kingdom of God is Christ himself and involves the resurrection.[42] In 24:19 the risen Savior questions Cleopas and company

---

40. One can make a good case for Luke's inclusion of healing, miracles, and exorcism within the scope of the Spirit's empowering based on other considerations as well. For example, Luke's multiple references to the ministries of Elijah and Elisha in relation to Christ imply that his miracles were performed by the same empowering Spirit. The miracles that followed Jesus's anointing with the Spirit as well as the healing of the lame man following Pentecost imply the agency of the Spirit. Also, Acts 2:22 connects Jesus's anointing with signs, Acts 10:38 connects his anointing with healing, and the opening of blind eyes in Luke 7:22 alludes to Luke 4:18. Tannehill also notes that the "release" in Luke 4:18 includes exorcism. Tannehill, *Narrative Unity*, 1:64.

41. The word βασιλεία occurs only a total of eight times in Acts, and the only time it does not occur in the full phrase "the kingdom of God" is in 1:6, where the disciples inquire if Jesus is restoring the kingdom to Israel. In 14:22 Paul speaks of entering the kingdom of God, but this passage is also connected with teaching about the kingdom. For the proclamation of the kingdom of God in Acts, see 1:3, 8:12; 19:8; 20:25; 28:23, 31.

42. Cho, *Spirit and Kingdom*, 182–83.

about what things had recently transpired, and they respond, "The things concerning Jesus of Nazareth [τὰ περὶ Ἰησοῦ τοῦ Ναζαρηνοῦ], a man who was a prophet powerful in deed and word before God and all the people." Heightening the suspense and irony in the passage, the two go on to speak of their dismay over reports of Jesus's resurrection (vv. 22–24). Similarly, Acts commences by referring to the Gospel of Luke as an account "concerning all [περὶ πάντων] that Jesus began to do and teach" (Acts 1:1), with "convincing proofs" of his resurrection (v. 2), and with a summation of the content of Jesus's speaking: "the things concerning the kingdom of God" (τὰ περὶ τῆς βασιλείας τοῦ θεοῦ; v. 3). The message of the kingdom is the message about Jesus of Nazareth and, specifically, about his death and resurrection.

In Luke 24:25–26 Jesus upbraids the two travelers for their failure "to believe all that the prophets have spoken" and asks, "Was it not necessary [ἔδει] for the Christ to suffer these things and to enter into his glory?" The next verse is telling: "And beginning with Moses and all the prophets, he interpreted to them in all the Scriptures the things concerning himself [τὰ περὶ ἑαυτοῦ]." This pattern is evident in Jesus's claim that Isa 53:12 is about him: "For I say to you that what is written must [δεῖ] be fulfilled in me [ἐν ἐμοί]: 'And he was numbered with the lawless'; for what is written concerning me [περὶ ἐμοῦ] has its fulfillment" (Luke 22:37). In the final words of Jesus in the gospel, he claims "that it is necessary [δεῖ] for all the things which have been written in the Law of Moses and the Prophets and the Psalms concerning me [περὶ ἐμοῦ] to be fulfilled" (24:44). Luke's account neatly condenses the teaching of the Old Testament about Jesus into three infinitives. The Christ is "to suffer" and "to rise from the dead on the third day," and "repentance for the forgiveness of sins is to be preached in his name to all nations" (v. 47). The disciples are "witnesses," and Jesus will send them the promise of his Father and clothe them with power from on high (vv. 48–49). The verbal parallels between the opening of Acts and the end of Luke confirms that the essence of Jesus's discussion of the kingdom over the forty-day period is contained at the end of Luke 24, which highlights Jesus's suffering and resurrection, the proclamation of forgiveness to all nations, and the promise of the Spirit (vv. 46–49).

One can hardly fault the disciples for asking a natural question, given their familiarity with Jewish eschatological expectations and the kingdom content of Jesus's teaching. They inquire, "Lord, are you at this time restoring the kingdom to Israel?" (Acts 1:6),[43] but Jesus redirects the disciples' question about the timing of the kingdom to the coming empowerment of the Spirit to be his "witnesses" (1:8). A substantial number of scholars have rightly observed the prophetic nature of Spirit-empowered utterances in Luke-Acts, but the more significant point is that the utterances are not only prophetic, but christocentric. The Gospel of Luke is about Jesus (περὶ αὐτοῦ; 2:33) and Acts records the proclamation about him (περὶ τοῦ Ἰησου; 18:25).[44]

Luke's concern with offering "many convincing proofs" (πολλοῖς τεκμηρίοις; 1:3)[45] of Jesus's resurrection makes it evident that the disciples will chiefly bear witness to Christ's resurrection. As Acts progresses, the message about the kingdom of God, Jesus, and his resurrection become practically synonymous. David saw in advance and "spoke concerning [περὶ] the resurrection of the Christ" (2:31).[46] When the Samaritans believed Philip as he preached the good news concerning [ἐπίστευσαν τῷ Φιλίππῳ εὐαγγελιζομένῳ περὶ] the kingdom of God and the name of Jesus Christ, they were baptized, both men and women" (8:12). The parallelism between "the kingdom of God" and "the name of Jesus Christ" assumes the inherent royal dimensions of Luke's conception of "the name" of Jesus and of him as "Christ." Luke could scarcely have made it clearer that the Samaritans had become full-fledged members of the church. They believed (not only in Philip, but also the good news, which is in the dative case along with Philip);[47] they came under the rule of the kingdom

---

43. Keener, *Acts*, 1:682; Fitzmyer claims Jesus's reply was not intended as a rebuke. Fitzmyer, *Acts of the Apostles*, 205.

44. Luke uses περί ("concerning," "about") forty-five times in his gospel and seventy-two times in Acts, and it often is in reference to Jesus (Luke 2:17–18, 33, 38; 4:10, 14, 37; 5:15; 7:3, 17; 9:9; 22:37; 23:8; 24:4, 19, 27, 44; Acts 1:1; 2:31; 7:52; 8:12, 34; 13:29; 17:32; 18:25; 22:18; 23:6, 11; 24:21, 24; 25:19; 26:7; 28:23, 31).

45. Witherington comments on the use of τεκμηρίοις as necessary proof: "Quintilian (Inst. Or. 5.9.3) puts it more strongly: τεκμηρία involve a conclusion, 'those which cannot be otherwise are called τεκμηρία by the Greeks, because they are indications from which there is no getting away.'" Witherington, *Acts of the Apostles*, 108.

46. Stephen also credits the Old Testament prophets with announcing in advance "about (περὶ) the coming of the Righteous One" (7:52).

47. Montague views the Samaritan episode as an "exception" in the normal pattern of receiving the Spirit at conversion. He explains the "exception" by arguing that their faith was tainted by associations with witchcraft. Evidence for this faulty faith is that they "believed Philip" rather than in the Lord. But Luke surely intends the reader to see the participle εὐαγγελιζομένῳ as typical of his salvation language. Montague also argues that Philip's ministry was not "officially commissioned by the Jerusalem church"

of God (the reign of Christ); they submitted to the name (authority) of Jesus as the Messiah; they were baptized as an act of submission to King Jesus; and both men and women participated as a Lukan illustration of salvation for all.[48]

One gets the impression that in Luke's day controversy existed over the referent of Isa 53. The Ethiopian eunuch reads Isa 53:7–8 and urgently entreats Philip: "Concerning whom [περὶ τίνος] does the prophet say this, concerning himself [περὶ ἑαυτοῦ] or concerning someone else [περὶ ἑτέρου τινός]?" (Acts 8:32–34). Isaiah then serves as the launching pad for Philip's preaching the good news about Jesus (v. 35; cf. 13:29). Luke can easily summarize the message as concerning Jesus (22:18; 23:11), the resurrection (17:32; 23:6; 24:21; 26:7), or the kingdom of God (19:8). Even Festus grasps the central idea when he explains Paul's case as "concerning a certain Jesus who had died, whom Paul claims is alive" (25:19).

The final occurrences of "the kingdom of God" in Acts both frame the book and encapsulate much of what Luke has previously established. "Paul was declaring and solemnly testifying about the kingdom of God [διαμαρτυρόμενος τὴν βασιλείαν τοῦ θεοῦ], and persuading them concerning Jesus [πείθων τε αὐτοὺς περὶ τοῦ Ἰησοῦ] from both the Law of Moses and the Prophets, from morning till evening" (Acts 28:23). The parallelism between the two present participles and their two objects illustrates the indissoluble relationship between the kingdom and Jesus and identifies the center of the testimony in Luke-Acts. Luke finally closes the book with Paul "preaching the kingdom of God [κηρύσσων τὴν βασιλείαν τοῦ θεοῦ] and teaching the things concerning the Lord Jesus Christ [διδάσκων τὰ περὶ τοῦ κυρίου Ἰησοῦ Χριστοῦ] with all boldness and unhindered" (v. 31). Just as in 28:23, Luke employs parallel participles with parallel objects along with his favorite proclamation preposition περί

---

and the delay allowed for a display of unity. Montague, *Holy Spirit*, 293–94.

48. Turner does a good job of summarizing the various views on the reason for the chronological separation between belief and reception of the Spirit in Acts 8. He effectively refutes Dunn's position that the Samaritan faith was deficient; however, Turner concludes that the episode is "anomalous" because it does not conform to Luke's pattern in Acts 2:38–39. While Luke may very well see a significant time span between salvation and Spirit reception as less than the ideal, this is not because he identifies regeneration with an experience of empowerment for service. It is problematic when scholars isolate more exceptions to a supposed pattern in Lukan theology than examples of the pattern. Turner, *Power from on High*, 360–75, especially 362–67, 374; Dunn, *Baptism in the Holy Spirit*, 46–49, 55–72; For a view that emphasizes the oneness of the church, see Thiselton, *Holy Spirit*, 65.

("concerning"). Jesus is given his threefold title with the pregnant terms "Lord" and "Christ," rounding out the parallelism and positioning "the Lord Jesus Christ" squarely in the center of "the kingdom of God." The Scriptures feature prominently by way of general reference (v. 23) and direct quotation (vv. 26–27; cf. Isa 6:9–10),[49] and Paul specifically attributes the quotation from Isaiah to the Holy Spirit (Acts 28:25). The attempt to narrow Luke's emphasis to only one body of literature is fruitless, for the Holy Spirit also speaks through David's psalms (1:16, 20; 4:25)[50] and Luke insists that all branches of Scripture are christocentric (Luke 24:44). The Spirit has spoken prophetically about Israel's opposition to the kingdom message, but Paul implies that the Spirit will continue to speak through messengers who testify to Christ (Acts 28:25–28).

The way Luke speaks of the kingdom of God, Jesus, and the resurrection in a practically interchangeable way and introduces them in an almost formulaic manner with περί ("concerning") suggests that Jesus is the key figure and his resurrection is the key event in the broader concept of the kingdom. The Spirit of God receives attention in Luke 24, Acts 1, and Acts 28. Jesus taught about the kingdom "through the Holy Spirit" (1:2) and promised the disciples an empowering experience (Luke 24:49; Acts 1:4, 5, 8) to be witnesses of the reality of his resurrection. In short, the Spirit is the empowering agent behind the testimony to Christ and his resurrection, both through Scripture and Spirit-filled messengers. The use of kingdom terminology in association with this is appropriate, as the resurrection is the means of Jesus's exaltation as King and the spread of the gospel is the increase of his kingdom.

The Word of God

Just as the kingdom of God relates to the person of Christ and his resurrection, so does ὁ λόγος ("the word") in Lukan usage. He incorporates the term thirty-two times in his gospel and sixty-five times in Acts. Although there is some overlap with the use of ῥῆμα ("word," "report"; occurring only nineteen times in Luke and fourteen times in Acts), he clearly prefers λόγος, and this term takes on somewhat of a technical use, especially in Acts. To illustrate, note the parallel but distinctive use of the two terms

---

49. Pao sees Luke's quotations of Isaiah as important indicators of Luke's hermeneutical framework in Luke-Acts. Pao, *Acts and the Isaianic New Exodus*, 70–110.

50. See also Acts 7:51–53 and possibly 15:28.

in Acts 10:44: "While Peter was still speaking these words [τὰ ῥήματα ταῦτα], the Holy Spirit fell on all those hearing the word [τὸν λόγον]." Luke often uses ῥῆμα to describe the particular words someone utters, but he usually uses λόγος to refer to the message of Christ.[51] The following survey reviews Luke's specialized use of λόγος, usually occurring in the singular in this regard, and especially taking on a clear connection with the proclamation of Christ in Acts.

That "the word" can refer to Christ directly is apparent from the opening of Luke's gospel, where he refers to his sources as "eyewitnesses and servants of the word" (1:2). Hearing "the word of God" is important in Luke's gospel (5:1; 8:21; 11:28), and he converts the farmer's sowing of the seed in Mark 4:14 to "the seed is the word of God" in Luke 8:11 (cf. Matt 13:18–20).[52] The narrative in Acts more often includes "the word of God" (Acts 4:31; 6:2, 7; 8:14; 11:1; 12:24; 13:5, 7, 46; 17:13; 18:11) or the similar expression "the word of the Lord" (Acts 8:25; 13:44, 48–49; 15:35–36; 16:32; 19:10), but often simply gives the shorter version, "the word."

A substantial amount of discussion surrounds the meaning of Luke's summary statements: "And the word of God was growing and the number of disciples in Jerusalem was multiplying exceedingly" (Καὶ ὁ λόγος τοῦ θεοῦ ηὔξανεν καὶ ἐπληθύνετο ὁ ἀριθμὸς τῶν μαθητῶν ἐν Ἰερουσαλὴμ σφόδρα; Acts 6:7); "But the word of God was growing and multiplying" (Ὁ δὲ λόγος τοῦ θεοῦ ηὔξανεν καὶ ἐπληθύνετο; 12:24); "So with power the word of the Lord was growing and becoming strong" (Οὕτως κατὰ κράτος τοῦ κυρίου ὁ λόγος ηὔξανεν καὶ ἴσχυεν; 19:20). Various scholars have noted the close connection with the Septuagint of Exod 1:7: "But the sons of Israel grew and multiplied and became numerous and were becoming very, very strong, and the land was multiplying them" (οἱ δὲ υἱοὶ Ισραηλ ηὐξήθησαν καὶ ἐπληθύνθησαν καὶ χυδαῖοι ἐγένοντο καὶ κατίσχυον σφόδρα σφόδρα ἐπλήθυνεν δὲ ἡ γῆ αὐτούς).[53] Pao finds in these passages a

---

51. Pao draws some clear distinctions between the two terms. Pao, *Acts and the Isaianic New Exodus*, 147–48. The term ῥῆμα is sometimes used in reference to a report, an event, or a prophetic utterance (Luke 1:38; 2:17, 19, 29; 3:2; 22:61; Acts 11:16). However, these passages refer to the utterances of specific personages, thus ῥῆμα is not used in a technical way to describe prophetic utterances as is commonly thought in some circles in popular movements. Kodell also notes the use of ῥῆμα for individual utterances. Kodell, "Word of God Grew," 509n1.

52. Kodell, "Word of God Grew," 505.

53. Keener notes that readers familiar with the Septuagint would have recognized the association with Exod 1:7 and the association with the be-fruitful-and-multiply

"hypostatization" of the word wherein "Luke understands the word as an independent reality that possesses an active will."[54] He views the word as prevailing, even in the face of opposition, and this "hypostatization" fits well with the exodus and Isaiah backdrop of the growth of the community in Acts.[55] While there is much to glean from Pao, it seems preferable to view the independence of the word in these passages as more closely related to the prophetic empowering of the word that is so heavily emphasized in Luke-Acts (Luke 21:33; 24:44; Acts 1:8; cf. Isa 55:10, 11),[56] and, as I will endeavor to demonstrate below, the essential element of the word in Acts is the life-giving message of the resurrection (Acts 13:26–49).[57]

At Pentecost Peter bids the Jewish men (ἄνδρες Ἰουδαῖοι) to pay attention to his "words" (τὰ ῥήματά μου; Acts 2:14c). There is a natural break in the message when he makes a similar appeal following the quotation from Joel: "Men, Israelites, listen to these words" (Ἄνδρες Ἰσραηλῖται, ἀκούσατε τοὺς λόγους τούτους; v. 22). At this point the subject of the resurrection and enthronement of Jesus dominates the speech until the narrator's voice returns (v. 37). Peter gives final instructions on repentance, water baptism, and Spirit reception in response to the audience's appeal, and the narrator summarizes how Peter "with many other words [ἑτέροις τε λόγοις πλείοσιν] solemnly testified" about their need to be saved (v. 40). The narrator gives a final summary describing how "those who accepted his word" (οἱ μὲν οὖν ἀποδεξάμενοι τὸν λόγον αὐτοῦ) were baptized and their numbers increased (v. 41). The final summary of the words as a "word" therefore includes a heavy emphasis on the resurrection/exaltation of Christ and a warning to repent of murdering him.

"The word" is once again used in a summary statement after the proclamation of the resurrection in the next story: "And many of those who heard the word [ἀκουσάντων τὸν λόγον] believed, and the number of men became about 5000" (Acts 4:4). Peter's speech following the healing of the lame man emphasizes the resurrection (3:13–14, 22, 26), and immediately

---

formula. Keener, *Acts*, 2:1290; Pao, *Acts and the Isaianic New Exodus*, 167–69; Kodell, "Word of God Grew," 510–11; Rosner, "Progress of the Word," 223; Tannehill, *Narrative Unity*, 2:82.

54. Pao, *Acts and the Isaianic New Exodus*, 160.
55. Pao, *Acts and the Isaianic New Exodus*, 160–80.
56. Keener appears to lean toward this understanding. Keener, *Acts*, 2:1289.
57. Pao's hypothesis that the word travels through Acts in a linear fashion runs into difficulty when Acts fails to produce any mention of λόγος in Rome or after Acts 22:22. Pao, *Acts and the Isaianic New Exodus*, 155.

before the summary of the people's faith in the word the reader learns that the apostles are arrested for teaching the people and proclaiming "in Jesus the resurrection from the dead" (4:2b). Peter, not demoralized by the arrest but "filled with the Holy Spirit" (v. 8), credits "the name of Jesus Christ of Nazareth" with the healing, confronts his captors with their murderous act, and proclaims the resurrection of Jesus (vv. 10–11). Upon release and further threats, the gathered believers petition the Lord: "Grant that your servants may speak your word with all boldness" (δὸς τοῖς δούλοις σου μετὰ παρρησίας πάσης λαλεῖν τὸν λόγον σου; 4:29b). The answer to prayer is described in similar terms: "And they were all filled with the Holy Spirit and were speaking the word of God with boldness" (καὶ ἐπλήσθησαν ἅπαντες τοῦ ἁγίου πνεύματος καὶ ἐλάλουν τὸν λόγον τοῦ θεοῦ μετὰ παρρησίας; v. 31b). Another summary passage immediately follows and prepares the reader for the selflessness of Barnabas and the selfishness of Ananias and Sapphira (4:32–37), but the summary also highlights the central element of apostolic proclamation: "And with great power [δυνάμει] the apostles were giving testimony [τὸ μαρτύριον] of the resurrection of the Lord Jesus [τοῦ κυρίου Ἰησοῦ]" (v. 33a).[58]

Several points deserve mentioning. First, "the word of God" (τὸν λόγον τοῦ θεοῦ) in Acts 2–4 is not as general an expression as one might think; it is clearly and consistently associated with the resurrection. Second, the filling experiences of the believers (4:8, 31) are following the anticipated pattern of Luke 12:12[59] and Acts 1:8; that is, the Spirit empowers believers to testify in the face of opposition (the Spirit does not baptize them into the body of Christ) and that testimony is specifically to the living status of Christ. Third, Luke's summary includes "of the Lord" (τοῦ κυρίου) in describing Jesus's resurrection, reflecting the clearly articulated message of resurrection/enthronement at Pentecost. Resurrection is never distant from enthronement in Lukan Christology. Thus, if this pattern holds in Acts, the word of God is not any general word and the Spirit does not empower for any general purpose; the Spirit primarily empowers testimony to the resurrected and exalted Christ.

---

58. That the community was experiencing the empowering of the Holy Spirit is evident from Acts 4:31, but I suspect that the apostles are singled out in verse 33 because of the close connection with the word μαρτύριον. For Luke, this word often signifies the eyewitness testimony of Jesus's resurrection and not witnessing in the modern, general sense of the word.

59. Mittelstadt, *Spirit and Suffering in Luke-Acts*, 70, 80–84.

The Center of Luke-Acts

In Acts 6 the apostles refused to be distracted from the ministry of the word (vv. 2, 4) so that "the word of God grew" (v. 7a), but Philip's preaching in Samaria offers more definition of "the word." The parallelism is revealing: "Those who were scattered went about preaching the word [εὐαγγελιζόμενοι τὸν λόγον]" (8:4). "And Philip went down to the city of Samaria and preached Christ to them [ἐκήρυσσεν αὐτοῖς τὸν Χριστόν]" (v. 5). To preach the word meant to preach Christ. Responding in a similar fashion as the Jews did to Peter's inaugural sermons (2:41; 4:3),[60] the Samaritans "believed Philip as he preached the good news [εὐαγγελιζομένῳ] concerning the kingdom of God and the name of Jesus Christ" and "were baptized" (8:12). To the Jerusalem apostles this meant that "Samaria had accepted the word of God" (δέδεκται ἡ Σαμάρεια τὸν λόγον τοῦ θεοῦ; v. 14; cf. ἀποδεξάμενοι τὸν λόγον αὐτοῦ; 2:41). The narrator concludes the episode: "Now when they had solemnly testified [διαμαρτυράμενοι] and spoken the word of the Lord, they returned to Jerusalem, and many villages of the Samaritans were evangelized [εὐηγγελίζοντο]" (v. 25).[61] "The word" at Samaria is that of Christ, the kingdom of God, the name of Jesus Christ, and the Lord (Jesus). "The word" is obviously christocentric, and the similarities to Peter's sermons as well as the christologically loaded term διαμαρτυράμενοι (used for testimony to Christ, and especially as risen; 2:40; 10:42; 23:11) hint at the implicit assumption that faith has the resurrected Christ as object.

"The word" appears again in Peter's speech in Acts 10: "The word which he sent to the sons of Israel, preaching good news of peace through Jesus Christ—this one is Lord of all" (τὸν λόγον [ὃν] ἀπέστειλεν τοῖς υἱοῖς Ἰσραὴλ εὐαγγελιζόμενος εἰρήνην διὰ Ἰησοῦ Χριστοῦ, οὗτός ἐστιν πάντων κύριος; v. 36).[62] C. K. Barrett voices the frustration of many over the perplexing Greek construction of Acts 10:36-38: "It is so difficult as to be untranslatable."[63] The verse as it stands in the Nestle-Aland text reads more like a title than a complete sentence, and most scholars view the final phrase as parenthetical, even if they see it as "the theme of the speech

---

60. The similar response to the initial converts gives additional confirmation of the genuineness of the Samaritan's conversion.

61. Although it is sometimes difficult to ascertain whether Luke means "Lord Jesus" or "Lord God," the presence of "the name of the Lord Jesus" in verse 16 and the parallel "solemnly testifying" in verse 25 suggests that the Lord in view is Jesus.

62. Textual evidence regarding the inclusion of ὃν is divided.

63. Barrett, *Acts of the Apostles*, 1:521.

conceptually."[64] Despite the grammatical difficulties, there may be some good reasons why Luke placed "the word" (τὸν λόγον) in the accusative case at this juncture in Peter's speech. Its location adds emphasis; it reflects Luke's habit of leading phrases in speeches with words (often pronouns) in the accusative case, thereby forming a grammatical connection with this structure in Peter's Pentecostal sermon (e.g., Acts 2:22–24, 32);[65] and "the word" matches the concluding summary in Acts 10:44: "While Peter was still speaking these words [τὰ ῥήματα ταῦτα] the Holy Spirit fell upon all those hearing the word [τὸν λόγον]."[66] This frame construction suggests that τὸν λόγον serves as a technical term referring to the essential elements of the gospel, including Jesus's life and ministry, death, resurrection, and exaltation (vv. 37–42).

The emphasis on Jesus's exaltation forms a second framing element. Jesus Christ as Lord of all (Acts 10:36) relates conceptually to "this is the one appointed by God as Judge of the living and the dead" (v. 42).[67] The Lord of all is Judge of all. The emphasis on Jesus's resurrection on the third day (v. 40), his appearance (v. 40), and his eating and drinking with the witnesses after he rose from the dead (v. 41) comports well with this emphasis on Christ's exalted position and identity and the universal availability of the gospel so central to Luke's interests. Thus, Luke provides a one-line description of whom "the word" is about: "Jesus Christ, this one is Lord of all." While "the word" is somewhat more encompassing in this passage,[68] the accent remains on the resurrection as the key event making possible the primary identification of "Jesus Christ—this one is Lord of all." Once again, the apostles acknowledged that the Gentiles "accepted [ἐδέξαντο] the word of God" (11:1b; cf. 2:41; 8:14).

---

64. Bock, *Acts*, 397.

65. This has to do with clearly identifying Jesus and will receive further elaboration later.

66. Scholars have offered a variety of explanations for the difficult Greek. Longenecker attributes it to Peter's lack of eloquence in speaking Greek to his Gentile audience. Thus, Luke follows Peter's speech quite closely here. His suggestion may partially explain the difficult Greek, but the literary reasons offered above and the attempt to draw parallels with Acts 2 by placing a series of accusatives in prominent places are also contributing factors. Longenecker, "Acts of the Apostles," 392.

67. Fitzmyer and Bock also make this conceptual connection. Fitzmyer, *Acts of the Apostles*, 466; Bock, *Acts*, 399–400.

68. Peter summarizes his message at Cornelius's house as "the word of the gospel" (τὸν λόγον τοῦ εὐαγγελίου; 15:7), employing a noun rarely used (εὐαγγέλιον; cf. Acts 20:24) in Luke's writings.

The λόγος ("word") is used as a shorthand term in Acts 11:19 (also 12:24; 13:5, 7), but the context makes it clear that this is the preaching of the good news about "the Lord Jesus" (v. 20c). After Paul finishes reviewing Israel's history at Pisidian Antioch, he transitions into his message of the resurrection with this line: "Men and brothers, sons of the family of Abraham and those among you who fear God, to us this word of salvation [ὁ λόγος τῆς σωτηρίας ταύτης] has been sent" (13:26). Paul argues the case for the resurrection in a manner similar to what Peter had done (vv. 30–37), and the summary of the preaching is repeatedly called "the word of the Lord" (vv. 44, 48, 49) as well as "the word of God" (v 46). This sermon is particularly significant because it presents Paul preaching the same word of resurrection (vv. 30–37) and salvation (vv. 26, 46–48) as Peter preached.

Once Peter and Paul have both established their use of "the word" in reference to the message of Jesus, and particularly of his resurrection and enthronement, there is little need to explain it in the later chapters of Acts. The shorthand expression occurs often (14:3, 25, 35–36; 16:6, 32; 17:11, 13; 18:5, 11; 19:10, 20; 20:32) with little or no defining context. The important point for this discussion is that the word of God, like the kingdom of God, focuses largely on the resurrection of Christ, so that the Lukan expressions for the content of the preaching are essentially christocentric and practically euphemisms for the resurrection in the narrative of Acts. That the Spirit empowers the preaching in the Lukan narrative scarcely needs defending, but the preaching is not public speaking in general. The speaking the Spirit inspires is the resurrection message of the Lord Jesus Christ.

Summary

Luke had several purposes in mind when he wrote Luke-Acts, but the central idea that towers above all others and contextualizes the others is the identity of Jesus as Lord and Christ. Two of the six passages that identify him as Lord and Christ frame Luke-Acts, while the other four occur at pivotal points in the narrative. The identifying terms point to the royal status of Jesus, and this is consistent with Luke's emphasis on the kingdom. He is especially concerned to present Jesus as a royal Davidite, and the unique ways he focuses on the kingdom in comparison to the other gospels makes this interest evident. The transfiguration manifests the royal glory of Christ, and this glory is also related to Jesus's resurrection.

The content of the preaching in Luke and Acts reveals Luke's interest in the kingdom concept and in his concern to present the Spirit as the one who energizes the proclamation. In Luke's gospel the Spirit anoints Jesus to preach the good news of the kingdom, and this message includes both healing and deliverance. In Acts the proclamation of the kingdom is the proclamation of Jesus and the message of his resurrection. The testimony of the Scriptures and of the disciples alike "concern" Christ, and the proclamation of "the word" is the proclamation of the resurrection of the Lord Jesus Christ.

With Christ in his proper place at the center of Luke-Acts, the discussion now turns toward an investigation of how the resurrection and the Spirit both function in relation to Jesus as Lord and Christ.

7

The Resurrection and the Spirit as Identifiers of the Lord Jesus Christ

IN THE PREVIOUS DISCUSSION I argued that Luke writes to demonstrate that the man from Nazareth is "the Lord Jesus Christ," that this central christological claim is foundational for the universal availability of salvation, and that the Spirit-anointed preaching of Christ focuses largely on his resurrection. Thus, there is an apologetic element to Luke's writings, and the Scriptures are the primary tool he uses to establish the identity of Jesus as Lord and Christ. Luke draws on various Old Testament themes and patterns to explain to Theophilus how a crucified man could be Lord and Christ. Jesus fulfills the promises to Abraham; he is a prophet like Moses, recapitulating the wilderness wanderings and accomplishing a new exodus; he fulfills the pattern of Elijah and Elisha; he is the Davidic king; and he is the servant from Isaiah. Luke also enlists various personages as witnesses to Jesus's exalted status and records miraculous events and healings to point in this direction. The following discussion highlights how two of Luke's most prominent themes—the resurrection and the Holy Spirit—function as key identifiers of the Lord Jesus Christ. Without the merging of these two themes in identifying Jesus, there would be no "Lord and Christ" in Acts 2:36.

The Spirit as Identifier of Jesus

In the previous chapter I pointed out how Luke views the Scriptures as the voice of the Spirit (Acts 1:16; 28:25) and as essentially christocentric in nature (4:25). Stephen also describes the opposition of the Jewish Council to the prophets, "who announced beforehand about the coming of the Righteous One" (7:52b), as their "always opposing the Holy Spirit" (v. 51c). However, the Spirit not only identifies Jesus as Christ through the ancient prophets, but he also identifies him in Luke's birth and inauguration narratives. The result of the Spirit's overshadowing of Mary is that "the holy one to be born will be called the Son of God" (Luke 1:35c), and Elizabeth prophesies by the Spirit that Mary is "the mother of my Lord" (vv. 41, 43b).[1]

Simeon, the Spirit, and the Lord's Christ

The narrative of Simeon's encounter with Jesus and his parents develops the theme of universal salvation[2] but also functions to clearly identify Jesus as the key to this salvation. Simeon has stellar qualifications for this encounter, including the prophetic presence of the thrice-mentioned Spirit in his life (Luke 2:25-27). The setting in the temple and Simeon's long wait for "the consolation of Israel" prepares the reader for a significant moment in redemptive history. The identification of Jesus comes through the Spirit's revelation that Simeon would see "the Lord's Christ/Messiah/Anointed" (τὸν χριστὸν κυρίου; 2:26) prior to the elderly prophet's death. No identical possessive phrase occurs in the New Testament, although Acts 4:26 is similar;[3] this passage quotes Ps 2:2 (LXX) and records how the rulers rose up "against the Lord and against his anointed" (κατὰ τοῦ κυρίου καὶ κατὰ τοῦ χριστοῦ αὐτου). However, the first occurrence of a similar phrase in the Old Testament comes in Hannah's prophetic praise, where the Lord "will exalt the horn of his anointed" (ὑψώσει κέρας χριστοῦ αὐτοῦ; 1 Sam 2:10 LXX). Similar phrasing occurs in a few other passages,[4] but the exact phrase "Lord's anointed" (χριστὸν κυρίου) is common in reference to Saul and David (1 Sam 26:9, 11, 16, 23; 2 Sam 1:14, 16; 2:5; 19:22) and is used once of Jehu (2 Chr 22:7). Luke appears to preserve the antiquated phrase because of its royal, Davidic

---

1. Zechariah also prophesies by the Spirit (Luke 1:67) a raising up of a "horn of salvation" (v. 69) and identifies John as a prophet who prepares the way for this Lord and Savior (v. 76).

2. See the discussion on salvation in Tannehill, *Narrative Unity*, 1:38-44.

3. Cf. Luke 9:20; 23:35; Acts 3:18; Rev 11:15; 12:10.

4. 1 Sam 12:3; 16:6; 24:7, 11; 2 Sam 23:1; Ps 20:7 (LXX); 27:8; 89:51; Amos 4:13; Lam 4:20; Sir 46:19; *Pss. Sol.* 17:32; 18:7.

implications, and the use of "the Lord's Christ" (τὸν χριστὸν κυρίου) identifies the "consolation" as the anointed one, the Messiah.[5]

Further identification takes place in the Nunc Dimittis (Luke 2:28–32), when Simeon declares that the babe in his arms is the fulfillment of God's promise to him and that he has seen God's salvation (Isa 40:5; 52:10) and light for the Gentiles and Israel alike (42:6; 49:6). Simeon further identifies Jesus as the center of the falling and rising theme that Luke develops in his gospel (Luke 2:34–35). What is important to keep in mind is that Luke has emphatically credited the Holy Spirit with these christocentric, prophetic utterances and with the identification of Jesus as the Christ. Anna, as a devout "prophetess" (v. 36), confirms by the Spirit Simeon's identification when she speaks "about" Jesus (περὶ αὐτοῦ) "to all those who were waiting for the redemption of Jerusalem" (2:38b).

The Messiah, the Spirit, and the Resurrection in Judaism

Simeon and Anna serve as additional witnesses among the devout Jews in the birth narratives who expect a coming Messiah, and this expectation is not a fabrication of the writers of the gospels.[6] Although there was some diversity of thought regarding messianic expectations during the Second Temple period,[7] the Psalms of Solomon evince a first-century-BC hope of a Messiah that combines several elements of the Hebrew tradition found also in Luke's writings.[8] The psalmist grieves the humiliation of Jerusalem, but he anticipates a reversal of circumstances and praises God at the end of the psalm (2:19–35). The reversal distinguishes between the destinies of the godly and the unrighteous: "He is the one who raises [ἀνιστῶν] me into glory and puts to sleep the arrogant unto eternal destruction in dishonor" (*Pss. Sol.* 2:31). The sinner "fell . . . and he will not rise up" (ἔπεσεν . . . καὶ οὐκ ἀναστήσεται; 3:10b; cf. Luke 2:34). The

---

5. Danker, *Jesus and the New Age*, 64.

6. Contra William Scott Green, who holds that the notion of messianic expectation was largely the invention of the New Testament writers. Green, "Messiah in Judaism," 1–5.

7. For a good discussion of the Jewish expectations of a Davidic Messiah, see Strauss, *Davidic Messiah*, 35–74; Marshall sees the title "Christ" used in Acts 17:3 as more primitive than some have suggested and not an example of Luke's reading a later notion back into the early church. Marshall, "Resurrection in the Acts," 98.

8. Wright dates these psalms to between 70 and 45 BC, and Evans dates them to about 50 BC. Wright, "Psalms of Solomon," 640–41; Evans, *Ancient Texts*, 58.

sinner has everlasting destruction (*Pss. Sol.* 3:11), "but those who fear the Lord will rise [ἀναστήσονται] unto eternal life" (3:12b; cf. 13:11). For this psalmist, reversal includes the resurrection of the righteous, while sinners inherit Hades (14:9; 15:10). The psalmist had even sunk so low at one point that his "soul was poured out to death, at the gates of Hades with the sinner" (16:2), which is similar to the earlier Hebrew notion of dire circumstances as a tasting of death. The psalmist expresses his alienation from God in terms of Isaiah's suffering servant, who "poured out his soul to death and was numbered with the transgressors" (53:12b).

The final chapters (*Pss. Sol.* 17–18) contain an impressive number of references to a Davidic kingdom and Messiah.[9] The psalmist cites the promises to David in 2 Sam 7 (*Pss. Sol.* 17:4) and appeals to the Lord to "raise up for them their king, the son of David" (17:21; cf. Luke 18:38, 39).[10] The psalmist emphasizes the Messiah's reign of righteousness (*Pss. Sol.* 17:26–32; cf. Isa 11:4, 5) and refers to him as a king who is "Christ the Lord" (χριστὸς κύριος; *Pss. Sol.* 17:32; cf. 18:7).[11] The only other place this double title occurs in biblical and Jewish literature is in Luke 2:11,[12] and Acts 2:36 provides the interpretive key to this passage. Luke sees both words as titles defining who Jesus is: "Lord and Christ" (κύριον ... καὶ χριστόν). The title χριστός ("Christ") largely maintains its meaning from the Hebrew Scriptures in Luke-Acts, for it has both royal and pneumatic associations,[13] and every one of the twelve occurrences of "Christ" in Luke's gospel directly relates to Jesus's identification.[14] Once again, the *Psalms of Solomon* provide a glimpse of these messianic expectations in at least one segment of Jewish society. The Messiah will "drive away sinners

---

9. Strauss goes so far as to say that chapter 17 "represents the strongest expression of this hope in the Second Temple period." Strauss, *Davidic Messiah*, 40.

10. Nolland points out that only in *Pss. Sol.* 17:21 is the phrase "Son of David" used as a messianic title before the New Testament. Nolland, *Luke 18:35—24:53*, 972.

11. This reading assumes the unamended text. Wright argues that there is neither textual evidence nor theological necessity to justify amending the text to χριστὸς κυρίου as found in Rahlfs's *Septuaginta*. Wright, "Psalms of Solomon," 667 n. z; Rahlfs and Hanhart, *Septuaginta*, 2:488.

12. It also occurs in Lam 4:20 (LXX), but this is apparently a mistranslation of the Hebrew text מְשִׁיחַ יְהוָה.

13. Regarding pneumatic associations, see for example Luke 3:15–16; Acts 2:26–38; 10:36–38. This will receive further discussion below.

14. Luke 2:11, 26; 3:15; 4:41; 9:20; 20:41; 22:67; 23:2, 35, 39; 24:26, 46. This trend continues in Acts, but there the use broadens out to also include functioning in the name of Christ (e.g., 3:6; 8:12; 10:48). However, even those passages play somewhat of a role in identifying Jesus in the narrative.

The Resurrection and the Spirit as Identifiers of the Lord Jesus Christ

by the strength of his word" (17:36b; cf. Isa 11:4), and he will not weaken because God made him "powerful in the Holy Spirit and wise [δυνατὸν ἐν πνεύματι ἁγίῳ καὶ σοφὸν] in the counsel of understanding with strength and righteousness" (*Pss. Sol.* 17:37; cf. Isa 11:2).[15] The psalmist even looks for "a day of election at the raising up of his Christ" (εἰς ἡμέραν ἐκλογῆς ἐν ἀνάξει χριστοῦ αὐτοῦ; 18:5b).[16]

To summarize, the psalmist yearns for a day of righteousness led by the Lord Christ, a son of David and future messianic figure who will fulfill the expectations of both 2 Sam 7 and Isa 11. He will rule by the power of his word and the power of the Holy Spirit. In association with the arrival of this future day, a time of reversal will take place for the righteous of Israel, and this reversal will include a resurrection to life for the righteous and an inheritance of Hades for the ungodly. Thus, Luke did not impose later Christian ideas onto his characters in the birth narratives, for some pious Jews of that early period were already steeped in key aspects of Luke's messianism.

The *Ethiopic Apocalypse* of Enoch (*1 Enoch*) shares some common threads with the *Psalms of Solomon* and with Luke. Throughout the various parts of *1 Enoch* it emphasizes an eschatological judgment on the wicked and a vindication of the righteous, and the latter vindication assumes a resurrection of the righteous (e.g., 1.8–9; chs. 62, 67; 103.4).[17] The *Book of the Similitudes* in *1 Enoch* holds special interest because of its messianic focus; the author refers to this future figure as the Righteous One (38.2–3; 53.6), the Elect One (e.g., 39.6; 40.6; 49.2), the Son of Man (e.g., 46.3–4; 48.2; 62.6–7, 9, 15), the Chosen One (48.6), the Before-Time (48.2–3), and the Messiah (48.10; 52.4). He is a pre-existent figure (46.1–3; 48.6–7) who is also the eschatological judge of sinners (38.3) and sits "in a throne of glory" (55.4).[18] In addition, this Messiah is "the light of the gentiles and he will become the hope of those who are sick in their hearts" (48.4; cf. Isa 42:6; 49:6; Luke 2:32).

---

15. The Messiah will also have "wisdom of Spirit" (*Pss. Sol.* 18:7b).

16. Because the Hebrew vorlage is no longer extant for the Psalms of Solomon, it is difficult to draw conclusions based on similar terminology, but it is possible that this "raising up" reflects the hope of Moses in Deut 18:15.

17. For an overview of resurrection passages in *1 Enoch*, see Wright, *Resurrection*, 153–57. For a brief introduction to the theology of *1 Enoch*, see Isaac, "1 (Ethiopic Apocalypse of) Enoch," 9.

18. All quotations from *1 Enoch* are from Isaac, "1 (Ethiopic Apocalypse of) Enoch."

The Spirit of God also plays a role in *1 Enoch*. Enoch claims possession of the prophetic Spirit when he informs Methuselah that "the spirit is poured over me so that I may show you everything that shall happen to you forever" (91.1).[19] The wicked receive judgment "because they believe in the debauchery of their bodies and deny the spirit of the Lord" (67.10–11). Previously the author notes, "Lust shall fill their souls so that their bodies shall be punished, for they have denied the Lord of the Spirits" (67.8). The author uses the expression "Lord of the Spirits" as a divine title over one hundred times in the *Similitudes*, indicating that the parallel "spirit of the Lord" is also referring to the divine Spirit. Given the author's incorporation of Isa 11:1–5 into his theology (see below), "Lord of the Spirits" is probably a title adapted from that text.

That the author views the Messiah in terms of Isa 11:2 is evident in *1 En.* 49.2–3: "The Elect One stands before the Lord of the Spirits; his glory is forever and ever and his power is unto all generations. In him dwells the spirit of wisdom, the spirit which gives thoughtfulness, the spirit of knowledge and strength, and the spirit of those who have fallen asleep in righteousness."[20] In reference to the Elect One, the apocalyptic writer records, "The spirit of righteousness has been poured out upon him. The word of his mouth will do the sinners in; and all the oppressors shall be eliminated from before his face" (62.2–3; cf. Isa 11:4). The exaltation, judgment, and pneumatological language surrounding the Elect One sounds similar to Jesus's exaltation, conquest, and reception of the Spirit in Peter's sermon at Pentecost (Acts 2:33–36), but Enoch's account stops short of the Messiah giving the Spirit.[21]

A few chapters at the center of the *Similitudes* (48–51) hold particular relevance to this study. Here the Son of Man (48.2) is "the light of the Gentiles" (48.4), the "Chosen One" (48.6), and the "Messiah" (48.10), whom kings and powerful landowners deny (48.8). They "shall be humiliated" (48.8) and "shall burn" (48.9), but the righteous "will be saved" and "have life" (48.7–8). In short, there will be a time of reversal when

---

19. Menzies cites this text in support of his argument for a prophetic view of the Spirit in Judaism. Menzies, *Empowered for Witness*, 65.

20. In *1 En.* 61.10–11 the Elect One and all the heavenly beings join in praise "in the spirit of faith, in the spirit of wisdom and patience, in the spirit of mercy, in the spirit of justice and peace, and the spirit of generosity." This passage may also have the divine Spirit in mind as another example of a reflection of Isa 11:1–5.

21. Menzies claims that "nowhere in Jewish intertestamental literature is it recorded that the Messiah will bestow the Spirit of God upon his followers." Menzies, *Empowered for Witness*, 67.

the righteous will no longer be oppressed by the rich and powerful but will triumph over the sinners (48.9). The Elect One, who has the Spirit after the fashion of Isa 11 (*1 En.* 49.2–3), will serve as the judge, and "oppression cannot survive his judgment" (50.4). This future day is one of resurrection and glorification of the Messiah (51.1–4a):

> In those days, Sheol will return all the deposits which she had received and hell will give back all that which it owes. And he shall choose the righteous and the holy ones from among (the risen dead), for the day when they shall be selected and saved has arrived. In those days, (the Elect One) shall sit on my throne, and from the conscience of his mouth shall come out all the secrets of wisdom, for the Lord of the Spirits has given them to him and glorified him.[22]

The apocalypticist records that "the Elect One has arisen," that is, been enthroned, on that day (51.4c). These few chapters read like a laundry list of important Lukan themes, connecting messianism with Isaiah's vision of a Spirit-empowered Davidite, a royal enthronement, a time of reversal, and a resurrection of the dead. This pseudepigraphical writing gives evidence that Luke's birth narrative characters were not alone in their messianic expectations and that a key identifying characteristic of the Messiah was the Spirit of Isa 11. And although the author of *1 Enoch* lacked the light of the New Testament and its highly developed Christology, his eschatological orientation clearly embraced a future resurrection related to the reign of a Spirit-anointed Davidite.

The two messiahs in the Dead Sea Scrolls (1QS IX, 11; 1QSa II, 11–22) present a somewhat confusing picture, but Strauss argues, "Various Cave 4 documents suggest an increase in royal-Davidic expectation in the sect's later years (c. 4 BC to AD 68)."[23] A fragment of a messianic apocalypse requires particular attention here (4Q521 2 II, 1–12):

> . . . [the hea]vens and the earth will listen to His Messiah, and none therein will stray from the commandments of the holy ones.
>
> Seekers of the Lord, strengthen yourselves in His service!
>
> All you hopeful in (your) heart, will you not find the Lord in this?
>
> For the Lord will consider the pious (*hasidim*) and call the righteous by name.

---

22. Translation by Isaac, "1 (Ethiopic Apocalypse of) Enoch."
23. Strauss, *Davidic Messiah*, 43.

> Over the poor His spirit will hover and will renew the faithful with His power.
>
> And He will glorify the pious on the throne of the eternal Kingdom.
>
> He who liberates the captives, restores sight to the blind, straightens the b[ent] (Ps. cxlvi, 7-8).
>
> And f[or] ever I will clea[ve to the h]opeful and in His mercy . . .
>
> And the fr[uit . . .] will not be delayed for anyone
>
> And the Lord will accomplish glorious things which have never been as [He . . .]
>
> For he will heal the wounded, and revive the dead and bring good news to the poor (Isa. lxi, I).
>
> . . . He will lead the uprooted and make the hungry rich . . .[24]

This fragment combines some of the key themes discussed above. It refers directly to the Messiah, parallels the hovering Spirit with God's power,[25] contains reversal imagery, reflects the language of Isa 61:1-2, and gives one of the clearest statements of the resurrection of the dead found among the Qumranites (cf. *Pseudo-Ezekiel* 4Q385; 4Q521 7, 5).[26] The concept of reversal is evident in the glorification of the poor, the straightening up of those bent over (or lifting up of those bowed down; Ps 146:8b), the making the hungry rich, and the reviving of the dead. The prominence of the Messiah at the beginning of the passage and the allusion to Isa 61:1-2 (cf. Luke 4:18-19; 7:22) suggests that the Spirit operates through the Messiah to effect the renewal envisioned.[27] The resurrection fragment assumes an eschatological relationship between the Messiah, the Spirit, and the resurrection, and it confirms the existence of a Jewish perspective akin to that in Luke's gospel.

---

24. Translations of the Dead Sea Scrolls are from Vermes, *Complete Dead Sea Scrolls*, 412-13.

25. Turner also notes the parallelism here. Turner, *Power from on High*, 117.

26. Charlesworth, "Resurrection," 145-53; Lichtenberger is less enthusiastic about the embracing of resurrection by the Essenes than Charlesworth is. He doubts that some of the resurrection texts are from the Essene community. However, Lichtenberger does see salvation beyond the grave at Qumran: "Der Tenor der Texte aber läßt keinen Zweifel daran, daß die Qumran-essenische Gemeinschaft auch über den Tod des einzelnen hinaus an eine Teilhabe am Heil glaubte, auch wenn sie dies nich mit dem Gedanken der leiblichen Auferstehung von den Toten in Verbindung brachte." Lichtenberger, "Auferstehung in Den Qumranfunden," 91.

27. Similarly, Turner, *Power from on High*, 117.

Because the Jewish literature of the time still anticipates the Messiah's coming, it does not have the same degree of identification language that Luke has, but it certainly identifies the Messiah with passages such as Isa 11 and connects him with an eschatological resurrection. Thus, Simeon and other witnesses in the birth narratives are not alone in their messianic expectations.

John the Baptist and the Spirit's Identification of Christ

From the outset Luke portrays John the Baptist as a Spirit-filled prophet (Luke 1:15-17), and his father Zechariah confirms this role by the prophetic Spirit (vv. 67, 75). John's role in identifying Jesus is evident in his response to speculation that he (John) might be the Christ (3:15): "I baptize you with water [ἐγὼ μὲν ὕδατι βαπτίζω ὑμᾶς], but one stronger than I is coming, of whom I am not worthy to untie the strap of his sandals; he will baptize you with the Holy Spirit and fire [αὐτὸς ὑμᾶς βαπτίσει ἐν πνεύματι ἁγίῳ καὶ πυρί]" (3:16). The emphatic "I" (ἐγὼ) and "he" (αὐτὸς) clearly distinguish John from the Christ, and the latter's roles as Spirit-baptizer and judge (v. 17) serve as identification markers. Scholars vary widely in their understanding of Luke 3:16-17 and particularly of the nature of the fire.[28] At this stage in the narrative Luke's primary interest is in identifying Jesus in his two roles; the timing and application of the two baptisms await further development as the story progresses.[29] It is commonly recognized that Israel did not expect the Messiah to give the Spirit,[30] but Turner's assertion that "God's Spirit was God himself present and active, and to make the messiah 'Lord of the Spirit' in such a way would inevitably have threatened Jewish exclusive monotheism" misses Luke's point in establishing Jesus's divine identity early in the narrative (1:32-33, 43).[31] The emphasis on wrath (3:7), an ax poised to chop down

---

28. See the discussion in Menzies, *Empowered for Witness*, 123-31; Turner, *Power from on High*, 175-87; Warrington, "Synoptic Gospels," 94-96; Wenk, *Community-Forming Power*, 182-90.

29. In response to Wenk, this approach observes the sequence of Luke-Acts and allows Luke to anticipate the words of Jesus in Acts 1:8 without expecting the reader to have full comprehension of the details of the baptism at this stage in the story. Wenk, *Community-Forming Power*, 182-83n22.

30. Lampe seems to be an exception, citing *T. Levi* 18 and *Gen. Rab.* 2. Lampe, "Holy Spirit in the Writings of St. Luke," 163.

31. Turner's eagerness to demonstrate a cleansing of Israel theme in Luke 3:16-17

the tree (v. 9), a clear distinction between wheat and chaff (v. 17), and a fire of judgment (vv. 9, 17) in the immediate context indicate that the baptism of fire is not a restorative fire but an eschatological judgment fire (v. 16). This picture fits well with the Jewish expectations outlined above and with the identification of Jesus as "Lord of all" (Acts 10:36), "anointed with the Holy Spirit and power" (v. 38), and "Judge of the living and the dead" (v. 42) at Cornelius's house. The emphasis remains on the identity of the Messiah, and this is fundamental to Isa 11, where "The Spirit of the LORD will rest" on the "branch" of Jesse (vv. 1–2) and "he shall strike the earth with the rod of his mouth, and with the breath of his lips he shall kill the wicked" (v. 4b ESV). The intentional omission of "and fire" to the experience of the disciples at Pentecost (Acts 1:5) and to those of Cornelius's household (11:16) clarifies the nature of a baptism with the Spirit in distinction from a baptism of fire. However, the emphasis remains on the greater point that there is one Baptizer who exercises the divine prerogative of giving the Spirit to the submissive and dispensing eschatological judgment to the rebellious. The unity is in the one performing the two functions, not in the functions themselves, and Pentecost is not a baptism in this kind of fire.

In the above discussion the Spirit identifies Jesus through the prophet John, but Luke also identifies Jesus by his roles as bearer of the Spirit and giver of the Spirit. With regard to the former, Luke records the descent of the Spirit in vivid terms: "And the Holy Spirit descended on him in bodily form [σωματικῷ εἴδει], like a dove; and a voice came from heaven, 'You are my beloved Son; with you I am well pleased'" (Luke 3:22; cf. v. 37). All four gospels describe the Spirit's descent as visible, but Luke clarifies for Theophilus how the Spirit appeared in an objectively observable manner.[32] The divine voice confirms the identification made by the previous voices in the narrative, and "it also underscores the bi-polarity of possible responses to Jesus."[33] Just as one's response determines which baptism the person will receive, so "one can join Elizabeth, the angels,

---

leads him to deny that John depicts Jesus as Giver of the Spirit and to conclude that John and Jesus/Luke understand this text differently. Turner, *Power from on High*, 179, 184–87; See Henrichs-Tarasenkova, *Luke's Christology of Divine Identity*.

32. Bock is probably right to emphasize the metaphorical aspect of the Spirit's descent "like" a dove, but Leaney goes too far in denying the objectively observable element of the Spirit's descent. Bock, *Luke*, 1:339; Leaney, *Gospel According to St. Luke*, 110.

33. Green, *Gospel of Luke*, 186.

the narrator, and others who affirm Jesus's exalted status and/or identity as God's Son, or one can reject this evaluation and so pit oneself over against God."[34]

The heavenly voice echoes the "beloved" of Gen 22:2 and the enthronement terminology of Ps 2:7,[35] and it also finds a parallel in Isa 42:1, which "links the object of divine pleasure with the anointing of the Spirit for divine mission."[36] Functionally speaking, Jesus's anointing empowers him as a prophet to fulfill the mission (Luke 4:1, 14, 18–19). From a literary standpoint, his anointing serves as a paradigm for the later experience of the disciples (Acts 2:1–4). But from a theological and christological perspective, his anointing identifies him as the long-awaited Messiah and Son of God. Thus, his anointing is unique with regard to the latter, but it is not entirely unique with regard to functionality.[37]

Peter makes Jesus's role as Spirit-giver abundantly clear at Pentecost: "Therefore, being exalted to the right hand of God, and having received from the Father the promise of the Holy Spirit, he has poured out this which you yourselves both see and hear" (Acts 2:33; cf. vv. 17–18). Few scholars offer comments on the timing of when Jesus received the Spirit to pour out to others,[38] but there appears to be both continuity with Jesus's

34. Green, *Gospel of Luke*, 186.

35. Edwards, *Gospel According to Luke*, 118.

36. Green, *Gospel of Luke*, 187.

37. Henrichs-Tarasenkova is right in asserting that Jesus is Christ from birth with regard to his unique status. Henrichs-Tarasenkova, *Luke's Christology of Divine Identity*, 162. At the same time, there must be a point in time when Jesus, as a man, must experience an anointing with the Spirit for vocational purposes. Regarding the vocational or charismatic element, see Stronstad, *Charismatic Theology of St. Luke*, 27–28. Keener's conclusions on this are similar to mine. See his discussion in Keener, *Acts*, 1: 957–58. There is no need to limit Jesus's anointing to either charismatic empowerment or messianic identification.

38. A few have ventured to comment on it. Fitzmyer suggests that the reason for the "received" language is that "Luke is concerned . . . to show the risen Christ subordinate to his heavenly Father." In light of the emphasis on enthronement, this does not seem likely. Fitzmyer, *Acts of the Apostles*, 259. Barrett argues that the Spirit was given to Jesus in connection with his exaltation for the purpose of giving the Spirit away. However, he builds his argument primarily on the premise that Acts 2:33 directly refers to Ps 68:18 (68:19 MT), and this is a disputable matter. Barrett, *Acts of the Apostles*, 1:150. Turner also depends on Ps 68:18 when he concludes that "2.33–34 affirms a New Moses fulfilment of Ps. 68.18, re-contextualized in the light of Joel and the Pentecost events." However, his argument depends too heavily on a supposed Sinai/Mosaic tradition in Acts 2. He acknowledges that these are not "in the surface structure of the argument." Turner, *Power from on High*, 286–87.

anointing at his baptism and a new era of exercising the divine prerogatives in his exaltation. Jesus ministers in the Spirit between his resurrection and ascension (Acts 1:2), and his identity as Lord and Christ does not change at any point, yet "the full authority of these titles is granted only through death, resurrection, and exaltation."[39] Thus, Christ begins to fully exercise his divine prerogative of distributing the Spirit at Pentecost.

At various points I have highlighted the Spirit's role in inspiring various kinds of speech and the often christocentric nature of it. This includes the inspiration of the Scriptures, of leaders such as the seventy elders (Num 11), of Old Testament prophets, of prophets in the birth and inauguration narratives, and of Spirit-filled preachers proclaiming the kingdom of God and "the word." Thus, it is fair to say that a major role of the Spirit is to identify Christ through the Scriptures, preaching, and anointed prophets, but one other manifestation of christocentric prophecy deserves comment—speaking in other tongues.

It is now generally recognized that the tongues of Pentecost are prophetic in nature.[40] This is evident from Peter's quotation of Joel 2:28–29 (Acts 2:17–18), his *pesher* style introduction of the quotation (Acts 2:16), and his repetition of "and they will prophesy" (2:18c), which occurs only one time in the Septuagint of Joel 3:1–2. It is also hard to miss the eschatological tone of the narrative with Luke's employment of the verb συμπληρόω ("to fulfill") at the outset (Acts 2:1) and Peter's substitution of Isaiah's "last days" (2:2) for Joel's "afterward" (3:1 LXX) at the beginning of his Old Testament quotation (Acts 2:17). However, the christocentric orientation of the speaking in tongues is not generally recognized.

The observers at Pentecost describe the content of tongues as speaking the τὰ μεγαλεῖα ("mighty deeds") of God (Acts 2:11). Most scholars view this as a form of praise,[41] and this is consistent with the emphasis on praise in Ps 70:19 (LXX); Sir 17:10; 42:21; and 43:15 (LXX). Luke uses the cognate participle μεγαλυνόντων of tongues as praise in Acts 10:46, and he also uses the verbal form as praise in the Magnificat (Luke 1:46)

---

39. Tannehill, *Narrative Unity*, 2:39.

40. E.g., Menzies, *Empowered for Witness*, 178–89; Peterson, *Acts of the Apostles*, 134; Polhill, *Acts*, 109; Stronstad, *Prophethood of All Believers*, 48–65; Turner, *Power from on High*, 348.

41. Menzies is among the minority who view this as proclamation rather than praise. Menzies, *Empowered for Witness*, 177. The adjective μεγαλεῖος rarely occurs in the Old Testament, but it occurs more often in the Apocrypha (Sir 17:8, 10, 13; 18:4; 36:7; 42:21; 43:15; 45:24; cf. Tob 11:15; 2 Macc 3:34; 7:17; 3 Macc 7:22).

and at Ephesus (Acts 19:17). Given the resurrection and ascension context of Acts 2, it is likely that the "mighty deeds" for which the disciples praise God center on Jesus's resurrection/enthronement. In response to the crowd's inquiry, "What does this mean?," Peter describes the nature of the tongues as prophetic utterance but the historical-redemptive significance of the event as indicative that the risen Jesus is Lord and Christ (Acts 2:36) and exercises the divine prerogatives of granting salvation and pouring out the Spirit. Luke uses various literary means of moving the narrative toward the recognition that Jesus is the Lord, including his direct address to the Israelite men (vv. 14, 22, 29), the use of the emphatic pronouns to identify Jesus (as detailed below), the piling on of Scripture references, and the repetition of the inferential particle οὖν ("therefore"; vv. 30, 33, 36) followed by a conclusion about Christ's resurrection in each occurrence.[42]

In the first occurrence of οὖν ("therefore"; Acts 2:30), the presence of David's tomb testifies to the fact that David prophesied about someone other than himself (Ps 16:8–11). He was "therefore" (οὖν) a prophet, and because he also knew of God's covenantal oath to seat David's offspring "on his throne" (ἐπὶ τὸν θρόνον αὐτοῦ; Acts 2:30), he looked ahead and "spoke concerning the resurrection of the Christ" (ἐλάλησεν περὶ τῆς ἀναστάσεως τοῦ Χριστοῦ; v. 31).[43] Peter clearly refers to Ps 132:11: "The LORD swore to David a sure oath from which he will not turn back: 'One of the sons of your body I will set on your throne'" (ESV; cf. Ps 89:3–4; Heb 6:13, 16–17). This ultimately refers to the Davidic covenant in 2 Sam 7:12–13. "What does this mean?" (Acts 2:12); it means Jesus is the resurrected Davidite.

The second "therefore" (οὖν; Acts 2:33) assumes the theological unity between the resurrection and Christ's exaltation to God's right hand: "Therefore [οὖν] having been exalted to the right hand of God . . ." And based on Jesus's having received the promised Spirit, Peter concludes, "He

---

42. Anderson highlights this structural element and its significance. Anderson, "*But God Raised*", 202, 209–19.

43. Not only does Ps 110:1 appear again in the Pentecostal narrative (Acts 2:34), but even the οὖν ("therefore") in the narrative seems to reflect the terminology found in Luke 20:44 (Δαυὶδ οὖν κύριον αὐτὸν καλεῖ). In Acts 2:30 David is a prophet (προφήτης οὖν ὑπάρχων) who foresees Jesus's enthronement, and in 2:36 Jesus is "therefore" both "Lord and Christ." Luke does not follow Mark on this, as the οὖν is absent in Mark (12:37; but see Matt 22:45), so it seems that Luke intends to emphasize that the logical conclusion the Scriptures lead to is that Jesus is Lord. Nolland notices the absence of "therefore" in Mark. Nolland, *Luke 18:35—24:53*, 973.

has poured out this that you both see and hear" (Acts 2:33).[44] And "What does this mean?" It means that the manifestations (the sound of wind, the speaking in tongues, and the fiery tongues) are due to the Davidic King having poured out the Spirit. Peter supports this with another mention of David and a quotation from Ps 110:1 (cf. Luke 20:42-43), from which Peter infers that David addresses Jesus as "Lord" (Acts 2:34-35).

The third οὖν occurs in Acts 2:36, where Peter concludes, "Therefore [οὖν] let all the house of Israel know for certain that God has made him both Lord and Christ, this Jesus whom you crucified." Several important literary elements converge in this verse: the use of the adverb ἀσφαλῶς ("certainty"), which alludes to the purpose of Luke-Acts;[45] the recurrence of emphatic pronouns in the accusative case identifying Jesus; the conclusion of the three particles (οὖν); and the threefold reference to the Davidic descendant as Jesus, Lord, and Christ. Thus, the explanation of the tongues of Pentecost travels along the path of prophetic speech, but the ultimate destination is the Lord and Christ. Speaking in tongues, then, is a form of prophetic praise that has both a theocentric and christocentric orientation, and because Luke so clearly attributes this kind of speech to the inspiration of the Holy Spirit (vv. 4, 17-18), speaking in tongues serves as an additional pneumatic response to and confirmation of Jesus's exalted status as Lord and Christ. Jesus's baptizing in the Spirit in fulfillment of John's prophecy results in a pneumatic response which further affirms the lordship of Christ.

Thus, there are several ways the Spirit identifies Jesus as the Messiah in Luke-Acts. The Spirit proclaims his identity through the Scriptures and through preachers of the kingdom and the word. The Spirit inspires prophets, including those who offer prophetic praise, to announce Jesus's universal lordship. The Spirit descends in bodily form at Jesus's baptism to identify him as the anointed one, and Jesus's gifting of the Spirit to others identifies him as the enthroned King who exercises the divine prerogative of pouring out the Spirit.

---

44. Some scholars see an allusion in Acts 2:33 to Ps 68:18 (68:19 LXX). Jesus's ascension is likened to Moses's ascending Mt. Sinai to receive the Law. Thus, Jesus has ascended to receive and pour out the Spirit, but the clear and overwhelming Davidic context makes this identification extremely unlikely. Fitzmyer is correct: "This suggestion . . . is eisegetical." Fitzmyer, *Acts of the Apostles*, 259; O'Toole, "Acts 2:30," 248.

45. Its cognate noun ἀσφάλειαν occurs in Luke 1:4.

The Resurrection as Identifier of Jesus

The focus of attention now turns to how the resurrection of Jesus serves to demonstrate Jesus's identity. After an overview of the topic in Luke's gospel and a brief examination of a couple significant passages, the bulk of the discussion highlights the resurrection preaching in Acts. Some conclusions about how the resurrection and the Spirit identify Jesus in the narrative follow.

Luke pays ample attention to the need for people to recognize Jesus's true identity, and even passages regarding Jesus's raising of others center on his own identity. After raising the widow's son, the people conclude that "a great prophet has risen among us" (Luke 7:16), and the raising of the dead is offered as proof to John (v. 22) in response to his query: "Are you the coming one, or should we look for another?" (v. 19). In the story of the raising of Jairus's daughter, the laughter of the people (8:53) draws attention to the question of Jesus's authority and identity in anticipation of Jesus's question: "But who do you say I am?" (9:20).[46] From there Luke repeats Jesus's prediction of his passion and resurrection both before (9:22; 18:31-33) and after the events (24:7, 46) in order to emphasize that these events are bound up with his identity as the Son of Man and the subject of the Scriptures.

At the eschatological resurrection the men of Jesus's generation will receive condemnation from the Queen of the South and the Ninevites because they failed to recognize Jesus (Luke 11:29-32; cf. 13:34-35). Jesus himself becomes the judge of those who killed him when his death results in a great resurrection reversal: "The stone which the builders rejected—this one has become the cornerstone" (λίθον ὃν ἀπεδοκίμασαν οἱ οἰκοδομοῦντες, οὗτος ἐγενήθη εἰς κεφαλὴν γωνίας; 20:17b; cf. Ps 117:22 LXX; Acts 4:11). Luke follows the Septuagint exactly and even includes the demonstrative pronoun οὗτος ("this one"), which is not found in the Masoretic Text (Ps 118:22). The stylistic elements, which include the frontloading of the noun λίθον ("stone") and the relative pronoun ὃν ("which") in the accusative case and οὗτος ("this one"), are significant because they place emphasis on the specific identity of the stone and because this practice becomes normal procedure for Luke in resurrection contexts in Acts.

The emphasis on recognition of Jesus's identity continues in the Third Gospel as the women find the tomb dispossessed of "the body of

---

46. Green, *Gospel of Luke*, 350.

the Lord Jesus" (24:3). The two travelers who had hoped that Jesus would redeem Israel did not recognize the risen Christ (vv. 16, 21, 26) until their eyes were opened at Jesus's breaking of bread (vv. 30–31, 35), resulting in a confession of faith: "Truly the Lord has risen and has appeared to Simon" (v. 34b). The appearance of Jesus to the eleven has an apologetic element in establishing the fact of Jesus's resurrection and identifies him as the prophesied Christ of Scripture and object of faith. Jesus's encouraging the disciples to look at his wounds, touch him, and give him some food establishes the veracity of the former (vv. 38–43) and his opening of their minds to understand the Scriptures accomplishes the latter (vv. 45–47).

At first glance Jesus's resolution of the question posed by the Sadducees regarding the resurrection does not appear to have much bearing on the relationship between Jesus's identity and the resurrection, but the following text suggests otherwise: "But he said to them, 'How is it that they say the Christ is David's son? For David himself says in the book of Psalms, "The Lord said to my Lord, 'Sit at my right hand until I make your enemies a footstool for your feet.'" David therefore calls him *Lord*, so how is he his son?'" (Luke 20:41–44; cf. Ps 109:1 LXX). Matthew and Mark both have the additional story of the Law expert inquiring about the greatest commandment sandwiched between the resurrection question and the Davidic son passage (Matt 22:23–46; Mark 12:18–37), but Luke omits this story in order to connect the resurrection question to the identity of David's Lord.[47] That Lukan redaction is at work is also suggested by Luke's substitution of David's citation of "the book of Psalms" for Matthew's and Mark's account of David speaking "by the Holy Spirit" (Mark 12:36) or "by the Spirit" (Matt 22:43). This is consistent with Luke's emphasis on the fulfillment of Scripture and anticipates Jesus's further comment in Luke 24:44 that "it is necessary for everything that has been written in the Law of Moses and the Prophets and the Psalms concerning me [περὶ ἐμοῦ] to be fulfilled." Luke intends to develop a relationship between the subject of the resurrection and the identity of the Messiah and to affirm that both are anticipated in Scripture and converge in Jesus. While Luke opts for mention of the Scriptures in 20:42, his record of Jesus's promise to send the Spirit in 24:49 indicates that christological pneumatology remains a priority. However, Luke has shown that he is

---

47. Kurz notes how Luke uses the conjunction δέ ("and") in 20:41 to connect the retreat of the Sadducees in verse 40 with Jesus's challenge in verses 41–44. Thus, there are literary, grammatical, and thematic reasons to believe that Luke intends the reader to recognize a relationship between the two pericopes. Kurz, *Reading Luke-Acts*, 56.

perfectly capable of omitting the direct mention of the Spirit when emphasis on the Scriptures better suits his christological agenda in identifying the Christ (Luke 11:20; 20:42).

Luke 20:41-44 is saturated with christological identification. "David" is mentioned three times, "Christ" is mentioned once, "son" occurs twice, and Luke wets his pen three times for "lord." In addition, the citation is an oft-quoted coronation psalm of David (Ps 110:1).[48] Because the entire issue focuses on the identity of this κύριος ("lord"), who, though rejected, will become the cornerstone (Luke 20:17), it becomes evident that Luke is developing a picture of Jesus as the one who is exalted as Lord via resurrection and even dispenses the Spirit. Although Christ's resurrection is not directly articulated in 20:27-40, the general resurrection in view anticipates the annoyance of the Sadducees over the disciples proclaiming "in Jesus the resurrection from the dead" (Acts 4:2).

Just as Luke's gospel contains some proofs of the resurrection, so Acts has its apologetic elements. Jesus gave "many proofs" (ἐν πολλοῖς τεκμηρίοις) that he was alive and made appearances over a forty-day period (1:3). Although the "witness" (μάρτυς) word group centers largely on Christ and the message of his resurrection from Luke 24:48 through Acts (e.g., 1:8, 22; 3:15; 4:33; 10:41),[49] it maintains an element of its legal use in establishing eyewitness proof of Jesus's resurrection. Paul also claims to have been chosen by God to see Jesus alive in order that he may be "a witness [μάρτυς] to all men" of what he has seen and heard (22:14-15; cf. v. 18).

At Athens Paul offers Jesus's resurrection itself as proof (πίστιν) that Jesus is the one appointed to judge the world (17:31), but the most common pattern in Acts in identifying Jesus is the repeated use of pronouns placed in an emphatic position and often occurring in the accusative case to identify Jesus as the resurrected Lord and Christ. In Acts 2 Peter's direct address to the Jewish men (ἄνδρες Ἰουδαῖοι; v. 14) is repeated with only a slight variation (Ἄνδρες Ἰσραηλῖται; "Israelite men"; v. 22), indicating a new segment of the argument.[50] The new division begins with "Jesus the

---

48. Edwards is right in saying that "the question of Jesus in vv. 41-44 seems not to introduce a messianic understanding of Ps 110, but to *presuppose* it." Emphasis his. Edwards, *Gospel According to Luke*, 583.

49. See the overview in Coenen, "Witness, Testimony," 1043-44.

50. Anderson also notices both the repeated use of the vocatives and the emphatic placement of "Jesus the Nazarene" and the two subsequent pronouns highlighted here. Anderson, *"But God Raised"*, 201, 202-3. Bruce also indicates that τοῦτον ("this man")

Nazarene, a man ['Ιησοῦν τὸν Ναζωραῖον, ἄνδρα] attested to you by God," and all four initial words are in the accusative case. After a description of his miraculous ministry, the accusative returns with "this man" (τοῦτον) as the one delivered up by God's foreknowledge and killed by Peter's audience (v. 23). In contrast to "you killed" (ἀνείλατε) and in reference to "this man," the accusative begins the next clause: "whom God raised" (ὃν ὁ θεὸς ἀνέστησεν; v. 24). The grammar seems a bit awkward, but the repetition and frontloading of accusative pronouns clearly identifies Jesus as the man from Nazareth whom they crucified but whom God raised.

A quotation of a psalm attributed to David follows and provides biblical support for the resurrection of a Davidite (vv. 25–28; Ps 15:8–11 LXX). Peter begins commenting on the text with another vocative ("Ἄνδρες ἀδελφοί; "Men, brothers"; v. 29), finds additional support in Ps 132:11, claims that Ps 15:10 (LXX) refers to the resurrection of the Christ, and returns to his identification formula: "This Jesus God raised; of this we are all witnesses" (τοῦτον τὸν Ἰησοῦν ἀνέστησεν ὁ θεός, οὗ πάντες ἡμεῖς ἐσμεν μάρτυρες; Acts 2:32). The identification reaches its pinnacle in 2:36, when Peter utters the central truth of the chapter: "God has made him both Lord and Christ, this Jesus whom you crucified." Notice the word order and repeated use of the accusative case:

καὶ κύριον αὐτὸν
καὶ χριστὸν   ἐποίησεν ὁ θεός,
τοῦτον τὸν Ἰησοῦν
ὃν   ὑμεῖς ἐσταυρώσατε.

Thus, the resurrection serves as a primary identifier of Jesus as the anointed one in the line of David and as the exalted Lord who reigns on David's throne.[51]

Peter's temple speech also commences with "Israelite men" (ἄνδρες Ἰσραηλῖται; Acts 3:12) and invests considerable time in identifying the roles of each actor in the story. The lame man walked not because of any divine quality of Peter and John, but because "God ... glorified his servant Jesus, whom you [ἐδόξασεν τὸν παῖδα αὐτοῦ Ἰησοῦν ὃν ὑμεῖς] handed over and denied before Pilate" (v. 13). Peter repeats the emphatic ὑμεῖς ("you") at the beginning of the next clause to contrast God's favor on and

---

in verse 23 is resumptive and emphatic. Bruce, *Acts of the Apostles*, 91.

51. The phrase diagram also clearly shows the contrast between divine activity and that of fallen humanity. This has also been emphasized throughout Peter's sermon as a means of bringing his audience to repentance.

glorification of Jesus with the Jewish audience's betrayal of "the Holy and Righteous one" (τὸν ἅγιον καὶ δίκαιον; v. 14a). Peter continues, "But the Originator of Life [τὸν δὲ ἀρχηγὸν τῆς ζωῆς] you killed, whom [ὃν] God raised from the dead; we [ἡμεῖς] are witnesses of this" (v. 15). The roles of God, the audience, and the disciples are clearly marked by strategically placed pronouns, but Jesus is marked by words in the accusative case, which find their way to the front of the clauses in verse 15. The christological titles are rich, and the glorifying of the "servant Jesus" not only evinces Isa 52:13 but establishes a strong relationship between Jesus's resurrection and exaltation (glorifying). Resurrection is not theologically or conceptually distinct from enthronement,[52] and the resurrection is central in identifying Jesus.[53]

The stylistic elements continue when Peter, full of the Spirit, addresses the Jerusalem leaders and "all the people of Israel" and asserts that "by the name of Jesus Christ of Nazareth, whom you [ὃν ὑμεῖς] crucified, whom God [ὃν ὁ θεὸς] raised from the dead—by him [ἐν τούτῳ] this man stands before you well" (Acts 4:10). Peter explicitly identifies Jesus with a quotation from Ps 118:22 (117:22 LXX) and he exposes the identification of the temple leaders when he personalizes the stone passage with "you [ὑμῶν] the builders" (v. 11). "He is 'the stone [οὗτός ἐστιν ὁ λίθος] which was rejected by you, the builders, which has become the cornerstone.'" The *pesher* style introduction here is similar to that used by Peter in Acts 2:16. Peter's message clearly identifies Jesus as the risen Christ prophesied in Scripture.

Once again Luke highlights the contrasting assessments of Jesus's identity. After the miraculous release of the apostles and continued preaching, Peter, in company with the others, confronts the Sanhedrin (Acts 5:30–32): "The God of our fathers raised [ἤγειρεν] Jesus, whom you murdered [ὃν ὑμεῖς διεχειρίσασθε] by hanging him on a tree. This one God exalted to his right hand as Leader and Savior [τοῦτον ὁ θεὸς ἀρχηγὸν καὶ σωτῆρα ὕψωσεν] to give repentance to Israel and forgiveness of sins. And we are witnesses [ἡμεῖς ἐσμεν μάρτυρες] of these things, and so is the Holy

---

52. Harrison is right to see Jesus's resurrection as a stage in his exaltation (Acts 2:32–33; 3:13–15; 5:30–31). Harrison, "Resurrection of Jesus," 223; cf. *T. Benj.* 10:6–7.

53. The parallel phrases in Acts 2:30–31 (ESV) evince the important relationship between Christ's resurrection and enthronement: "Being therefore a prophet, and knowing that God had sworn with an oath to him that he would set one of his descendants on his throne, he foresaw and spoke about the resurrection of the Christ, that he was not abandoned to Hades, nor did his flesh see corruption."

Spirit whom God gave to those who obey [πειθαρχοῦσιν] him." The similar structure and themes found in other resurrection passages make it highly likely that the raising is in reference to resurrection and not merely an appearance on the stage of history (3:15).[54] Once again accusative pronouns accentuate the identity of Jesus, a second-person pronoun emphatically identifies the religious leaders as murderers, and another pronoun defines the role of the apostles as "witnesses." The intentional placement of τοῦτον ("this one") at the front of the sentence with ἀρχηγὸν καὶ σωτῆρα ("Leader and Savior") following ὁ θεὸς ("God") makes the phrase seem clumsy, but it shows Luke's interest in identifying Jesus.[55]

It is more difficult to define the precise manner in which the Spirit testifies in Acts 5:32. Some scholars see the gift of the Spirit to the church as testimony to Christ's exaltation.[56] Keener also refers to the Pentecostal gift, along with repentance (Acts 2:38), as the beginning point of obedience.[57] The latter point merits consideration particularly because of the conceptual similarities to Acts 5:30–32 found in the titles of Moses as "ruler and judge" (7:27, 35), the refusal of "our fathers" to obey Moses (v. 39), and the resistance to the Holy Spirit (v. 51).[58] At the same time, the verb πειθαρχέω ("to obey") is also found in 5:29 in reference to the disciples' obedience to God in preaching. Thus, the effect is that the apostles received the Holy Spirit in the past (aorist ἔδωκεν) and now obediently preach (present πειθαρχοῦσιν) so that they are the possessors of the Spirit (in contrast to the religious leaders), and the Spirit testifies through them to the resurrection and exaltation of Christ.[59] This is consistent with

---

54. With Barrett, *Acts of the Apostles*, 1:289; Witherington, *Acts of the Apostles*, 232n155; contra Bruce, *Acts of the Apostles*, 143. The theme of "witness" is so bound up with the resurrection that it would be very surprising if the resurrection were not in view.

55. Bock also notices that the word order is "unusual." Bock, *Acts*, 247.

56. E.g., Marshall, *Acts of the Apostles*, 120.

57. Keener, *Acts*, 2:1220.

58. Luke identifies Moses in a manner similar to the way he identifies Jesus, and this appears to be intentional as Stephen reports, "This is the Moses who said to the sons of Israel, 'God will raise up for you a prophet like me from your brothers'" (Acts 7:37; cf. Deut 18:15). Thus, his emphatic style reinforces the identity of Jesus as the new ruler and deliverer (v. 35) in the tradition of Moses. Note the numerous emphatic pronouns in verses 35–38.

59. Bock notes the trinitarian dimensions of this passage and concludes that "the testimony of the human witnesses is actually God's voice and message." Bock, *Acts*, 248.

Luke's emphasis on inspired utterance, and the center of all this is the identification of Christ.

Peter's resurrection message at Caesarea is framed by "the word" (τὸν λόγον; 10:36, 44) and the exalted status of Jesus (vv. 36, 42). Peter speaks of the preaching of the gospel of "peace through Jesus Christ—this one is Lord of all" (εἰρήνην διὰ Ἰησοῦ Χριστοῦ, οὗτός ἐστιν πάντων κύριος; v. 36b), and toward the end of the speech he speaks of the apostles' charge to preach and testify "that this is the one appointed [οὗτός ἐστιν ὁ ὡρισμένος] by God as Judge of the living and the dead" (v. 42). It appears that the attempt to identify Jesus's exalted status with similar language (οὗτός ἐστιν) explains some of the difficult grammar in verse 36.[60] The pattern observed in other passages reappears in 10:38, with "Jesus of Nazareth" in the emphatic position: "Jesus of Nazareth, how God anointed him with the Holy Spirit and power" (Ἰησοῦν τὸν ἀπὸ Ναζαρέθ, ὡς ἔχρισεν αὐτὸν ὁ θεὸς πνεύματι ἁγίῳ καὶ δυνάμει). The effort to identify Jesus of Nazareth as the Lord and Christ anointed with the Spirit by God is so extensive that it strains the Greek language. The Spirit's anointing clearly identifies Jesus, the disciples play their usual role as witnesses (ἡμεῖς μάρτυρες; v. 39), the Jews are held accountable for killing Jesus (ὃν καὶ ἀνεῖλαν; v. 39), and "God raised this one on the third day" (τοῦτον ὁ θεὸς ἤγειρεν [ἐν] τῇ τρίτῃ ἡμέρᾳ; v. 40a). The emphatic noun and pronouns in the accusative case (Ἰησοῦν, ὃν, τοῦτον) are followed by two other clear references to the resurrection: God caused Jesus "to appear" (v. 40) to appointed witnesses "after he rose [ἀναστῆναι] from the dead" (v. 41c). It is this risen one that God appointed as "Judge of the living and the dead" (v. 42). Both the Spirit and Jesus's resurrection serve as key identifiers of Jesus as the Christ, the Lord, and the Judge. The Spirit relates more particularly to Jesus as Christ, and the resurrection points clearly to Jesus as Lord of all and Judge of all. Forgiveness of sins is received by coming under Christ's lordship through faith in his name. Once the Gentiles realize that the invitation is for all, then they can also experience the benefits of knowing Christ as Lord and receive the gift of the Spirit, for the benefits are not reserved for Jews only.

The stylistic features highlighted in the speeches of Acts 2–10 diminish in the rest of the book. Probably one major reason for this is that the emphatic identification of Jesus as the one raised in contrast to those

---

60. Fitzmyer holds that the "miserable Greek" in this verse is an "echo of primitive kerygmatic preaching." Fitzmyer, *Acts of the Apostles*, 460; Bruce speculates that the rough Greek reflects an Aramaic source. Bruce, *Acts of the Apostles*, 225.

who killed him no longer applies directly to audiences outside of Judea. In other words, the Jews who actually killed Jesus are no longer in the vicinity, so the emphatic second-person plural pronouns will be reduced in number, and the contrasting roles of the characters in the story will lessen a little in intensity. At the same time, some contrast is retained between human misdeeds and God's raising Jesus when the story is retold: "But God raised him from the dead" (13:30).

Another reason for the reduction in the use of the emphatic style after chapter 10 may be that Pentecost has reached its most important echo in Caesarea. It is also possible that Paul made less use of those grammatical patterns than Peter did (although Stephen's speech has some of the Petrine elements).[61] In addition, there are simply less gospel speeches later in Acts where the setting is conducive to the kinds of arguments made by Peter. In any event, the primary themes of the speeches continue in the later ones, and the resurrection continues to serve as a primary identifier of Jesus. As is commonly pointed out, Paul's speech in Pisidian Antioch mirrors Peter's earlier speeches in numerous ways, yet it does not exhibit the same extensive use of emphatic pronouns. The closest parallel to Peter's speeches in this regard occurs when Paul contrasts the decay of David's body with Jesus's resurrection: "But he whom God raised did not see corruption" (ὃν δὲ ὁ θεὸς ἤγειρεν, οὐκ εἶδεν διαφθοράν; Acts 13:37). However, one finds both the emphasis on Jesus's identity as superior to that of John (v. 25) and the emphasis on the resurrection of Jesus as the fulfillment of Scripture (vv. 29-37) and as the identifying characteristic that demonstrates his authority to forgive sins and justify those who believe (vv. 37-39).

Luke summarizes Paul's preaching in Thessalonica as a time of proving from the Scriptures "that the Christ had to suffer and to rise from the dead" (τὸν χριστὸν ἔδει παθεῖν καὶ ἀναστῆναι ἐκ νεκρῶν; Acts 17:3). Luke continues with a one-line quotation of Paul: "This one is the Christ, Jesus, whom I am proclaiming to you" (οὗτός ἐστιν ὁ χριστὸς [ὁ] Ἰησοῦς ὃν ἐγὼ καταγγέλλω ὑμῖν; v. 3c). The identification of Jesus as the risen Christ is explicit here.

A clear picture of Luke's agenda in identifying Jesus as Lord and Christ on the basis of his resurrection emerges in the Third Gospel and Acts. In his gospel Luke relies on narrative structure and key Old Testament quotations (e.g., Ps 117:22; 109:1 LXX) to prepare for the

---

61. The discussion of the Law and justification in Acts 13:39 sounds very Pauline and suggests that Luke's source preserves genuine Pauline material.

resurrection preaching in Acts. In Acts, Luke accentuates the identity and exalted status of Jesus by the generous use and strategic placement of pronouns in the sermons. Peter's Pentecostal sermon establishes a pattern for this and develops a line of reasoning that identifies Jesus as the one who fulfills Old Testament expectations of a resurrected Messiah and who now reigns as Lord and Christ.

Summary

One of the most important ways that the Spirit and resurrection relate to each other in Luke-Acts is that they both identify Jesus as Lord and Christ. Luke builds on an Old Testament pattern, also observable in Judaism, of associating a coming Messiah who is characterized by the anointing of the Spirit with an eschatological resurrection. In Luke-Acts the Spirit identifies Jesus as that Messiah in several ways. The Spirit identifies Jesus through the Scriptures, inspired preaching, and prophetic utterances. However, the Spirit not only identifies Jesus as Christ through the ancient prophets, but he also identifies him through the prophetic voices in Luke's birth and inauguration narratives. Through the Spirit, Simeon identifies Jesus as "the Lord's Christ," and John identifies Jesus as the one who baptizes "with the Holy Spirit and fire." Even the Pentecostal speaking in tongues is a form of prophetic praise manifesting the identity of Jesus as "Lord and Christ." The Spirit also identifies Christ by descending on him bodily and thereby anointing him for ministry. Finally, Jesus's role as giver of the Spirit identifies him as Lord and Christ.

Luke also offers proofs of the resurrection to identify Jesus as the long-expected Lord and Christ, but his primary purpose in alluding to the resurrection is not to prove that Jesus has risen, but to demonstrate that the one who has risen is the Christ predicted in the Old Testament. Luke emphasizes Jesus's identity as the Lord and Christ by means of a generous use of pronouns, often occurring in an emphatic position and in the accusative case. The sermons in Acts especially exhibit this grammatical tendency. The pronouns point directly to Jesus as the one whom God raised from the dead. The Spirit and the resurrection receive great emphasis in Acts 2, where both identify Jesus as Lord and Christ. At the same time, it is easy to see how the Spirit particularly identifies Jesus as the Christ, the anointed one, and how the resurrection as an act of enthronement identifies Jesus as the royal Lord.

8

Resurrection and Spirit
The Risen Lord Bestows the Spirit

LUKE HAS THE PRIVILEGE of recording the fulfillment of many of the eschatological expectations found in the Pentateuch and the Scriptures that built on its foundation. At the center of it all is Jesus, the one God has made "both Lord and Christ" (Acts 2:36). This chapter further examines the centrality of Christ and how his resurrection and enthronement prepare the way for his bestowal of the divine Spirit. The discussion highlights how Christ fulfills an ancient pattern of falling and rising, a reversal that has been well articulated by the prophet Isaiah and comes to fruition in Christ's humiliation, death, and resurrection. In turn, Christ's exaltation results in the bestowal of the Spirit on God's humble children who have submitted to Christ's lordship. This chapter also explores how Luke employs cultic images in order to describe Christ's resurrection, his ascension to God's right hand, and the outpouring of the Spirit. Luke gathers the threads of multiple ancient themes, such as that of the temple, and draws them together in Christ. Finally, a brief survey of pneumatic texts in Acts confirms the christocentric nature of the Spirit's activity throughout Acts. The Spirit is the Spirit of the risen Lord Jesus.

The Resurrection Reversal, the Lordship of Christ, and the Spirit

The Scriptures exhibit an eschatological perspective from Gen 1:1 forward and anticipate an ultimate reversal of the devastating effects of sin (Acts 3:21). Reversals of varying magnitudes in redemptive history have already been highlighted in previous chapters. Examples include the re-emergence of dry ground after the flood, the release of Israel from Pharaoh's oppression, the multiple cases of barren women having children, the return of Israel from captivity, the rise of David from shepherd to king, and the exaltation of Jesus from suffering servant to enthroned King. The discussion to follow takes a closer look at how Luke draws on the reversal pattern to inform Theophilus that suffering is not antithetical to God's favor, to show the appropriateness of a divine economy in which the humble receive the eschatological Spirit, and to portray Jesus as the exalted Lord who exercises multiple divine prerogatives including fulfilling the role of distributor of the eschatological Spirit.

Humble Recipients of the Spirit

One need not search long in Luke's gospel for examples of the opposite poles of pride and humility and the reversal of status that often accompanies the pair. Mary announces both an individual and national reversal of circumstances in the Magnificat (1:46–55; cf. v. 71); the widow of Zarephath and Naaman unexpectedly receive divine favor (4:24–27); Luke's Beatitudes have blessings for the poor and hungry as well as woes for the rich and full (6:20–26; cf. Matt 5:3–12); and Peter's confession of Christ provides the platform for Jesus's prediction of his own humiliation then resurrection (Luke 9:20–22). Theophilus must understand that the identification of Jesus as Lord in the birth narratives and Christ by Petrine confession does not exempt Jesus from suffering but virtually requires it in fulfillment of historical-redemptive patterns (11:50–51; 13:33–35). Yet Jesus's suffering only temporarily masks his true identity, as he is vindicated in his resurrection on the third day (9:22; 18:33). Reversal of status is also evident in the least-and-greatest saying (9:48); in the surprising guest list at the eschatological feast (13:28–30; 14:12–14, 22–24; 15:28–32); and in the honor given to the persistent widow (18:1–8), the tax collector (in contrast to the Pharisee; 18:9–14), Zachaeus (19:1–10), the impoverished widow (21:1–4), and the thief on the cross (23:43). James Arlandson demonstrates how Luke presents men and women as experiencing a reversal of status with regard to the kingdom of God. Simon the wealthy Pharisee descends from his position of power when confronted by Jesus, but the sinful woman emerges as favored in the kingdom of God (7:36-50).[1]

Consistent with Luke's kingdom values, he also presents those who bear the Spirit as humble recipients of the Father's gift (11:13). Roger Stronstad has noted how "Luke typically states the spiritual qualifications of those who will receive the Holy Spirit at the beginning of his narrative."[2] In so doing, Luke highlights the essential prerequisite for bearing the Spirit, that is, a heart submitted to God's rule. Elizabeth is barren but blameless (Luke 1:6-7), and she proclaims by the Spirit the identity of her "Lord" Jesus (vv. 41-44). The young virgin Mary is fit to bear the Spirit because she is "the Lord's servant" and filled with faith (vv. 35-38, 45). Another woman, Anna, is an elderly widow who fasts and prays continually and prophesies about Jesus (2:36-38). Zechariah is also upright in character, but the filling of the Spirit is temporarily postponed precisely because of his lack of faith and submission to Gabriel's message (1:18-20, 67). Simeon is "righteous and devout" and living in expectation of Israel's consolation (2:25). John the Baptist's filling is unusual in its timing, but his lifestyle of consecration is consistent with humility. Those who bear the Spirit in the birth narratives provide a proleptic picture of the "sons and daughters" Peter refers to at Pentecost (Acts 2:17-18; cf. Joel 2:28-29). They are the faithful and humble who are fit to bear the Spirit and announce Messiah's advent.

The promise of the gift of the Spirit is for those who call God "Father" when they pray, who demonstrate faith by their persevering and bold prayers, and who simply ask their Father for the gift of the Spirit (Luke 11:1-13). Their prophetic endowment of the Spirit becomes evident during persecution and in the midst of fearful circumstances (12:11-12). The disciples themselves might not be high on the list of likely people to function in the power of the Spirit, but Jesus calls them "little children" who receive revelation in contrast to "the wise and learned" who remain in the dark (10:21). And the disciples, rather than the religious elites, lead the way in experiencing the Pentecostal outpouring. Likewise, the Samaritans (Acts 8:14-17), the Gentiles of Cornelius's circle (10:44-48),

---

1. Arlandson, *Women, Class, and Society*, 158-62.

2. Stronstad, *Charismatic Theology of St. Luke*, 79. He argues this point in order to establish that the coming of the Spirit in Luke-Acts is charismatic in nature and distinct from regeneration.

and a humbled Paul (9:1-19) receive the Spirit. The twelve disciples of Ephesus also receive the Spirit and speak in tongues, but only after they submit to Christ as Lord, being "baptized into the name of the Lord Jesus" (19:5). And Christ himself is the ultimate example of one humbled through crucifixion yet uniquely entrusted with the Spirit (2:33).

Luke concerns himself with the necessary prerequisite to bear the eschatological Spirit, that is, the proper humble response to the lordship of Christ. He assumes that his readers realize that the Spirit does not come in charismatic power automatically, but the Spirit falls on the humble righteous in a manner similar to that of certain Old Testament characters (e.g., Moses; Num 12:3).[3] Luke knows nothing of the contemporary debate over the timing of the Spirit's coming in relation to regeneration. The Spirit often falls after conversion because the humble heart is the prerequisite for the blessing. Luke's primary concerns surround the christocentric nature of the Spirit testifying to the risen Christ and the eschatological availability of the charismatic Spirit to all God's children who have submitted to Christ (Acts 2:38-39). Luke assumes continuity with the Old Testament, in which God's humble servants receive and maintain an endowment of the Spirit to advance the divine agenda.[4]

The Falling and Rising of Many in Israel

The Lord Jesus serves as both the ultimate example of an individual reversal and the cause of reversal in others. Luke gives substantial weight to Simeon's comments about Jesus's identity and mission early in the narrative (2:29-32), and in this setting he tells Mary (2:34b-35):

> Behold, this one is set for a fall and resurrection of many in Israel and for a sign that is spoken against (and a sword will pierce your own soul also) so that the thoughts of many hearts may be revealed.
>
> ἰδοὺ οὗτος κεῖται εἰς πτῶσιν καὶ ἀνάστασιν πολλῶν ἐν τῷ Ἰσραὴλ καὶ εἰς σημεῖον ἀντιλεγόμενον— καὶ σοῦ [δὲ] αὐτῆς τὴν ψυχὴν διελεύσεται ῥομφαία—ὅπως ἂν ἀποκαλυφθῶσιν ἐκ πολλῶν καρδιῶν διαλογισμοί.

---

3. Of course there are some notable exceptions to the general pattern. For example, God sovereignly empowers the pagan diviner Balaam (Num 24:2).

4. Saul serves as a good example of one whose loss of humility also precedes his loss of the Spirit (1 Sam 10-16). Moses, Joshua, Caleb, the seventy elders, Bezalel, Elijah, Elisha, and David serve as appropriate models for Lukan pneumatology.

Several scholars have noted a probable connection between Isaiah's stone passages and Simeon's comment in Luke 2:34b.[5] This assessment is based on the conceptual similarities, such as the christocentric cause of the status changes and the suggestive nature of a couple terms. The "fall" (πτῶσιν) may relate to the stumbling stone of Isa 8:14–15 (LXX), where the Lord will be to Israel "as a rock of stumbling" (ὡς πέτρας πτώματι; v. 14) by which "many will fall" (πολλοὶ . . . πεσοῦνται; v. 15), and to Isa 28:13–16 (LXX), where those who mock God's Word "will fall backward" (πέσωσιν εἰς τὰ ὀπίσω; v. 13).[6] In addition, the term κεῖμαι can mean "to set" or "to lay" something down, such as a stone.[7]

The comparison between Luke 2:34 and Isa 8:14–15 is valid not only on the basis of similar terminology and the fact that Luke later develops stone imagery (20:18), but also because Isa 8 is part of a similar, messianic reversal passage as well as part of a broader emphasis on reversal in Isaiah. The stumbling of Israel results in gloom and darkness (8:22), but the conjunction כִּי ("but," "nevertheless") in 8:23 (MT; 9:1 ET) signifies a reversal: "But there will be no gloom for her who was in anguish" (9:1a ESV). Light replaces darkness for Galileans because of the birth of a Davidic king (vv. 1–7). Simeon's allusion to Isa 49:6 (cf. 40:5; 42:6; 52:10),[8] the application to the babe in his arms, and the eschatological perspective he espouses points to a Lukan dependence on Isaiah's worldview. At Pentecost Peter quotes Joel 2:28 (3:1 LXX) but borrows from the reversal in Isa 2:2 (LXX) for his opening line: "it will be in the last days" (ἔσται ἐν ταῖς ἐσχάταις ἡμέραις; Acts 2:17). Isaiah again announces a coming reversal in 4:2–6, when "the branch of Yahweh will be beautiful and glorious" and the Spirit will bring judgment to Jerusalem.[9] Isaiah's remnant theology expresses a similar idea when the Lord cuts down the tree of Assyria but brings forth a shoot from the stump of Jesse upon whom the Spirit rests (10:20—11:5). In like manner to the Assyrians, the

---

5. E.g., Fitzmyer, *Gospel According to Luke*, 1286; Jeremias, "Λίθος," 271; Stein, *Luke*, 493.

6. See Bock, *Luke*, 2:246.

7. For a detailed survey of uses, see Liddell and Scott, *Greek-English Lexicon*, 934; See also Hübner, "Κεῖμαι," 280.

8. "I will make you as a light for the nations, that my salvation may reach to the end of the earth" (Isa 49:6b ESV; cf. Luke 2:32).

9. Despite the substantial list of scholars who hold that Isaiah 4 is the product of another hand, the reversal here is quite typical of both Isaiah and Hebrew style in general. See the list of scholars provided by Ma, *Until the Spirit Comes*, 137n134.

Resurrection and Spirit

king of Babylon embodies the arrogance Luke detests and the king will be brought down to Sheol (14:12–15). Similarly, the proud oppressor Moab sees his end and gives way to the establishment of a throne occupied by someone from the house of David (16:4–6). It is fitting that the resurrection passage (26:19; see ch. 5 above) occurs in the midst of a unit (Isa 24–27) in which the enthronement of the Lord is celebrated in contrast to the humbling of the nations in judgment (13–23) and woe (28–33).

Isaiah foresees a day when "a king will reign in righteousness and rulers will rule with justice" (32:1 NIV) and when the time of women mourning over destruction concludes with this reversal: "till the Spirit is poured upon us from on high, and the desert becomes a fertile field, and the fertile field seems like a forest" (v. 15 NIV).[10] Isaiah characterizes the period as a time of justice, righteousness, peace, and blessing (vv. 16–20). The Lord's reign in righteousness is associated with the outpouring of the Spirit from "on high" (ἀφ' ὑψηλοῦ; 32:15 LXX; cf. Luke 24:49),[11] and although neither Isaiah nor Luke often speak directly of an outpouring in fructifying, life-giving, and transformative terms (but see the similar reversal in Isa 44:3), the association with the reign of the Lord is very important for Luke (cf. Isa 33:5, 10, 22).[12] Pentecost for Luke is an outpouring of the Spirit on a group of people (Acts 2:17), from on high (Luke 24:49), and evincing the exaltation and reign of Christ (Acts 2:36). The Spirit is not directly mentioned in association with the reversal described as a blossoming desert in Isa 35, but his activity may be assumed as the

---

10. The outpouring and reversal in 32:15–20 is typical of Isaiah and has not "been deliberately interpolated by a later hand to tone down the threat of punishment (vv. 9–14)." Ma, *Until the Spirit Comes*, 80. The modern critical divisions of Isaiah into three parts (as reflected in Ma's book) and the assumption that Isaiah could not have forecast the future would not have been comprehensible to the author of Luke-Acts, as Pao notes. This makes such critical approaches to Isaiah practically irrelevant to understanding Luke. Pao, *Acts and the Isaianic New Exodus*, 19.

11. The interest in height or exaltation is reflected in Isaiah's employment of ὑψηλός, ὕψος, ὕψιστος, or ὑψόω seventy-seven times. Only Psalms has more occurrences with ninety-seven, and Sirach is third with sixty-four. These words are used sparingly in the New Testament, and Luke has no close competitor with twenty-two occurrences in his gospel and six in Acts.

12. Oswalt also notices the kingdom implications of this text: "If God's people were ever to share his character, an outcome devoutly to be hoped for, then it would have to come about through an infusion of God's Spirit into human beings. This development relates fundamentally to a crisis of Lordship. God cannot fill where he does not rule. Thus, it is no accident that this statement occurs in this context of divine kingship." Oswalt, *Book of Isaiah*, 1:88–89.

healing of the blind, deaf, and lame obtains at least partial fulfillment in Jesus's ministry (Luke 7:22). Jesus makes the reference to Isa 35:5-6 in response to the inquiry of John's messengers about Jesus's identity, and Jesus concludes his comments with reference to humility and the kingdom of God: "I tell you, among those born of women none is greater than John. Yet the one who is least in the kingdom of God is greater than he" (Luke 7:28 ESV). These kingdom values are essential to Isaiah's reversal, which is followed by the account of Sennacherib's arrogant threats to Hezekiah and Hezekiah's prayer: "O LORD of hosts, God of Israel, enthroned above the cherubim, you are the God, you alone, of all the kingdoms of the earth; you have made heaven and earth" (Isa 37:16 ESV). The story of Hezekiah's rescue and Sennacherib's demise illustrates the reversal of Isa 35 and contrasts the pride of man with the majesty of God. Jesus (and Luke) clearly understood the kingdom implications of Isaiah.[13]

The prosperity of Hezekiah's time is only a temporary reprieve from the judgment looming over Jerusalem (Isa 39:5-8), but a future day of comfort will come in association with one who prepares the way (40:3-5; Luke 3:4-6). Thus, Isa 40:1 marks the beginning of a great reversal, but does not necessarily mark the hand of a new writer. This chapter also magnifies God as King in contrast to human weakness and the vanity of idols. In contrast to those idols, Yahweh says, "Behold my servant, whom I uphold, my chosen, in whom my soul delights; I have put my Spirit upon him; he will bring forth justice to the nations" (42:1 ESV). Oswalt notes that this is presentation language (1 Sam 9:17) commonly applied to kings (2 Sam 3:18), who were responsible for establishing judicial order.[14] He rightly sees the servant here as a messianic figure like that in Isa 11:1-9 and observes the connection between the emphasis on divine lordship in Isa 42 and the New Testament emphasis on Christ as Lord.[15]

The reversal in Isa 52:1-3 depicts Jerusalem as rising up from the dust to sit (evidently) on a throne.[16] So also the servant experiences exaltation after a period of suffering (52:13; 53:12). Isaiah's later chapters continue to describe the conditions at the time of eschatological reversal, and the Spirit's resting on the Messiah effects the turn-around through the proclamation of good news (61:1-2). When Simeon sees "the Lord's

13. Note also the Davidic element in Hezekiah's story, as God defends Jerusalem for the sake of David (Isa 37:35).
14. Oswalt, *Book of Isaiah*, 2:109-10.
15. Oswalt, *Book of Isaiah*, 2:109-11.
16. Young, *Book of Isaiah*, 3:326.

Christ" (Luke 2:26), quotes Isaiah, and prophesies a fall and resurrection of many in Israel, he is drawing on an entire perspective set forth by Isaiah. It is one in which Yahweh is Lord over all the kingdoms of the earth, Yahweh brings about an eschatological reversal that affects Jew and Gentile alike, the central figure responsible for the turn-around is the Spirit-anointed servant, and the servant himself experiences both humiliation and exaltation. This humiliation and opposition to the servant also results in Mary experiencing the pain of a sword piercing her soul (Luke 2:35b). Luke's dependence on Isaiah for elements of his pneumatology is not surprising when the bulk of Isaiah's references to the Spirit pertain to either the identification and authentication of the Messiah and his prophetic empowerment to proclaim justice, righteousness, healing, and release (11:1-5; 42:1-7; 61:1-2), or to the prophetic empowering of his ancient people (30:1; 48:16; 63:10-11, 14) and eschatological people (59:21).[17] The latter text promises a covenantal blessing of inspired speech, which Peter alludes to at Pentecost (Acts 2:39).[18]

Through Simeon the Spirit affirms that the babe in his arms is the Christ who will suffer, bring salvation to the nations, and cause the fall and resurrection of many in Israel. I have translated the noun ἀνάστασις as "resurrection" in Luke 2:34 because Luke uses it only in reference to resurrection from the dead in the sixteen other places it occurs.[19] Also, the translators of the Septuagint use the verbs ἀνίστημι ("to rise") and πίπτω ("to fall") in combination in Isa 26:19 to contrast the resurrection of the righteous with judgment on the ungodly. Second Maccabees employs similar terminology to describe the seven brothers facing martyrdom (7:9, 14, 36) and in reference to Judas's attempts to atone for the idolatrous sins of his fallen soldiers: "For if he were not expecting those who had fallen to rise . . ." (εἰ μὴ γὰρ τοὺς προπεπτωκότας ἀναστῆναι προσεδόκα; 12:44). There may also be echoes of the rising (ἀναστήσονται)

---

17. Isa 30:1 laments the refusal of Israel to listen to God's prophets in favor of uninspired plans. Other activities of the Spirit in Isaiah include his role in judgment (4:4; 34:16), eschatological renewal (32:15; 44:3), and wisdom (40:13-14). For a discussion of the Spirit in Isaiah, see Block, "View from the Top," 175-207; Hildebrandt, *Old Testament Theology*; Ma, "Isaiah," 34-45.

18. For an in-depth discussion of Peter's use of this passage at Pentecost, see Ruthven, *On the Cessation of the Charismata*, 221-55.

19. Luke 14:14; 20:27, 33, 35-36; Acts 1:22; 2:31; 4:2, 33; 17:18, 32; 23:6, 8; 24:15, 21; 26:23. While the verb ἀνίστημι 'to rise' occurs much more frequently (seventy-two times in Luke-Acts) and in both resurrection contexts and in a variety of more mundane settings, this consistent use of the noun is rather remarkable.

of Daniel's "many" (πολλοί) and the clear separation in the ultimate destinies of people (Dan 12:2) when Simeon announces the fall and resurrection of πολλῶν in Israel due to the babe in his arms.[20] For Luke, resurrection is so enmeshed in the broader concept of rising in exaltation that he could scarcely find a better term than ἀνάστασις. Fitzmyer's comments, however, well summarize the general consensus regarding the mention of ἀνάστασις in Luke 2:34: "Though *anastasis*, which usually means 'resurrection,' is employed here, its meaning is rather more generic and contrasted with *ptōsis*, 'fall, failure.'"[21] It seems more likely that Luke purposely uses ἀνάστασιν to evoke images of resurrection in connection with Jesus early in the narrative to centralize resurrection in Jesus by use of the stone symbolism (John 11:25 says it more directly) and to identify Jesus as the source of resurrection realized by his followers (Acts 4:2; 23:6).[22] Perhaps Luke's habit of using double entendres with resurrection terminology is at work here (cf. Acts 3:7, 22, 26; 7:37).

Luke presents Simeon as a submissive prophet of God, endowed with the Spirit. He announces the coming salvation to both Israel and Gentiles, the divided response (cf. Luke 3:16) in Israel to the Messiah, and the exposure of the condition of human hearts. Christ is both salvation and a stumbling stone, and his voluntary humiliation, despite his identity as Lord, shows his worthiness to bear the Spirit. Luke portrays him as having humble human origins and, as a contrasting figure to Adam, fasting where Adam feasted and refusing the path of pride to royal rule (Luke 3:38; 4:2, 5-8). Thus, Luke repeatedly records Jesus's anointing with the Spirit (3:22; 4:1 (2x), 14, 18 [2x]).

Luke must face two precarious realities of history that would likely seem counterintuitive to Theophilus and the rest of his audience. First,

---

20. Other parallels to Daniel, such as Daniel's heavy emphasis on the kingdom of God, the cutting off of the anointed one (9:26), and the emphasis on resurrection immediately before the death of the prophet (12:1-4, 13), add to the likelihood that the echoes may be deliberate.

21. Fitzmyer, *Gospel According to Luke*, 1:429n34.

22. Note also that the *Nunc Dimittis* (Luke 2:29-32) creates a context ripe for allusions to resurrection. The phrase "glory of your people Israel" (v. 32, cf. Isa 40:5) primes the reader for the ἀνάστασιν πολλῶν. Jewish literature had made a connection between the restoration of Israel's glory and their eschatological resurrection (Ezek 37; 1 *En.* 62:15-16; 2 *Bar.* 51:5, 10), but Simeon focuses the national glory on the baby in his arms. The glory of Christ is preliminarily manifest at the transfiguration (Luke 9:32), but Jesus specifically tells the two on the road to Emmaus that the Christ had "to suffer these things and enter his glory" (24:26).

the death by crucifixion of the hero and Savior in the story requires Luke to draw heavily on the prophecies of Scripture and the Spirit's testimony for evidence of God's plan. Second, the rejection of the Savior by his own people, and their continued animosity toward his followers, requires Luke to offer explanations of how the Jewish Messiah could be rejected by many Jews. The seed for these explanations is found on Simeon's lips and in the Isaianic perspective he adopts. Luke incorporates the kingdom principles of humility and vindication in reversal as major elements in the unfolding story and accentuates Christ's humiliation and then resurrection/exaltation as a fitting precursor to the exercising of the divine prerogative of giving the Spirit.

"The Stone Which the Builders Rejected"

Psalm 118:22 as the Key to the Parable of the Tenants

The Parable of the Tenants, with its Old Testament references, fits well into the above narrative with this climax: "But he looked straight at them and said, 'What then is this which has been written: "The stone which the builders rejected—this has become the cornerstone"? Everyone who falls on that stone will be broken to pieces, but on whomever it may fall, it will crush him'" (Luke 20:17–18; par. Matt 21:42, 44 and Mark 12:10–11; cf. Isa 8:14–15; 1 Pet 2:7–8). That the reversal here refers to Christ's resurrection is more obvious in Acts 4:11 than in Luke 20:17–18, but readers with some knowledge of the resurrection of Christ or the Jewish tradition of messianic interpretation of the stone passages will understand the application to Christ and the allusion to Ps 118:22 (117:22 LXX). Snodgrass rightly sees the quotation as integral to the parable and as the *nimshal*, apart from which the parable lacks its explanation.[23] Luke alone reserves the record of murder for the son only (cf. Matt 21:35–36; Mark 12:3–5); thus, the reversal and vindication provides a particularly fitting exclamation point to the progression from dishonored and injured prophets to the death of the son.

Psalm 117:22–23 (LXX) closely follows the Masoretic Text (118:22–23), and all three Synoptics follow the Septuagint verbatim in verse 22. However, each has a different introductory formula, and Luke's is the most dramatic when he records, "But he looked straight at them and said." This

---

23. Snodgrass, *Stories with Intent*, 291.

follows the μὴ γένοιτο ("May it never be!") response of the Jewish people to the parable (v. 16).[24] Luke and Mark are alike in that the response to Jesus's inquiry about what the owner of the vineyard should do is heard on the lips of Jesus rather than from the crowd (as in Matthew), but only Luke further heightens the drama with the people's response, adds to the tension, and makes the emphasis on judgment all the more poignant. Jesus then asks, "What then is this which has been written . . . ?" (τί οὖν ἐστιν τὸ γεγραμμένον τοῦτο; v. 17). This is a typical Lukan expression (cf. 4:17; 18:31; 21:22; 22:37; 24:44; Acts 13:29; 24:14), and as Bock observes, "It is more direct" than in the parallels.[25]

Matthew includes the warning about the crushing stone after a statement about the transfer of the kingdom to those who will bear fruit (21:43-44), but Luke immediately adds, "Everyone who falls on that stone will be broken to pieces, but on whomever it may fall, it will crush him" (20:18). Jesus draws on texts related by a common word and alludes here to Isa 8:14-15 and Dan 2:34, 44-45.[26] Luke 20:18 does not directly quote any passage, but it emphasizes the concept of a stumbling stone (Isa 8:14) and a crushing stone (Dan 2).[27] Luke omits Ps 118:23 ("This was from the Lord, and it was marvelous in our eyes") in order to maintain the link between stone passages and the emphasis on judgment, but Matthew (21:42) and Mark (12:11) retain it exactly as in the Septuagint. Luke's sobering warning of judgment on the religious leaders in the parable is consistent with similar warnings of woe to those who mistreat and kill God's prophets (11:45-54; 13:32-35). The warning in the parable acquires an even more ominous tone when one considers that Jesus's encounter takes place in the temple and that the vineyard imagery of Isa 5:1-7, which likely exerted some interpretive influence in the parable, was understood to be associated with the temple.[28]

---

24. This is the only place this expression is found in Luke's writings, but it is more commonly found in Paul's letters (Rom 3:4, 6, 31; 6:2, 15; 7:7, 13; 9:14; 11:1, 11; 1 Cor 6:15; Gal 2:17; 3:21; 6:14).

25. Bock, *Luke*, 2:1604.

26. Peter (1 Pet 2:4-9; cf. Ps 118:22; Isa 8:14; 28:16) and Paul (Rom 9:32-33; cf. Isa 8:14; 28:16), apparently taking their cues from Jesus, also combine stone passages with theological intent, although each author has his own method of combining texts. Oss, "Interpretation of the 'Stone' Passages," 184.

27. Bock, *Luke*, 2:1605.

28. See the discussion about Jewish references to the temple (such as in 4Q162) in Snodgrass, *Stories with Intent*, 288.

That the various stone images had acquired a messianic understanding in Judaism is evident in the literature. For example, Josephus says of Dan 2, "Daniel did also declare the meaning of the stone to the king but I do not think proper to relate it, since I have only undertaken to describe things past or things present, but not things that are future" (*Ant.* 10.210).²⁹ Apparently, Josephus was hesitant to expound on messianic claims before his Roman superiors.³⁰ The *Isaiah Targum* 28:16b also understands the cornerstone messianically and royally: הָאֲנָא מְמַנֵּי בְצִיּוֹן מַלַךְ מַלַךְ תַּקִּיף ("Behold, I appoint in Zion a king, a king mighty . . ."), and the *Psalms Targum* 118:22 interprets the stone in personal terms: "The child the builders abandoned was among the sons of Jesse; and he was worthy to be appointed king and ruler."³¹ It is noteworthy that Luke also presents Jesus as a ruler and a judge (Luke 20:18; Acts 7:35-37; 10:42), and as some scholars have observed, the "stone" (*'eben*) of Luke 20:17 appears to have been a play on words with the "son" (*ben*) in Hebrew.³² Thus, Jesus's original spoken words would have lent themselves to a christocentric understanding of the stone (cf. Luke 3:9). The metaphor has changed since Simeon's falling and rising statement, but Simeon's essential points continue to develop.

To Luke, Jesus is the fulfillment of the Jewish messianic expectation of a rejected stone becoming the cornerstone, and the imagery is sufficiently broad to include the event of Jesus's resurrection and the exercise of his lordship in carrying out judgment. Reflection on some important elements in the Parable of the Tenants reinforces the centrality of Christ as Lord in Luke's stone passages. This point gains momentum when one considers that Luke has already quoted Ps 118:26 in Luke 13:35 and 19:38 and that the latter passage assumes a royal reading of the psalm and possibly reflects a use as "an annual rite of reenthronement of the king."³³ Of the Synoptics, only Luke designates "he who

---

29. Translation of Josephus used here is by Whiston, *New Complete Works of Josephus*.

30. Paul Maier makes this observation in Whiston, *New Complete Works of Josephus*, 353. For a substantial list of Jewish references to the stone passages as messianic, see Jeremias, "Λίθος," 272-73.

31. Cook, *Psalms Targum*.

32. Nolland, *Luke 18:35—24:53*, 949; Snodgrass, *Stories with Intent*, 290.

33. This interpretation assumes an earlier application of the psalm. Green, *Gospel of Luke*, 709. Psalm 118 is the last of the "Egyptian Hallel" psalms and was used in various Jewish settings, such as at the Feast of Tabernacles (*m. Sukkah* 3:9; 4:5). See VanGemeren, "Psalms," 713; Goldingay, *Psalms*, 3:354-55.

comes in the name of the Lord" as "the king" (19:38);[34] therefore Luke has primed the reader to understand the royal implications of Ps 118 in the stone passage in Luke 20:17.

Salvation History, Resurrection, and Lordship

Several scholars have noticed that the Parable of the Tenants (Luke 20:9–16; cf. Isa. 5:1–7) assumes a salvation-historical perspective.[35] History records the master of the vineyard sending one servant (Luke 20:10–11) or prophet after another (including John the Baptist in 20:4–6), but in the parable a defining moment in history arrives when the master sends someone in the tradition of the prophets who is greater than the prophets: "I will send my beloved son" (πέμψω τὸν υἱόν μου τὸν ἀγαπητόν; v. 13; cf. 3:22; Gen 22:2). The quotation of Ps 118:22, which is eschatologically oriented in its Hebrew setting, provides the biblical precedent for the rejection and exaltation of this son, making it evident that this entire program is part of the divine necessity emphasized by Luke.[36] The mention of the "beloved" son is perhaps a not-so-subtle hint of the Abrahamic covenant, and the mention of an "heir" and an "inheritance" (Luke 20:14) may remind the reader of how Abraham's heir, Isaac, faced imminent death and so prefigured the one who actually tasted it.[37] Thus, Luke uses Ps 118:22 to place the events of Christ's death, resurrection, and exaltation in their proper salvation-historical context.

Jesus refuses to give the religious leaders a direct answer to their inquiry about the source of his authority (Luke 20:2), but the following parable and allusions to the stone passages (v. 18) make it evident that the source of his authority comes from his identification as the son and heir of "the Lord of the vineyard" (vv. 13, 15)[38] and by virtue of his inherited

---

34. John adds that he is "the king of Israel" (12:13; cf. Matt 21:9; 11:9).

35. E.g., Bock, *Luke*, 2:1596; Fitzmyer, *Gospel According to Luke*, 2:1281; Green, *Gospel of Luke*, 704–5; Nolland, *Luke 18:35—24:53*, 943.

36. Green, *Gospel of Luke*, 709; Pao and Schnabel, "Luke," 364.

37. Green sees several hints of the Abrahamic covenant in this text, including the unspoken contract between the master of the vineyard and the tenants. Green, *Gospel of Luke*, 707–8.

38. Johnson sees the "Lord" (κύριος) of verse 13 as an allusion to Isa 5:7. He argues that the vineyard is Israel and that the tenants in Luke's gospel are therefore Israel's leaders. Several scholars recognize the difficulty of applying the symbolism of the vineyard as Israel in Isa 5 to that of Luke 20 directly. Johnson, *Gospel of Luke*, 305, 308–9.

position as Lord and Judge (v. 18; cf. Eph. 2:20).[39] That Luke is developing his redemptive history with the key elements of resurrection and lordship in mind is borne out by the cotexts. The issue of authority continues at the forefront when the question of paying taxes to Caesar arises (Luke 20:20–26). Next the Sadducees test Jesus with their question about resurrection (vv. 27–40) and Jesus educates his audience about the nature of resurrected people when he affirms that "they are sons of God, being sons of the resurrection" (v. 36). He grounds his teaching on corporate resurrection in the life of God, for whom death is no barrier to relationship and to whom all are alive (vv. 37–38).

The ink is still wet from writing Jesus's reference to Exod 3:6 ("the God of Abraham and the God of Isaac and the God of Jacob"; Luke 20:37) when Luke broaches the subject of Christ's Davidic descent and his lordship: "For David himself says in the Book of Psalms, 'The Lord said to my Lord, "Sit at my right hand, until I make your enemies your footstool." David thus calls him Lord, so how is he his son?'" (vv. 42–44; cf. Ps 110:1). From the passages above, it is clear that both Father and Son are Lord, that Jesus fulfills a Davidic expectation, and that Christ reigns over his enemies. These strands of salvation-historical theology, reversal of messianic circumstances, resurrection, and reign are all mingled together and receive prominence and clarification in Acts, especially when Peter's Pentecostal sermon reaches its pinnacle and he declares that "God has made him both Lord and Christ, this Jesus whom you crucified" (Acts 2:36).

In Acts 4:2 the Sadducees are annoyed not only over the preaching about Jesus's resurrection, but that the disciples proclaim "in Jesus the resurrection of the dead." Paul also preaches this salvation-historical theology summed up in the eschatologically rich word "hope." He appeals to his own background in Judaism, affirms his position as a Pharisee, and divides his audience of Pharisees and Sadducees when he claims that he endures judgment on the basis of "the hope, even [καὶ] the resurrection of the dead" (23:6).[40] Paul appeals to salvation history before Felix when he mentions the Law and the Prophets as the source of his "hope" that "there is going to be a resurrection of the just and the unjust" (24:14–15). When Paul defends himself before Agrippa, he once again refers to his

---

39. Stein sees the mention of the son as "heir" as christological and implying the son's future lordship of the vineyard. Stein, *Luke*, 495.

40. Some translations reflect the close relationship between "the hope" and "the resurrection" by making it "the hope of the resurrection" (e.g., NIV). The resurrection is the essential hope of which Paul speaks.

background in Judaism as a Pharisee and to God's promise to the fathers. Paul refers to the "hope" three times, cites it as the reason for the accusations against him, and defines it as the belief that "God raises the dead" (26:5–8).[41] Paul's eschatological presuppositions surface later in the same speech when he aligns himself with the predictions of the prophets and Moses "that the Christ would suffer and be the first to rise from the dead, and that he would proclaim light both to the people and to the Gentiles" (vv. 22–23). The "first" to rise indicates the tight (and even causative) relationship between Christ's resurrection and the believer's resurrection (cf. 1 Cor 15:20, 23; Col 1:18). Luke further augments the emphasis on the resurrection and other essential elements of the kerygma by placing them in the propositio of Paul's speech (Acts 26:22–23).[42]

The Parable of the Tenants, therefore, typifies Luke's salvation-historical perspective, which involves a clear line of continuity from the Pentateuch forward and encompasses the rest of the Scriptures; Judaism; the sermons of Peter, Stephen, Philip, and Paul; and the entirety of Luke-Acts.[43] Christ is central in all this, and his resurrection secures the believer's resurrection. The stone the builders rejected has indeed become the cornerstone, and because of him many other stones will rise to prominence too.

Luke uses Ps 118:22 to support his salvation-historical approach and to announce the arrival of the days of eschatological fulfillment in Jesus Christ. He sees this passage and the other stone passages as prophesying the rejection and resurrection/rule of Christ. The religious leaders of the day will experience the judgment of the enthroned king, resulting in "others" (Luke 20:16) replacing them, experiencing solidarity with Christ, and ultimately sharing in his resurrection and rule.

Peter's encounter with the religious leaders in Acts 4 reflects Jesus's encounter in Luke 20 and confirms the christological interpretation of Ps 118:22. As in Luke 20, the leaders approach Peter inquiring about the source of his authority in healing the lame man: "By what power or what name did you do this?" (Acts 4:7b; cf. Luke 20:2). Peter's Spirit-filled

---

41. Paul also cites "the hope of Israel" as the reason for his chains when he reaches Rome (Acts 28:20). Once again the context emphasizes the fulfillment and christocentric nature of Scripture (v. 23).

42. Witherington notes this in his outline of the various rhetorical elements of Paul's speech. Witherington, *Acts of the Apostles*, 737, 747–48.

43. Dunn also notices the continuity in the message between Paul and Peter and John. Dunn, *Acts of the Apostles*, 331.

response draws on the terminology of Acts 2:36. Peter replies, "Let it be known [γνωστὸν ἔστω] to all of you and to all the people of Israel that by the name of Jesus Christ of Nazareth, whom you crucified [ὃν ὑμεῖς ἐσταυρώσατε], whom God raised from the dead—by this name this man stands before you well" (4:10). At Pentecost Peter proclaims, "Therefore let all the house of Israel know [γινωσκέτω] for certain that God has made him both Lord and Christ, this Jesus whom you crucified [ὃν ὑμεῖς ἐσταυρώσατε]" (Acts 2:36). The similar language, appeal to the people of Israel, focus on resurrection, and emphasis on Christology creates a clear path from Luke 20 to Acts 2 to Acts 4. Peter quotes Ps 118:20 but adds "you the builders" (Acts 4:11) to specify who the despisers are in the psalm.[44] Peter's version of the psalm substitutes ἐξουθενέω ("to despise") for the more typical ἀποδοκιμάζω ("to reject") found in Ps 117:20 (LXX), and in Jesus's assertions of the necessity of his suffering and rejection (δεῖ ... πολλὰ παθεῖν καὶ ἀποδοκιμασθῆναι; Luke 9:22; 17:25).[45] Both Greek terms can mean "rejection" (cf. 1 Sam 8:7), and the use of ἐξουθενέω ("to despise") was no less confrontational than ἀποδοκιμάζω ("to reject") in a context where Peter singles out the Jewish leaders as "you, the builders" (Acts 4:11; cf. Luke 11:47). The more significant point is that an amazing reversal has taken place, and the divine necessity of the rejection and suffering of the Christ has led to the recognition of him as the sole source of salvation and the divine necessity of finding salvation in him (δεῖ σωθῆναι; "it is necessary to be saved"; Acts 4:12). That the apostles have experienced the power of a resurrection/reversal is also evident in that Peter speaks by the Spirit (Acts 4:8) and the religious leaders recognize the boldness of Peter and John and that their education in the Scriptures has come from outside the usual, approved channels—it has

---

44. The Septuagint follows the Masoretic Text of Ps 118:22 quite closely, but Peter's quotation of the Septuagint (Acts 4:11) contains adjustments to the cases of the nouns and to the forms of the verbs and participles in order for his speech to flow smoothly. Only εἰς κεφαλὴν γωνίας ("unto a cornerstone") remains identical to the Septuagint.

45. Scholars have offered a variety of explanations for the change in terminology, but one of the better suggestions is that Luke draws the term from a Greek translation of Isa 53:3 in an attempt to allude to the suffering servant passage. Bock says the terminology in Acts 4:11 occurs in Isa 53:3 of Symmachus, Aquila, and Theodotion, but he opts for the view that "ἐξουθενηθεὶς represents an independent rendering of the Hebrew term נמאס by a tradition which is independent of the LXX and other NT uses of this text." Bock, *Proclamation*, 199-200; See also Barrett, *Acts of the Apostles*, 1:229-30; Rese, *Alttestamentliche Motive*, 113-15.

come through Jesus (v. 13; cf. Eph 2:17–23). Having experienced a life-altering humbling, Peter preaches Christ and no longer centers on self.

As discussed in chapter 6, the characters in the Lukan narrative struggle to come to grips with the full significance of Jesus as Lord (κύριος), and C. Kavin Rowe correctly observes that Luke also employs "dramatic irony, that is, the literary technique that allows for characters to say more than they know or more than they can retain."[46] Thus, the reader feels both the tension and development in the narrative when characters such as Peter (Luke 5:8), the leper (v. 12), the centurion (7:6), James and John (9:54), Martha (10:40), an unnamed person (13:23), the blind man (18:41), and Zacchaeus (19:8) all address Jesus as Lord (κύριε), but with obviously varying degrees of faith and gravity in the use of the title. Twice in the final chapters leading up to Jesus's crucifixion he identifies himself as the "Lord" in the full, royal sense of the word. He instructs his disciples to bring a colt and explains that "the Lord needs it" (19:31), and he publicly points to his identity as Lord when he refers to Ps 110:1 in Luke 20:41–44. These are the final references to Jesus as Lord (κύριος) before a series of disastrous references to him that intensify the sense of irony and tragedy felt by the reader. Peter boasts, "Lord [κύριε], I am prepared to go with you both to prison and to death" (22:33). The disciples are more than helpful when they point out, "Lord, look, there are two swords here" (v. 38). Jesus is certainly "impressed" when they inquire, "Lord, shall we strike with the sword?" (v. 49). Finally, "The Lord [ὁ κύριος] turned and looked straight at Peter, and Peter remembered the word of the Lord [τοῦ κυρίου], how he said to him, 'Before the rooster crows today, you will deny me three times'" (22:61). Peter's denial of the Lord is a microcosm of humanity's denial of Christ as Lord in his rejection and crucifixion. The title "Lord" is noticeable by its complete absence throughout the crucifixion narrative, and "Christ" is used only in mockery (22:67; 23:2, 35, 39).

The stage has been set for the announcement of history's greatest reversal, the reintroduction of "Lord" (κύριος), and the post-resurrection designation of Jesus as the "Lord Jesus" (Luke 24:3).[47] Upon their return to Jerusalem, the travelers on the road to Emmaus announce that "truly the Lord [ὁ κύριος] has risen and has appeared to Simon" (v. 34). Talbert observes how the resurrection in Luke serves to establish continuity in

---

46. Rowe, *Early Narrative Christology*, 91.

47. Rowe highlights the strategic placement of κύριος after its absence during the crucifixion. Rowe, *Early Narrative Christology*, 183.

the identity of Jesus from before and after Easter,[48] as the Lord of the birth narrative (2:11) and the body of the gospel is the same one the disciples recognize as the risen and royal Lord thereafter. The disciples continually proclaim this reversal when they emphasize the activity of God in raising Jesus in contrast to the murderous activity of man (Acts 1:23-24; 3:15; 4:10; 5:30; 10:39-40; 13:29-30).

The Parable of the Tenants and its accompanying stone passages is crucial in Luke's development of Jesus's credentials as the divine Lord. Through this resurrection reversal the reader learns that Jesus is the exalted Lord and the Judge. With such a divine identity, it is not a very large leap for Luke to also affirm that, in the course of salvation history, this Lord becomes the dispenser of the Spirit at Pentecost and the means of eternal salvation.

Christ's Expectation of Exaltation

The latter portion of the Third Gospel contains several pointers to Jesus's expectation of a reversal, that is, a vindication and exaltation after a period of suffering. Charles Talbert recognizes that Luke "has an interest in individual eschatology,"[49] and this is particularly important for Luke in demonstrating the continuity of Christ's identity and his relationship with the Father despite the temporary limitations in exercising divine prerogatives imposed by the incarnation and crucifixion. The eschatology presented earlier in this work forms a crucial component of Luke's view of Jesus's status and how he can be Lord at his birth and yet become Lord in his exaltation and dispenser of the Spirit.

Throughout Luke's narrative Jesus has repeatedly prophesied or implied his rejection and resurrection (Luke 9:22, 31; 16:31; 18:33; cf. 24:26), and his appeal to the stone passage in Ps 118:22 (Luke 20:17) enhances the expectation of a reversal. The addition of "for all are alive to him" (πάντες γὰρ αὐτῷ ζῶσιν; 20:38) in Luke's version of the resurrection question of the Sadducees suggests that the children of the resurrection are never separated from the Father (20:36). Jesus also envisions his coming in Danielic terms (Dan 7:13): "coming on a cloud with power and great glory" (Luke 21:27), and he confers a kingdom on the disciples and promises they will eat and drink at his table in his kingdom

---

48. Talbert, "Place of the Resurrection," 21-22.
49. Talbert, *Reading Luke*, 221.

(22:29-30) after they learn a lesson in servanthood (vv. 24-27). Despite the momentary "rule of darkness" (v. 53), "from now on the Son of Man will be seated at the right hand of the power of God" (v. 69). The two criminals crucified next to Jesus depict the falling and rising principle of Luke 2:34,[50] and the penitent thief expects Jesus to rule in a future kingdom but does not expect to join Jesus in the kingdom immediately after death.[51] Nevertheless, Jesus promises him that "today you will be with me in paradise" (σήμερον μετ' ἐμοῦ ἔσῃ ἐν τῷ παραδείσῳ; 23:43). Much as in Luke's description of Abraham's bosom (16:19-31), there is a place of blessing that the righteous occupy immediately after death, and the criminal will join Jesus there.[52]

Paradise in the New Testament is the equivalent of heaven (2 Cor 12:4; Rev 2:7), and the term is used in the Septuagint of a garden or park (2 Chr 33:20), especially of the garden of Eden in Genesis (2:8, 9-10, 15-16; 3:1-3, 8, 10, 23-24). In Judaism it refers to the abode of the righteous dead.[53] Jesus functions as God's "viceroy" in using the divine prerogative to grant salvation to the criminal even during the hour of darkness.[54] "Today" in Luke's gospel is a theologically loaded term for the time of God's visitation in salvation (2:11; 4:21), especially with regard to Zachaeus (19:5, 9).[55] This in combination with the criminal's direct address, Ἰησοῦ ("Jesus"; which is rare in Luke and reminiscent of Gabriel's announcement of Jesus's saving name; 1:31),[56] further depicts him as exercising royal and divine power even before his full exaltation. In fact, the combination of "Jesus" and "kingdom" is getting remarkably close to the "Lord Jesus" in 24:3. Luke portrays Jesus as exercising authority to grant access to the eternal rest promised to the righteous in the Old Testament (see chapter 5). Luke's view of Jesus's lordship is expansive and extends

---

50. Danker, *Jesus and the New Age*, 378.

51. Bock, *Luke*, 2:1857; Marshall, *Gospel of Luke*, 873.

52. There is no room in Lukan eschatology for a messianic visit to hell in which the Christ preaches to ancient sinners, performs a ransom, or does similar exploits. The resurrection of Jesus's body from the grave (Acts 2:26-27) must be understood from the vantage point of the Third Gospel's eschatology rather than from that of later church tradition.

53. E.g., see *Apoc. Ab.* 21; *1 En.* 17-19; 32:3; 60:8, 23; 61:12; *2 En.* 65:10; 70:4; *T. Dan.* 5:12; *T. Levi* 18:10-11; *Pss. Sol.* 14:3; Bock, *Luke*, 2:1857; Marshall, *Gospel of Luke*, 1872-73; Talbert, *Reading Luke*, 221.

54. Danker, *Jesus and the New Age*, 378.

55. Bock, *Theology of Luke and Acts*, 135; Danker, *Jesus and the New Age*, 377.

56. Green, *Gospel of Luke*, 822.

even over the issues of individual eschatology, so that the acquisition of the authority to grant the Spirit becomes another prerogative in a series of divine prerogatives attributed to Jesus.

Another remark of Jesus's anticipation of vindication comes near the climactic moment of his death in Luke 23:46: "Father, into your hands I entrust my spirit. And when he had said this, he breathed his last" (πάτερ, εἰς χεῖράς σου παρατίθεμαι τὸ πνεῦμά μου. τοῦτο δὲ εἰπὼν ἐξέπνευσεν). Luke omits the more difficult cry of abandonment from Ps 22:1, found in Matt 27:46 and Mark 15:34, and adds this quotation from Ps 31:5 (31:6 MT; 30:6 LXX).[57] This psalm is an appeal to God for deliverance from enemies and expresses confident trust in God that he will distinguish between the wicked and the righteous. "Love the LORD, all you his saints! The LORD preserves the faithful but abundantly repays the one who acts in pride" (v. 23 ESV). Bock well captures the appropriateness of and reason for the quotation in Luke: "The use of the psalm is typico-prophetic: Jesus is the righteous sufferer *par excellence*. As he faces death, he expresses his trust that God will care for him. In fact, this is a call to resurrect him."[58] Thus, the quotation of the psalm emphasizes the twin themes connected with reversal: Jesus humbly submits to the Father's will but expects vindication via resurrection.[59] Jesus's addition of "Father" to the psalmist's prayer underscores the trusting relationship the Son has with the Father and further dispels any notion that death will separate them.[60] The completion of a reversal and the ultimate exaltation of Christ are never in question.

---

57. Opinions vary as to why Luke differs from the other gospels. For example, Johnson holds that Luke "omits the cry of anguish from the cross, and the accompanying confusion over whether he was calling Elijah. Again the effect is to remove attention from the bystanders and their misunderstanding, and place attention on the death of Jesus." Johnson, *Gospel of Luke*, 381. Matera concludes that Luke wants to emphasize the continued obedience of Jesus to the Father while Mark emphasizes abandonment. Matera, "Death of Jesus," 476.

58. Bock, *Luke*, 2:1862. Emphasis original.

59. Pao and Schnabel, "Luke," 399.

60. The entrusting of Jesus's spirit (πνεῦμα) to the Father and his breathing his final breath (ἐξέπνευσεν) does not appear to have the pneumatological significance of Jesus's giving up the spirit (παρέδωκεν τὸ πνεῦμα) in John's gospel (19:30). John's account may point to the Spirit's availability through Jesus's death and resurrection. See the discussion in Burge, *Anointed Community*, 134–35.

The Ascension and the Promise of the Spirit

Luke certifies the resurrection of Jesus in chapter 24 "with many convincing proofs" (Acts 1:3) and climaxes the narrative with his entrance into "glory" (Luke 24:26, 50-53). The disciples are expected to lay to rest any lingering doubts on the basis of Jesus's own prophecies (v. 7), physical evidence (vv. 30, 37-43), and the totality of biblical testimony (vv. 25-27, 32, 44-47). The resurrection account also establishes continuity between the identity of the crucified Jesus and the risen Lord, as they are one and the same.[61] The final chapter of the Third Gospel also records the progress of the disciples coming to the place of full faith in the resurrected Christ in preparation for their mission. The slowness of the travelers to believe the Scriptures turns to recognition of Jesus and their proclamation that "truly the Lord has risen" (ὄντως ἠγέρθη ὁ κύριος; Luke 24:34). The fear and unbelief of the disciples (vv. 37, 41) give way to open minds and are transformed into the highest and most clear expression of faith and adoration in the Third Gospel: "And after they worshiped him they returned to Jerusalem with great joy" (v. 52).[62] In Luke's gospel the outpouring of the Spirit must await the day of Pentecost because of historical-redemptive timing, but this does not mean the disciples lack salvation as they await the outpouring of the Spirit. Soteriological terminology in relation to the experience of the disciples is noteworthy by its absence in Jesus's forecasting of Pentecost and mission, but their mission to proclaim forgiveness appears as a key element in the scriptural plan, and their occupation as witnesses provides the platform for Jesus to admonish them to wait in Jerusalem for the clothing with power (24:46-49). The outpouring occurs at Pentecost because the timing of the event fulfills (συμπληροῦσθαι; Acts 2:1)[63] the Hebrew Scriptures and because the disciples must first express faith in the risen Christ and see his ascension and glorification before they can engage in mission and provide testimony to it. Thus, their personal regeneration must precede the outpouring of the missional Spirit.

---

61. Carroll, *Luke*, 491; Danker, *Jesus and the New Age*, 400; Green, *Gospel of Luke*, 862.

62. Regarding the opening of the disciples' eyes, see Bock, *Luke*, 2:1937; Green, *Gospel of Luke*, 858, 862. The longer reading of the text, which includes προσκυνήσαντες αὐτὸν (and καὶ ἀνεφέρετο εἰς τὸν οὐρανόν in v. 51), has superior textual support. See Metzger, *Textual Commentary*, 189-90; Osborne, *Resurrection Narratives*, 104n4.

63. Luke is certainly aware of the significance of his terminology and does not use it merely as a transition in the story (cf. Luke 9:51).

Several elements in the commissioning and ascension narrative attest to Christ's royal and divine status finally comprehended after the reversal of his death. Jesus's claim that every corpus of the Hebrew Scriptures centers on him (περὶ ἐμοῦ; Luke 24:44) would be narcissistic in the extreme were his place not actually at God's right hand (22:69). The same applies to his assertion that forgiveness would be preached to all nations "in his name" (24:47), that is, by Jesus's authority. The authority of the Lord God has been transferred to the Lord Jesus,[64] and the church functions in this name throughout Acts (e.g., 2:38; 3:6; 4:10, 30; 8:12; 19:5). A similar transfer is evident in Jesus's promise of the Spirit: "And behold, I am sending the promise of my Father upon you" (καὶ [ἰδοὺ] ἐγὼ ἀποστέλλω τὴν ἐπαγγελίαν τοῦ πατρός μου ἐφ᾽ ὑμᾶς; Luke 24:49a). The "I am sending" (ἐγὼ ἀποστέλλω) is emphatic, the expression "of my Father" (τοῦ πατρός μου) shows the intimacy between Jesus and the Father, and the passage indicates that Jesus assumes the role of distributing the Spirit—a role that was the sole prerogative of the Father (Exod 31:3; Isa 44:3; Joel 2:28–29; Luke 11:13).[65] Just as Jesus promises the Spirit immediately following his assertion that the disciples are "witnesses" (μάρτυρες; Luke 24:48) of his death and resurrection, so Peter ties their role as "witnesses" (μάρτυρες; Acts 2:32) of Jesus's resurrection directly to Jesus's possession of the Spirit, pouring out of the Spirit, and reign as Lord (vv. 32–36). The "therefore" (οὖν) in Acts 2:36 signals the conclusion that, based on Jesus's resurrection and his pouring out of the Spirit, Jesus now exercises the divine prerogative as Lord and Christ.

The conclusion of Luke's gospel confirms the superior and royal status of Jesus in a few different ways.[66] Jesus's leading the disciples out

64. Bock, *Luke*, 2:1939.

65. Although the distribution of the Spirit from Moses to the seventy elders anticipates the distribution of the Spirit from Christ to his disciples, God remains the active agent in Num 11. Christ exceeds this model in personally giving the Spirit. See also Bock, *Luke*, 2:1942; Danker, *Jesus and the New Age*, 399; Nolland, *Luke 18:35—24:53*, 1220.

66. There is a substantial amount of scholarly debate regarding whether or not the ascension occurs on Easter Sunday evening and as a separate event from the ascension in Acts 1. However, there are good reasons to believe that Luke simply telescoped his gospel conclusion to bring closure while anticipating volume 2. The following items point in this direction: the open-endedness of the gospel anticipates Pentecost; there is no firm temporal marker in the narrative of the gospel's ascension; Luke affirms the gospel account in Acts 1:2; and there is a clear theological unity between the two accounts. See Bock, *Luke*, 2:1944n23; Green, *Gospel of Luke*, 860; Osborne, *Resurrection Narratives*, 137–38.

to Bethany (Luke 24:50) is reminiscent of Jesus's leading the disciples to Bethany on Palm Sunday (19:28–29). The effects of the rejection and death of Jesus after the latter event are now wholly reversed.[67] Green captures the significance of Jesus's ascension: "In this account, movement 'upward' signifies in a visible and concrete way the elevated status of Jesus. The glory and regal power anticipated of Jesus (9:26, 32, 51; 19:12) is now made visible to his followers."[68] Jesus's superior status is also suggested in his reception "into heaven" (εἰς τὸν οὐρανόν), a phrase which Luke uses four times in Acts 1:10–11 in anticipation of the outpouring of the Spirit "from heaven" (ἐκ τοῦ οὐρανοῦ; 2:2). In addition, the fact that Luke can unapologetically record that the disciples worshiped Jesus outside of the temple and then blessed God in the temple has both Trinitarian implications and implications for the future role of the temple. Luke has prepared the way for the christocentric sights and sounds of Pentecost with the divine status of Jesus firmly fixed in place.

Pentecost, the Temple, and Christ

No scholarly consensus exists regarding the extent to which Pentecost employs temple imagery and the significance of this for Lukan pneumatology. The following discussion examines Luke's perspective on the temple in relation to the outpouring of the Spirit at Pentecost and his doctrine of the resurrection. This segment begins with a resumption of the discussion of the ascension in Luke 24, where Luke describes Jesus as lifting his hands and blessing the disciples while ascending into heaven (vv. 50–51).

The High Priest, the Temple, and Pentecost

Many scholars point out the similarities between Jesus's blessing (Luke 24:50–51) and that of the high priest Simon II (Sir 50:20–21),[69] but they

---

67. Mikeal Parsons connects Jesus's departure with Palm Sunday and calls it a "Triumphal Exit," but Nolland rejects this terminology. Parsons, *Departure of Jesus*, 104; Nolland, *Luke 18:35—24:53*, 1227; Carroll also makes a connection between the two events. Carroll, *Luke*, 495.

68. Green, *Gospel of Luke*, 861–62.

69. E.g., Edwards, *Gospel According to Luke*, 739; Fitzmyer, *Gospel According to Luke*, 2:1590; Lohfink, *Himmelfahrt Jesu*, 167–69; Nolland, *Luke 18:35—24:53*, 1227; Van Stempvoort, "Interpretation of the Ascension," 34.

differ widely in their understanding of the significance of the allusion. Gerhard Lohfink and others see Luke depicting Jesus as a priest,[70] while Richard J. Dillon and others find no evidence for a Lukan portrait of a priestly Jesus.[71] The latter are correct in observing that Luke does not exercise himself in developing the theme of a priestly Christ, but as Lohfink has demonstrated, the Greek language similarities between Luke's account and the account of Simon II are too compelling to dismiss altogether the priestly implications of the comparison.[72] Although the royal theme dominates Luke's presentation of Jesus, Luke's dependence on all the Scriptures and his generally exalted view of Jesus easily allows him to draw on a variety of images to affirm Christ's superior status. Thus, Jesus performs a divine/priestly function when he announces, "Your sins are forgiven" (Luke 5:20; 7:48). Jesus shows himself superior to the priesthood when he touches a leper without incurring uncleanness and effects healing (5:12–16), and he is "the Son of Man" and "Lord of the Sabbath" (6:5; cf. Acts 7:56), following the Davidic pattern of eating what was reserved only for the priests (Luke 6:1–11).[73] These hints in the narrative point to Jesus as fulfilling the Old Testament cultic system and surpassing in greatness the priests of the old system. Therefore, even though Luke emphasizes the royalty of Jesus, he is not beyond portraying him as also priestly.

This emphasis on fulfillment of Israel's cultic system gains traction within the Lukan inclusio formed by statements regarding Jesus's

---

70. Lohfink, *Himmelfahrt Jesu*, 167–69; Danker, *Jesus and the New Age*, 399–400; Geldenhuys, *Commentary on the Gospel of Luke*, 645–46; Parsons, *Departure of Jesus*, 105; Van Stempvoort, "Interpretation of the Ascension," 34. Brown agrees with others who hold the position that "the priestly blessing that could not be given at the beginning of the Gospel by Zechariah will be given at the end of the Gospel by Jesus." Brown, *Birth of the Messiah*, 280.

71. Dillon, *From Eye-Witnesses to Ministers*, 222; Carroll, *Luke*, 495; Green, *Gospel of Luke*, 861; Nolland, *Luke 18:35—24:53*, 1227. Fitzmyer admits the priestly element but marginalizes it: "Though Luke depicts Christ performing a hieratic act, his theology is not concerned with Jesus as priest (this is the sole reference to it and it is implicit, rather than explicit)." Fitzmyer, *Gospel According to Luke*, 2:1590.

72. Both Lohfink and Nolland compare the Lukan ending with Sir 50:20–22 and Aaron's blessing in Lev 9:22. Luke appears to be aware of both texts. Lohfink, *Himmelfahrt Jesu*, 168; Nolland, *Luke 18:35—24:53*, 1227.

73. Perrin, *Jesus the Temple*, 62. Luke demonstrates the superior status of Jesus using a variety of images. A few other examples not so closely connected with priestly images include his position as bridegroom (5:33–39), his power over demons (11:20) and the ability to give authority over demons to others (10:19), and his wisdom exceeding that of Solomon (11:31).

teaching each day in the temple (19:47; 21:37).[74] After Jesus's cleansing of the temple (19:45-46), Luke notes the murderous desires of the Jewish officials and their questioning Jesus's authority (19:47—20:2). This leads to Jesus's Parable of the Tenants, in which "others" will care for the vineyard (20:16), and then to Jesus's quotation of the stone passage from Ps 118:22, which I have already argued is a reversal and a reference to Christ's resurrection (Luke 20:17). Jesus's previous references to stones crying out (19:40) and not one stone being left on another (v. 44), along with the temple context of both Ps 118 and Luke 20, suggest that the cornerstone in mind is the cornerstone of the temple. Jesus thus rises from the dead as the cornerstone of a new and greater temple (cf. John 2:19-22).[75] J. Bradley Chance also summarizes a similar line of reasoning but rejects any notion of an identification of the temple with Jesus or the church in Luke's writings. He argues that stone terminology does not necessarily imply a reference to the temple,[76] but as pointed out above, the emphasis on the temple in the context of Luke 20:17 is too overwhelming to dismiss the association with Jesus. However, the cautions raised by various scholars regarding Jesus's identification as a priest or with the temple are not entirely without merit, as Luke's primary interest is not to present Jesus as a new temple or as a high priest but as one exalted through resurrection to a place of recognized divine status. But Luke seems comfortable with using multiple images and touching on various elements of the Hebrew Scriptures in order to show Christ as fulfilling the Law, the Prophets, and the Psalms (24:44). Even the stone falling in judgment on the builders who reject the cornerstone (20:17-18) points to Christ as replacing the corrupt power structure in the temple system (19:45-47).[77]

Acknowledging Christ's priestly function in his ascension has some bearing on one's understanding of Pentecost, for it is immediately after Jesus claims that he will exercise the divine prerogative of sending the promise of the Father (Luke 24:49) that Jesus leads the disciples out to Bethany and exercises the role of the high priest in blessing the disciples as he ascends into heaven (vv. 50-51). The juxtaposition of the promise of the Spirit ("until you are clothed with power from on high"; ἕως οὗ ἐνδύσησθε ἐξ ὕψους δύναμιν; Luke 24:49c) with the blessing is reminiscent

74. Head, "Temple in Luke's Gospel," 115.

75. I am following Head's line of reasoning here, and he draws a similar conclusion. Head, "Temple in Luke's Gospel," 115-16.

76. Chance, *Jerusalem, the Temple, and the New Age*, 44-45.

77. Perrin, *Jesus the Temple*, 62.

of the reversal from judgment to blessing in Isaiah ("until the Spirit comes upon you from on high"; ἕως ἂν ἐπέλθῃ ἐφ᾽ ὑμᾶς πνεῦμα ἀφ᾽ ὑψηλοῦ; 32:15a LXX). The activity of God in Isaiah is now effected by the risen Christ as an eschatological fulfillment. The promise also brings to mind the prophetic word to Mary ("the Holy Spirit will come upon you, and the power of the Most High will overshadow you"; πνεῦμα ἅγιον ἐπελεύσεται ἐπὶ σὲ καὶ δύναμις ὑψίστου ἐπισκιάσει σοι; Luke 1:35b),[78] so that the image of God's glory overshadowing the temple applied as an act of God's power in the birth narrative is reapplied to the experience of the disciples at Pentecost. While the temple imagery may not be prominent, it is present in the form of divine power. Furthermore, the blessing is not merely a matter of wishing the disciples well. Consistent with Luke's heavy emphasis on the prophetic word and the often prophetic nature of Hebrew blessings (Gen 49), Jesus both announces and effects the impartation of the Spirit through his blessing, or as Edwards comments, "Jesus not only prophesies the event, but he blesses it into being."[79] Edwards also grasps the significance of Jesus's body language: "The raising of Jesus's hands in blessing provides the symbolic (even sacramental?) accompaniment of the prophecy."[80] It "is liturgical body language in which the body enacts what the will resolves and mouth declares."[81]

Thus, multiple images point to the centrality of Christ in fulfilling the Old Testament. He is at once the cornerstone of a new temple and the high priest who blesses the true followers of God. Worship centers on Christ and can even occur apart from the temple complex (Luke 24:50–53), so that a shift away from the Jerusalem temple has begun in Christ's death, resurrection, and ascension. The rending of the temple curtain in Luke 23:45 also points in this direction, as the mention of it occurs between Jesus's promise to the criminal of access to the kingdom (v. 43) and Jesus's final words of trusting in the Father's deliverance from death (v. 46). Access to the kingdom centers on Christ's exalted status (soon to

---

78. Edwards notices these connections and makes this thought-provoking comment: "The similarity with the annunciation is striking, for it applies incarnational language to the missionary witness of the church." Edwards, *Gospel According to Luke*, 737.

79. Edwards, *Gospel According to Luke*, 740.

80. Edwards, *Gospel According to Luke*, 740.

81. Edwards, *Gospel According to Luke*, 740. It is also important to note that drawing this connection between the promise of the Spirit and the blessing mitigates the force of the argument that the two ascension accounts in Luke 24 and Acts 1 are theologically distinct from one another (as held by Van Stempvoort). See Van Stempvoort, "Interpretation of the Ascension," 39.

become obvious through resurrection and ascension) independent of the temple system.[82] How ironic it is that the religious rulers, as representatives of a waning system, along with the soldiers and one of the thieves, all mock Jesus's ability to save immediately before he demonstrates his saving authority to the penitent criminal (Luke 23:35-43).

The point of all this is that Luke has no aversion to incorporating cultic concepts in his description of Jesus in his exalted role as giver of the Spirit or in his description of the coming of the Spirit at Pentecost. These images add to the exalted portrait of Christ and further establish his worthiness to pour out the Spirit as the one risen from the dead and ascended into heaven. The reader might expect Luke to employ additional cultic images in his account of Pentecost and as a means of further emphasizing the centrality of Christ.

Resurrection and Temple at Pentecost

The discussion now addresses the question of whether or not Luke presents Pentecost in terms of the temple and, if he does, what theological significance this might have. The difficulty in establishing the presence of temple imagery and determining its significance is evident from Gregory Beale's detailed study of the subject. Even after surveying numerous ancient texts, studying the background of the quotations in Acts 2, and arguing in favor of the descent of a heavenly temple in Acts 2, he makes some concessions. "Among the eight Old Testament references . . . surveyed in the main body of this essay, except 1 Kings 8/1 Chronicles 7, none refer explicitly to the temple."[83] Again he notes, "The lines of evidence adduced in favour of this thesis have only indirectly and implicitly supported it." He then speaks in terms of "plausibility" and "probability."[84] Beale offers his stronger arguments in the first of his two articles,[85] yet Steve Smith entirely dismisses Beale's thesis in favor of a christocentric understanding of the temple: "As such, Greg Beale is wrong to understand

---

82. Green sees the rending of the veil as indicating both the obsolescence of the symbolic world of the temple and as preparation for the "centrifugal" mission to the world. Green, *Gospel of Luke*, 826.

83. Beale, "Descent of the Eschatological Temple: Part 2," 82.

84. Beale, "Descent of the Eschatological Temple: Part 2," 83.

85. Beale approaches this topic with some caution throughout his writings. For example, he also speaks of "hints" and a lack of direct references to the Sinai theophany. Beale, *Temple and Mission*, 204-5.

the descent of the Spirit at Pentecost as the replacement of the temple; it is Jesus."[86] The depiction of Jesus as the center of a new temple and the use of temple imagery to describe the nature of the eschatological people of God, however, are not mutually exclusive, and I will argue that Luke incorporates a variety of Old Testament allusions into his Pentecostal narrative, baptizes them into the service of his own agenda, and employs them in a christocentric and missional manner.

Luke presents the temple in a generally positive light (e.g., Luke 1:8–22; 2:21–50; 24:53; Acts 2:46; 3:1), yet he also records its predicted destruction (Luke 21:6) and presents the church as transitioning away from its central role in worship (Acts 7:48–50).[87] Ironically, Cornelius's Gentile "house" (οἶκος) is a place of prayer (Acts 10:30), complete with a vision and an angelic visitation (10:3; 11:13; cf. Luke 1:11), while God's "house" (οἶκος) has become a "den of robbers" (Luke 19:46). However, the temple remains the primary gathering place of the disciples in the early chapters of Acts, and it appears that some or all of the Pentecostal events transpire there. Luke makes no clear statement to this effect, and F. F. Bruce suggests that perhaps the disciples began in a private house and then moved to the temple courts.[88] At least the Petrine speech likely takes place in the temple courts in order to accommodate the crowds, and several hints in the text point in this direction. First, the temple is mentioned several times as the place where the disciples frequently gathered (Luke 24:53; Acts 2:46). Second, Peter specifically gives the hour as nine in the morning (2:15). This is the hour of prayer at the temple, and Luke mentions such an hour in Luke 1:10 and immediately after the Pentecostal story when Peter and John go to the temple for prayer at three in the afternoon (3:1). Third, the celebration of Pentecost increases the likelihood that devout Jews would be found in the temple precincts.[89] Fourth, it is possible that the "house" (οἶκος) where the disciples were sitting (Acts 2:2) is a reference to the temple, as Luke occasionally refers to it as such

---

86. Smith, *Fate of the Jerusalem Temple*, 187. Beale actually emphasizes Christ as the temple in other passages in Acts in his monograph. Beale, *Temple and Mission*, 216–22, 232–37.

87. McKelvey affirms the latter point when he describes the significance of the Jerusalem church's reception of the Spirit-filled Samaritans "without reference to the question of their worshipping at the temple of Jerusalem." This "goes to show that whatever importance the temple previously had for the Christian movement it was no longer seen to possess any essential importance." McKelvey, *New Temple*, 88.

88. Bruce, *Book of the Acts*, 51.

89. Rea, *Holy Spirit in the Bible*, 169.

(e.g., Luke 6:4; 19:46; Acts 7:47, 49) and the Septuagint commonly calls it such (e.g., 2 Sam 7:13; 1 Kgs 6:2; 2 Chr 5:1).

The opening verses in Acts 2 offer the most fruitful possibilities for a temple theme in the Pentecostal narrative. Luke records in verse 2, "And suddenly a sound like a violent rushing wind came from heaven and filled [ἐπλήρωσεν] the whole house where they were sitting." The language is reminiscent of God's glory filling the tabernacle and temple in the Old Testament, and the mention of the 120 (1:15; 2 Chr 5:12) invites a comparison with the completion and dedication of the temple in 2 Chr 5–7. In these chapters the temple is referred to as a "house" (οἶκος) thirty-three times (LXX). Once the author records that "the house was filled [ἐνεπλήσθη] with the cloud of the glory of the Lord" (2 Chr 5:13; cf. 1 Kgs 8:10 LXX); once he says that "the glory of the Lord filled [ἐνέπλησεν] the house of God" (2 Chr 5:14; cf. 1 Kgs 8:11 LXX); and twice he mentions that "the glory of the Lord filled [ἔπλησεν] the house" (7:1–2 LXX). In 2 Chr 5:12 the 120 are priests engaged in worship, and there is an emphasis on praise throughout the proceedings. Likewise, with the descent of the Spirit at Pentecost the 120 respond to Christ's resurrection and enthronement with praise: "We hear them speaking in our own tongues the mighty deeds of God" (Acts 2:11b). Both authors describe the event in theophanic language and include the descent of fire or what appears to be tongues of fire (2 Chr 7:1–2; Acts 2:3).[90]

The emphasis on Davidic fulfillment in Christ's resurrection and enthronement (Acts 2:24–36) is also reminiscent of the chronicler's record of an eternal Davidic throne (1 Chr 17:10–14, 23–27; 2 Chr 6:3–18), and the repeated mention of a house for God's name (2 Chr 6:5, 7–10) finds a counterpart in the name of the Lord Jesus (Acts 2:21, 38; 3:6, 16; 4:10, 12, 17). Even when Stephen quotes Isa 66:1–2 (Acts 7:49–50) in exposing the inadequacy of any handmade house for God, his claim rests on Solomon's prayer of dedication in 2 Chr 6:18.

Luke uses πληρόω ("to fill") to describe the filling of the house (Acts 2:2), but he switches to πίμπλημι ("to fill") to describe how the disciples "were all filled with the Holy Spirit" (2:4). This could be simply a stylistic adjustment or a habit of using πίμπλημι in the passive voice.[91] It is

---

90. Horton views the mass of fire as first representing God's acceptance of the corporate body as the temple and then each flame as representing his acceptance of the disciples as individual dwelling places of the Spirit. Horton, *What the Bible Says*, 140–42.

91. Stronstad points out Luke's common practice of using πίμπλημι in the passive

also possible that Luke uses his preferred term for the filling of the Spirit (Luke 1:15, 41, 67; Acts 4:8, 31; 9:17) to conform to the Septuagintal use and draw attention to the sanctuary filling passages (Exod 40:34–35; 1 Kgs 8:10, 11; 2 Chr 7:1, 2). The effect of this would be to de-emphasize the filling of the Jerusalem temple and apply πίμπλημι to the believers in order to indicate a shift in the locus of God's presence from inanimate buildings to his people. Regardless of Luke's reasons for altering his terminology, the terminology of "filling" invokes sanctuary images. I have already argued in chapter 2 that Acts 1:8 has ties with Luke 1:35 and Isa 32:15 and that Luke 1:35 has roots in Exod 40:35. Therefore Jesus's promise of the Spirit's power to bear witness to him has associations with the divine presence filling sanctuaries—associations that extend back to the Pentateuch. Luke's description of the healing effects of Peter's shadow builds directly on this sanctuary background, for he employs the identical term used of the glory overshadowing the tabernacle (Exod 40:35) and the Spirit overshadowing Mary (Luke 1:35) to describe the people's desire that Peter's shadow "might overshadow" (ἐπισκιάσῃ) the sick and heal them (Acts 5:15). This hope does not reflect the overzealous longings of the desperate, but a Lukan understanding of the healing presence of God's glory emanating from Jesus's disciples (cf. Luke 6:19). Luke describes the Spirit-filled disciples of Jesus with sanctuary terminology, but he does not do so in order to define the moment of their personal regeneration; he does so to portray them as Christ's charismatic agents of eschatological healing and restoration.

It also seems that the common thread among passages containing tongues of fire is simply the divine presence, whether there are direct temple associations or not.[92] However, to speak of divine presence is essentially to define what a temple is all about. The *Liturgy of Three Tongues of Fire* from Qumran (1Q29, partially overlapping with 4Q376) evinces similarities with Acts 2:3. This document is based on Exod 28:9–12 and describes the use of the gemstones set on the shoulders of the high priest's ephod in a ritual for testing prophets.[93] "And he shall go out with it with tongues of fire. The left-hand stone on his left side will show itself to

---

voice. Stronstad, *Spirit, Scripture and Theology*, 82.

92. Some relevant texts concerning tongues of fire include: Isa 5:24; 30:27–28; *1 En.* 14:8–25; Philo, *Decal.* 1:46; *Gen. Rab.* 59:4.

93. Menzies, "Pre-Lucan Occurrences," 58. For a description of how the stones function, see Josephus, *Ant.* 3:214–18.

the eyes of all the assembly until the priest has completed his speech."[94] Fragments 2–7 of 1Q29 contain the unusual phrase "three tongues of fire," which apparently "come to rest on the high priest."[95] The tongues of fire both represent the divine presence and relate to the high priest's prophetic activity. Thus, the cult, prophetic activity, and tongues of fire combine in this text at Qumran (cf. Luke 2:25–38).

Beale argues that the "tongues as of fire" of Acts 2:3 "appears to be a theophany associated with the descending divine presence of the heavenly temple."[96] To make such an argument, he depends heavily on the notion that Pentecost reflects the Sinai tradition and on the further thought that Luke views Sinai in terms of a sanctuary. Opinions vary widely on the degree to which Sinai forms the backdrop of Pentecost, whether or not Luke depicts Jesus's ascent to heaven in a manner similar to Moses's ascent of Sinai, and the possible implications for viewing Pentecost as a new covenant event like Moses's giving of the law.[97] Beale also develops the idea of "tongues of fire" as having temple associations by tracing similar phrases through the Scriptures and ancient literature.

Regardless of whether or not one can follow Beale entirely in his thesis, there does appear to be enough evidence to conclude that Luke employs some temple imagery.[98] When one combines the temple imagery with the priestly blessing of Jesus in Luke 24:50–53 and his exaltation as Lord, it starts to sound like how the Pentateuch presents Adam as priest-king and as God's vice-regent (cf. Luke 3:38—4:1). In addition,

---

94. 4Q376 Fr. 1 II, 1–3. English translation from Vermes, *Complete Dead Sea Scrolls*, 578.

95. Menzies, "Pre-Lucan Occurrences," 55; Beale emphasizes the relation of the high priest to the temple as well as the prophetic function in this text. Beale, "Descent of the Eschatological Temple: Part 1," 89–91.

96. Beale, "Descent of the Eschatological Temple: Part 1," 76.

97. These scholars favor a Sinai background to Pentecost: Dunn, *Baptism in the Holy Spirit*, 48–49; Niehaus, *God at Sinai*, 350–53, 371–72; Turner, *Power from on High*, 279–89; The following scholars reject or limit images of Sinai at Pentecost: Bock, *Acts*, 96; Keener, *Acts*, 1:787; Levison, *Filled with the Spirit*, 325; Menzies, *Empowered for Witness*, 191–92.

98. Although I disagree with Beale at various points, his work does add to the probability that Luke draws from the Sinai theophany and that Acts 2 contains temple imagery. I disagree with Beale that Pentecost is a reversal of Babel, preferring to see references to that story as pointing to the promises of Abraham in Gen 12. I also question his equation of the fire of Pentecost with that of John's prophecy (Matt 3:11; Luke 3:16) and his identification of John 20:22 with Pentecost. See Beale, "Descent of the Eschatological Temple: Part 1."

the emphasis on missions at Pentecost suggests that this new "temple will not fail to fulfil the intention of Eden's and Israel's temples to expand its borders until the entire earth comes under its roof."[99] Given the identification of Christ as the cornerstone in his resurrection (Acts 4:11), one can find temple imagery applied both to Christ and, by extension, to the disciples at Pentecost as well. Luke is not averse to using multiple Old Testament images to describe the eschatological events unfolding at Pentecost. However, the larger question is not simply whether Luke employs temple terminology, but how he applies it.

Luke's view of Christ as the eschatological fulfillment of the entire Old Testament (Luke 24:44–49) leads him to interpret the cultic images of Israel as christocentric. Pentecost in particular becomes a christocentric event. This is accomplished by framing the Pentecostal outpouring with proofs of Christ's resurrection and his ascension in Acts 1 and with a sermon declaring his resurrection and exaltation in Acts 2. Even the addition of Matthias to the eleven (1:23–26), with all its symbolism of twelve (6:2), has more to do with the necessity of having another eyewitness of the resurrection than with the numerical symbol itself (1:22). In fact, the number twelve receives no mention in the story of Judas's replacement. It would be easy to assume that the Spirit descends from the heavenly temple at Pentecost, yet Luke does not direct the reader's attention to a temple so much as to Christ himself. Luke's fourfold repetition of "into heaven" at the ascension (1:9–11) anticipates the sound "from heaven" (2:2). Luke's use of the aorist passive ἐπλήσθησαν ("they were filled"; v. 4) to describe the filling of the disciples implies divine activity,[100] and the actor here is the Christ who has gone "into heaven" (cf. Luke 3:16; Acts 2:33). At the same time, Pentecost's theophanic language, reminiscent of Sinai (Exod 19:16–19) and especially the temple (40:34–35; 2 Chr 5:13–14; 7:1–3), becomes more of a Christophany, as the God who pours out the Spirit (Acts 2:17, 18) delegates this role to the Lord Jesus (vv. 33, 36). The glory commonly associated with Old Testament theophanies is now associated with Christ in his transfiguration (Luke 9:30–32) and ascension (as implied by the cloud; Acts 1:9), his future coming (Luke

---

99. Beale, *Temple and Mission*, 208; He recognizes that "Joel and Acts do not have in mind primarily the regenerating function of the Spirit but that function which would enable people to serve in various capacities." Beale, "Descent of the Eschatological Temple: Part 1," 94.

100. Lenski, *Interpretation of the Acts*, 60.

21:27), his death and resurrection (24:26; Acts 3:13–16; 22:11), and his presence with the Father (Acts 7:55).

The latter text is particularly relevant to the discussion of how Luke Christianizes Hebrew cultic symbols and concepts. The "God of glory" (θεὸς τῆς δόξης; Acts 7:2) and Stephen's vision of the "glory of God and Jesus standing at the right hand of God" (δόξαν θεοῦ καὶ Ἰησοῦν ἑστῶτα ἐκ δεξιῶν τοῦ θεοῦ; 7:55) frames Stephen's speech and recontextualizes the concept of glory from temple to Jesus. The Jews confronting Stephen err twice in that they mistakenly limit God's presence to a temple "made by hands" (v. 48; cf. 2 Chr 6:18) and fail to see the glory of God in Christ (John 1:14).[101] The significance of all this is that Luke can draw on a number of related concepts from the Old Testament, including the theophanic cloud, temple, fire, divine presence, glory, filling, and the Holy Spirit, and relate them all to Christ's resurrection, ascension, and exaltation to the right hand of God.[102]

The disciples become empowered bearers of the divine presence/Spirit by virtue of Christ's glory and for the express purpose of testifying to his resurrection and exalted status. Consequently, Luke's primary themes of empowerment, prophetic speech, eschatological fulfillment, Davidic reign, and testimony to the resurrection remain in clear sight in the narrative, but he employs other more subtle images to enrich his heavily christocentric and missional emphases. Some temple terminology applies to both Christ and the church, but the terminology serves his more dominant themes. Luke does not use temple terminology to develop a regenerational pneumatology in the Pauline sense of ontological indwelling, but to enrich his charismatic pneumatology with Hebrew

---

101. The latter point mitigates some of Chance's argument that Luke presents the tabernacle in a more favorable light as a model for a God on the move. For Luke any Old Testament image of dwelling place must be understood in relation to the glory of Christ. In any event, there is little to go on to draw a major distinction between tabernacle and temple theology in Luke-Acts (Acts 7:44; 15:16). Chance, *Jerusalem, the Temple, and the New Age*, 40–41. Regarding the significance of "David's fallen tabernacle" in Acts 15:16, the same principle applies in that the mention of David and the contextual emphasis on the "Lord Jesus" (as discussed in chapter 6 of this work; Acts 15:11, 26) makes any cultic reference subject to a christocentric understanding. Strauss seems to have the right idea in interpreting the rebuilding of the fallen tabernacle as a reference to "the restoration of the Davidic dynasty accomplished through the life, death, resurrection and exaltation of Jesus." Strauss, *Davidic Messiah*, 190. Keener's understanding is similar to that of Strauss. Keener, *Acts*, 3:2255–57.

102. Baltzer also notes how glory and Spirit are related concepts in Luke. Baltzer, "Meaning of the Temple," 277.

images and magnify the glory of Jesus, who is "both Lord and Christ" (Acts 2:36). Luke employs temple images to describe both Christ's resurrection and the disciples' reception of the Spirit. Christ is the cornerstone of a new temple, and his people are "filled" with the Holy Spirit as the temple of old. But the terminology and concepts of glory related to the exalted Christ and the filling with the Spirit make it evident that the disciples' filling with the Spirit is an experiencing of the glory of Christ realized through his resurrection and exaltation. Once again, the Spirit ultimately points to the Lord Jesus in Luke-Acts.

The Spirit of Jesus in Acts

When the risen Lord poured out the Spirit at Pentecost, "they were all filled with the Holy Spirit and began to speak in other tongues as the Spirit was giving them utterance" (Acts 2:4). The multiple languages symbolize the missional purpose of the Spirit's filling, and the Spirit empowers the proclamation of Christ throughout Acts. The Holy Spirit directs the missionary efforts of Paul and his travelling companions (Acts 16:6), but Luke best expresses his christological perspective of the Spirit when he comments that "the Spirit of Jesus did not allow them" to go into Bithynia (v. 7). The designation "Spirit of Jesus" occurs only here in the New Testament (cf. Phil 1:19), but the expression encapsulates the intimate relationship between Christ and the Spirit at Pentecost and reminds the reader that Jesus continues to work by his Spirit.[103] A brief survey of the activity of the Spirit in Acts demonstrates Luke's continued intention to depict the Spirit as the Spirit of the risen Lord Jesus.

Peter informs his Pentecostal audience that the gift of the Spirit is a promise available for everyone the Lord calls, but first he instructs them in repentance and baptism "in the name of Jesus Christ" (Acts 2:38). The emphasis is on submission to Christ, especially since some of that audience had approved of his crucifixion. Likewise, the Samaritans had received baptism in "the name of the Lord Jesus" some time before receiving the Spirit (8:16). In addition, the narrative implies a contrast between Simon's greedy motives for desiring the Spirit (vv. 18–19) and the faithful proclamation of "the word of the Lord" by Peter and John (8:25). Baptism "into the name of the Lord Jesus" also precedes Paul's laying hands on the

---

103. Kurz and Peterson also see theological significance in Luke's use of the phrase. Kurz, *Acts of the Apostles*, 251; Peterson, *Acts of the Apostles*, 455.

twelve Ephesian men for their reception of the Spirit. The emphasis is not on a baptismal formula as such, but on the necessity of submission to the exalted Lord as a prerequisite for the filling of the Spirit.[104]

When Luke associates the Spirit with the Scriptures, the biblical texts often prophesy the coming of Christ (Acts 4:25–26; 7:51; cf. 8:29–33). When the Spirit appoints overseers in the church in Ephesus, they are specifically overseers of the church "he bought with his blood" (20:28). The Spirit's operation in connection with Cornelius and his household (10:19, 38, 44–45, 47; 11:12, 15–17; 15:8, 28) revolves around the proclamation that Jesus Christ is Lord of all (10:36). Ananias and Sapphira test "the Spirit of the Lord," that is, the Lord Jesus (5:3, 9). Likewise, Philip was taken away by "the Spirit of the Lord" (8:39). The church multiplied by living in "the fear of the Lord" and the encouragement of "the Holy Spirit" (9:31). Paul was filled with the Holy Spirit and pronounced a temporary judgment of blindness on Elymas for perverting "the way of the Lord" (13:9–11). It was while the prophets at Antioch were worshiping the Lord that the Spirit instructed them to send Paul and Barnabas on their missionary journey (13:1–4). Luke describes Barnabas as a man "full of the Holy Spirit" who encouraged the people of Antioch to remain faithful to the Lord and influenced people to come to the Lord (11:23–24).[105]

Luke often uses the terminology of "filled" or "full" to describe the Spirit's enablement in the proclamation of Christ's resurrection or exaltation. Peter was "filled with the Holy Spirit" in order to proclaim "the name of Jesus Christ" and the resurrection message to the adversarial Jewish leaders (Acts 4:8–12). The gathered believers were "filled with the Holy Spirit" to boldly proclaim "the word of God" (v. 31), and the apostles were testifying "to the resurrection of the Lord Jesus" (v. 33; cf. 13:52—14:3). Stephen was "full of the Holy Spirit" when he saw Jesus standing at God's right hand and gave testimony to Jesus's exalted status (7:54–56). Paul also needed to "be filled with the Holy Spirit" (9:17) in order to testify of his encounter with the risen Christ and carry his name before the

---

104. The fact that water baptism takes place after the reception of the Spirit at Cornelius's household demonstrates that the ritual of baptism was not the primary issue. Peter's audience grasped his announcement of Christ's lordship (Acts 10:36) and submitted their hearts to him before Peter could even finish his sermon (11:17; 15:8–9).

105. Peter's application of Joel's "day of the Lord" and "name of the Lord" (Joel 3:4–5 LXX; Acts 2:20–21) is indicative of the ease with which Luke applies the divine title to Jesus. This precedent, in combination with the immediate context of the texts cited, justifies interpreting the "Lord" in these passages as the "Lord Jesus."

Gentiles (v. 15). Peter and the apostles also described the Spirit's role in witnessing to the death, resurrection, and exaltation of Jesus (5:29–32).

To be sure, the Spirit's functioning in Acts is charismatic and prophetic in nature. This is evident not only at Pentecost (Acts 2:17–18), but wherever Spirit-filled proclamation is in view and also in the daily activity of the church (11:28; 20:22–24; 21:4, 10–14).[106] However, every pneumatic text in Acts is ultimately oriented toward the risen and exalted Lord Jesus Christ. He is the tie that binds the various texts together. The Spirit at Pentecost and the Spirit throughout Acts is always the Spirit of the risen Lord Jesus.

Summary

The themes of resurrection and Spirit converge most clearly in the ending of Luke's gospel and in the Pentecostal narrative, for it is through the resurrection as part of the one theological motion of resurrection, ascension, and exaltation that Christ's divine status is observed and that he exercises the divine prerogative to pour out the Spirit on his waiting followers. Through the Pentecostal event, Theophilus not only learns about empowerment for ministry, but he also learns that Jesus's suffering and death does not impinge on his royal identity but serves as a climax of an ancient pattern of reversals, fulfills an eschatological expectation of one who is uniquely anointed, and enables the launching of a global mission.

Luke portrays Jesus as the "Lord and Christ" (Acts 2:36) who is recognized through his resurrection and exaltation as fully suited to exercise various divine prerogatives including judging, granting salvation, and pouring out the Spirit. Luke shows Theophilus that Jesus's humility fulfills a pattern that has its roots in the Old Testament, serves as a model for others, typifies people of the Spirit, and results in honor. Luke employs Simeon's falling and rising terminology (Luke 2:34), the reversal theme from Isaiah, and the stone passage of Ps 118:22 to demonstrate

---

106. Agabus and other prophets operating under the Spirit's influence repeatedly warned Paul about the coming persecution in Jerusalem. Paul chose to travel to Jerusalem in spite of the warning, as the purpose of the warnings was not to keep Paul from Jerusalem but to prepare Paul and the church for the events to come (Acts 21:13–14). Horton also suggests that the Spirit's warnings may have helped defend the church from the claims of the Judaizers that Paul's arrest was a divine judgment. Horton, *Book of Acts*, 246. For the prophetic emphasis in Luke-Acts, see Johnson, *Prophetic Jesus*; Stronstad, *Prophethood of All Believers*.

that Christ's path of humiliation and resurrection was anticipated by the prophets and offers an explanation for the rejection Christ received from his own people. At the same time, those who follow Christ in humility and submit to his lordship can enjoy the blessing of the outpouring of the eschatological Spirit.

The salvation-historical perspective of the Parable of the Tenants and all of Luke-Acts confirms the divine necessity of Christ's sufferings, but Jesus's adoption of an Old Testament perspective of individual eschatology bolsters his unwavering certainty that death cannot separate him from his Father.[107] He fully expects a resurrection and exaltation. Likewise, his followers should expect resurrection (Acts 4:2) and royal honors (Luke 22:29–30), as their resurrection is secured in Christ's resurrection.

In the meantime, Jesus's followers have the opportunity to experience the eschatological blessing of the Spirit. Luke describes Christ in priestly terms and as one who has the authority to bless into being the bestowal of the Spirit.[108] Luke also reaches back to the Hebrew Scriptures to borrow tabernacle and temple images to describe both Christ as the corner of a new temple and the descent of the Spirit on the believers, but the cultic terminology serves the greater purpose of pointing to the glory of Christ as the one who fills others with the divine presence. The disciples do not become believers at Pentecost, but they become bearers of the divine presence to the nations and empowered proclaimers of the Lord Jesus Christ. Christ is the risen Lord, and the Lord pours out the Spirit.

A review of the Spirit's activity throughout Acts reinforces and confirms Luke's core convictions about the christocentric nature of the Spirit's work. The Spirit is given after one submits to the lordship of Christ, and Luke often associates this submission with baptism in the name of the Lord Jesus. The Spirit functions as "the Spirit of the Lord" (Jesus), and Luke even calls him "the Spirit of Jesus" (Acts 16:7). When believers are filled with the Spirit, they testify to his resurrection and exalted status. The risen Lord bestows the Spirit, and the Spirit testifies to the risen Lord Jesus Christ.

---

107. E.g., Luke 20:36–38 with Exod 3:6; Luke 23:46 with Ps 31:5b; Luke 23:43; 24:49.

108. Edwards, *Gospel According to Luke*, 740.

9

Conclusion

PETER EXPRESSES THE CENTRAL truth of Luke-Acts when he explains the Pentecostal effusion of the Spirit as a consequence of the resurrection and exaltation of Jesus: "Therefore let all the house of Israel know for certain that God has made him both Lord and Christ, this Jesus whom you crucified" (Acts 2:36). Other important themes in Luke-Acts, such as universal salvation, derive from this identification of Jesus, and this pinnacle of Pentecostal pronouncements also serves as the focal point at which the royal exaltation of Jesus via resurrection and the bestowment of the eschatological gift of the Spirit converge. The following concluding thoughts highlight four ways Luke's doctrine of the resurrection and his pneumatology intersect and then draw out some implications for critical scholarship and for the ongoing Pentecostal debate.

Luke taps into an eschatological perspective that has origins in the opening verses of Gen 1. Thus, the first intersection of resurrection and Spirit for Luke is not so much in a theological proposition as in a fundamental presupposition, that is, that God continues to advance his plan in history toward an ultimate goal and that his plan reaches a new stage of development in Jesus Christ. The resurrection of Jesus, as a distinct eschatological event within a single theological motion consisting of resurrection, ascension, and exaltation to the right hand of God, marks the enthronement of the long-awaited Messiah. Upon this enthronement another eschatological event unfolds in Christ's exercising the divine prerogative to pour out the Spirit in fulfillment of Joel 2:28–29. The Pentateuch lays the groundwork for anticipating a Spirit-filled Messiah and the democratization of the Spirit, on the one hand, and the eventual conquest of death and enthronement of a Messiah in the tradition of Enoch's translation, on the other hand. The eschatological Spirit and the hope of resurrection meet in Christ at Pentecost.

Along with Luke's evident emphasis on fulfillment of Scripture and some new creation images, Luke has a robust individual eschatology drawn from conceptions of God's faithfulness beyond the grave (Luke 20:37–38), a place of rest and security with the people of God (16:23), judgment for the wicked (vv. 23–24; Acts 3:23), and resurrection (2:26–27). The resurrection of Jesus requires reflection on the hereafter, and Luke makes eternal destinations dependent on one's response to Christ (Luke 23:42–43; Acts 2:38). In short, eschatology is christocentric for Luke.

A second way that resurrection and Spirit converge in Luke's perspective is through the Spirit-empowered proclamation of the resurrection. Many have recognized Luke's emphasis on prophecy inspired by the Spirit, but the object of such utterances is even more important than the prophetic means, for such utterances are typically christocentric. Upon Jesus's resurrection and the subsequent outpouring of the Spirit, the central subject matter of inspired utterance is the resurrection of Christ. This is reflected in the preaching of the kingdom, the proclamation of "the word," and clear statements that the disciples receive the power of the Holy Spirit to be witnesses of Christ's resurrection (Acts 1:8, 22). Even the Pentecostal tongues, symbolic of the spread of Christ's rule over the nations, are an inspired response to the resurrection and enthronement of Christ.

Luke does not primarily set out to prove that Jesus has risen from the dead, but rather to inform his readers of the identity of the risen one. In this one sees a third manner in which resurrection and Spirit converge in Luke-Acts: the resurrection serves to identify Jesus as the Lord and the Spirit identifies him as the Messiah/Christ ("anointed one"). The Lord and Christ concepts have a royal lineage dating back to Adam, who, as God's vice-regent, was given the task of tending the garden sanctuary and expanding it over the globe. Enoch, Moses, Elijah, and others anticipate the coming of a royal Messiah, but the life of David and the narrative of 1 and 2 Samuel most clearly depict the coming of a king who will experience a falling and rising. Isaiah, Ezekiel, Daniel, and Hosea each develop various strands of this history and conceive of an anointed but suffering servant who rises again. This expectation spills over into some branches of Judaism, so that the expectation is alive and well in Luke's birth narratives. Luke relies heavily on biblical history, the charismatic life of Jesus, and the clever use of grammar in order to present Jesus as the "Lord and Christ" of Pentecost. God anointed Jesus for his ministry and delegated to him the responsibility of pouring out the Spirit upon his resurrection/enthronement; therefore, "all Israel," Theophilus, and the ends of the earth should know that Jesus is the long-expected Messiah, the "Lord and Christ" (Acts 2:36).

A fourth convergence of resurrection and Spirit relates directly to the third, involves Jesus's bestowing of the Spirit, and concerns the availability of eschatological blessings to believers in Jesus. Peter makes it evident at Pentecost that Jesus exercises the divine prerogative of pouring out the Spirit. This speaks to his divine identity and fits well with his other roles including granting forgiveness, dispensing salvation, and judging the nations. Although Jesus has always been Lord (Luke 2:11), it was necessary for him to fulfill the historical-redemptive plan of God in time in order for him to fully exercise the divine prerogative of bestowing the Spirit. Thus, there is a historical and theological necessity for Jesus to first rise from the dead in order for people to realize his true identity, and the bestowing of the Spirit evinces that identity. Luke's depiction of Jesus as the risen and enthroned Lord and bestower of the Spirit at Pentecost signifies that a new stage in the history of redemption has begun. Consequently, the blessings of Christ's resurrection and Spirit are available for the followers of Jesus; the nations apprehend the hope of the future resurrection and experience a baptism in the Spirit. In Christ's resurrection and anointing of the Spirit, the believers have resurrection and fullness of the Spirit.

The conclusions drawn from the biblical-theological approach employed in this study have a direct bearing on various critical issues. The framing element between Gen 1 and Deut 32 suggests continuity within the Pentateuch itself and contributes to the eschatological perspective on pneumatology and the hope of resurrection. Regarding the latter, all the core elements of a doctrine of resurrection are present in the Pentateuch, including pointers to the demise of death itself, anticipation of resurrection (Gen 22:5), God's sovereignty over life and death, the covenantal and eternal faithfulness of God to his children (Exod 3:6), and the solidarity of God's people. Luke and other New Testament writers did not impose a doctrine of resurrection on the ancient texts of Scripture; rather, they clearly understood the implications of occasions when God brought life to barren lands and barren wombs. Therefore it is unnecessary to limit

Hebrew hopes only to continued existence via one's offspring or to posit the arrival of a doctrine of resurrection in the Maccabean period.

Neither does Luke derive his pneumatology primarily from later Judaism or Greek influence. He relies heavily on the Pentateuch for pneumatic themes, images, and language. His christocentric view of the Spirit has its roots in the story of Moses, and this perspective receives substantial support from the life of David.

Luke's reliance on the ancient Scriptures and his assumption of a basic unity to them also speaks to the matter of Lukan hermeneutics. Modern source-critical theories regarding the Pentateuch and Isaiah offer little assistance to the interpreter who desires to understand Luke on his own terms and from his eschatological and historical-redemptive perspective.

A christocentric approach to Luke's doctrine of resurrection and the Spirit has implications for the ongoing Pentecostal debate and the relationship of Luke's pneumatology with the rest of the canon. What is of primary importance is that Luke's writings are entirely consistent with the New Testament's ubiquitous emphasis on the Lord Jesus Christ, eschatological perspective, and basically christocentric orientation of pneumatology (John 14:25–26; Rom 8:9; 1 Cor 12:3; 1 Pet 4:14; Rev 1:10–20). Paul directly relates the Spirit to Jesus's resurrection and to his identity as the Son of God in Rom 1:4.[1] If one must apply a lens to the pneumatology of the various New Testament authors, then let that lens be Christ.

In an attempt to conform Luke's pneumatology to a conversion-initiation or new birth model, several scholars have sought alternative explanations for the apparent distinction between the moment of faith and the gift of the Spirit in various stories in Luke's narrative (e.g., Luke 24:50–53; Acts 2:4; 8:12, 15–17).[2] But Luke does not exercise himself at all to explain what some contemporary scholars see as self-contradictory or "anomalous."[3] For Luke, a delay in the reception of the eschatological blessing after Pentecost may not be necessary or ideal, but it is entirely

---

1. Luke does not attribute the resurrection of Jesus to the activity of the Holy Spirit, but it is a matter of debate whether or not Paul does. Burke accepts this notion and Fee rejects it. See Burke, "Romans," 131–34; Fee, *God's Empowering Presence*, 478–84.

2. For a summary of the debate especially between Dunn and various Pentecostals, see Atkinson, *Baptism in the Spirit*; Mittelstadt, *Reading Luke-Acts*.

3. Turner rightly rejects the notion that the subsequent outpouring at Samaria is "problematic" for Luke, but he cannot accept the notion that it is in any way normal. Turner, *Power from on High*, 374.

consistent with the Old Testament model where people in a covenant relationship with Yahweh receive an empowering endowment of the Spirit. Luke reinforces this idea by portraying the recipients of the Spirit as humble people who are living in submission to Yahweh. The heavy christological language applied to the Samaritan's conversion experience leaves no room for a deficient conversion. The timing of their reception of the Spirit is no problem at all for Luke, for his assumption of an Old Testament model makes the timing of the event less relevant to him than the christocentric and missiological nature of it.[4]

Those who allow for an empowering of the Spirit logically distinct from salvation can also benefit from this study. It is neither necessary nor helpful to narrow Luke's pneumatology solely to his emphasis on prophecy or missiological empowerment. There is room in Luke's pneumatology for an eschatological Spirit who advances God's plan, does creative acts, empowers the working of miracles, directs the affairs of the church, brings joy to God's people, and inspires prophecy. Whatever the functional means of his work, in all his activity the Spirit points to the resurrection and enthronement of Christ. Even the tongues of Pentecost occur in response to Christ's enthronement, so that a christocentric pneumatology is a more balanced pneumatology.

In addition to this, the reader should allow for the full expression of Luke's diverse Old Testament and cultic images without denying them, on the one hand, or attempting to pigeonhole them into a preconceived conversion-initiation model, on the other hand. Luke embraces the image of Jesus as a high priest blessing his servants with the eschatological Spirit, the Spirit filling the disciples in a manner like that of Bezalel and the temple itself, and the resurrection of Christ as the cornerstone in a new temple. Such cultic language is not antithetical to a Pentecostal perspective but heightens Luke's exalted Christology and depicts the disciples as bearers of the divine presence to the nations. Just as fire has various kinds of symbolic significance in the Bible (and even within Luke's own writings; Luke 3:16; Acts 2:3), so Paul directly uses metaphorical temple language in reference to the unity of the corporate church body at Corinth (1 Cor 3:16–17), to the ethical implications of the individual's body as a temple of the Spirit (6:18–20), to Gentile inclusion into the one body (Eph 2:11–22), and in connection with the man of lawlessness (2 Thess 2:4). Luke and Paul adopt similar language to address a separate

---

4. That a missiological purpose exists in the Samaritan reception of the Spirit is implied by the type scene established at Pentecost.

set of concerns. Paul's metaphors emphasize ontology and lack the missiological and enthronement emphases present in Luke's context, but they both draw on the same image because of its association with God's presence.

Luke has gifted the church with a rich Christology that serves as an umbrella under which all his themes find definition. To understand his doctrine of the resurrection is to comprehend the enthronement of Christ. To understand his pneumatology is to comprehend the glory of Christ. The two themes converge in Christ, and today's reader would do well to heed the words of Peter: "Therefore let all the house of Israel know for certain that God has made him both Lord and Christ, this Jesus whom you crucified" (Acts 2:36).

Bibliography

Alexander, T. D. *From Paradise to the Promised Land: An Introduction to the Pentateuch*. 2nd ed. Grand Rapids: Baker Academic, 2002.

Allen, Leslie C. *Ezekiel 20–48*. Word Biblical Commentary 29. Grand Rapids: Zondervan, 1990.

Allen, Ronald B. "Numbers." In *The Expositor's Bible Commentary*, edited by Frank E. Gaebelein, 2:655–1008. Grand Rapids: Zondervan, 1990.

Anderson, Kevin L. *"But God Raised Him from the Dead": The Theology of Jesus's Resurrection in Luke-Acts*. Paternoster Biblical Monographs. Eugene, OR: Wipf & Stock, 2006.

Arlandson, James Malcolm. *Women, Class, and Society in Early Christianity: Models from Luke-Acts*. Peabody, MA: Hendrickson, 1997.

Ashley, Timothy R. *The Book of Numbers*. New International Commentary on the Old Testament. Grand Rapids: Eerdmans, 1993.

Atkinson, William P. *Baptism in the Spirit: Luke-Acts and the Dunn Debate*. Eugene, OR: Pickwick, 2011.

Averbeck, Richard E. "Breath, Wind, Spirit and the Holy Spirit in the Old Testament." In *Presence, Power, and Promise: The Role of the Spirit of God in the Old Testament*, edited by David G. Firth and Paul D. Wegner, 25–37. Nottingham, England: Apollos, 2011.

Baer, D. A., and R. P. Gordon. "חסד." In *New International Dictionary of Old Testament Theology and Exegesis*, edited by Willem A. VanGemeren, 2:211–18. Grand Rapids: Zondervan, 1997.

Bailey, Randall C. "The Redemption of YHWH: A Literary Critical Function of the Songs of Hannah and David." *Biblical Interpretation* 3 (1995) 213–31.

Baldwin, Joyce G. *Daniel: An Introduction and Commentary*. Tyndale Old Testament Commentaries 21. Downers Grove, IL: InterVarsity, 1978.

Baltzer, Klaus. "The Meaning of the Temple in the Lukan Writings." *Harvard Theological Review* 58 (1965) 263–77.

Barré, Michael L. "New Light on the Interpretation of Hosea VI 2." *Vetus Testamentum* 28 (1978) 129–41.

Barrett, C. K. *A Critical and Exegetical Commentary on the Acts of the Apostles*. 2 vols. International Critical Commentary on the Holy Scriptures of the Old and New Testaments. New York: T. & T. Clark, 1994, 1998.

Bauckham, Richard. *Jesus and the Eyewitnesses: The Gospels as Eyewitness Testimony*. Grand Rapids: Eerdmans, 2006.

Bauer, Walter, William F. Arndt, F. Wilbur Gingrich, and Frederick W. Danker. *A Greek-English Lexicon of the New Testament and Other Early Christian Literature*. 2nd ed. Chicago: University of Chicago Press, 1979.

Beale, G. K. "The Descent of the Eschatological Temple in the Form of the Spirit at Pentecost: Part 1: The Clearest Evidence." *Tyndale Bulletin* 56.1 (2005) 73–102.

———. "The Descent of the Eschatological Temple in the Form of the Spirit at Pentecost: Part 2: Corroborating Evidence." *Tyndale Bulletin* 56.2 (2005) 63–90.

———. *The Temple and the Church's Mission: A Biblical Theology of the Dwelling Place of God*. New Studies in Biblical Theology 17. Downers Grove, IL: InterVarsity, 2004.

Bergen, Robert D. *1, 2 Samuel*. New American Commentary 7. Nashville: Broadman & Holman, 1996.

Block, Daniel I. *The Book of Ezekiel*. 2 vols. New International Commentary on the Old Testament. Grand Rapids: Eerdmans, 1997, 1998.

———. *Deuteronomy*. NIV Application Commentary. Grand Rapids: Zondervan, 2012.

———. "The View from the Top: The Holy Spirit in the Prophets." In *Presence, Power and Promise: The Role of the Spirit of God in the Old Testament*, edited by David G. Firth and Paul D. Wegner, 175–207. Nottingham, England: Apollos, 2011.

Bock, Darrell L. *A Theology of Luke and Acts: God's Promised Program, Realized for All Nations*. Biblical Theology of the New Testament. Grand Rapids: Zondervan, 2012.

———. *Acts*. Baker Exegetical Commentary on the New Testament. Grand Rapids: Baker Academic, 2007.

———. *Luke*. 2 vols. Baker Exegetical Commentary on the New Testament. Grand Rapids: Baker Academic, 1994, 1996.

———. *Proclamation from Prophecy and Pattern: Lucan Old Testament Christology*. Journal for the Study of the New Testament Supplement 12. Sheffield, England: Sheffield Academic, 1987.

Brauner, Reuven, ed. *Online Soncino Babylonian Talmud Translation*. Translated by Isidore Epstein. *The Ancient World Online*, January 2012. http://ancientworldonline.blogspot.com/2012/01/online-soncino-babylonian-talmud.html.

Brown, Francis, S. R. Driver, and Charles A. Briggs. *A Hebrew and English Lexicon of the Old Testament*. Oxford: Clarendon, 1951.

Brown, Raymond E. *The Birth of the Messiah: A Commentary on the Infancy Narratives in Matthew and Luke*. New York: Doubleday, 1977.

Bruce, F. F. *The Acts of the Apostles: The Greek Text with Introduction and Commentary*. Grand Rapids: Eerdmans, 1984.

———. *The Book of the Acts*. Rev. ed. New International Commentary on the New Testament. Grand Rapids: Eerdmans, 1988.

———. *The Epistle to the Hebrews*. Rev. ed. New International Commentary on the New Testament. Grand Rapids: Eerdmans, 1990.

Brueggemann, Walter. "From Dust to Kingship." *Zeitschrift Für Die Alttestamentliche Wissenschaft* 84 (1972) 1–18.

Buber, Martin. *Die Schrift und ihre Verdeutschung*. Berlin: Schocken, 1936.

Budd, Philip J. *Numbers*. Word Biblical Commentary 5. Waco, TX: Word, 1984.

Burge, Gary M. *The Anointed Community: The Holy Spirit in the Johannine Tradition*. Grand Rapids: Eerdmans, 1987.

Burke, Trevor J. "Romans." In *A Biblical Theology of the Holy Spirit*, edited by Trevor J. Burke and Keith Warrington, 129–45. Eugene, OR: Cascade, 2014.

Cadbury, Henry J. *The Making of Luke-Acts*. 2nd ed. Peabody, MA: Hendrickson, 1999.

Bibliography

Carroll, John T. *Luke: A Commentary*. New Testament Library. Louisville: Westminster John Knox, 2012.

Carson, D. A. "Current Issues in Biblical Theology: A New Testament Perspective." *Bulletin for Biblical Research* 5 (1995) 17–41.

Chance, J. Bradley. *Jerusalem, the Temple, and the New Age in Luke-Acts*. Macon, GA: Mercer University Press, 1988.

Charles, R. H. *Eschatology: The Doctrine of a Future Life in Israel, Judaism, and Christianity: A Critical History*. New York: Schocken, 1963.

Charlesworth, James H. "Resurrection: The Dead Sea Scrolls and the New Testament." In *Resurrection: The Origin and Future of a Biblical Doctrine*, by James H. Charlesworth, C. D. Elledge, James L. Crenshaw, Hendrikus Boers, and W. Waite Willis Jr., 138–86. Faith and Scholarship Colloquies. New York: T. & T. Clark, 2006.

Childs, Brevard S. *Introduction to the Old Testament as Scripture*. Philadelphia: Fortress, 1979.

———. *Isaiah*. Old Testament Library. Louisville: Westminister John Knox, 2001.

Cho, Youngmo. *Spirit and Kingdom in the Writings of Luke and Paul: An Attempt to Reconcile These Concepts*. Paternoster Biblical Monographs. Eugene, OR: Wipf & Stock, 2005.

Clowney, Edmund P. *The Unfolding Mystery: Discovering Christ in the Old Testament*. 2nd ed. Phillipsburg, NJ: P&R, 2013.

Cockerill, Gareth Lee. *The Epistle to the Hebrews*. New International Commentary on the New Testament. Grand Rapids: Eerdmans, 2012.

Coenen, Lothar. "Witness, Testimony." In *The New International Dictionary of New Testament Theology*, edited by Colin Brown, 3:1038–47. Grand Rapids: Zondervan, 1978.

Cole, R. Dennis. *Numbers*. New American Commentary 3B. Nashville: Broadman & Holman, 2000.

Conzelmann, Hans. *The Theology of St. Luke*. Translated by Geoffrey Buswell. New York: Faber and Faber, 1960.

Cook, Edward M. *The Psalms Targum: An English Translation*. Edward M. Cook, 2001. http://www.targum.info/pss/tg_ps_index.htm.

Cornelius, I., Andrew E. Hill, and Cleon L. Rogers Jr. "אסף." In *New International Dictionary of Old Testament Theology and Exegesis*, edited by Willem A. VanGemeren, 1:468–72. Grand Rapids: Zondervan, 1997.

Cotton, Roger D. "The Pentecostal Significance of Numbers 11." *Journal of Pentecostal Theology* 10.1 (2001) 3–10.

Craigie, Peter C., and Marvin E. Tate. *Psalms 1–50*. 2nd ed. Word Biblical Commentary 19. Grand Rapids: Zondervan, 2004.

Crenshaw, James L. "Love Is Stronger than Death: Intimations of Life beyond the Grave." In *Resurrection: The Origin and Future of a Biblical Doctrine*, by James H. Charlesworth, C. D. Elledge, James L. Crenshaw, Hendrikus Boers, and W. Waite Willis Jr., 53–78. Faith and Scholarship Colloquies. New York: T. & T. Clark, 2006.

Danker, Frederick W. *Jesus and the New Age: A Commentary on Luke's Gospel*. Rev. ed. Philadelphia: Fortress, 1988.

Dearman, J. Andrew. *The Book of Hosea*. New International Commentary on the Old Testament. Grand Rapids: Eerdmans, 2010.

deClaissé-Walford, Nancy, Rolf A. Jacobson, and Beth LaNeel Tanner. *The Book of Psalms*. New International Commentary on the Old Testament. Grand Rapids: Eerdmans, 2014.

Delling, Gerhard. "Πίμπλημι, Ἐμπίπλημι, Πλησμονή." In *Theological Dictionary of the New Testament*, edited by Gerhard Friedrich and Geoffrey W. Bromiley, translated by Geoffrey W. Bromiley, 6:128–34. Grand Rapids: Eerdmans, 1968.

Dillon, Richard J. *From Eye-Witnesses to Ministers of the Word: Tradition and Composition in Luke 24*. Analecta Biblica: Investigationes Scientificae in Res Biblicas 82. Rome: Biblical Institute Press, 1978.

Dumbrell, William J. *The End of the Beginning: Revelation 21–22 and the Old Testament*. Eugene, OR: Wipf & Stock, 2001.

Dunn, James D. G. *The Acts of the Apostles*. Grand Rapids: Eerdmans, 1996.

———. *Baptism in the Holy Spirit: A Re-Examination of the New Testament Teaching on the Gift of the Spirit in Relation to Pentecostalism Today*. Philadelphia: Westminster, 1970.

Dupont, Jacques. *The Salvation of the Gentiles: Essays on the Acts of the Apostles*. Translated by John R. Keating. New York: Paulist, 1979.

Edwards, James R. *The Gospel According to Luke*. Pillar New Testament Commentary. Grand Rapids: Eerdmans, 2015.

Elledge, C. D. "Resurrection of the Dead: Exploring Our Earliest Evidence Today." In *Resurrection: The Origin and Future of a Biblical Doctrine*, by James H. Charlesworth, C. D. Elledge, James L. Crenshaw, Hendrikus Boers, and W. Waite Willis Jr. Faith and Scholarship Colloquies. New York: T. & T. Clark, 2006.

Ellingworth, Paul. *The Epistle to the Hebrews: A Commentary on the Greek Text*. New International Greek Testament Commentary. Grand Rapids: Eerdmans, 1993.

Els, P. J. J. S. "לקח." In *New International Dictionary of Old Testament Theology and Exegesis*, edited by Willem A. VanGemeren, 2:812–17. Grand Rapids: Zondervan, 1997.

Evans, Craig A. *Ancient Texts for New Testament Studies: A Guide to the Background Literature*. Grand Rapids: Baker Academic, 2005.

Fee, Gordon D. *The First Epistle to the Corinthians*. New International Commentary on the New Testament. Grand Rapids: Eerdmans, 1987.

———. *God's Empowering Presence: The Holy Spirit in the Letters of Paul*. Peabody, MA: Hendrickson, 1994.

Firth, David. "The Historical Books." In *A Biblical Theology of the Holy Spirit*, edited by Trevor J. Burke and Keith Warrington, 12–23. Eugene, OR: Cascade, 2014.

Fishbane, Michael. *Biblical Text and Texture: A Literary Reading of Selected Texts*. Oxford: Oneworld, 1998.

Fitzmyer, Joseph A. *The Acts of the Apostles: A New Translation with Introduction and Commentary*. Anchor Bible 31. New York: Doubleday, 1998.

———. *The Gospel According to Luke*. 2 vols. Anchor Bible 28, 28A. Garden City, NY: Doubleday, 1981, 1985.

France, R. T. *The Gospel of Matthew*. New International Commentary on the New Testament. Grand Rapids: Eerdmans, 2007.

Garrett, Duane A. *Hosea, Joel*. New American Commentary 19A. Nashville: Broadman & Holman, 1997.

Geldenhuys, Norval. *Commentary on the Gospel of Luke: The English Text with Introduction, Exposition, and Notes*. New International Commentary on the New Testament. Grand Rapids: Eerdmans, 1951.

Goldingay, John E. *Daniel*. Word Biblical Commentary 30. Dallas: Word, 1989.

———. *Psalms*. 3 vols. Baker Commentary on the Old Testament: Wisdom and Psalms. Grand Rapids: Baker Academic, 2006–2008.

Gowan, Donald E. *Bridge between the Testaments: A Reappraisal of Judaism from the Exile to the Birth of Christianity*. Pittsburgh Theological Monograph Series 14. Eugene, OR: Pickwick, 1986.

Green, Gene L. *Jude and 2 Peter*. Baker Exegetical Commentary on the New Testament. Grand Rapids: Baker Academic, 2008.

Green, Joel B. *The Gospel of Luke*. New International Commentary on the New Testament. Grand Rapids: Eerdmans, 1997.

Green, William Scott. "Messiah in Judaism: Rethinking the Question." In *Judaisms and Their Messiahs at the Turn of the Christian Era*, edited by Jacob Neusner, William Scott Green, and Ernest S. Frerichs, 1–14. New York: Cambridge University Press, 1987.

Grogan, Geoffrey W. "Isaiah." In *The Expositor's Bible Commentary*, edited by Frank E. Gaebelein, 6:1–354. Grand Rapids: Zondervan, 1986.

———. *Psalms*. Two Horizons Old Testament Commentary. Grand Rapids: Eerdmans, 2008.

Gunkel, Hermann. *Genesis*. Translated by Biddle. Macon, GA: Mercer University Press, 1997.

———. *The Influence of the Holy Spirit: The Popular View of the Apostolic Age and the Teaching of the Apostle Paul*. Translated by Roy A. Harrisville and Philip A. Quanbeck II. Minneapolis: Fortress, 2008.

Hamilton, Victor P. *The Book of Genesis*. 2 vols. New International Commentary on the Old Testament. Grand Rapids: Eerdmans, 1990, 1995.

———. *Exodus: An Exegetical Commentary*. Grand Rapids: Baker Academic, 2011.

Harman, Allan M. "נפל." In *New International Dictionary of Old Testament Theology and Exegesis*, edited by Willem A. VanGemeren, 3:129–31. Grand Rapids: Zondervan, 1997.

Harrison, Everett F. "The Resurrection of Jesus Christ in the Book of Acts and in Early Christian Literature." In *Understanding the Sacred Text: Essays in Honor of Morton S. Enslin on the Hebrew Bible and Christian Beginnings*, edited by John Reumann, 217–31. Valley Forge, PA: Judson, 1972.

Harrison, R. K. *Numbers*. Wycliffe Exegetical Commentary. Chicago: Moody, 1990.

Hasel, Gerhard F. "New Light on the Book of Daniel from the Dead Sea Scrolls." *Archaeology and Biblical Research* 5 (Spring 1992) 45–53.

———. "Resurrection in the Theology of Old Testament Apocalyptic." *Zeitschrift Für Die Alttestamentliche Wissenschaft* 92 (1980) 267–84.

Haya-Prats, Gonzalo. *Empowered Believers: The Holy Spirit in the Book of Acts*. Edited by Paul Elbert, translated by Scott A. Ellington. Eugene, OR: Cascade, 2011.

Head, Peter. "The Temple in Luke's Gospel." In *Heaven on Earth: The Temple in Biblical Theology*, edited by T. Desmond Alexander and Simon Gathercole, 101–20. Waynesboro, GA: Paternoster, 2004.

Henrichs-Tarasenkova, Nina. *Luke's Christology of Divine Identity*. Library of New Testament Studies 542. New York: T. & T. Clark, 2016.

Hess, Richard S. "Bezalel and Oholiab: Spirit and Creativity." In *Presence, Power, and Promise: The Role of the Spirit of God in the Old Testament*, edited by David G. Firth and Paul D. Wegner, 162–72. Nottingham, England: Apollos, 2011.

Hildebrandt, Wilf. *An Old Testament Theology of the Spirit of God*. Peabody, MA: Hendrickson, 1995.

Hock, Ronald F. "Lazarus and Micyllus: Greco-Roman Backgrounds to Luke." *Journal of Biblical Literature* 106 (1987) 447–63.

Horton, Stanley M. *The Book of Acts*. Springfield, MO: Gospel Publishing, 1981.

———. *What the Bible Says about the Holy Spirit*. Rev. ed. Springfield, MO: Gospel Publishing, 2005.

Hubbard, David Allan. *Hosea: An Introduction and Commentary*. Tyndale Old Testament Commentaries 22A. Downers Grove, IL: InterVarsity, 1989.

Hübner, Hans. "Κεῖμαι." In *Exegetical Dictionary of the New Testament*, edited by Horst Balz and Gerhard Schneider, 2:280. Grand Rapids: Eerdmans, 1991.

Isaac, E. "1 (Ethiopic Apocalypse of) Enoch: A New Translation and Introduction." In *The Old Testament Pseudepigrapha*, edited by James H. Charlesworth, 1:5–89. Peabody, MA: Hendrickson, 1983.

Jeremias, J. "Λίθος." In *Theological Dictionary of the New Testament*, edited by Gerhard Kittel and Geoffrey W. Bromiley, translated by Geoffrey W. Bromiley, 4:268–80. Grand Rapids: Eerdmans, 1967.

Johnson, Luke Timothy. *The Gospel of Luke*. Sacra Pagina 3. Collegeville, MN: Liturgical, 1991.

———. *Prophetic Jesus, Prophetic Church: The Challenge of Luke-Acts to Contemporary Christians*. Grand Rapids: Eerdmans, 2011.

Kaiser, Walter C. "The Pentateuch." In *A Biblical Theology of the Holy Spirit*, edited by Trevor J. Burke and Keith Warrington, 1–11. Eugene, OR: Cascade, 2014.

Kalland, Earl S. "Deuteronomy." In *The Expositor's Bible Commentary*, edited by Frank E. Gaebelein, 3:1–235. Grand Rapids: Zondervan, 1992.

Keener, Craig S. *Acts: An Exegetical Commentary*. 4 vols. Grand Rapids: Baker Academic, 2012–2015.

Kidner, Derek. *Genesis: An Introduction and Commentary*. Tyndale Old Testament Commentaries 1. Downers Grove, IL: InterVarsity, 1967.

———. *Psalms 1–72: An Introduction and Commentary on Books I and II of the Psalms*. Tyndale Old Testament Commentaries 14A. Downers Grove, IL: InterVarsity, 1973.

Kline, Meredith G. *Kingdom Prologue: Genesis Foundations for a Covenantal Worldview*. Eugene, OR: Wipf & Stock, 2006.

Koch, Robert. *Der Geist Gottes Im Alten Testament*. Frankfurt am Main: Peter Lang, 1991.

Kodell, Jerome. "The Word of God Grew: The Ecclesial Tendency of Logos in Acts 6,7; 12,24; 19,20." *Biblica* 55.4 (1974) 505–19.

Kraus, Hans-Joachim. *Psalms 1–59*. Translated by Hilton C. Oswald. Continental Commentaries. Minneapolis: Fortress, 1993.

Kurz, William S. *Acts of the Apostles*. Catholic Commentary on Sacred Scripture. Grand Rapids: Baker Academic, 2013.

———. *Reading Luke-Acts: Dynamics of Biblical Narrative*. Louisville: Westminster, 1993.

Lampe, G. W. H. "The Holy Spirit in the Writings of St. Luke." In *Studies in the Gospels: Essays in Memory of R. H. Lightfoot*, edited by D. E. Nineham, 159–200. Oxford: Blackwell, 1955.

Lane, William L. *Hebrews 9–13*. Word Biblical Commentary 47B. Mexico City: Thomas Nelson, 2000.

LaSor, William Sanford, David Allan Hubbard, and Frederick Wm. Bush. *Old Testament Survey: The Message, Form, and Background of the Old Testament*. 2nd ed. Grand Rapids: Eerdmans, 1996.

Leaney, A. R. C. *The Gospel According to St. Luke*. Harper's New Testament Commentaries. Peabody, MA: Hendrickson, 1966.

Bibliography

Lenski, R. C. H. *The Interpretation of the Acts of the Apostles*. Columbus, OH: Wartburg, 1957.

Levenson, Jon D. *Resurrection and the Restoration of Israel: The Ultimate Victory of the God of Life*. New Haven, CT: Yale University Press, 2006.

Levine, Baruch A. *Numbers 1–20: A New Translation with Introduction and Commentary*. Anchor Bible 4A. New York: Doubleday, 1993.

Levison, John R. *Filled with the Spirit*. Grand Rapids: Eerdmans, 2009.

Lichtenberger, Hermann. "Auferstehung in Den Qumranfunden." In *Auferstehung-Resurrection*, edited by Friedrich Avemarie and Hermann Lichtenberger, 79–91. Wissenschaftliche Untersuchungen zum Neuen Testament 135. Tübingen: Mohr Siebeck, 2001.

Liddell, Henry George, and Robert Scott. *A Greek-English Lexicon*. Rev. ed. Oxford: Clarendon, 1968.

Lohfink, Gerhard. *Die Himmelfahrt Jesu: Untersuchungen Zu Den Himmelfahrts—Und Erhöhungstexten Bei Lukas*. Studien zum Alten und Neuen Testament 26. Munich: Kösel, 1971.

Longenecker, Richard N. "The Acts of the Apostles." In *The Expositor's Bible Commentary*, edited by Frank E. Gaebelein, 9:205–573. Grand Rapids: Zondervan, 1981.

Louw, Johannes P., and Eugene A. Nida, eds. *Greek-English Lexicon of the New Testament Based on Semantic Domains*. 2 vols. New York: United Bible Societies, 1988.

Ma, Wonsuk. "Isaiah." In *A Biblical Theology of the Holy Spirit*, edited by Trevor J. Burke and Keith Warrington, 34–45. Eugene, OR: Cascade, 2014.

———. *Until the Spirit Comes: The Spirit of God in the Book of Isaiah*. Journal for the Study of the Old Testament Supplement Series 27. Sheffield, England: Sheffield Academic, 1999.

Macchia, Frank D. "Groans Too Deep for Words: Towards a Theology of Tongues as Initial Evidence." *Asian Journal of Pentecostal Studies* 1.2 (July 1998) 149–73.

Maddox, Robert. *The Purpose of Luke-Acts*. Göttingen: Vandenhoeck & Ruprecht, 1982.

Marshall, I. Howard. "Acts." In *Commentary on the New Testament Use of the Old Testament*, edited by G. K. Beale and D. A. Carson, 513–606. Grand Rapids: Baker Academic, 2007.

———. *The Acts of the Apostles: An Introduction and Commentary*. Tyndale New Testament Commentaries 5. Grand Rapids: Eerdmans, 1996.

———. *The Gospel of Luke: A Commentary on the Greek Text*. New International Greek Testament Commentary. Grand Rapids: Eerdmans, 1978.

———. *Luke: Historian and Theologian*. Grand Rapids: Zondervan, 1970.

———. "The Resurrection in the Acts of the Apostles." In *Apostolic History and the Gospel: Biblical and Historical Essays Presented to F. F. Bruce on His 60th Birthday*, edited by W. Ward Gasque and Ralph P. Martin, 92–107. Grand Rapids: Eerdmans, 1970.

Martin-Achard, Robert. *From Death to Life: A Study of the Development of the Doctrine of the Resurrection in the Old Testament*. Translated by John Penney Smith. Edinburgh: Oliver and Boyd, 1960.

Matera, Frank J. "The Death of Jesus According to Luke: A Question of Sources." *Catholic Biblical Quarterly* 47 (1985) 469–85.

Maurer, Christian. "Τίθημι." In *Theological Dictionary of the New Testament*, edited by Gerhard Friedrich and Geoffrey W. Bromiley, translated by Geoffrey W. Bromiley, 8:152–68. Grand Rapids: Eerdmans, 1972.

McCasland, Selby Vernon. "The Scripture Basis of 'On the Third Day.'" *Journal of Biblical Literature* 48 (1929) 124–37.

McComiskey, Thomas Edward. "Hosea." In *The Minor Prophets: An Exegetical and Expository Commentary*, edited by Thomas Edward McComiskey, 1:1–237. Grand Rapids: Baker, 1992.

McKelvey, R. J. *The New Temple: The Church in the New Testament*. Oxford Theological Monographs. Oxford: Oxford University Press, 1969.

Menzies, Glen. "Pre-Lucan Occurrences of the Phrase 'Tongue(s) of Fire.'" *Pneuma* 22.1 (Spring 2000) 27–60.

Menzies, Robert P. *Empowered for Witness: The Spirit in Luke-Acts*. New York: T. & T. Clark, 2004.

———. *The Language of the Spirit: Interpreting and Translating Charismatic Terms*. Cleveland, TN: CPT, 2010.

Metzger, Bruce M. *A Textual Commentary on the Greek New Testament: A Companion Volume to the United Bible Societies' Greek New Testament*. Stuttgart: United Bible Societies, 1975.

Milgrom, Jacob. *Numbers*. JPS Torah Commentary. Philadelphia: Jewish Publication Society, 1990.

Mittelstadt, Martin William. *Reading Luke-Acts in the Pentecostal Tradition*. Cleveland, TN: CPT, 2010.

———. *The Spirit and Suffering in Luke-Acts: Implications for a Pentecostal Pneumatology*. Journal of Pentecostal Theology Supplement Series 26. New York: T. & T. Clark, 2004.

Moessner, David P. "Reading Luke's Gospel as Ancient Hellenistic Narrative: Luke's Narrative Plan of Israel's Suffering Messiah as God's Saving 'Plan' for the World." In *Reading Luke: Interpretation, Reflection, Formation*, edited by Craig G. Bartholomew, Joel B. Green, and Anthony C. Thiselton, 125–54. Scripture and Hermeneutics Series 6. Grand Rapids: Zondervan, 2005.

Montague, George T. *The Holy Spirit: The Growth of a Biblical Tradition*. Eugene, OR: Wipf & Stock, 1976.

Moore, George Foot. *Judaism in the First Centuries of the Christian Era: The Age of the Tannaim*. Vol. 2. Cambridge, MA: Harvard University Press, 1955.

Motyer, J. Alec. *The Prophecy of Isaiah: An Introduction and Commentary*. Downers Grove, IL: InterVarsity, 1993.

Müller, Paul-Gerd. "Ἀρχηγός." In *Exegetical Dictionary of the New Testament*, edited by Horst Balz and Gerhard Schneider, 1:163–64. Grand Rapids: Eerdmans, 1990.

Neve, Lloyd R. *The Spirit of God in the Old Testament*. Centre for Pentecostal Theology Classics Series. Cleveland, TN: CPT, 2010.

Niehaus, Jeffrey J. *God at Sinai: Covenant and Theophany in the Bible and Ancient Near East*. Studies in Old Testament Biblical Theology. Grand Rapids: Zondervan, 1995.

Nolland, John. *Luke 1—9:20*. Word Biblical Commentary 35A. Nashville: Thomas Nelson, 2000.

———. *Luke 9:21—18:34*. Word Biblical Commentary 35B. Nashville: Thomas Nelson, 1993.

———. *Luke 18:35—24:53*. Word Biblical Commentary 35C. Nashville, TN: Thomas Nelson, 1993.

Noth, Martin. *Numbers: A Commentary*. Translated by James D. Martin. Old Testament Library. Philadelphia: Westminster, 1968.

Bibliography

Nötscher, F. "Zur Auferstehung Nach Drei Tagen." *Biblica* 35.3 (1954) 313–19.

O'Brien, Peter T. *The Letter to the Hebrews*. Pillar New Testament Commentary. Grand Rapids: Eerdmans, 2010.

Osborne, Grant R. *The Resurrection Narratives: A Redactional Study*. Grand Rapids: Baker, 1984.

Oss, Douglas A. "The Interpretation of the 'Stone' Passages by Peter and Paul: A Comparative Study." *Journal of Evangelical Theological Society* 32.2 (June 1989) 181–200.

Oswalt, John N. *The Book of Isaiah*. 2 vols. New International Commentary on the Old Testament. Grand Rapids: Eerdmans, 1986, 1988.

O'Toole, Robert F. "Acts 2:30 and the Davidic Covenant of Pentecost." *Journal of Biblical Literature* 102.2 (1983) 245–58.

Palma, Anthony D. *The Spirit—God in Action*. Springfield, MO: Gospel Publishing, 1974.

Pao, David W. *Acts and the Isaianic New Exodus*. Biblical Studies Library. Grand Rapids: Baker Academic, 2002.

Pao, David W., and Eckhard J. Schnabel. "Luke." In *Commentary on the New Testament Use of the Old Testament*, edited by G. K. Beale and D. A. Carson, 251–414. Grand Rapids: Baker Academic, 2007.

Parsons, Mikeal C. *The Departure of Jesus in Luke-Acts: The Ascension Narratives in Context*. Journal for the Study of the New Testament Supplement Series 21. Sheffield, England: Sheffield Academic, 1987.

Perrin, Nicholas. *Jesus the Temple*. Grand Rapids: Baker Academic, 2010.

Peterson, David G. *The Acts of the Apostles*. Pillar New Testament Commentary. Grand Rapids: Eerdmans, 2009.

Phillips, Richard D. *Hebrews*. Reformed Expository Commentary. Phillipsburg, NJ: P&R, 2006.

Plummer, Alfred. *A Critical and Exegetical Commentary on the Gospel According to S. Luke*. 1896. Reprint, London: Forgotten Books, 2015.

Polhill, John B. *Acts*. New American Commentary 26. Nashville: Broadman & Holman, 1992.

Rahlfs, Alfred, and Robert Hanhart, eds. *Septuaginta*. Rev. ed. Germany: Deutsche Bibelgesellschaft, 2006.

Rea, John. *The Holy Spirit in the Bible: All the Major Passages about the Spirit: A Commentary*. Lake Mary, FL: Creation House, 1990.

Rese, Martin. *Alttestamentliche Motive in der Christologie des Lukas*. Studien zum Neuen Testament 1. Gütersloh: Gütersloher Verlagshaus, 1969.

Rosner, Brian. "The Progress of the Word." In *Witness to the Gospel: The Theology of Acts*, edited by I. Howard Marshall and David Peterson, 215–33. Grand Rapids: Eerdmans, 1998.

Rowe, C. Kavin. *Early Narrative Christology: The Lord in the Gospel of Luke*. Beihefte zur Zeitschrift für die Neutestamentliche Wissenschaft und die Kunde der Älteren Kirche 139. New York: De Gruyter, 2006.

Ruthven, Jon Mark. *On the Cessation of the Charismata: The Protestant Polemic on Post-Biblical Miracles*. Rev. ed. Word and Spirit Press Monograph Series 1. Tulsa, OK: Word and Spirit, 2011.

Sailhamer, John. *Genesis Unbound: A Provocative New Look at the Creation Account*. Colorado Springs, CO: Dawson, 2011.

———. "Genesis." In *The Expositor's Bible Commentary*, edited by Frank E. Gaebelein, 2:1–284. Grand Rapids: Zondervan, 1990.

———. *The Pentateuch as Narrative: A Biblical-Theological Commentary*. Grand Rapids: Zondervan, 1992.

Sarna, Nahum M. *Genesis*. JPS Torah Commentary. Philadelphia: Jewish Publication Society, 1989.

Schmidt, Werner H. *Die Schöpfungsgeschichte der Priesterschrift*. Edited by Günther Bornkamm and Gerhard von Rad. Wissenschaftliche Monographien zum Alten und Neuen Testament. Neukirchen-Vluyn: Neukirchener, 1964.

Schweizer, Eduard. "Πνεῦμα, Πνευματικός." In *Theological Dictionary of the New Testament*, edited by Gerhard Friedrich and Geoffrey W. Bromiley, translated by Geoffrey W. Bromiley, 6:389–451. Grand Rapids: Eerdmans, 1968.

Seebass, H. "נָפַל." In *Theological Dictionary of the Old Testament*, edited by G. Johannes Botterweck, Helmer Ringgren, and Heinz-Josef Fabry, translated by David E. Green, 9:488–97. Grand Rapids: Eerdmans, 1998.

Sellin, Gerhard. *Der Streit um die Auferstehung der Toten: Eine Religionsgeschichtliche und Exegetische Untersuchung von 1 Korinther 15*. Edited by Wolfgang Schrage and Rudolf Smend. Forschungen zur Religion und Literatur des Alten und Neuen Testaments. Göttingen: Vandenhoeck & Ruprecht, 1986.

Smith, Steve. *The Fate of the Jerusalem Temple in Luke-Acts: An Intertextual Approach to Jesus' Laments over Jerusalem and Stephen's Speech*. Library of New Testament Studies 553. New York: T. & T. Clark, 2017.

Snodgrass, Klyne R. *Stories with Intent: A Comprehensive Guide to the Parables of Jesus*. Grand Rapids: Eerdmans, 2008.

Stein, Robert H. *Luke*. New American Commentary 24. Nashville: Broadman & Holman, 1992.

Strauss, Mark L. *The Davidic Messiah in Luke-Acts: The Promise and Its Fulfillment in Lukan Christology*. Journal for the Study of the New Testament Supplement Series 110. Sheffield, England: Sheffield Academic, 1995.

Stronstad, Roger. *The Charismatic Theology of St. Luke: Trajectories from the Old Testament to Luke-Acts*. 2nd ed. Grand Rapids: Baker Academic, 2012.

———. *The Prophethood of All Believers: A Study in Luke's Charismatic Theology*. Cleveland, TN: CPT, 2010.

———. *Spirit, Scripture and Theology: A Pentecostal Perspective*. Baguio City, Philippines: Asia Pacific Theological Seminary Press, 1995.

Stuart, Douglas. *Hosea–Jonah*. Word Biblical Commentary 31. Mexico City: Thomas Nelson, 1987.

Talbert, Charles H. "The Place of the Resurrection in the Theology of Luke." *Interpretation* 46.1 (1992) 19–30.

———. *Reading Luke: A Literary and Theological Commentary on the Third Gospel*. New York: Crossroad, 1984.

Tannehill, Robert C. *The Narrative Unity of Luke-Acts: A Literary Interpretation*. 2 vol.s Philadelphia: Fortress, 1986, 1994.

Thiselton, Anthony C. *The Holy Spirit—In Biblical Teaching, through the Centuries, and Today*. Grand Rapids: Eerdmans, 2013.

Thompson, Alan J. *The Acts of the Risen Lord Jesus: Luke's Account of God's Unfolding Plan*. New Studies in Biblical Theology 27. Downers Grove, IL: Apollos, 2011.

Tsumura, David Toshio. *The First Book of Samuel*. New International Commentary on the Old Testament. Grand Rapids: Eerdmans, 2007.

Bibliography

Turner, Max. *Power from on High: The Spirit in Israel's Restoration and Witness in Luke-Acts*. Sheffield, England: Sheffield Academic, 2000.

VanGemeren, Willem A. "Psalms." In *The Expositor's Bible Commentary*, edited by Frank E. Gaebelein, 5:1–880. Grand Rapids: Zondervan, 1991.

Van Pelt, Miles V., and Walter C. Kaiser Jr. "מלא." In *New International Dictionary of Old Testament Theology and Exegesis*, edited by Willem A. VanGemeren, 2:939–41. Grand Rapids: Zondervan, 1997.

———. "רחף." In *New International Dictionary of Old Testament Theology and Exegesis*, edited by Willem A. VanGemeren, 3:1098. Grand Rapids: Zondervan, 1997.

Van Stempvoort, P. A. "The Interpretation of the Ascension in Luke and Acts." *New Testament Studies* 5.1 (1958) 30–42.

Vermes, Geza. *The Complete Dead Sea Scrolls in English*. Rev. ed. London: Penguin, 2011.

———. *The Resurrection*. New York: Doubleday, 2008.

Vos, Geerhardus. *Biblical Theology: Old and New Testaments*. Grand Rapids: Eerdmans, 1948.

———. *The Eschatology of the Old Testament*. Edited by James T. Dennison Jr. Phillipsburg, NJ: P&R, 2001.

Warrington, Keith. "The Synoptic Gospels." In *A Biblical Theology of the Holy Spirit*, edited by Trevor J. Burke and Keith Warrington, 84–103. Eugene, OR: Cascade, 2014.

Webb, Barry G. *The Book of Judges*. New International Commentary on the Old Testament. Grand Rapids: Eerdmans, 2012.

Wenham, Gordon J. *The Book of Leviticus*. New International Commentary on the Old Testament. Grand Rapids: Eerdmans, 1979.

———. *Genesis 1–15*. Word Biblical Commentary 1. Waco, TX: Word, 1987.

———. *Genesis 16–50*. Word Biblical Commentary 2. Waco, TX: Word, 1994.

———. *Numbers: An Introduction and Commentary*. Tyndale Old Testament Commentaries 4. Downers Grove, IL: InterVarsity, 1981.

———. "Sanctuary Symbolism in the Garden of Eden Story." *Proceedings of the Ninth World Congress of Jewish Studies, Division A: The Period of the Bible* 9 (1986) 19–25.

Wenk, Matthias. *Community-Forming Power: The Socio-Ethical Role of the Spirit in Luke-Acts*. New York: T. & T. Clark, 2000.

Whiston, William, trans. *The New Complete Works of Josephus*. Commentary by Paul L. Maier. Rev. ed. Grand Rapids: Kregel, 1999.

Wijngaards, J. "Death and Resurrection in Covenantal Context (Hos. VI 2)." *Vetus Testamentum* 17 (1967) 226–39.

Wilson, Robert R. "Prophecy and Ecstasy: A Reexamination." *Journal of Biblical Literature* 98 (1979) 321–37.

Witherington, Ben, III. *The Acts of the Apostles: A Socio-Rhetorical Commentary*. Grand Rapids: Eerdmans, 1998.

Wolff, Hans Walter. *Hosea: A Commentary on the Book of the Prophet Hosea*. Edited by Paul D. Hanson, translated by Gary Stansell. Hermeneia. Philadelphia: Fortress, 1974.

Wood, Leon J. *The Holy Spirit in the Old Testament*. Grand Rapids: Zondervan, 1976.

Woods, Edward J. *The "Finger of God" and Pneumatology in Luke-Acts*. Journal for the Study of the New Testament Supplement Series 205. Sheffield, England: Sheffield Academic, 2001.

Wright, N. T. *The Resurrection of the Son of God*. Christian Origins and the Question of God 3. Minneapolis: Fortress, 2003.

Wright, R. B. "Psalms of Solomon (First Century B.C.): A New Translation and Introduction." In *The Old Testament Pseudepigrapha*, edited by James H. Charlesworth, 2:639–70. Peabody, MA: Hendrickson, 1983.

Young, Edward J. The *Book of Isaiah: The English Text, with Introduction, Exposition, and Notes*. Vol. 3. New international Commentary on the Old Testament 3. Grand Rapids: Eerdmans, 1972.

Author Index

Alexander, T.D., 60
Allen, Leslie C., 113
Allen, Ronald B., 36, 37, 43
Anderson, Kevin L., 3, 113, 114, 127, 155, 159
Arlandson, James Malcolm, 84, 167, 168
Ashley, Timothy R., 37, 39, 40, 48, 49, 50, 96
Atkinson, William P., 206
Averbeck, Richard E., 11, 35

Baer, D. A., 93
Bailey, Randall C., 76
Baldwin, Joyce G., 114, 115
Baltzer, Klaus, 198
Barre, Michael L., 104, 105, 106
Barrett, C. K., 97, 98, 122, 139, 153, 162, 181
Bauckham, Richard, 70
Bauer, Walter, 129
Beale, G. K., 14, 16, 17, 18, 19, 62, 192, 193, 196, 197
Bergen, Robert D., 76, 78, 79
Block, Daniel I., 12, 113, 173
Bock, Darrell L., 23, 66, 67, 68, 69, 74, 76, 93, 94, 97, 100, 101, 102, 116, 119, 122, 140, 152, 162, 170, 176, 178, 181, 184, 185, 186, 187, 196
Brauner, Reuven, 13
Brown, Francis, 37
Brown, Raymond E., 66, 73, 75, 189
Bruce, F. F., 65, 159, 160, 162, 163, 193
Brueggemann, Walter, 109

Buber, Martin, 18
Budd, Philip J., 39
Burge, Gary M., 185
Burke, Trevor J., 206

Cadbury, Henry J., 118, 119, 120
Carroll, John T., 186, 188, 189
Carson, D. A., 5
Chance, J. Bradley, 190, 198
Charles, R. H., 9
Charlesworth, James H., 150
Childs, Brevard S., 77, 83, 109, 111
Cho, Youngmo, 4, 131
Clowney, Edmund P., 46
Cockerill, Gareth Lee, 64, 65
Coenen, Lothar, 159
Cole, R. Dennis, 39, 43, 49, 50
Conzelmann, Hans, 98, 119
Cook, Edward M., 177
Cornelius, I., 86, 87
Cotton, Roger D., 36, 37, 39, 43, 44, 45
Craigie, Peter C., 93
Crenshaw, James L., 93

Danker, Frederick W., 145, 184, 186, 187, 189
Dearman, J. Andrew, 104
deClaisse-Walford, Nancy, 92
Delling, Gerhard, 25, 26
Dillon, Richard J., 189
Dumbrell, William J., 20
Dunn, James D. G., 2, 3, 82, 111, 134, 180, 196, 206
Dupont, Jacques, 91, 119

Edwards, James R., 67, 153, 159, 188, 191, 202
Elledge, C. D., 115
Ellingworth, Paul, 64
Els, P. J. J. S., 56
Evans, Craig A., 145

Fee, Gordon D., 90, 206
Firth, David, 78, 79
Fishbane, Michael, 16
Fitzmyer, Joseph A., 66, 122, 124, 130, 133, 140, 153, 156, 163, 170, 174, 178, 188, 189
France, R. T., 100

Garrett, Duane A., 103
Geldenhuys, Norval, 189
Goldingay, John E., 114, 116, 177
Gordon, R. P., 93
Gowan, Donald E., 57, 93
Green, Gene L., 59
Green, Joel B., 24, 70, 72, 127, 152, 153, 157, 177, 178, 184, 186, 187, 188, 189, 192
Green, William Scott, 145
Grogan, Geoffrey W., 92, 110
Gunkel, Hermann, 33, 34, 44, 45, 63

Hamilton, Victor P., 21, 55, 58, 60, 62, 63, 65, 87, 89, 96
Harman, Allan M., 110
Harrison, Everett F., 161
Harrison, R. K., 39
Hasel, Gerhard F., 109, 114
Haya-Prats, Gonzalo, 130
Head, Peter, 190
Henrichs-Tarasenkova, Nina, 152, 153
Hess, Richard S., 22
Hildebrandt, Wilf, 11, 14, 31, 32, 37, 41, 48, 77, 79, 130, 173
Hock, Ronald F., 101
Horton, Stanley M., 194, 201
Hubbard, David Allan, 90
Hubner, Hans, 170

Isaac, E., 147, 149

Jeremias, J., 170, 177
Johnson, Luke Timothy, 178, 185, 201

Kaiser, Walter C., 11, 21, 33, 39
Kalland, Earl S., 12
Keener, Craig S., 42, 119, 124, 127, 133, 136, 137, 153, 162, 196, 198
Kidner, Derek, 57, 58, 87, 92, 94
Kline, Meredith G., 18
Koch, Robert, 39
Kodell, Jerome, 136, 137
Kraus, Hans-Joachim, 91, 92
Kurz, William S., 158, 199

Lampe, G. W. H., 151
Lane, William L., 64, 65, 66
LaSor, William Sanford, 49
Leaney, A. R. C., 102, 152
Lenski, R. C. H., 197
Levenson, Jon D., 13, 55, 62, 80, 87, 88
Levine, Baruch A., 37
Levison, John R., 33, 34, 35, 196
Lichtenberger, Hermann, 150
Liddell, Henry George, 170
Lohfink, Gerhard, 188, 189
Longenecker, Richard N., 140
Louw, Johannes P., 58, 129, 130

Ma, Wonsuk, 170, 171, 173
Macchia, Frank D., 15
Maddox, Robert, 119
Marshall, I. Howard, 6, 42, 67, 91, 97, 98, 119, 127, 130, 145, 162, 184
Martin-Achard, Robert, 55, 90, 104, 106
Matera, Frank J., 185
Maurer, Christian, 58
McCasland, Selby Vernon, 106,
McComiskey, Thomas Edward, 90
McKelvey, R. J., 193
Menzies, Glen, 195, 196
Menzies, Robert P., 2, 3, 47, 82, 129, 130, 148, 151, 196
Metzger, Bruce M., 83, 186
Milgrom, Jacob, 37, 39, 43, 45, 46
Mittelstadt, Martin William, 2, 4, 81, 138, 206
Moessner, David P., 97
Montague, George T., 39, 43, 133, 134

Author Index

Moore, George Foot, 59
Motyer, J. Alec, 69, 108, 109, 110
Müller, Paul-Gerd, 127

Neve, Lloyd R., 13, 78
Nida, Eugene A., 58, 129, 130
Niehaus, Jeffrey J., 196
Nolland, John, 23, 125, 126, 130, 146, 155, 177, 178, 187, 188, 189
Noth, Martin, 50
Nötscher, F., 106

O'Brien, Peter T., 64, 65
Osborne, Grant R., 186, 187
Oss, Douglas A., 176
Oswalt, John N., 109, 110, 171, 172
O'Toole, Robert F., 124, 156

Palma, Anthony D., 4
Pao, David W., 119, 128, 135, 136, 137, 171, 178, 185
Parsons, Mikeal C., 188, 189
Perrin, Nicholas, 189, 190
Peterson, David G., 154, 199
Phillips, Richard D., 58
Plummer, Alfred, 119
Polhill, John B., 154

Rahlfs, Alfred, 146
Rea, John, 12, 23, 49, 193
Rese, Martin, 129, 181
Rosner, Brian, 137
Rowe, C. Kavin, 182
Ruthven, Jon Mark, 173

Sailhamer, John, 10, 11, 14, 16, 17, 18, 35, 58, 59
Sarna, Nahum M., 55, 56
Schmidt, Werner H., 11
Schnabel, Eckhard J., 178, 185
Schweizer, Eduard, 129
Scott, Robert, 170
Seebass, H., 110

Sellin, Gerhard, 106
Smith, Steve, 192, 193
Snodgrass, Klyne R., 100, 101, 102, 175, 176, 177
Stein, Robert H., 100, 101, 170, 179
Strauss, Mark L., 145, 146, 149, 198
Stronstad, Roger, 4, 25, 43, 45, 46, 60, 67, 153, 154, 168, 194, 195, 201
Stuart, Douglas, 89, 90, 103, 106, 107

Talbert, Charles H., 182, 183, 184
Tannehill, Robert C., 45, 98, 119, 128, 129, 131, 137, 144, 154
Tate, Marvin E., 93
Thiselton, Anthony C., 134
Thompson, Alan J., 111, 124
Tsumura, David Toshio, 76
Turner, Max, 2, 3, 10, 111, 130, 134, 150, 151, 152, 153, 154, 196, 206

VanGemeren, Willem A., 177
Van Pelt, Miles V., 11, 21
Van Stempvoort, P. A., 188, 189, 191
Vermes, Geza, 5, 6, 56, 150, 196
Vos, Geerhardus, 5, 6, 10, 19, 29, 32

Warrington, Keith, 151
Webb, Barry G., 68, 69
Wenham, Gordon J., 13, 14, 15, 16, 17, 18, 39, 43, 50, 54, 61, 87, 96
Wenk, Matthias, 151
Whiston, William, 177
Wijngaards, J., 105, 106
Wilson, Robert R., 41, 43
Witherington, Ben, III, 122, 133, 162, 180
Wolff, Hans Walter, 103, 104
Wood, Leon J., 39
Woods, Edward J., 130
Wright, N. T., 114, 115, 147
Wright, R. B., 145, 146

Young, Edward J., 172

Index of Ancient Documents

OLD TESTAMENT

Genesis

1–11	54
1:1—2:3	14
1	11, 15, 29, 72, 203, 205
1:1–3	51, 69
1:1	10, 11, 114, 167
1:2	9, 10, 11, 13, 14, 15, 22, 23, 24, 28, 29, 31, 33, 34
1:3	11, 16, 31
1:6	16, 31
1:9	16, 31
1:11	31
1:14	16, 31
1:20	16, 31
1:22	21
1:24	16, 31
1:26	16, 31
1:28	18, 21, 48
1:31	16
2:1–3	16, 19
2:2	19
2:4	15
2:7	9, 109, 112
2:8	184
2:9–10	184
2:9	17, 54
2:10	17
2:11–12	16
2:12	16
2:15–17	18
2:15–16	184
2:15	16, 17
2:16–17	18
2:17	32, 54, 62
3	17
3:1–3	184
3:3	54
3:4	54
3:8	17, 58, 184
3:10	184
3:15–16	62
3:15	32, 124
3:19	54, 109, 114
3:20	32
3:22	11, 32, 54
3:23–24	184
3:24	16
5	54, 59
5:5	54, 55
5:8	54, 55
5:11	54, 55
5:14	54, 55
5:17	54, 55
5:20	54, 55
5:21–24	54
5:22	55, 58
5:24	55, 56, 58, 93
5:27	54, 55
5:31	54, 55
6:3	34
6:8–9	58
6:9	58
6:11	21
6:13	21

225

Genesis (*cont.*)

7:22	56
9:1	21
9:11	95
9:29	54
10	47
11:10–27	61
11:28	61
11:30	61, 67
11:32	61
12	196
12:1–3	42
12:2a	61
12:7–8	62
12:17	61
13:4	62
13:10	62
13:14–18	62
15:2	63, 67
15:5	51
15:6	63
15:8	67
15:12–21	32
15:15	86, 87, 102
16:5	101
17:1	58, 65
17:4	95
17:5	63
17:6	49, 124
17:14	95, 96
17:16	49
17:17–18	67
17:17	67
17:19	67
18:14	71
20:6–7	32
20:7	62
20:18	62
20:30	61
21–22	66
21:2	62
21:6	67
21:16	63
21:18–19	63
21:18	63
21:19	21
21:33	65
22:2	65, 153, 178
22:5	65, 205
22:8	65
22:14	65
22:18	98
23:1–20	63
23:20	63
24:16	21
25:8–9	87
25:8	86, 87
25:10	87
25:17	86, 87, 88
25:19–21	66
25:21	67
25:24	21
25:26	66
26:15	21
29:21	21
29:27–28	21
29:31	67
30:22	66
35:11	49, 124
35:29	86
37:1–11	33
37:5–11	42
37:35	88
38	35
39:2–3	35
39:21	35
39:23	35
41:16	33
41:25	33
41:28	33
41:32	33
41:38	9, 33
41:39	33
42:2	35
42:20	35
42:25	21
42:38	88, 89
43:8	104
44:1	21
44:29	88
44:31	88
45:26	89
45:27	89
45:28	89
46:3–4	89
47:30	86
49	191

49:1	50	28:3	9, 20, 26, 28, 48
49:8–12	124	28:9–12	195
49:10–11	88	28:41	25
49:10	35, 42, 50	30:11	16
49:29–33	87	30:17	16
49:29–32	63	30:22	16
49:29	86, 88	30:33	95
49:33	86, 88	30:34	16
50:3	21	30:38	95
50:19–21	42	31	17
		31:1–11	20

Exodus

		31:1–6	21
1:6	21	31:1	16
1:7	21, 136	31:3	9, 20, 21, 25, 26, 28, 187
1:8	21		
1:13	130	31:5	11
3:6	97, 99, 179, 202, 205	31:12–18	20
		31:12	16
3:18	20	31:14	95, 96
4:16	45	35–40	17, 20, 22
4:23	20	35	20
4:25	95	35:1–3	20
6:7	130	35:4–29	20
8:9	95	35:30—36:7	20
8:20	20	35:30–34	21
9:13	20	35:31	9, 20, 21, 22, 25, 26, 28, 48
12:15	95, 96		
12:19	95, 96	39:32	16
14:22	48	39:42–43	22
15:1–21	42	39:43	16
15:1	13	40:2	16
15:8	9, 130	40:17	16
15:10	9, 130	40:33	16
15:20	45	40:34–35	22, 26, 195, 197
19:5–6	18	40:35	23, 24, 30, 48, 195
19:16–19	197	40:36–38	22
20:8–11	19		

Leviticus

25–31	20		
25–30	20	7:20–21	95
25:1	16	7:20	95
25:3	16	7:21	95
25:7	16	7:25	95
25:8	20	7:27	95
25:8–9	22	8:22	21
25:11	16	8:33	21
25:18–22	16	9:17	21
25:31–40	17	9:22	189
26:1	16	12:3	21

Leviticus (*cont.*)

12:6	21
15:31	96
16:32	21
17:4	95, 96
17:9–10	95
17:9	95
17:10	95, 96
17:14	95
18	95
18:19	95
18:29	95
19:8	95
19:29	21
20:3	95, 96
20:5–6	95
20:5	95, 96
20:6	95, 96
20:17–18	95
21:10	21
22:3	95, 96
23:9	96
23:26–32	97
23:29	95, 97
25:30	21
26:11	17
26:12	17

Numbers

1:53	36
3:3	21
3:7–8	18
4:18	95
5:3	36
5:14	24
5:30	24
6:1–12	69
6:5	21
6:13	21
8:26	18
9:13	95, 96
9:15–23	36
9:20	95
10:33–36	36
11–12	31, 45, 46, 47, 52
11	4, 7, 35, 36, 37, 38, 39, 41, 42, 43, 44, 45, 47, 48, 51, 52, 84, 154, 187
11:1–3	36
11:1	36
11:12	37
11:14	37
11:17	9, 37, 38
11:18	36
11:19–20	36
11:24–30	47
11:25–27	39, 40, 41
11:25–26	9, 10, 38, 39
11:25	37, 38, 42, 47
11:26	38, 43
11:27	43
11:29	9, 10
11:29b	38
12	45
12:3	46, 169
12:5–8	46
12:6–8	46
12:6	42
12:7	46
12:8	46
14:21–23a	28
14:21	28, 29
14:24	28, 45
14:30	19
15:30–36	96
15:30–31	95
15:30	95
15:31	95, 96
16:30	89
16:33	89
18:5–6	18
18:7	18
19:13	95
19:20	95
20:24	86, 87
20:26	86
23:3b	49
23:7	49
23:10	49
23:18	49
23:19–20	49
23:21b	49
23:23	49
24	50, 51
24:1	49

Index of Ancient Documents

24:2	9, 79, 169	23:1	95
24:2b	49	30:15–16	59
24:3	49	30:19	59
24:4	49	31:16	102
24:5–7a	49	32	12, 14, 15, 29, 90, 205
24:7–24	50	32:6	11, 90
24:7b	49	32:10	11
24:9	42, 49	32:11	11
24:14	50	32:15	17
24:15	49	32:18	90
24:16	49	32:22	89
24:17	42, 50, 51	32:24	91
24:17a	50	32:28–29	90
24:17b	50	32:36–43	91
24:19	50	32:36	12, 14
24:20–21	49	32:39	12, 80, 90, 104
24:23	49	32:40	12
27	47	32:50	86, 87
27:12–18	48	34:4	88
27:13	86, 87	34:5–9	48
27:17b	47	34:6	88
27:18	9, 28, 47	34:7	88
31:2	86	34:9	9, 25, 28, 47, 48
31:16	79	34:10–11a	48
32:11	28		
32:12	28	**Joshua**	
		3:7	48
Deuteronomy		3:17	48
1:35	19		
1:36	28	**Judges**	
5:12–15	19	2:10	86, 102
6:11–12	21	11:39	69
8:15	130	12:4–6	69
11:16	18	13:2–5	66
12:29	95	13:2–3	67
12:30	18	13:3–23	68
13:1–5	18	13:5	68, 69
13:4	18	13:10–11a	68
13:5	18	13:14	68
18:15–19	96	13:22–23	68
18:15	46, 48, 96, 147, 162	13:24	66
18:15c	130	13:24b–25	69
18:16	96	13:25	69
18:18	48	14:6	78
18:19	96, 99	14:19	78
19:1	95	15:14	78
19:15	127		

1 Samuel

1:17–18	75
1:18	75
1:19	66
2	83
2:1–10	75
2:1	77
2:2	77
2:3–5	77
2:4	77
2:5	67
2:5b	80
2:6–8	109
2:6	77, 80, 89
2:8	77
2:10	76, 77, 144
2:10b	77
2:35	77
8:7	181
9:17	172
10–16	169
10:1–13	78
10:5–6	39, 40
10:6	10, 35, 78, 79
10:7	35
10:9–13	79
10:9	79
10:10	10, 39, 40, 78, 79
10:11	40
10:13–14	35
10:13	39, 40
10:18	35
11:6–11	78
11:6	78, 79
12:3	144
15:23	78
16:6	144
16:13–14	78
16:13	78
16:14	34, 78, 79
16:18	79
18:10	40
18:12	35, 79
18:14	35, 79
18:18	46
18:28	79
19:20–21	39
19:20	40
19:21	40
19:23–24	39, 40, 79
19:23	79
23:1–2	78
24:6	78
24:7	144
24:10	78
24:11	144
25:28	77
26:9	78, 144
26:11	78, 144
26:16	78, 144
26:23	78, 144

2 Samuel

1:14	78, 144
1:16	78, 144
2:1–10	75
2:5	144
2:8	76
3:18	172
6:20–23	79
7	75, 77, 146, 147
7:5	46
7:6–7	17
7:8	46
7:11	75
7:12–16	123
7:12–13	155
7:12	124
7:13	75, 194
7:16	75, 124
19:22	144
21	77
22–23	76
22:1	77
22:2	77
22:3	77
22:5–7	77
22:6–7	89
22:6	80, 89
22:14	77
22:16	77
22:28	77
22:32	77
22:35	77
22:47	77
22:51	77

23:1–2	49, 116
23:1	144
23:1a	49
23:2	77, 78
23:3	77
23:5	77

1 Kings

2	109
6:2	194
6:23–28	16
8	192
8:10	194, 195
8:11	194, 195
8:15	21
9:1	18
9:6–7	18
17:17–24	60
17:21	112
18:29	40, 41
22:8	40
22:10	40
22:11	40
22:18	40

2 Kings

2	55, 56
2:3	56, 93
2:5	56, 95
2:9–10	56
2:9	93
2:11–12	60
2:11	57
2:15	38, 60
4:31	114
8:1	104
9:10	93
13:21	104, 105
22:20	86
22:30	87

1 Chronicles

7	192
17:10–14	194
17:23–27	194

2 Chronicles

5–7	194
5:1	194
5:12	194
5:13–14	197
5:13	194
5:14	194
6:3–18	194
6:5	194
6:7–10	194
6:18	194, 198
7:1–3	197
7:1–2	194
7:1	195
7:2	195
15:1	10
18:7	40
18:9	40
18:11	40
18:17	40
20:14	10
20:37	40
22:7	144
24:20	10
33:20	184
34:28	86, 87

Nehemiah

9:20	37

Job

1:19	24
4:15	24
7:9	89, 105
11:8	89
14:7–14	105
14:13	89
17:13	89
17:16	89
19:25–26	105
19:25	104
21:13	89
24:9	89
26:6	89

Psalms

1:3	17
2	81
2:2	144
2:7	153
6:5	89
8:3	51
9:17	89
15:5b LXX	94
15:8–11 LXX	75, 91, 160
15:10 LXX	93, 94, 160
16	91, 93, 94
16:1	92
16:3	93
16:5–6	92, 94
16:8–11	155
16:9–11	92
16:9–10	92
16:9	93
16:10	81, 82, 89, 91, 93
17:7	92
17:14a	92
17:15	92, 114
18:5	89
20:7 LXX	144
22	110
22:1	185
22:1a	92
22:14–18	81
22:24	81, 92
22:30	110
27:8	144
30:3	89
30:6 LXX	185
31:5	185
31:5b	63, 202
31:6 MT	185
31:23	185
46:5	17
49	92, 93
49:12–13	92
49:14–15	81, 93
49:15	57, 89
49:17	93
51:11	78
51:13	44
68:18	153, 156
68:19 LXX	156
68:19 MT	153
70:19 LXX	154
73	93
73:17	93
73:24	57, 93
73:26	93
77–78	62
89:3–4	155
89:51	144
90:4 LXX	23
91:6	91
95:10	19
105	32
105:10 LXX	68
105:15	32, 33, 62
105:17–19	32
109:1 LXX	158, 164
110	159
110:1	75, 81, 155, 156, 159, 179, 182
116:3–4	89
117:20 LXX	181
117:22–23 LXX	175
117:22 LXX	157, 161, 164, 175 177, 178, 190
118	
118:20	181
118:22–23	175
118:22	81, 157, 161, 175, 176, 178, 180, 181, 183, 190, 201
118:23	176
118:26	177
132:11–12	124
132:11	75, 155, 160
132:17	124
139:8	89
139:8 LXX	23
143:10	44
146:7–8	150
146:8b	150

Proverbs

7:27	89
15:11	89
18:11	23
27:20	89
30:16	89

Ecclesiastes

3:16–17	105
12:14	105

Isaiah

2:2	50, 104, 154, 170
4	170
4:2–6	170
4:4	173
5	178
5:1–7	176, 178
5:7	178
5:24	195
6:9–10	135
7:11	89
8	170
8:14–15	72, 170, 175, 176
8:14	170, 176
8:15	170
8:22	170
8:23	170
9:1–7	170
9:1	170
9:1a	170
9:2–7	69
9:2	69
10:20—11:5	170
11	147, 149, 151, 152
11:1–9	172
11:1–5	148
11:1–2	69, 152
11:1	26, 39, 44
11:2	38, 44, 147, 148
11:3	25, 26
11:4	146, 147, 148
11:4b	152
11:5	146
11:9	29
13–23	171
14:9	89, 109
14:12–15	171
14:13	50
16:4–6	171
24–27	171
25:6–7	108
25:6	108
25:7–8	108
25:8c	109
25:8b	109
25:12	109
26:5	109
26:13–19	108
26:13	109
26:14	104, 105, 109
26:15	105
26:18–19	113
26:19	72, 92, 102, 105, 108, 109, 113, 114, 171, 173
28–33	171
28:2	91
28:6	44
28:13–16	72, 170
28:13	170
28:16	176
30:1	173
30:27–28	195
32:1	171
32:9–14	171
32:15–20	44, 171
32:15	24, 171, 173, 195
32:15a	191
32:16–20	171
33:5–6	172
33:5	171
33:10	171
33:22	171
34:11	14
34:16	173
35	171, 172
35:5–6	172
37:16	172
37:35	172
39:5–8	172
40:1	172
40:3–5	172
40:5	145, 170, 174
40:9	128
40:13–14	173
42	172
42:1	39, 82, 127, 153, 172
42:1b	38
42:6	145, 147, 170
42:7	39
44–45	14
44:3	171, 173, 187

Isaiah (*cont.*)

44:28	14
45:6	14
45:7	14
45:13	14
45:18	14
49:6	145, 147, 170
49:6b	170
51:17	72
52–53	114, 115
52:1–3	172
52:10	145, 170
52:13	39, 46, 98, 114, 115, 161, 172
52:14–15	115
52:14	111
52:15	111
53	116, 134
53:3	181
53:7–8	97, 134
53:8–9	39
53:8	113, 116
53:10–12	39, 102, 106, 108
53:10	39, 111
53:11–12	115
53:11	111
53:11b	114
53:12	97, 111, 115, 132, 172
53:12b	146
54	66
55:3	111
55:10	137
55:11	137
57:7	128
58:6c	129
60:6	128
61:1–2	130, 150, 172
61:1	39, 128, 150
61:1a	82
61:1b	129
61:2a	130
61:3	13
63:9b	37
63:10a	37
63:11–12	130
63:11	37, 38
63:14	37
65:17–25	111
66:1–2	194
66:14	112

Jeremiah

2:8	40
4:23	14
14:14	40
23:9	11
23:13	40
26:20	40

Lamentations

4:20	144, 146

Ezekiel

1:3	112
2:2	112
3:14	56
3:22	112
3:24	112
8:1	112
8:3	112
11:1	112
11:5	112
11:19	112
11:24	112
13:7	41
24:16	55, 56
24:18	55, 56
25:8–14	50
31:16	89
33:22	112
34:23	113
34:24	113
36:26	112
36:27	44, 112
37	106, 108, 113, 174
37:1–14	13, 102, 111, 112
37:1	112
37:4–10	112
37:5	112
37:6	112
37:8	112
37:9	40, 112
37:10	41, 112
37:10b	113

Index of Ancient Documents

37:11b	113	12:25	116
37:14	112		
37:14b	113	**Hosea**	
37:24	113	1:10–11	90, 103
37:25	113	1:11	113
39:22	111	2:14–23	90
40:1	112	2:14–15	103
40:6	16	3:5	50, 104
43:5	112	5	103
47:1–12	17	5:13	103
		5:14	103
Daniel		5:15	103
1:4	114	6:1–3	103, 104, 108
1:17	114	6:1	103
2	176, 177	6:2	90, 102, 104, 106, 107, 108, 113
2:34	50, 176		
2:44–45	50, 176	6:2b	107
2:44	115	6:4—7:16	103
4:3	115	6:4	103
4:34	115	11:8–11	103
7:13–14	50, 115	13	90
7:13	183	13:1	104
7:18	115	13:13–14	91
7:22	115	13:13	90
7:27	115	13:14	90, 91, 103, 104, 108
8:10	51		
9:21	116	13:14a	90
9:22	114	14:1–9	103
9:23	116	14:1–3	103
9:24	116	14:2	103
9:25–26	116	14:3	103
9:25	50, 114, 116	14:4–9	103
9:26	116, 174	14:4–7	90
10:14	50	14:4	103
11:33	114	14:5	103
11:35	114	14:9	90
12	102, 108		
12:1–4	174	**Joel**	
12:1–3	102, 113	2	4
12:2–3	114	2:28–29	10, 154, 168, 187, 203
12:2	92, 106, 109, 114, 174		
		2:28	170
12:3	50, 51, 114, 115, 116	3:1–2 LXX	42, 44, 154
		3:1 LXX	41, 104, 154, 170
12:3b	115	3:4–5 LXX	200
12:13	102, 113, 114, 115, 174		

Amos

4:13	144
9:2	89
9:11–15	90
9:11–12	103, 122
9:12	122

Jonah

2:2	89
4:3	56

Micah

2:12–13	103
3:8	25

Habakkuk

2:5	89
2:14	29

Malachi

4:5–6	116

APOCRYPHA

Tobit

11:15	154

Sirach

17:8	154
17:10	154
17:13	154
18:4	154
36:6	25
36:7	154
42:21	154
43:15	154
45:24	154
46:19	144
50:20–22	189
50:20–21	188

Baruch

51:5	174
51:10	174

2 Maccabees

3:34	154
7	65, 71
7:9	173
7:9b	65
7:11	65
7:14	173
7:17	154
7:22–23	66
7:28b	66
7:36	173
12:44	173

3 Maccabees

7:22	154

4 Maccabees

13:17	101

PSEUDEPIGRAPHA

Apocalypse of Abraham

21	184

2 Baruch (Syriac Apocalypse)

51:5	174
51:10	174

1 Enoch (Ethiopic Apocalypse)

1:8–9	147
1:9	59
10:17–19	59
14:8–25	195
17–19	184
32:3	184
38:2–3	147
38:3	147
39:6	147
40:6	147
46:1–3	147
46:3–4	147
48–51	148
48:2–3	147
48:2	147, 148
48:4	147, 148

48:6–7	147		**4 Ezra**	
48:6	147, 148		7:36	101
48:7–8	148		7:75–99	101
48:8	148			
48:9	148, 149		**Jubilees**	
48:10	147, 148		4:23–24	55
49:2–3	148, 149			
49:2	147		**Psalms of Solomon**	
50:4	149		2:31	145
51:1–4a	149		3:10b	145
51:4c	149		3:11	146
52:4	147		3:12b	146
53:6	147		13:11	146
55:4	147		14:3	184
60:8	184		14:9	146
60:23	184		15:10	146
61:10–11	148		16:2	146
61:12	184		17–18	146
62	147		17	146
62:2–3	148		17:4	146
62:6–7	147		17:21	146
62:9	157		17:26–32	146
62:15–16	174		17:32	144, 146
62:15	59, 147		17:36b	147
67	147		17:37	147
67:8	148		18:5b	147
67:10–11	148		18:7	144, 146
70:1–4	55			
71	55			
91:1	148			
102:4	59			
103–4	101			
103:2–4	59			
103:4	147			
104:4	59			
106:7–8	55			
108:11	59			
108:13	59			

TESTAMENTS OF THE TWELVE PATRIARCHS

Testament of Benjamin

10:6–7	161

Testament of Daniel

5:12	184

2 Enoch (Slavonic Apocalypse)

22:8	55
22:10	55
65:10	184
70:4	184

Testament of Levi

18	151
18:10–11	184

NEW TESTAMENT

Matthew

1:1	123
2:1–2	50
2:2	125
2:9–12	50
2:22	123
3:2	125
3:11	196
3:17	126
4:17	125
4:23	128
5:3–12	167
5:3	125
5:10	125
5:19	125
5:20	125
6:10	125
7:9–11	131
7:11	131
7:21	125
8:11–12	125
9:27	123
9:35	128
10:7	125, 128, 129
11:9	178
11:11	125
11:12	125
12:23	123
12:28	130
12:40	106, 108
13:18–20	136
13:24	125
13:31	125
13:33	125
13:38	125
13:43	125
13:44–45	125
13:47	125
15:22	123
16:6	126
16:21	106, 107
16:27	126
17:5	23, 126
17:23	106, 107
18:1	125
18:3	125
18:4	125
18:23	125
19:14	125
19:23–24	125
20:1	125
20:18–19	92
20:19	106, 107
20:19c	107
20:30	123
20:31	123
21:5	46
21:9	123, 178
21:15	123
21:31	125
21:35–36	175
21:42	175, 176
21:43–44	176
21:43	125
21:44	115, 175
22:2	125
22:10	25
22:23–46	158
22:23–33	99
22:32b	100
22:42	123
22:43	158
22:45	155
23:13	125
24:14	128
25:1	125
25:14–30	125
25:31–46	125
26:61	106
27:11	125
27:29	125
27:37	125, 126
27:37b	125
27:40	106, 125, 126
27:42	125, 126
27:43	125, 126
27:46	92, 185
27:48	25
27:51–54	113
27:63	106
27:64	106

Mark

1:1	128

Index of Ancient Documents

1:14–15	128	1:10	193
1:15	128	1:11–20	68
4:14	136	1:11	193
6:7–11	129	1:13	67
8:31	106, 107	1:15–17	27, 68, 151
8:35	128	1:15	14, 24, 25, 68, 69, 195
8:38	126	1:17	24, 26, 60, 116
9:7	23	1:18–20	168
9:31	106, 107	1:18	67
10:29	128	1:20	26, 69
10:34	106, 107	1:23	26
10:34c	107	1:25	67
12:3–5	175	1:27	75, 123
12:10–11	175	1:28	116
12:11	176	1:30	75
12:18–37	158	1:31	24, 184
12:18–27	99	1:32–33	115, 151
12:27b	100	1:32	24, 75, 116, 123
12:36	158	1:33	75, 123, 124
12:37	155	1:35–38	168
13:10	128	1:35	11, 14, 15, 23, 24, 26, 29, 30, 195
14:9	128	1:35b	191
14:44	120	1:35c	144
14:58	106	1:36	67
15:2	125	1:38	75, 136
15:9	125	1:41–45	24
15:12	125	1:41–44	168
15:18	125	1:41–42	10
15:26	125	1:41	14, 25, 26, 67, 144, 195
15:26b	125	1:43	27, 74, 151
15:29	106	1:43b	144
15:32	125	1:45	74, 168
15:34	185	1:46–56	81
16:15	128	1:46–55	24, 75, 76, 167
16:19	57	1:46	154
		1:47–55	15
Luke		1:48	76
1	29	1:49	2
1:1	5, 10, 29, 67, 70	1:50	76
1:2	70, 71, 136	1:51–53	76
1:3–4	67	1:54–55	76, 124
1:4	71, 119, 156	1:57	26, 27
1:5–17	81	1:67–79	10, 24
1:5–6	67	1:67–75	81
1:6–7	168	1:67	14, 25, 26, 67, 144, 151, 168, 195
1:7	67		
1:8–22	193		
1:8–11	116		

Luke (cont.)

1:68–79	15
1:68–73	124
1:69–75	68
1:69	27, 46, 68, 123, 144
1:70	68
1:71	68, 167
1:72–73	68, 123
1:74	68
1:75	151
1:76–77	68
1:76	144
1:77	68
1:79	69
1:80	69
2:4	123
2:6	26
2:10	83, 122
2:11	74, 81, 83, 85, 121, 122, 123, 146, 183, 184, 205
2:17–18	133
2:17	136
2:19	136
2:21–50	193
2:21	26
2:22	26
2:25–38	196
2:25–35	10, 24
2:25–27	81, 144
2:25	14, 168
2:26	14, 144, 146, 173
2:28–32	145
2:29–35	81
2:29–32	169, 174
2:29	136
2:32	147, 170, 174
2:33	33, 133
2:34–35	145
2:34b–35	169
2:34	3, 72, 145, 170, 173, 174, 184, 201
2:34b	170
2:35b	173
2:36–38	168
2:36	145
2:38	133
2:38b	145
2:46–55	75
2:49	2
3:2	136
3:4–6	172
3:7	151
3:9	152, 177
3:15–16	146
3:15	81, 146, 151
3:16–17	151
3:16	82, 151, 152, 174, 197, 207
3:17	151, 152
3:21–22	82
3:22	39, 152, 174, 178
3:31	123
3:37	60, 152
3:37—4:15	111
3:38—4:13	19
3:38—4:1	196
3:38	174
4:1	112, 153, 174
4:2	174
4:5–8	174
4:10	133
4:14	133, 153, 174
4:17	176
4:18–19	39, 111, 128, 150, 153
4:18	128, 129, 131, 174
4:18a	82, 128
4:18b	128, 130
4:18c	129
4:19	128, 130
4:21	74, 184
4:24–27	38, 167
4:24	128
4:25–26	60
4:25	46
4:37	133
4:41	146
4:43	128
5:1	71, 136
5:8	182
5:12–16	189
5:12	182
5:15	133
5:20	189
5:33–39	189
6:1–11	189

Index of Ancient Documents

6:3	123	9:60	128
6:4	194	10:1–17	47
6:5	74, 189	10:1	47
6:10	94	10:9	125, 128, 129
6:19	195	10:10–24	130
6:20–26	167	10:11	125, 128
6:20	125	10:19	131, 189
6:46	74	10:21	168
7:3	133	10:40	182
7:6	182	11:1–13	168
7:11–17	3, 60	11:2	125, 131
7:13	74	11:11–12	131
7:16	157	11:13	112, 131, 168, 187
7:17	133	11:20	125, 129, 130, 159, 189
7:19	157		
7:22	130, 131, 150, 157, 172	11:28	71, 136
		11:29–32	157
7:28	125, 172	11:30	108
7:36–50	168	11:31	189
7:48	189	11:39	74
8:1	128	11:45–54	176
8:11	71, 136	11:47	181
8:21	71, 136	11:50–51	167
8:49–56	3	12:11–12	168
8:53	157	12:12	138
9:2	128, 129	12:32	125
9:9	133	13:15	74
9:11	128, 129	13:18	125
9:20–22	167	13:20	125
9:20	126, 144, 146, 157	13:23	182
9:22	63, 97, 101, 106, 107, 126, 157, 167, 181, 183	13:28–30	101, 167
		13:28–29	102, 125
		13:32–35	176
9:26	126, 127, 188	13:32	106
9:27	126	13:33–35	167
9:28–36	126	13:34–35	157
9:28	126	13:35	177
9:30–33	60	14:12–14	167
9:30–32	197	14:14	3, 72, 173
9:30	38, 127	14:15	125
9:31	127, 130, 183	14:22–24	167
9:32	126, 174, 188	15:28–32	167
9:34	23	15:31	104
9:35	126, 127	15:32	3
9:35c	130	16:14–15	100
9:37–45	130	16:16–18	100
9:48	167	16:16	125, 128
9:51	186, 188	16:19–31	100, 184
9:54	182		

Luke (cont.)

16:22–33	101
16:23–24	204
16:23	204
16:31	3, 63, 100, 183
17:20–21	125
17:25	181
18:1–8	167
18:9–14	167
18:16–17	125
18:17	125
18:24–25	125
18:31–33	157
18:31	176
18:31b	108
18:32–33	108
18:33	101, 106, 107, 108, 167, 183
18:33c	107
18:38–39	123
18:38	146
18:39	146
18:41	182
19:1–10	167
19:5	74, 184
19:8	182
19:9	74, 184
19:11–27	125
19:11	125
19:12	188
19:14	123
19:27	123
19:28–29	188
19:31	182
19:38	177, 178
19:40	190
19:44	190
19:45–47	190
19:45–46	190
19:46	193, 194
19:47—20:2	190
19:47	190
20	178, 180, 181, 190
20:2	178, 180
20:4–6	178
20:9–16	178
20:10–11	178
20:13	178
20:14	178
20:15	178
20:16	175, 180, 190
20:17–18	72, 175, 190
20:17	159, 175, 176, 177, 178, 183, 190
20:17b	157
20:18	115, 170, 176, 177, 178
20:20–26	179
20:27–40	99, 159, 179
20:27–37	3
20:27	72, 173
20:33	72, 173
20:34–35	100
20:35–36	72, 173
20:36–38	202
20:36	179, 183
20:37–38	12, 179, 204
20:37	97, 179
20:37b	99
20:38	100, 183
20:40	158
20:41–44	158, 159, 182
20:41	123, 146, 158
20:42–44	179
20:42–43	156
20:42	74, 123, 158, 159
20:44	74, 123, 155
21:1–4	167
21:6	193
21:22	27, 176
21:24	27
21:27	183, 198
21:31	125
21:33	137
21:37	190
22:7–22	97
22:16	124
22:18	124
22:24–27	184
22:29–30	124, 184, 202
22:29	125
22:30	125
22:33	182
22:37	97, 132, 133, 176
22:38	182
22:49	182
22:53	184

22:61	136, 182	24:32	186
22:67	146, 182	24:34	182, 186
		24:34b	158
22:69	81, 184, 187	24:35	158
23:2–3	124	24:37–43	186
23:2	125, 146, 182	24:37	89, 186
23:3	125	24:38–43	158
23:4	97	24:41	89, 186
23:8	133	24:44–49	97, 197
23:14–15	97	24:44–47	186
23:20	97	24:44–46	70, 71, 82
23:22	97	24:44	71, 132, 133, 135, 137, 158, 176, 187, 190
23:34	97		
23:35–43	192		
23:35	82, 126, 144, 146, 182	24:45–47	158
		24:46–49	132, 186
23:37–38	124, 125	24:46	71, 106, 107, 146, 157
23:37	126		
23:38	126	24:47	71, 132
23:38b	125	24:48–49	132
23:39	126, 146, 182	24:48	70, 71, 159, 187
23:41	97	24:49	82, 135, 158, 171, 190
23:42–43	204		
23:42	124, 125, 126	24:49a	187
23:43	63, 125, 167, 184, 191, 202	24:49c	190
		24:50–53	19, 186, 191, 196, 206
23:45	191		
23:46	63, 185, 191, 202	24:50–51	188, 190
23:47	97, 187	24:50	188
23:51	124, 125	24:51	186
24	3, 132, 135, 186, 188, 191	24:52	57, 186
		24:53	193
24:3	75, 158, 182, 184		
24:4	133	**John**	
24:7	106, 107, 157, 186	1:14	198
24:11–12	89	1:18	102
24:11	89	2:19–22	190
24:16	158	6:12	25
24:19	131, 133	11:25	174
24:21	106, 158	12:13	178
24:22–24	132	13:23	102
24:25–27	82, 186	14:25–26	206
24:25–26	132	19:19b	125
24:26	127, 146, 158, 174, 183, 186, 202	19:30	185
		20:19	106
24:27	127, 133	20:20	106
24:30–31	158	20:22	112, 113, 196
24:30	186		

Acts

1	135, 187, 191, 197
1:1–11	3
1:1	71, 132, 133
1:2	57, 135, 154, 187
1:3	124, 131, 132, 133, 159, 186
1:4	2, 135
1:5	135, 152
1:6	94, 124, 131, 133
1:8	2, 19, 24, 43, 70, 112, 133, 135, 137, 138, 151, 159, 195, 204
1:8a	24
1:9–11	197
1:9	38, 197
1:10–11	60, 188
1:10	57
1:11	57
1:15	194
1:16	123, 135, 143
1:20	135
1:21	75
1:22	24, 57, 70, 71, 72, 159, 173, 197, 204
1:23–26	197
1:23–24	183
2–10	163
2–4	98, 138
2	29, 39, 44, 60, 94, 99, 104, 109, 140, 153, 155, 159, 165, 181, 192, 194, 196, 197
2:1–4	153
2:1	154, 186
2:2	57, 193, 194, 197
2:3	47, 194, 195, 196, 207
2:4–12	83
2:4	23, 25, 26, 27, 34, 156, 194, 197, 199, 206
2:5	57
2:11	43, 57, 154
2:11b	194
2:12	155
2:13	43
2:14	155, 159
2:14c	137
2:15	193
2:16–18	36
2:16	154, 161
2:17–21	15
2:17–18	43, 153, 154, 156, 168, 201
2:17	27, 104, 154, 170, 171, 197
2:18	197
2:18c	154
2:20–21	200
2:21	194
2:22–36	61, 75
2:22–24	140
2:22	3, 131, 137, 155, 159
2:23–24	82
2:23	160
2:24–36	194
2:24–35	27
2:24	160
2:25–28	75, 91, 160
2:25	75, 123
2:26–38	146
2:26–27	184
2:26	93
2:27	91
2:27b	93
2:29–31	82
2:29	75, 123, 155, 160
2:30–31	161
2:30	75, 155
2:31	72, 81, 91, 133, 155, 173
2:31c	94
2:32–36	187
2:32–33	161
2:32	70, 140, 160, 187
2:33–36	148
2:33–34	153
2:33	2, 82, 153, 155, 156, 169, 197
2:34–36	75
2:34–35	156
2:34	57, 75, 123, 155

2:36	1, 3, 8, 27, 43, 51, 71, 74, 82, 83, 94, 111, 120, 121, 122, 127, 143, 146, 155, 156, 160, 166, 171, 179, 181, 187, 197, 199, 201, 203, 205, 208	3:26	39, 46, 97, 98, 137, 174
		4	180, 181
		4:2	72, 98, 159, 173, 174, 179, 202
		4:2b	138
		4:3	139
		4:4	61, 71, 137
2:37	137	4:7	3, 97
2:38–39	82, 134, 169	4:7b	180
2:38	2, 23, 162, 187, 194, 199, 204	4:8–13	27
		4:8–12	200
2:39	2, 173	4:8	25, 26, 138, 181, 195
2:40	3, 137, 139		
2:41	3, 61, 71, 137, 139, 140	4:10–11	138
		4:10	3, 97, 161, 181, 183, 187, 194
2:42–47	45	4:11	157, 161, 175, 181, 197
2:44–45	47		
2:46	193	4:12	3, 98, 181, 194
3	97, 99	4:13	181
3:1	193	4:17	194
3:6–7	3	4:25–26	200
3:6	3, 97, 146, 187, 194	4:25	112, 123, 135, 144
3:7	174	4:26	144
3:12	160	4:27	39
3:13–16	198	4:29	3, 71
3:13–15	161	4:29b	138
3:13–14	97, 137	4:30	3, 39, 187
3:13	39, 46, 97, 98, 160	4:31–33	27
3:13a	127	4:31	25, 26, 71, 136, 138, 195, 200
3:14	61, 97, 98		
3:14a	161	4:31b	138
3:15	70, 97, 98, 127, 159, 161, 162, 183	4:32–37	138
		4:33	3, 72, 75, 159, 173, 200
3:16	3, 97, 194		
3:18–21	15	4:33a	138
3:18	97, 98, 144	5:3	200
3:19	23, 98	5:9	200
3:20	97, 98	5:15	23, 195
3:21	23, 25, 51, 94, 97, 98, 167	5:23	120
		5:29–32	201
3:22–23	96	5:29	3, 162
3:22	38, 46, 97, 137, 174	5:30–32	161, 162
3:23	96, 98, 99, 204	5:30–31	161
3:24–26	23	5:30	183
3:25	98, 99	5:31–32	23
3:25b	98	5:31	127

Acts (*cont.*)

5:32	70, 112, 162
5:40	3
5:42	82
6	46, 139
6:2	71, 136, 139, 197
6:4	71, 139
6:7	71, 136
6:7a	139
7:2	198
7:27	162
7:35–38	162
7:35–37	177
7:35	162
7:37	162, 174
7:39	162
7:44	198
7:45	123
7:47	194
7:48–50	193
7:48	198
7:49–50	194
7:49	194
7:51–53	135
7:51	162, 200
7:51c	143
7:52b	143
7:53	133
7:54–56	200
7:55	57, 198
7:56	3, 189
7:59	75
8	134
8:4	71, 139
8:5	139
8:12	128, 131, 133, 139, 146, 187, 206
8:14–17	168
8:14	71, 136, 139, 140
8:15–17	206
8:16	75
8:21	71
8:25	71, 136, 139
8:29–33	200
8:29	112
8:32–34	134
8:32–33	97, 116
8:34	133
8:35	133
8:39	200
9:1–19	169
9:3–16	3
9:15	201
9:17	25, 26, 195, 200
9:20	27
9:22	82
9:31	200
9:40–41	3
10	139
10:3	193
10:13–15	3
10:19	200
10:30	193
10:35	83, 128
10:36–42	71
10:36–38	139, 146
10:36	61, 71, 83, 121, 122, 139, 140, 152, 163, 200
10:36b	163
10:37–42	140
10:38	130, 131, 152, 163, 200
10:39–40	183
10:39	70, 163
10:40	106, 140, 163
10:40a	163
10:41	70, 140, 159
10:41c	163
10:42	51, 139, 140, 152, 163, 177
10:44–48	168
10:44–45	200
10:44	61, 71, 107, 112, 136, 140, 163
10:45	2
10:46	154
10:47	200
10:48	146
11:1	71, 136
11:1b	140
11:12	112, 200
11:13	193
11:15–17	200
11:15	112
11:16	136, 152
11:17	2, 83, 121, 122, 200

Index of Ancient Documents 247

11:19	71, 141	15:8–9	200
11:20c	141	15:8	2, 112, 122, 200
11:23–24	200	15:11	122, 198
11:28	201	15:12	122
12:24	71, 136, 141	15:14	98
13	94	15:16–17	122
13:1–4	200	15:16	123, 198
13:2	112	15:17	122
13:5	71, 136, 141	15:26	83, 121, 122, 198
13:6–12	27	15:28–29	122
13:7	71, 136, 141	15:28	122, 135, 200
13:9–11	200	15:35–36	71, 136
13:9	25, 26	16:6	71, 141, 199
13:22	123	16:7	199, 202
13:25	164	16:23	120
13:26–49	137	16:31	75
13:26	71, 141	16:32	71, 136, 141
13:29–37	164	17:3	82, 145, 164
13:29–30	183	17:3c	164
13:29	133, 134, 176	17:11	71, 141
13:30–37	141	17:13	71, 136, 141
13:30	164	17:18	72, 173
13:31	70	17:31	159
13:33	74	17:32	72, 133, 134, 173
13:34	111, 123	18:5	71, 82, 141
13:35	91	18:9–10	3
13:36	123	18:11	71, 136, 141
13:37–39	164	18:25	133
13:37	164	18:28	82
13:39	164	19:5	169, 187
13:42	49	19:6	112
13:44	71, 136, 141	19:8	131, 134
13:46–48	141	19:10	71, 136, 141
13:46	71, 136, 141	19:17	155
13:48–49	71, 136	19:20	71, 136, 141
13:48	141	20:7	71
13:49	141	20:9–10	3
13:50	26	20:21	83
13:52—4:3	200	20:22–24	201
13:52	26, 27	20:24	128, 140
14:3	27, 71, 141	20:25	131
14:12	71	20:28	200
14:17	25	20:32	71, 141
14:22	51	21:4	201
14:25	71, 141	21:10–14	201
14:35–36	141	21:11	112
15:5	121	21:13–14	201
15:7	71, 128	22:11	198

Acts (*cont.*)

22:14–15	159
22:18	133, 134, 159
22:22	137
23:6	72, 133, 134, 173, 174, 179
23:8	3, 72, 173
23:11	3, 133, 134, 139
24:14–15	179
24:14	176
24:15	3, 72, 173
24:15b	115
24:21	72, 133, 134, 173
24:24	133
25:19	133, 134
26:5–8	180
26:7	133, 134
26:22–23	180
26:23	72, 173
28	135
28:20	180
28:23	131, 133, 134, 135, 180
28:25–28	135
28:25	112, 135, 143
28:26–27	135
28:28–31	122
28:28	124
28:29	83
28:31	83, 121, 122, 124, 131, 133, 134

Romans

1:4	206
1:18	61
3:4	176
3:6	176
3:31	176
4	66
4:3	63
4:17	66
4:17b	64
4:18–21	71
4:19	64
4:24b	64
4:25b	64
6:2	176
6:15	176
7:7	176
7:13	176
8:9	34, 206
8:11	113
8:29	93
9:14	176
9:32–33	176
11:1	176
11:11	176
15:24	25

1 Corinthians

3:16–17	207
6:15	176
6:18–20	207
12:3	206
13:12	46
15	106
15:4	106, 107, 108
15:20	180
15:23	180
15:54	108
15:55	90, 108

2 Corinthians

12:4	184

Galatians

2:17	176
3:21	176
6:14	176

Ephesians

2:11–22	207
2:17–23	182
2:20	179

Philippians

1:19	199

Colossians

1:18	180
3:5	64
4:14	6

1 Thessalonians

5:3	120

2 Thessalonians

2:4	207

1 Timothy

3:16	57

Hebrews

2:17	64
3:1	64
4:1–13	19
4:3	19
6:13	155
6:16–17	155
7:25	64
8:3	64
9:9	64
9:18	64
11	66
11:5	58
11:6	58
11:11–12	65, 71
11:12	64
11:16	63
11:17–19	65
11:17–18	65
11:19	64, 65, 71
11:21	63

1 Peter

2:4–9	176
2:7–8	175
4:14	206

Jude

14–15	59

Revelation

1:10–20	206
2:7	184
11:1	113
11:15	144
12:10	144
21:4	109
22:1–2	17
22:2	10
22:16	50

DEAD SEA SCROLLS

1QapGen 2:23	55
1QDana	114
1QDanb	114
1QS IX, 11	149
1QSa II, 11–22	149
1Q29Lit. of 3 Tongues of Fire	195
1Q29Lit. of 3 Tongues of Fire 2–7	196
4QDana	114
4QDanb	114
4QDanc	114
4QDand	114
4QDane	114
4QFlor	114
4Q162pIsa	176
4Q385psEzek	150
4Q385psEzek 2	112
4Q376Lit. of 3 Tongues of Fire	195
4Q376Lit. of 3 Tongues of Fire 1 II, 1–3	196
4Q521MessAp 2 II, 1–12	149
4Q521MessAp 7, 5	150
6QDan	114
CD VII, 15–20	50

RABBINIC WRITINGS

ibn Ezra

Gen 5:24	56

Rabbah Exodus

31:5	101

Rabbah Genesis

2	151
59:4	195

Rabbah Pesiq

43:4	101

b. Sanhedrin

90a	13
90b	13
91b	13

m. Sukkah

3:9	177
4:5	177

Targum Isaiah

28:16b	177

Targum Onkelos

Num 24:17	50

Targum Psalms

118:2	177

Targum Pseudo-Jonathan

Gen 5:24	55

JOSEPHUS

Jewish Antiquities

3.145	17
3.214–18	195
10.210	177

Philo

De decalogo	195

GRECO-ROMAN WRITINGS

Lucian

Cataplus	101

Quintilian

Institutio oratoria 5.9.3	133